INDIA CHINA BOUNDARY
IN
KASHMIR

INDIA CHINA BOUNDARY
IN
KASHMIR

H.N. KAUL

Published by

GYAN

Gyan Publishing House
5, Ansari Road
Daryaganj, New Delhi-110002
Phone: 011-47034999, 9811692060
E-mail: books@gyanbooks.com

Distribution Network
gyanbooks.com
India, USA, Canada, UK, Australia, France

ISBN: 978-81-212-0826-0 (HB)

Reprint in India, 2024
First Published, 2003

Printed at: Gyan Press, Delhi.

India China Boundary in Kashmir
Author: H.N. Kaul

Contents

List of Maps

Preface

India-China boundary dispute is now 50 years old and yet not near an amicable settlement. The intractable nature that the conflict has assumed has soured bilateral relations between the two countries, which have a great bearing on Asia. The dispute has given rise to many myths, some of them quite disingenuous. It is claimed that the boundary dispute in Kashmir arose between England and China in the 19th century because there is no definite frontier between Kashmir and Tibet to the east and Xinjiang to the north, both now in China, and that the Karakoram ridge is the traditional boundary in the north and also the watershed between South and Central Asia. The averments do not stop here but go on to suggest that the Indian claim that the Kuen Lun (-Bolor Tagh) mountains to the north of the Karakoram are the real limit between India and China has no credibility. Many of these myths were swallowed, hook, line and sinker, by the successor government to the British Empire, the Government of India.

The dispute burst into open soon after India's independence in early 1950s. Few in India had then even the haziest idea about the northern boundary in Kashmir. After the departure of the British from India, there was a complete break in administration. Pakistan, perhaps, for historical reasons, was somewhat better informed than India but not having any part of the northern boundary running over its territorial limits, save in the seized districts of Skardo and Gilgit in Jammu and Kashmir, chose to remain silent for strategic considerations. As China nibbled at Aksai Chin, Pakistan followed the British line on the northern boundary. Confusion over the boundary issue was worst confounded by Jawaharlal Nehru, India's Prime Minister, for one person perhaps well acquainted with British machinations in Kashmir, Maharaja Hari Singh, the last Maharaja, was exiled by him from his State within months of India's independence. The Maharaja was the one authority who could have bridged the gap between the pre-and post-independence administrations, after the departure of the British. Much later the Indian Ministry of External

Affairs did examine the boundary issue but very superficially. The Ministry's findings, incorporated in the India-China Officials Report, 1960, did more damage than good to India. To Nehru personally and to the ignorance of the Government of India are to be attributed the fatal agreement with China over Tibet, the boundary dispute, the 1962 border war and the stalemate thereafter. Whatever leverage India had over the boundary dispute it lost in the agreement over the Tibet.

For any in-depth study of the boundary dispute between India and China a complete understanding of British India's relations with China is necessary. In this relationship is to be found the beginning of the boundary dispute for before the arrival of England in Kashmir there was no boundary dispute either with Tibet or Xinjiang, or Kashgaria as it was then known. For this we have the authoritative work the "Tarikh-i-Rashidi" of Mirza Mohammad Haider Dughlat, who invaded Ladakh and Tibet, just after Babar stormed India. The Mirza categorically recalls the boundary of Ladakh as the scrap of the Tibetan (Kuen Lun) mountains. The reason for England to question the northern boundary of India in Kashmir was the advent of Russia in Central Asia and British fears of a Russian invasion of India. Britain was not weighed down by any military superiority of Russia even in Central Asia. Rather England feared the repercussions of such an invasion of India. A thousand insurrections, the British feared, would break out to throw their rear into disarray. To contain Russia in Central Asia England wooed China. The fear of Russia also persuaded England to formulate the forward policy, or British advance into trans-Indus regions of India and Kashmir. The Anglo-Russian rivalry, military and political, in Central Asia, or the "Great Game," as it came to be called, was an extension of Anglo-Russian rivalry in eastern Europe.

By the beginning of the 19th century the British power in India had reached the foothills of the Himalaya. It had only to forge past the Sikh State of Lahore to reach Peshawar and beyond to encompass the whole of India. The question then the British asked themselves was: what should be the northern boundary of the British Empire? England thus not only questioned the northern boundary of India but soon enough began to change it in British imperial interests. It was the Himalaya, in preference to the Kuen Lun, the British rooted for. The almost contemporary interposition of the Lahore State first in Ladakh, to ensure assured supplies of 'pashm' wool to Kashmir's shawl industry, and then in Skardo and Gilgit for a route to Badakashan to encircle Kabul and prevent British India becoming contiguous to Afghanistan, stalled the British. Even before the Sikh interposition in Ladakh British political agent and traveller in Central Asia, William Moorcraft, had rejected the Himalaya as the British boundary in these parts and proposed the East India Company take Ladakh under its protection. He thus impliedly suggested the Kuen Lun as the British Empire's northern boundary.

England inspired diversion of the 'pashm' trade from Gartok, Leh and Srinagar to British protected Bashahr or Rampur. This was not merely to enrich the British woollen industry but ignite widespread unrest in Kashmir Valley where the 'pashm' shawl industry, directly or indirectly, provided sustenance to more than half the population. The Sikh power in Kashmir valley, within the limits of the Himalaya, would have been shaken. When the Sikhs invaded Tibet in 1841, the British Indian Government took pains to explain to Tibet and China that it favoured its own and Lahore State's boundary to rest on the Himalaya, thus leaving out the trans-Himalayan Ladakh. The present day huge territorial claims of China in Ladakh are related to the 19th century British intrigue with and overtures to Tibet and China and bear a remarkable likeness to British views then on the boundary issue. But England failed to change the northern boundary in Kashmir by the treaty of Amritsar, 1846, which gave birth to the present state of the Jammu and Kashmir. Subsequent British moves on the boundary issue only precipitated a confrontation between the Maharajas of Kashmir and British Indian Government. The boundary issue was not therefore, one between England and China but one between the Maharajas of Kashmir and England.

Ladakh, Skardo and Gilgit, frontier districts of Kashmir, have, from ancient times, served as advance bases for periodic forward moments of India into Central Asia. Khotan was part of ancient Hindu Kingdoms of Kashmir and Skardo. Sallies from Kashmir into Central Asia were made by several routes, into Tibet by the Shipki la, Demchok and Pal (Rudok), into Khotan, north of Aksai Chin, by the Keria la, Polur, Yangi dawan, Hindutash dawan, and into Yarkand and Kashgar by the Walaghat, or Sanju or Grim, Kilian, Kokyar, Mintaka, Baik, Shinde and Baroghil. Traders and trading caravans crossed and recrossed these passes and outposts where "rahdaris," or passports as these were then called, were checked and custom duties paid. Until the end of the 19th century these passes and posts were, indeed, the northern boundary. Two commercial lines, readily served as military roads, ran, one over eastern Aksai Chin by the Keria la and Polur, the northern limit of Ladakh, to Khotan, and the other from Chitral over the Baroghil pass to the Pamirs or forked to Sirikul, at the head of the trough between the Kashgar and Sirikul ridges of the Bolor Tagh, to end in Ferghana in the present day Tajikistan. The two roads, the British feared, could become routes of invasion. This induced them to opt for the Karakoram as the boundary in the north. The

British resolve tore asunder from Jammu and Kashmir the territories intervening between the Kuen Lun to the north and the Karakoram to the south–Aksai Chin, Yarkand valley, Taghdumbash, Pamir and Little Pamir, over which ran these roads. This immense region, other than the two Pamirs, was declared as no man's land, being, the British argued, beyond the Karakoram watershed, which to this day remains an unverified watershed. To make over these territories to China, the British deposed the third Maharaja, Pratap Singh, and the fourth Maharaja, Hari Singh, almost as well, and fought a little war with Hunza, a vassal State of Kashmir. In return England looked to China for countenance in Central Asia against a marauding Czarist Russia becoming conterminous with the Indian empire and in a position to stoke the fires of Indian unrest. Thus was the Karakoram projected as the northern boundary of British Empire in Ladakh. Thus also arose the dispute over the northern boundary in Kashmir.

Military considerations no less influenced the British decision to trade off Kashmir territory for support of China, which ultimately could not fight its own battles. England had a warped view of Ladakh's defences. Traditionally Ladakh had relied on the arctic region between the Karakoram and the Kuen Lun for its defence. An invader was allowed to pass through this unpopulated desert before reaching Leh and beyond. If the invader succeeded and crossed the deserts, he was met south of the Karakoram where lay the populated areas. The attrition in men, beasts of burden and materials in crossing the deserts would certainly be prohibitive, making the invasion uninviting. The British took a contrary view. They saw themselves in occupation of and, therefore, in defence of the arctic region, where military operations were considered not feasible and even if feasible forbiddingly costly in terms of logistics. Withdrawal from, say, Aksai Chin, during the invasion would surely have invited a political disaster in the plains of India. Ultimately dependence on China proved quixotic by the turn of the 19th century, compelling first Sir L.W. Dane and then Sir Henry MacMohan in the British Indian Foreign Department, and the Viceroy, Lord Hardinge, totally to reverse British frontier policy. Collapse of central authority in China was the reason why China did not respond to MacDonald proposal on the boundary made in 1899, which Beijing now flaunts. Russia did not take long to occupy Xinjiang and intrigue in Tibet, just across the Himalaya. British frontier policy, based on several disastrous decisions, collapsed. Since then China has learnt that roads do not lead in only one direction, from Central Asia into India but can also lead from India into Central Asia or China.

This work, first of a trilogy on Kashmir, has taken long to complete. The delay was largely on account of inaccessibility of Government records in the National Archives of India, on which much of this volume is based. Some, not very consequential, relaxations were made by the National Archives with the prior permission of the Government of India. But more closed records being thrown open remained only a fond hope. On the basis of the research completed many material inferences were drawn. These needed to be supported with papers which were not forthcoming. The alternative was to drop this project. But the relaxation made by Government somewhat helped to proceed further into the first one or two decades of the 20th century, which nevertheless remain thinly researched. There are significant areas where the British records are silent, notably on the deposed Maharaja Pratap Singh's interventions on the boundary issue. These are readily available in the Jammu and Kashmir State Archives, Jammu, and have been, for the first time, used in this volume. Early Government reports and the Survey of India papers, having a bearing on the boundary issue, have too strengthened the conclusions reached in this volume.

Hriday Nath Kaul

Acknowledgments

It was in the course of research on a geo-political history of Kashmir at the National Archives of India, New Delhi, that I came across abundant references to the India China boundary in Kashmir. These references clearly revealed a contrary view on the boundary issue than was prevalent. This curious finding I discussed with Professor Devender Swarup, a fellow researcher at the National Archives. He advised me to pursue the subject and write on it. The result is this volume, though it has taken very long to complete the work and unconscionably delayed my original project, a geo-political history of Kashmir.

In the course of the long years of research I met with enormous courtesy and enjoyed the ready cooperation of Archivists of the National Archives and librarians of its magnificent library without whose willing assistance this volume would never have been completed. To them all I owe my deep gratitude. The National Archives did its best to make available to me as much of the closed records as possible. I am obliged to it.

Acknowledgements

Chapter 1
Northern Boundary in Kashmir Evidence

Historically India's boundary to the north, in Jammu and Kashmir State, with Tibet has fluctuated, presently resting on the outer Himalaya. With Chinese Turkistan the boundary ran over the Kuen Lun mountain and its continuation, the Kashgar chain, the eastern ridge of the Bolortagh (tagh-mountain). The Kuen Lun the Tibetan call by its near Sanskrit name, Angartaksia, (angar-fire) probably because of volcanic eruptions and the innumerable hot springs around its course. Mauryan and Kushan empires were exceptions. Both these included, at least, the bulk of Chinese or Eastern Turkistan, Four Garrisons, Altyshahr, Moghalistan, Kashgaria, Sinkiang or Xinjiang, as it has been called from time to time, to the north of the Kuen Lun. To the southwest of the Angirtaksia, the present day Afghan districts of Balkh, or Bactria of ancient times, and Badakshan or Tokharistan, as it was earlier known, were provinces of the Mauryan empire. The boundary westward of the Kuen Lun, therefore, lay to the north of Sirikul, or Sarikul, and the Pamirs, or the 'Nabapanktis' of the Asokan inscription. Incorporated within its fold was Lake Sirikul or Sarikul, a source of the Oxus river, or the Vanku of the Hindus. Emperor Asoka built a stupa at Varshdi, presently Tashkurgan, the site of the Sirikul fort, traces of which Sir Aurel Stein, eminent historian, came upon in the course of his archaeological explorations in the beginning of the 20th century.[1] To the southeast of Sirikul, near Aktagh, at the head of the Aksai Chin plains in Ladakh, was found by the Filippo De Filippi's Italian expedition of the Himalaya and Karakoram, 1914, a Ladakhi 'mani' wall with usual invocation "Om Mane Padme Om."[2] Both these, the remains of the stupa at Tashkurgan and the 'mani' wall, bear mute testimony to the extent of India to the north. Other Indian empires, Moghal apart, never reached even the Kuen Lun. But for a brief while Skardo, or Baltistan, north of Kashmir valley and Khotan in Eastern Turkistan were united under the Balti king, Vijayavarman. Obvious economic and geographical considerations, however, warrant the assumption that Kashmir, Ladakh, Baltistan and the Bolor States–Gilgit, Hunza, Nagar Yasin, or ancient Warshgam, Chitral, all northwest of Kashmir Valley and Kafiristan, now in Afghanistan, became successor States to these empires. The Bolor States, excluding Kafiristan, but with Baltistan or Skardo, now comprise the "Northern Territories" under Pakistan. Kashmir, principally, did not neglect to control the trade lines passing over Skardo and Ladakh.[3] This is evident from the campaigns of the kings of Kashmir in these parts. Moghal frontier touched the Kuen Lun through Skardo and Ladakh, its vassals. Such a boundary line placed, at least, the bulk of the Yarkand valley in India with China, or Kashgaria, avowdly confined to the Sanju, Kilian and Kukyar boundary passes over the Kuen Lun. The Kuen Lun was not a boundary drawn under a treaty but was laid down by nature and sanctioned by time and usage. No boundary marks, like pillars, could be set on so high and inaccessible mountain chains as the Kuen Lun partly, if not wholly, covered with huge glaciers, and even if erected could not have lasted, at least, for a period of time, amidst adverse weather conditions, as the British themselves were to concede in the context of the chain of mountains that they later caused to be called the Karakoram.

The Yarkand valley, stretching from the southern base of the Kuen Lun to the northern foot of the Karakoram pass (18,500 feet) astride the Karakoram ridge, has a few populated and cultivated tracts towards the north. In these tracts are to be found an Indian race or a race of Indian extraction, far more allied to the Indo-European than to any Mongol, Chinese, Tibetan or Turk race with which they may have been recently admixed[4], the Pakhpos as they are locally known. The celebrated Chinese pilgrim, Hiuen-tsang, narrates the legend about the sun origin of the founder of the Sirikul royal dynasty, w hich could well be the story of a Suryavanshi Indian prince. Hence, perhaps, the name Sirikul, or the illustrions clan, which the British fudged into Sirikul, head of the lake in Persian, or yellow valley, yellow from sariq in Turki. West and northwest of the Karakoram pass there were a few villages, inhabited by the Kanjutis, or people of Kanjut or Hunza, until the beginning of the 20th century. In Sirikul again are to be found a people whom Robert Shaw, a 19th century Kangra tea-planter, who doubled up as a British political agent, calls "Aryans,"[5] distinct from the Turks of Kashgar and Yarkand in Eastern Turkistan. All these people, the flotsam and jetsam of Indian history, couped up in these mountain fastnesses, lend an ethnic credibility to the Kuen Lun as the northern boundary in these regions. Together with the

Taghdumbash and Little Pamirs, north of the Hindu Kush mountains, or the Gravakasas of the Hindus, the region witnessed a demographic change in the beginning of the 19th century, if not a little earlier, with the advent of the Kirghiz from Kokand in the present day Tajikistan. Their arrival sparked a fierce ethnic conflict that virtually depopulated the Pamirs and largely the Yarkand valley. This depopulated nature of the country heavily weighed on British military strategists and influenced them to change the boundary of India in these parts.

That the northern boundary ran over the Kuen Lun-Kashgar chains is confirmed by a 15th century work, 'Tarikh-i-Rashidi,' chronicled by Mirza Mohammad Haidar Daughlat, a cousin of emperor Babar, who served under the sultans of Moghalistan or Kashgaria. He defined the limits of Eastern Turkistan thus: "...on the south along the whole length of the country the mountains forming the scarp of Tibetan highlands shut it off from all beyond. Towards the west the Pamirs, generally speaking constituted its extreme limits..."[6] As if to leave no room for doubt, Mirza Haidar described the "mountains of Tibet" as the source of the Karakash, or the Gomati, as it was called in ancient times. The Karakash flows down the south face of the Kuen Lun into Aksai Chin, runs west and finally north into Khotan. The name Tibet is generally applied to Ladakh by Mirza Haidar. 'Tarikh-i-Rashidi' also helps in knowing almost the exact limits of Bolor which has a significant bearing on the Sino-Indian boundary issue since it establishes Hunza, or Kanjut, included trans-Hindu Kush territories of the Taghdumbash Pamir and Sirikul. In an annotation for its English translation, British political agent, Ney Elias, rather, grudgingly concedes that "possibly even the comparatively low lying district of Tashkurgan (Sirikul), though to the north of the Hindu Kush watershed, may also have been included in Bolor. Thus it would, perhaps, be more correct to say that the province of Yarkand and Baltistan formed the eastern boundary of the region in question. "Bolor in a British map, to which Eilas' note refers, embraced greater part of eastern Pamirs also. That Bolor extended to the north of the Hindu Kush is also evident from Marco Polo's travels. Tashkurgan in Sirikul district is the northern end of the Taghdumbash Pamir. Consequently Taghdumbash was in Bolor, so also Raskam to its east, where it was bounded by Yarkand and Baltistan. Both Raskam, or the western part of the Yarkand valley, and Taghdumbash are contiguous to Hunza and Taghdumbash formed part of this chiefship to the north of the Hindu Kush. Elias, however, excludes Raskam from Hunza. Mirza Haidar claimed it formed part of Altyshahr.

Unlike the firm but traditional Ladakh–Eastern Turkistan frontier, the

Ladakh–Tibet sector of the northern boundary in Jammu and Kashmir drastically changed more than once as Ladakh's power waxed and waned in the last millennium. At the zenith of her power, the Gangri range, separating the Brahmaputra river basin from that of the Indus river, was Ladakh's eastern frontier, leaving Mnah-ris-skor-gsum, or western Tibet, which includes Changthang, in Ladakh. When Ladakh's power declined, the boundary shrank to the outer Himalaya, to the Lhari stream, near Demchok, on the Indus, Ladakh losing western Tibet. This frontier line, the present boundary of Ladakh with the addition of Minsar enclave, near Guge in Tibet, was laid down in the treaty of Tingmosgong* of 1683, that ended a three year long war, 1681-1683, between Ladakh and Tibet, then ruled by Qosot Mongols. From south, Spiti, to north, at least, Lanak la (la-pass), over the Karakoram chain, this boundary is well marked such as with large distinctive stones that serve the purpose of boundary pillars.

Such a boundary to the north left within India the extensive plateaux of Aksai Chin, or (western) Changthang as it was known until the end of the 17th century and which the Ladakhis have, thereafter, called Lingzithang, upper and lower Yarkand valley, Taghdumbash Pamir and Sirikul, all, except the last, arctic or sub-arctic wastes and very largely unpopulated. Not only was the Kuen Lun a firm and well recognised boundary in the north but Aksai Chin, a desert, to its south, held no inducement for Turks, living in Khotan, Yarkand and Kashgar, to venture into it except for trade. The region even though largely sterile, is highly strategic. The military importance of Ladakh, Skardo and Gilgit particularly is reflected in the titanic struggle between Tibet and China in the 8th century for supremacy in the Four Garrisons. Possession of Ladakh, Skardo, Gilgit and Warshgam, or Yasin, enabled Tibet to out flank China in the Four Garrisons. In the event Tibet in the 8th Century posed a great threat to Kashmir for all these territories are but outlying districts of hers in a political sense. Tibet's challenge was effectively met by China for a while, under General Kao Hsien-chih, in 747 A.D. No less spirited was Kashmir's response. King Lalitaditya put back India's frontier over the Kuen Lun, or, perhaps, beyond, in Kashgaria, defeating a combined Tibetan and Dard= force.[7]

Military considerations have no less contributed to settling Ladakh's northern boundary over the Kuen Lun. South of the Kuen Lun lies the

* For text of the treaty see appendix I.

= People of Gilgit, Yasin, Nagar and Hunza.

dreary desert of Aksai Chin, largely devoid of even sweet water and grass. Any invader, like Mirza Haidar in the 15th century, had, therefore, to carry his own supplies, including fodder, from Eastern Turkistan, the nearest sources were to the north of the Kuen Lun in the villages of Sanju, Kilian and Kukyar, well nigh 150 miles distant from Nubra valley to the south of the Karakoram pass where the invading armies were confronted by Ladakh army, or, if attacking Ladakh from the east as Tibetans certainly did in the 8th and 17th centuries, the invaders had to victual themselves from Guge, Rudok and Gartok in Western Tibet. Transport of supplies, even for a small force, over the desert was possible at only prohibitive cost, including large scale destruction of carriage animals. En route the invading force had also to endure effects of high altitude. These same considerations might well have persuaded Ladakhis to meet the Qosot Mongol-Tibetan invasion of Mnah-ris-skor-gsum in 1681, only around Mount Kailash and Lake Mansarovar, the area behind right up to the boundary pass of Mayur la and ahead no less, was an unpopulated desert. South of the Karakarom pass, supplies of all kinds were plentifully at hand, the country productive, the altitude lower. For these reasons all defence works of Ladakh were built on the Karakoram. North of the ridge only a civil presence was maintained through mining, pasturing, hunting and trading. The desert was left undeveloped, without roads particularly, to impede the progress of an invading force as much as possible. When the British arrived in Ladakh they shared this traditional thinking on the defence of Ladakh around the Karakoram but with a rider that was partly a departure from it as will be seen.

'Pashm' wool was another major factor to shape the Ladakh-Tibet part of the northern boundary. Most of 'pashm' imported by Kashmir came from Tibet. Extension of Moghal power to Ladakh during Moghal emperor Shahjahan's rule seems to have been in pursuit of control over 'pashm' wool trade to ensure increasing supplies to Kashmir's shawl industry. In the wake of Moghal court's summer visits to Kashmir its shawl industry had witnessed a phenomenal growth. It was set to acquire, in a few decades, worldwide markets. Moghal intervention in the three years long Ladakh-Tibet war was, therefore inevitable. The Qosot Mongols were driven out of what is now Ladakh. But the Moghals were disinclined to chase them out of Mnah-ris-skor-gsum for fear of being trapped in Tibet for the winter, cut off from all supplies by snow-bound passes. The boundary came to be fixed, as the Italian historian, Dr. Luciano Petech, puts it on the *uti possidetis* principle.[8] This is the present boundary of Ladakh-shorn of Mnah-ris-skor-gsum, including Chanthang, the habitat of the 'pashm' bearing ibex goat. Ladakh was still allowed to retain monopoly in 'pashm' wool trade, a concession entirely dictated by the direct Moghal presence in the neighbouring Kashmir. The 'pashm' factor continued to influence the course of history of Ladakh and, no less, of Tibet. For the war the Qosot Mongols had enlisted military assistance of Bashahr, now in Himachal Pradesh State, in return for unimpeded right to its subjects to travel and trade in Mnah-ris-skor-gsum, a right that, with British encouragement, degenerated into contraband trade in 'pashm' in the early 19th century, and led to occupation of Ladakh by the Sikhs and their invasion of Tibet.

The three years long Ladakh-Tibet war indisputably establishes that the Himalaya are not an insurmountable military barrier and were not looked upon as a political or even a geographical limit of India in the northwest, which the British later attempted to make them for the reason the Lahore State of Maharaja Ranjit Singh occupied the country up to the Kuen Lun. Easy passage by fairly large bodies of men must have been a common occurrence along the course of the Sutlej from Bashahr and Spiti in to Tibet and vice versa. Because of this knowledge Tibet, to ensure her victory against Ladakh, enlisted the military assistance of Bashahr, a State to the south of the Himalaya. The free movement of Bashahr troops across the Himalaya ultimately changed British thinking on the northern boundary in the region and persuaded them to seize Spiti and incorporate it in British India, that the treaty of Amritsar, 1846, which gave birth to modern Jammu and Kashmir State, did not provide for. The inner Himalaya then ceased to be projected by the British as India's frontier in the north in Jammu and Kashmir.

Their geo-political importance Ladakh, Yarkand valley, Sirikul and the Taghdumbash Pamir owed to some major and minor roads that ran through them from Central Asia to the plains of India. These were essentially trade lines, yet no less military routes for where caravans ventured easily, armies followed. The more important of these lines were : (i) From Polur, north of the Kuen Lun on the Ladakh-Eastern Turkistan boundary, to Keria la, Lanak la and Leh. It largely ran over what may conveniently be called east Aksai Chin, stretching to 82^0 E longitude. Keria la is a pass over the Kuen Lun in east Aksai Chin. A variation of this important highway led from the Lanak la to Rudok in Tibet and beyond to Lhasa. Deteruil de Rhins, a 19th century French explorer, "discovered" his own by pass of this road from Lake Yeshil Kul, south of Keria la, to Rudok further south. The main line and its variation was, probably, the principal route of commerce, before its use was proscribed, as also a military road that was probably used by the Dzungar invaders of Tibet. (ii) Yarkand-Shahidulla-Karakoram-Leh highway became the main trade route for Central Asian commerce after traffice was prohibited on the east Aksai Chin road. It had a winter and summer variation. Shahidulla, on the southern foot of the Kuen Lun, was a Ladakh boundary post on this route. A rival route to this line went over the glacier covered Muztagh pass (19019 ft.), west of the Karakoram pass, via Skardo. Mirza Haidar invaded Ladakh by the Yarkand-Leh road. (iii) Ferghana-Kizil Art-Sirikul line started in present day Tajikistan. This road bifurcated at Tashkurgan, one branch led to Shahidulla and Leh by the Yarkand valley and another via the Taghdumbash Pamir ended in Hunza across the Hindu Kush, or went by the Shinde pass over the Sirikul chain of the Bolortagh to Little Pamir, or over the Baroghil pass (12,400 ft.), across the Hindu Kush, into Chitral and down the Indus valley to Peshawar or Jallalabad. This was the nearest and, in some respects, the easiest road to India, militarily of great significance. Mirza Haidar used the bifurcations to escape from Ladakh to Badakshan. By this line Russia in the 19th century briefly acquired access to the Hindu Kush. Among the minor roads, one took off from Khotan to Yangi dawan (dawan-pass) (19092 ft.) overlooking Aksai Chin, through which it ran to the boundary pass of Lanak and thence to Rudok. This road China surreptitiously built into a motorable highway in 1950s. Entering Indian territory just east of Sarig Jilgang it courses northwest to Amtogor, Yangpa and then, across the Lanak la, into Tibet. China calls this road "Yehcheng-Gartok," or Sinkiang-Tibet highway.[9] Another minor route ascended the Hindutash pass over the Kuen Lun from Bushia in Khotan, ran over Lingzithang plains to the Lanak la or crossed one of the two main passes, Changlungbarma and Changlungyogma, over the Karakoram ridge, into Changchenmo valley in Ladakh. Khotan-Shahidulla-Karakash valley, along the Karakash river, was another minor road negotiable during the winter when the water level was low or the river frozen. This was reputedly a military road used by a mythical hero, Rustom, to attack Tibet.

Towards the east, Ladakh and Tibet were connected by three major highways, all commercial or military lines. The first road led from Leh by Rudok to Lhasa and beyond to Beijing, the Junglam highway as it was known. Mirza Haider invaded Tibet by this road. From Demchok ran the second line, along the course of the Indus, to the 'pashm' market town of Gartok. The Qosot Mongols were beaten back on this road in their attempt to enter Ladakh. The third route started in Spiti, ascended the Shipki la, and led to Lake Mansarovar and Mount Kailash. Roads also led from Gilgit to Yasin and Chitral or to Little Pamir, to Kashmir over the Brazil pass (13,300 ft.) and via Chilas, over the Babusar pass, to the Indus valley. What lines Kao, Mir Wali and Mirza Haidar, the latter both in the service of the sultans of Moghalistan, followed to reach the Bolor States is not known. But these could only have been from Yarkand and Kashgar via the Gez defile and the eastern face of the Kashgar range respectively to Sirikul, by the Khorabort and Ishkoman or Karambar passes to Yasin, or by the Kilik or Mintaka to Hunza and Gilgit. These Hindu Kush passes were negotiable by small bodies of men as the British and the Russians later proved in the 19th century in the course of their long political and military rivalry.

Earliest recorded British views on Ladakh's geo-political importance are those of William Moorcroft, Superintendent of East India Company's Stud, and early 19th century traveller. Moorcroft travelled to Ladakh with the concurrence of the Governor General-in-Council.[10] Once in Leh in 1820, Moorcroft proposed to enter Tibet, then closed to Europeans, and travel to Kokand, evidently to judge for himself how negotiable roads from Central Asia to India were. The intercession of the 'Kalon,' or minister, of Ladakh, on his behalf with the Gartok and Lhasa authorities failed. But the correspondence fully establishes independence of Ladakh.[11] The provision in the Tingmosgong treaty for the despatch of the triennial 'Lapchak' mission with gifts for Lhasa is seen by some western historians as the basis of Ladakh's subordination to Tibet. The correspondence should set at rest China's similar claims made during negotiations with India on the boundary issue. Moorcroft secured submission of the Gyalpo (Raja) of Ladakh to the British Indian Government,[12] as anticipated by Maharaja Ranjit Singh. Envoys were despatched to Ladakh by Lahore[13] to exact tribute from the Gyalpo. Moorcroft himself confirms this to Charles Metcalfe, Secretary, Secret Department, Calcutta. Anglo-Sikh rivalry over Ladakh later became intense.

Moorcroft was impressed by the convenience Ladakh afforded "as an advanced post preparatorily to the invasion of China." Quite evidently Moorcroft had the Lanak la-Keria la-Polur road in mind. His appraisal of Ladakh's geo-political importance he made in the context of a Russian invasion of China. But if the occupation of Ladakh was important to Russia in case of hostilities with China, it could scarcely have been less favourable to England in a similar contingency. No "political blunder," he wrote to Matcalfe, could have been, therefore, greater than that committed by China in permitting a country so important to its tranquillity by situation as Ladakh and of which the inhabitants were, in a degree, attached to the interests of China by the same religion to remain unannexed to the empire. That Ladakh could have equally served British interests against China Moorcroft himself alludes to. Information of Ladakh coming under the protection of the East India Company, Moorcroft elaborated, "must create alarm in the Chinese Government," for from Ladakh the "British power has the extraordinary facility of keeping in awe both China and the government that may hold Kashmir."[14] This is evidently how China saw Ladakh in 1950s and made up for the past blunder. China's failure to incorporate Ladakh and Baltistan in her empire, Moorcroft ascribed to her "ignorance or timidity." Her occupation of the whole tract of the country between Lhasa and Yarkand would have, he thought, rounded in this direction all possessions of China or its dependencies without the intervention of a single foreign territory but leaving as their barrier the Himalaya mountains[15]. This still could be the strategic objective of China in Ladakh.

Even after they reached the Himalaya in the beginning of the 19th century, the British hardly had any precise knowledge of this great range of mountains and much less, indeed, of the parallel chains running northeast to northwest of the Himalaya. In fact the countries between India and China were *terra incognita* to the British. Little was known to Europeans about them then other than that the vast tract of land was a labyrinth of mountains and narrow valleys. These mountains were then known by the collective name of the Kuen Lun, and to traders and travellers as mountains of Tibet or Khotan. Westward Angartaksia recedes and its continuation is regarded to be the Kashgar range over which towers the Tagharma or the Muztagh. This Muztagh is not to be mixed up with the Muztagh over the range which, before the arrival of Englishmen, was part of the Kuen Lun system but later came to called the Karakoram chain. Running parallel to the Kashgar mountains is the Sirikul chain, the two separated by a high level trough at the southern end of which are situated Sirikul and Taghdumbash Pamir. West of the Kashgar ridge are the Pamirs, largely arctic but partly a rich pasturage. Eastward along the Kuen Lun stretches (western) Changthang or, now, Aksai Chin plains. Of vital importance was the knowledge of this tract, particularly its mountain passes and passages, many carved out by the flood tides of the rivers Indus, Sutlej, Ghagra and Brahmaputra through the Himalaya and by the Yurungkash, Karakash and Yarkand through the Kuen Lun. For these passes and passages were also the routes of trading caravans. This large mountainous area, therefore, awaited to be probed by British military officers, political agents and surveyors, among the latter two many Indians. For the accomplishment of this immense and, in those early years, dangerous task the British virtually spent the whole of the 19th century. Their studies and reports provide ample evidence on India's northern boundary in Jammu and Kashmir State before and after the advent of the British in Ladakh.

Of the explorers the earliest were Moorcroft, who probed Mnah-ris-skor-gsum in Tibet in 1811, and Mir Izzatullah, an employee of the British Residency in Delhi, who travelled to Central Asia 1812. In Moorcroft's travel journal mention is made of the Niti-Gartok road,[16] which he later elaborated, was the Moghal line of commerce with Central Asia, running from Niti in the present day Garhwal to Gartok-Rudok-Keria la and Polur. The purpose of his visit to Tibet was to divert 'pashm' wool from Ladakh and Kashmir to British India which, indeed, had already started through an Englishman of Bareilly, one Gilman, in clear infraction of the treaty of Tingmosgong. Mir Izzatullah's journey was in the nature of a politico-economic reconnaissance, for Central Asia was then seen in Europe to provide an overland invasion route to India. In his travelogue the Mir no where calls any of the parallel chains of mountains by the name of the Karakoram or Muztagh which he refers to as passes. A sharp observer, Izzatullah does not mention the Karakoram as Ladakh's northern boundary. On the country he clearly states "from this place (The Karakoram pass) the territory of Khotan is 12 days journey to the north."[17] On one side of the Karakoram, he notes, "is Tibet Baltoo and on the other Sur-i-kool (Sirikul) which is Badakshan frontier." By the Karakoram referred to here the Mir means the Kuen Lun. A route is said by Izzatullah to have run through the Muztagh pass to Yarkand while a shorter one reputedly existed but the Baltis refused to reveal it to him. Several camping sites are also mentioned by him as he rode over the Leh-Yarkand road of commerce, including Brangsa, in Ladakhi traveller's shelter, Tugnuh, copper in Ladakhi and Kirghiz Jungle. He appears to have been unaware of its local name, Kokart. One day's journey from Kirghiz Jungle, Izzatullah mentions, was Shahidulla Khoja, Ladakh's boundary out-post. Two days journey beyond Shahidulla was again a mine from which agate or cornelian was mined. The Mir saw people going in that direction from Kukyar, a boundary village of Eastern Turkistan, to purchase these stones. Significantly Izzatullah does not say that the mine was Chinese, a claim which later day Englishmen made about a jade mine to the south of Shahidulla, obliquely to suggest that China's boundary touched these Ladakh areas. At Kirghiz Jungle the Mir saw ruins of houses which he says were destroyed by Chinese in reprisals against the plundering of caravans by Kirghiz. Kirghiz Jungle was a Kashmir boundary pass and the valley site of a Ladakh guard-house. Other places of interest mentioned by Izzatullah were the Ladakh boundary passes or posts–Yangi dawan, overlooking the Yarkand valley, Kulanuldi, where the road left Yarkand river that rises on the north face of the Karakoram pass, Chiragsaldi, Mazar and Karghalik, the last two on Chinese side. Mazar was a Chinese customs post and Karghalik a Turkistan border trading town. Turkish language was spoken from Kukyar and beyond, the Mir does not refer to these passes and places in the context of boundary between India and China. But this is brought out by his noticing them as Ladakhi or Turkish names.

Earliest reference by an Englishman to Ladakh's boundary is made by Walter Hamilton, in his "Geographical, Statistical and Historical Description of Hindustan." It precedes Moorcroft's visit to Ladakh in 1820. Other than with Kashmir, Hamilton says, "all other boundaries are wholly undefined, the interior never having been explored by any European." Yet he went on to indicate Ladakh-Tibet boundary being five days journey from Gurden–latitude 30°32'N, longitude 81°7'E, "Chinese regular station," 17 miles from Mansarovar[18]. Such a boundary with Tibet excluded the Lanak la-Keria la-Polur road from Ladakh which ran over east Aksai Chin. Hamilton's boundary is what later came to be adopted as Ladakh's northeastern limit with Tibet by England and, erroneously, accepted by India. Yet Hamilton's boundary was in the realm of speculation. As then England had no fixed ideas on the northern boundary, one reason why British explorers like J.B. Fraser and Captain Alexander Gerard persisted exploring Himalaya, the upper waters of the Sutlej in Spiti and the Tsomerreri (Tso=lake) in south Ladakh. Fraser considered the chains of mountains south of the Indus in Ladakh, which later came to be named Kailash, as a ramification of the Himalaya, stretching westward from the Mansarovar. Gerard was prevented from entering Tibet. He consequently had only a distant look at the Kailash from what he calls as the border pass of Keurbung. He saw Kashmir "the true limits of the Himalaya range," an observation which, together with their explorations suggests British interest in making it as the limit of the British empire. Credence is lent to this view by both Fraser and Gerard declaring, erroneously though, Tsomerreri as the source of the Para river, an affluent of the Sutlej. Tsomerreri was thus sought to be the watershed for a possible Himalaya boundary in the region. Six passes leading from Kinnaur, now in Himachal Pradesh, to Tibet were explored by Gerard, all were found practical for loaded sheep. Three frequented routes to Tibet were the Shipki, Shalkur and Guntung. By the latter the Sutlej was crossed at Chaksum Sango. Another all weather line led from Shalkur to Leh and beyond to Central Asia.[19]

With the routes of commerce and invasion passing through Ladakh, Moorcroft became familiar during his two year long stay there from 1820. He dismissed the Yarkand-Leh trade route as "most rugged." Emergency, he thought, might yet again "discover that taken by the Kalmaks," as Moorcroft called the Dzungars, "when they invaded Tibet," said to be "both shorter and more level but proscribed."[20] He only feared, as he was told, that this line did not run over the desert of Kolu, "a fact which he believed would prevent China to allow its use by Englishmen for their commerce with Khotan and Yarkand. This road could only be the Rudok-Lanak la-Keria la-Polur highway, the two end places separated by merely a "chain of mountains," which he further, though in a different context, elaborates were, "low." The "desert of Kolu" could only be Aksai Chin, more specifically east Aksai Chin and the "low" chain of mountains the Kuen Lun. Evidently the name Aksai Chin was not current in 1820 or else Moorcroft would have used it instead of an obscure name like "Kolu desert." That Moorcroft felt an emergency would again discover the Lanak la-Polur line of commerce suggests that it had been the trade route before the Dzungars seized it in 1717. Reference to the Niti-Gartok road by Moorcroft, briefly noticed earlier, became numerous in his despatches to senior officials of the East India Company. His keenness for this road stemmed from his belief that the Moghals had an extensive commerce with Central Asia by this line, which he suggested British trade could follow. The road, Moorcroft traced, started at Najibabad, in the present day State of Uttar Pradesh, ran to Niti-Gartok-Rudok, along the Karakash river to Sarekia, Shahidulla, Kilian, Karghalik and Yarkand."[21] Apart from the error of placing Sarekia to the south of Shahidulla–it is to its north–this road necessarily ran through Western Aksai Chin after Rudok and from the Karakash river to Shahidulla came later to be known as the Changchenmo road. The road existed all right but its use by caravans of any size was unlikely then. In the 19th century it was not used at all. Probably the caravans headed for Polur from Rudok. Here again Moorcroft does not mention Aksai Chin at all. The importance of Sarekia he attributed to its jasper mines which were frequented by merchants from India. The materials for flower work and tracery in the Taj Mahal he speculated "may have been from the mountains of Khotan" where he places Sarekia. No mention is made by Moorcroft also of China or Chinese owning the mines.

Geographical notices of Moorcroft convincingly establish the northern boundary of Ladakh and no less that there was no mountain range known then as the Karakoram. He certainly refers to "the Mountains of Karakoram" in his despatch, dated 29 September 1820, but categorically states that "the most rugged" Leh-Yarkand road ran over these chains that took 35 days to cover, end to end. The line ascended the Karakoram pass, astride the ridge now known as the Karakoram mountains, Sogat, Sanju or Kilian saddles, all over the Kuen Lun. Evidently Moorcroft was altogether unaware of the Kuen Lun name. This is confirmed by some other observations of Moorcroft. In noticing the limits of Khotan he wrote "It is bounded by the mountains of Tibet to the south[22]...," a nomenclature earlier used by Mirza Haidar. Again in his memorandum on Khotan Moorcroft remarks that the Karakash river, "proceeds from the mountains of Khotan[23]..." The southern boundary of Khotan was the Kuen Lun until 1950s and the Karakash, of course, springs from the Kuen Lun. As the name of the mountain chains, the Kuen Lun, to the north of the outer Himalaya, was evidently unknown among local people in general and traders in particular, Moorcroft used the names commonly in use. His informants appear to have been traders. Moorcroft goes on to define the boundary of Ladakh with Chinese Turkistan as the "Muztagh or Karakoram[24]..." Here again it is evident that the Karakoram or Muztagh, names of two passes, was the local name of the Kuen Lun, alongwith the mountains of Tibet or Khotan. Referring to Mirza Haidar's invasion of Ladakh, Moorcroft notes the Mirza marched across the Muztagh at Karakoram. Again he refers to the Karakoram Muztagh as Ladakh's boundary. Evidently he means the Kuen Lun. Once this is accepted Moorcrofts boundary of Ladakh is easily comprehended :

> "...on the northeast and north by part of Balti and Kufilong (Skardo) and by Muztagh or Karakoram mountains forming the boundary of Chinese Turkistan."

This boundary puts, at least, one part of theYarkand valley in Skardo and another in Ladakh. So, does it enclose Lingzithang or Aksai Chin in the Gyalpo's dominion. Again, agreeably, Muztagh-Karakoram forms the southern boundary of Chinese Turkistan. Moorcroft's view, conveyed to Metcalfe, that the Kokand-Ladakh line via Sirikul was a desideratum with Russia yet again confirms the accuracy of his boundary of Ladakh for this road passed through bulk of the Yarkand valley from Sirikul. Russia was also credited by Moorcroft with a request to the Gyalpo to remove difficulties en route. This would not have been possible were

Yarkand valley and Aksai Chin–or a loop line to Khotan–not in Ladakh. That there is no error in the assumption that the Kuen Lun and Karakoram are but one range of mountains is evident from Moorcroft's remonstrance with Metcalfe. Were Ladakh's allegiance accepted, Moorcroft assured Metcalfe, the use of the prohibited Aksai Chin route would be permitted by Ladakh[25]. Such permission could not have been given by the Gyalpo were the Kuen Lun and Karakoram two different ranges of mountains. In that eventuality, with the Karakoram as the northern boundary of Ladakh, Aksai Chin would be outside the territorial limits of the Gyalpo. Besides, Moorcroft truthfully states that the Dzungar attack was "invasion of Ladakh." The road by which they entered this principality "was closed and travelling upon it prohibited under pain of death by the order of the Government.[26] "The situation of this road and the existence of the Sirikul-Ladakh and Sirikul-Hunza parts of the Kokand highway are the heart of the India-China boundary dispute. In commending the Gyalpo's submission to the Governor General in Council, Moorcroft anticipated several objections, including that the British empire would pass beyond its natural–the Himalaya–limit. Moorcroft rejected the Himalaya as the British empire's northern boundary. To Metcalfe he wrote, "I have seen no features which announce a natural division between the Rajas of Kulu and Ladakh, nor can I learn that such boundary exists between Ladakh and Bashahr."[27] Here was an attempt by Moorcroft to influence British thinking on the northern boundary of the British empire. But it was too early for the British to rush in. Even so Moorcroft's view was not rejected.

There is no unanimity over the road the Dzungars took in 1717 to reach Tibet. Lieutenant George Hayward, a British explorer connected with the Royal Geographical Society, was of the view that the Dzungars set off from Yarkand, crossed the Yangi dawan into the Yarkand valley and thence went across Aksai Chin to Lanak la, to Rudok. This view is shared by Margaret Fisher and others.[28] But the Dzungars are said to have been 7000 strong cavalrymen! A force that could hardly have survived more than a few days, if at all even that long, in the arctic Aksai Chin desert. The almost insurmountable difficulties faced even on the fringe of the Lingzithang plains can be gauged from Mirza Haidar's experiences during his flight from Ladakh to Badakshan. Near Aktagh, a road junction well to the south of the Kuen Lun, they could not get water. The fairly large Yarkand river froze by sunset though it was only September. Try hard as they did, Mirza Haidar and a score of his companions could not break the ice. Even the strongest among his beasts of burden died. The 300 strong Forsyth expedition to Yarkand, 1870, which despite supplies laid on in advance, nearly perished in Lingzithang. Evidently even small bodies of men and beasts could not safely travel in Aksai Chin. In any event this Aksai Chin road was too long and the Yarkand valley part of it too frequented by trading caravans to ensure secrecy of approach of the Dzungars, a reason for which, presumably, they would have preferred this road to their usual northeast route to Tibet. Tibetan historian, Tespon W.D. Shakabpa, does not clearly indicate the road Dzungars took to reach Tibet. He merely says they "entered Tibet in the northwest."[29] Moorcroft, who explored the region along the Pangong lake, south of the Lanak la, half way across which the Ladakh-Tibet boundary runs, was told that the "Kalmaks" had come from the north,[30] that is Khotan and not Yarkand. The route from the north by which the Dzungars could have arrived, was only the Polur-Keria la-Lanak la-Rudok line. The noted Swedish explorer, Sven Hedin, who more than once explored Aksai Chin, confirms the Dzungars had, indeed, used the Polur-Keria la-Lanak la-Rudok line.[31] From Rudok they reached Lhasa by the Junglam highway. The Polur-Keria la-Lanak la-Rudok line over eastern Aksai Chin was far better than the one that traversed the Yarkand valley–western Aksai Chin regions. More water and grass were available en route and the altitude is generally lower. The two Aksai Chin roads are, indeed, but one.

Moorcroft was fully aware and conveyed it to Calcutta that strategically important roads passed over Lingzithang. One Aksai Chin road, he described to Metcalfe, ran over a low chain of mountains (Kuen Lun), four days journey north of Rudok. This was the bypass of the Polur-Keria la-Lanak la route. Both the main line and its variation mostly traversed east Aksai Chin approximately 82^{0}E. longitude. The road to Khotan was described to Moorcroft, during his explorations in the Pangong lake region, as both "shorter and more level" but "blocked up by the order of the Government of Ladakh[32]..." Following a portion of it himself, he found it, in a military view, some what difficult in parts. But if followed in a suitable season, Moorcroft saw it offered no material difficulties except in transport of artillery which could be overcome by the aid of Pioneers and robust porters of Kashmir and the Balti. The other Aksai Chin route was the Niti-Rudok-Lanak la-Sarekia line. That Moorcroft's despatches influenced British policy on the northern boundary is evident from the Forsyth expedition insisting on taking this rarely used route to Yarkand in 1870. His explorations in the Pangong-tso region also revealed to Moorcroft the road the Qosot Mangols successfully took to invade Ladakh in 1681, after their annexation of Mnah-ris-skor-gsum, and the ruins of the defence works of Sakti, to be further probed by British surveyors some years hence.

What were the frontiers of Ladakh on its annexation by the Sikhs in 1834? Dr. A.H. Francke, in an updated work of his, quotes Tse-brtan of Khalatse in Ladakh, who had fought in the "Dogra Wars" of 1834-42. From Tse-Brtan's testimony it is evident that in the west the boundary with Kashmir valley was Hdu-zi pass or Zoji la, in the northwest with Sbal-ti-yul, Baltistan or Skardo, it was Chos-hbad pass or Chorbut village and pass, in the southeast the boundary line passed over Pho-lon-hdra-hdra, or Fa-lung-danda, or Lingti. In the north Ladakh's territorial limit was Se-hdu-la pass, which is explained in the Index of the books as "Shahidulla, a place between Kuen Lun and Karakoram."[33] Shahidulla Khoja itself is at the south foot of the Kuen Lun, on the left bank of the Karakash or Gomati river. But the actual frontier line was up northward on the creast of the Kuen Lun, hence Shahidulla pass.

Tse-brtan's silence over Ladakh's eastern boundary is significant. He appears to have been a too well informed man to be ignorant about Ladakh's eastern limit. Therefore, the only rational explanation for his refraining from spelling the eastern boundary was Ladakh's irredentist claim to Mnah-ris-skor-gsum. This claim came to the fore during Lahore's invasion of Tibet in 1841. Moorcroft confirms Ladakh's boundary with Lahaul was a huge rock called Fa-lung-danda by Ladakhis and Lingti by the people of Lahaul[34]. Yet the British were to contest this claim. This rock, along with another set up near Rudok[35], after the Qosot Mongols retired from Ladakh, the Lha-ri-stream, near Demchok, and the fort at Shahidulla, are definite boundary marks and there is nothing vague or traditional about the eastern boundary of Ladakh as will be seen.

Over Spiti Moorcroft was initially, rather, equivocal. He declared it to be one of the two major 'parganahs' of Ladakh but with a rider that Lhasa was suspected to have jurisdiction over its south eastern part where a lama resided. One reason for Moorcroft's equivocation was the strategic importance of Spiti. It provides easy access to Tibet on the east, to the plains of northern India on the south and to Leh and beyond to Central Asia on the north. This factor as, indeed, Bashahr's possession then of trans-Himalayan Kinnaur had influenced Moorcroft to reject inner Himalaya as the British empire's ultimate boundary in this region. But after the Gyalpo's tender of submission to the British Indian Government, Moorcroft declared Spiti belonged to Ladakh. The arrival of Sikhs in Spiti, after annexation of Ladakh, persuaded the British to undertake surveys of the cis-Himalayan territories, Spiti and Kinnaur, with an eye to the Lahaul road to Tibet and Ladakh.

Whole of the Yarkand valley came to be controlled by Lahore after the annexation of Skardo in 1840. Skardo's appropriation, together with the tender of submission by Gilgit, Hunza and Nagar soon after, notionally made Lahore State a Central Asian State, its frontier in the north touching the Kuen Lun through Ladakh and Bolortagh through Hunza, the historical boundary of India. Of the submission of Hunza and Nagar to Lahore, the British appear to have been altogether ignorant for a long while, one reason why they did not, initially, acknowledge Kashmir's suzerainty over Hunza. The other reason was that Hunza then stretched across the Hindu Kush to include the Taghdumbash Pamir and Sirikul. England's policy on the northern boundary had not by then firmed up. Nor had any development occurred to induce a precipitous recognition of Kashmir rights. Skardo's boundary in the north, its Gyalpo had confided in Captain C.M. Wade, Governor General's Agent. North West Frontier, NWF, touched Chinese Turkistan.[36] To Wade the Gyalpo described Skardo's situation to be a point where Bolortagh (Kashgar range) and Muztagh (Karakoram) mountains converge and separate the lofty ledges of Tibet-Changthang-from the plains and valleys of Turkistan. This convergence occurs in the Taghdumbash Pamir. A high road over the mountains, evidently the route over the Muztagh pass, led from Skardo to Yarkand. G.T. Vigne, an English traveller who visited Skardo in 1835, partly explored the Muztagh. Vigne refers to Aksai Chin by its Ladakhi name of Changthang. He placed it north of Ladakh, or outside it. Calling the desert Changthang again suggests that Aksai Chin name was not current in 1830s. His observation that the road over Changthang to Yarkand was closed by "the jealousy of the Chinese"[37] contradicts Moorcroft both on the boundary of Ladakh and the prohibition enforced by the Gyalpo on travel through Aksai Chin. But Moorcroft's account was certainly based on information provided to him by the Government of Ladakh. Changthang was placed outside Ladakh by Vigne because over it ran the potential invasion route of Polur-Lanak la. Thus, preventing convergence of Central Asian roads on India was an early British policy objective. Vigne meditated an "excursion" over the Muztagh to Hunza and thence to the Pamirs and Kokand. His keenness to travel to Kokand was prompted by the mounting Russian pressure on the Khanate and its war with China in some way over Sirikul. Sirikul was seized and Kokand went on to capture Yarkand, evicting the Chinese.[38] British political agent, Alexander Burnes, from Kabul viewed Kokand as the key of Turkistan, on the high road to Chinese settlements of Kashgar, Yarkand and Khotan to the north of the Yarkand valley, where its Khan exercised much influence.[39] Russian predominance in Kokand was, therefore, a worrying situation for England in the context of the Indian empire.

Infraction of the Tingmosgong treaty by Tibet's "export" of "pashm" wool to British India prompted the Sikhs, as rulers of Kashmir, to revive Ladakh's claim to western Tibet. Between 1839 and 1840 "pashm" wool "export" to British India from Tibet had more than trebled, from 1013 maunds to 3496 maunds (1 maund=80 lbs) to cripple Kashmir's shawl industry on which subsisted, directly or indirectly, half the valley's 5 lakh population.[40] A Sikh invasion of Tibet was widely anticipated in 1840. A Nepalese contingent of 250 to 300 men appear to have entered Tibet, before the Sikh general Wazir Zorawar Singh's attack. The British suspected the Nepalese would join the Sikhs. But apprehensions that British protected Sutlej States would be attacked were dismissed unless there really was a coalition between Lahore, Nepal and China.[41] Implied is the possibility of movement of troops from trans to cis-Himalayan territories and the threat such a movement posed to the British in northern India.

The Sikh invasion of Tibet, under Zorawar Singh, was finally launched in 1841 from Dansikang, Sianguj and near the Pangong-tso.[42] The three columns together occupied the whole of Mnah-ris-skor-gsum, virtually without a contest. George Lushington, Commissioner of Kumaon, described to Government the object of invasion was "to secure for the Skihs the command of the trans-Himalayan traffic (salt, borax, shawl wool etc.)."[43] Bashahr, the centre of contraband "pashm" wool trade, was cut off from Tibet to prevent ingress of traders from the upper Kinnaur.[44] No evil other than immediate stoppage of contraband trade was apprehended by "the abrupt appearance of Sikh force." Nevertheless the Sikh movement in trans-Himalaya was seen as out flanking the British in northern India and, therefore, "fraught with much mischief." If not promptly met, the British apprehended, it would "eventually... imperil the prosperity and tranquillity not only of Kumaon but of all our frontier provinces."[45] Viewed thus how awesome are the consequences now for India of the Chinese presence in Tibet? What particularly alarmed the British was any proximity of Sikh positions to Nepal. Such proximity the Governor General-in-Council saw "as fraught with danger and inconvenience."[46] All these anxieties of England came to be reflected, on the founding of Jammu and Kashmir State in 1846, in the instructions given to the first boundary commission and in its proceedings. To arrest

Zorawar Singh in his tracks, George Clerk, Governor General's Agent, NWF, proposed to depute Lieutenant Joseph Cunningham, Assistant Agent, to Kinnaur frontier with Tibet to observe and report. A definite date, Clerk suggested to the Foreign Department at Fort William, Calcutta, should be named for withdrawal of Zorawar Singh "to within the commonly understood boundary of Ladakh."[47] Of this commonly understood boundary, the British must also have been aware to ensure complete Sikh withdrawal from Mnah-ris-skor-gsum. It could not, therefore, be argued, as the British did, and Chinese followed, that Ladakh's boundary was undefined.

On the annihilation of the little Sikh force in the winter of 1841 and Tibet's recovery of Mnah-ris-skor-gsum, the British saw Ladakh exposed to an invasion.[48] The Sikhs, Joseph Cunningham fancied, would seek their mediation to restrain the "Chinese"–as he called the Tibetans–from invading Ladakh. He was advised to be equivocal over any "Chinese" attempt to seize Ladakh but to remonstrate and signify the probability of the British Government having an interest "in preserving the State of dominion subsisting" before the annexation of Ladakh, that is Zoji la (Himalaya), being restored as the boundary.[49] This view Clerk also conveyed to T.H. Maddock, Secretary, Secret Department, as well, only little more explicitly.[50] Evidently the British had remained irreconciled to the Sikh conquest of Ladakh, involve as it did "extension" of India's frontier and Lahore's influence beyond the inner Himalaya. But the Governor General, Lord Ellanborough, did not wish to authorize any declaration to be made by Joseph Cunningham to either the Sikhs or the Tibetans regarding the future disposal of Ladakh or any other matter in dispute between them.[51] Not that Clerk had erred though as Governor General's Agent he should have known better. A British-Indian army, sent to Kabul to install Shah Shuja as the Amir was, on his overthrow, trapped near Jallalabad amidst Afghan insurrections that ended in the first Anglo-Afghan war. Aid from Sikhs was crucial for relieving Jallalabad. Yet it was not forthcoming what with the hated Raja Golab Singh, Commander-in-Chief of Sikh forces at Peshawar, sitting pretty. But for the Kabul factor, British opinion was extremely hostile to Sikhs, in particular to Jammu brothers, Rajas Golab Singh and Dhyan Singh, Lahore Prime Minister. British sentiment was well reflected in Joseph Cunningham's remark to Clerk, "...Chinese rule in Ladakh would, perhaps, be less disadvantageous to our interests than Sikh rule has been."[52] In this and similar British sentiments as, indeed, in the deliberate British references to Tibet as Chinese Tartary and Tibetans as Chinese must be seen England's desire to forge an entente with China, certainly to the north of India in Central Asia.

British countenance for the defence of Ladakh was, therefore, readily forthcoming. Clerk proposed to Meddock" ...not to hold any language towards the 'Darbar' (court) that would lead the Sikhs or the "Jammuies" (the Jammu Rajas) to apprehend that the British Government desires to prevent their protecting Ladakh."[53] The Governor General-in-Council took pains to explain the policy reversal. The British, it was pointed out, demanded cooperation of Raja Golab Singh in the direction of Peshawar. "...We cannot expect his cordial aid or that of his brother, Raja Dhyan Singh, if we at the same time offer any obstacle to the maintenance of their authority in the province of Ladakh."[54] Covertly, however, British opposition to Sikh presence in Ladakh persisted. After the destruction of Zorawar Singh's army, Tibetan views over the future of Ladakh markedly approximated the initial British opinion, ably projected by Joseph Cunningham in a stream of communications to Tibetan officials from the Indo-Tibetan boundary. 'Kalon' Surkhang of Tibet favoured status quo as it existed before Zorawar Singh annexed Ladakh–that is Ladakh's vassalage to Kashmir[55]. But British reverses in Afghanistan made impossible return to this status quo. Being thus forced to support Lahore, England still ensured that Sikh military operations did not exceed restoration of their power in Ladakh within Tingmosgong treaty limits. British acquiescence to the operations for the restoration of Ladakh was considered useful to the purposes of Jammu Rajas at Lahore 'Darbar' "and it is all the assurance we can give...in return for the aid which their relation to the 'Darbar' compels them unwillingly, it would seem, to give to our cause in Afghanistan."[56]

British political support to Lahore was nominal, limited to exchanges between Raja Dhyan Singh and Clerk. Indeed, even while offering political support, the British, rather coyly wished to deny them the use of their own territories for marching troops to Ladakh. Clerk justified demonstrating only limited interest in Ladakh, arguing any greater degree of encouragement would enthuse Raja Dhyan Singh to make propositions which, if not objectionable, were better avoided. For instance, Clerk noted, "he would probably ask permission to march reinforcement through that portion of Kulu which is under the protection of British Government."[57] Kulu was a Sikh protectorate and "that portion of Kulu which is under the protection of the British Government" was none other than Lahaul. With its excellent road to Leh it was, as Captain Alexander Cunningham had, during explorations in cis-Himalayan territories in the neighbourhood of Spiti, found to be tributary to Ladakh and, on that ground, Wazir Zorawar Singh had increased taxes.[58] Clerk's concern was, evidently, more for the road than any territory, the route leading to Spiti and beyond. It is debatable if the Sikhs would have ventured to recover Mnah-ris-skor-gsum. Yet the British continued to credit them with such an intention[59]. Invasions of countries beyond the Himalaya, it was feared by the British, would bring armies from beyond those mountains into India. It was, therefore, undesirable to extend the external political relations of Lahore, practically to extend British relations too. Seemingly the intention was to prepare for British intervention in Ladakh.

The spectre of foreign armies marching into India was conjured by Joseph Cunningham. From the Tibet boundary he reported to Clerk supplies having been laid on the Rudok-Yarkan road for a body of "genuine" Chinese troops[60]. The Rudok-Yarkand route was evidently the one over the Keria la to Polur, Guma and Yarkand, the line the Dzungars took for their invasion of Ladakh and Tibet. It linked up with the Lahaul road, referred to by Clerk, and made a credible invasion line from Central Asia to India. Six Ambans*, were also to reach Gartok to take charge of affairs. But a day later he wrote that the march of "genuine" Chinese troops was stayed "for the present" by Gumbo,[61] the Ladakh Raja's "Treasurer," who did not fancy Chinese presence in Ladakh. Joseph Cunningham having conjectured intervention in Ladakh, Clerk proposed that the Sikh-Tibetan conflict be patched up through British mediation. The Rajas of Jammu were not expected to desist from conflict with Tibet without establishing their frontier towards Tibet on such a footing" as to place the wool and tea trade of Kashmir beyond all risk of deterioration such as it has been suffering."[62] Chinese intervention, more fancied than real, beleaguered as China's sea-board provinces by England were then in the ongoing opium war, was a strong enough inducement for the British to initiate peace moves. However remote the passibility, spill over of these hostilities to the Indo-Tibetan border was undesirable.

Chinese assistance to Ladakh was forthcoming only on conditions. Ladakh, "as before," was to offer obeisance to Lhasa. Sikhs were to retain no area in Ladakh or Skardo and were to levy no tribute on either of these principalities. This would have brought down the boundary from the Kuen Lun to the inner Himalaya. The Gyalpos of both Ladakh and Skardo were to acknowledge Chinese supremacy as "before." Nothing

* Generally Chinese officials, the two at Lhasa were considered by the British to be "Residents," with imagined power to intervene.

more was heard of these conditions for the Chinese were in no position to dictate them, having no effective military presence in Tibet and negligible in Yarkand, to enforce them even if the Gyalpos of Ladakh and Skardo had really approached China. More credibly, however, the Ladakh Gyalpo *directly* petitioned Maharaja Sher Singh of Lahore, In this move to bypass Raja Dhyan Singh must be seen British hand. The Maharaja was promised the "usual services," or payment of tribute.[63] To such an arrangement, the revival of an "old custom," the Tibetans, or "Chinese," as the British pleased to call them, were also agreeable. If, however, the Rajas of Jammu did not leave, the Gyalpo threatened, the Chinese would, indeed, be inducted into Ladakh. The petition was sought to be despatched to Lahore through Joseph Cunningham, a service far too visible to be performed by the Assistant Agent to the Governor General. In Joseph Cunningham, the Gyalpo and his people also confided that Ladakh was "now within (Chinese) possessions."[64]

The threatened Chinese intervention, British records suggest, induced Raja Golab Singh to "seek cooperation" of England, at least, the Indian Government showing a front from Almora.[65] But the Rajas do not appear to have been unduly hard pressed. The intervention was too apparently British imagined. If Raja Golab Singh still urged the British Government to show a front from Almora; it was, perhaps, to mollify opinion in Lahore where opposition to Rajas, thanks to British intrigues, was simmering. The venom against the Jammu Rajas, the offer of submission of the Gyalpo, who seems to have been more under Joseph Cunninghm's spell than in counsel with 'Kalon' Surkhang of Tibet or even "genuine" Chinese, only reflected British desperateness at the despatch of a newly equipped force under Dewan Hari Chand, from Kashmir. Joseph Cunningham's despatches, one from Shalkur on the Indo-Tibetan boundary in particular[66], bring our boldly British interest to step into Ladakh conflict in one way or another, so also their keenness to limit the boundary in the north to the inner Himalaya in Kashmir. There was, as the British were soon to insist, nothing to covet beyond the Himalaya in Kashmir. It is very unlikely that Lahore, or even the Rajas themselves, as then grasped that the real reason for British hostility to the Sikhs holding Ladakh was not so much extension of India's limits beyond the inner Himalaya but access Lahore gained to Central Asia.

The long anticipated triumph of Lahore arms over Tibet put on hold British intentions on the northern boundary. In a "parwana" (communication) to Clerk, the Lahore 'Darbar' agreed to British mediation, through Joseph Cunningham, consistent with old treaties, incorporated in a 4 article draft peace treaty :

1. To preserve the old boundaries of Ladakh as possessed by the ancient Rajas.
2. To continue the import of shawl wool and tea as usual towards Kashmir.
3. To restore in original or its value the property, guns and baggage, that were plundered on the death of Wazir Zorawar Singh.
4. To mutually release prisoner.[67]

Two treaties were signed on 15th August 1842 at Leh or its neighbourhood. The first treaty, according to its Persian (Jammu) version was signed on behalf of the "Lhasa country" by 'Kalon' Surkhang and Bakshi Sapju, commander of the forces of "Empire of China" and in the name of Raja Golab Singh by Dewan Hari Chand and Wazir Ratnu. The Persian version, reproduced in the Golabnama*, does not mention the Dalai Lama while the Tibetan text prominently mentions him but is silent about the Chinese.[68] The Tibetan text of the treaty bears the names of 'Kalon' Surkhang and Depon Pishi on behalf of the Dalai Lama. The second treaty, also signed on 15th August 1842, was concluded on behalf of Maharaja Sher Singh and Raja Golab Singh, the 'Khakan' (emperor) of China and the Dalai Lama[69]. The British version of the treaty includes the name Shah Golam, which appears to be the same as Lala Golana in the Tibetan text, as the representative of the Ruler of Lahore[70]. That two treaties were concluded reflected the de facto and de jure positions of Jammu and Tibet. Both were virtually independent of Lahore and China and yet in a degree dependent on them. The virtue in singing the two treaties was that they bound all parties to their provisions.

The texts** of the treaties have one clause relating to trade in shawl wool and tea in common. This trade was to be "without restrictions" and in accordance with the "old established custom." The restrictions evidently were those placed after the outbreak of the opium war. The stipulation in accordance with the "old established customs" implied restoration of the Kashmir-Ladakh monopoly in 'pashm' wool. The article relating to the Ladakh-Tibet boundary is again common in all texts. The Persian text suggests that it was thoroughly discussed at the negotiating table and the contracting parties were to act in a prescribed manner. The Tibetan text refers to the restoration of peace and declares there was to be no cause for enmity in future between the two countries regarding their frontier. This avers to the fact that war broke out between the Sikhs

* A biography of Maharaja Golab Singh in Persian.

** See appendix 2 for texts of the treaties.

and Tibetans not because of doubt or dispute over the boundary but over diversion and, later, denial of 'pashm' wool. The treaties, therefore, only put an end to hostilities and restored the status quo in all matters. The boundary between Ladakh and Tibet was well known and for long under observation and use. Therefore, there was no actual need afresh to lay it down and the substantive treaty referred to only the "old, established frontiers." A clause of significance in the Tibetan text relates to the despatch of "annual tribute" to the Dalai Lama which the Maharaja was not to interfere with. The Persian text does not have this clause at all. No annual tribute was ever sent by Ladakh to the Dalai Lama but under the treaty of Tingmosgong, 1683, gifts were triennially sent to Lhasa. This triennial visit came to be known as the "Lapchak" mission. Annually, however, only the Tibetan traders visited Ladakh with tea and this come to be called the "Chhaba" mission. The substantive treaty puts the issue correctly thus: "In case the Rajas of Ladakh should (desire to) send their usual presents to the Lama Guru Sahib of Lhasa (The Dalai Lama) this will not concern us and we shall not interfere." Thus, the treaty of 1842 was a reiterated commitment to the provisions of the Tingmosgong accord, 1683.

The Tibetans appear to have calculatedly kept the Chinese out of the negotiating team. The little contingent of Chinese troops near Mansarovar, accompanied by the representatives of Ambans at Lhasa, were altogether ignored by the Tibetan plenipotentiaries, headed by 'Kalon' Surkhang himself. All that the detachment seemingly did, under the circumstances, was to impede the negotiations between the Sikhs and Tibetans and towards that objective intercepted messengers headed to or leaving the camp of 'Kalon' Surkhang[71]. Consistent with his line of thinking that the Chinese were the sovereign power in Tibet, which they, indeed, do not appear to have been, Joseph Cunningham opined that the peace treaty could only be regarded as a "suspension of hostilities until it was confirmed by the Chinese deputies at Lhasa, or by the emperor himself."[72] This prognosis of his was no better than his earlier prophesies. Not only was the treaty final but its principal negotiators, including 'Kalon' Surkhang, were honoured[73]. It is not a coincidence that the present views of China on the peace accord of 1842 approximate those of England in the 19th century.

This then was the historical basis for the northern boundary at the birth of Jammu and Kashmir State in 1846 after the defeat of the Sikhs in the first Anglo-Sikh war. The boundary of the new State in the northwest now extended to the Pamirs, with the inclusion of Gilgit and Yasin, Sikh dependencies of Kashmir. The Rajas, Thums or Mirs of Hunza and Nagar had already tendered their submission. In the north the boundary ran along the Angartaksia in Ladakh, as noticed in the Tarikh-i-Rashidi of Mirza Haidar confirmed by Mir Izzatullah and Tse-brtan, some three centuries later. The succeeding pages unveil evidence that such, indeed, was the boundary. The eastern part of the northern boundary, or the Tibet-Ladakh sector, remained the same as under the treaty of 1842, except for the exclusion of Spiti.

In the context of the northern boundary, articles I, II, IV, and V of the treaty of Amritsar*, 1846, arrest attention. Under article I territories eastward of the River Indus and westward of the River Ravi were transferred and made over to Maharaja Golab Singh. This suggests that the entire territories were actually transferred. Yet these were not and a point of importance is to determine what areas were actually transferred. The treaty of Lahore, between the Lahore State and the British Indian Government[74] stipulated surrender by the Lahore State of the district of Hazara, which is eastward of the Indus, and the valley of Kashmir together with its dependencies. Both these territories were not contiguous to British but touching Lahore dominions and were not, therefore, mentioned in article II for the purposes of demarcation of the territories forfeited by Lahore in the east, only Chamba was to the west of the Ravi. From Chamba itself Lahaul, because of its excellent road to Tibet and Central Asia, was excluded from transfer to Maharaja Golab Singh under the treaty of Amritsar. Conceivably its limits could have been defined by the boundary commissioners. The neighbouring Spiti district of Ladakh was literally seized by England. There was no mention of Spiti in the treaty and Maharaja Golab Singh was not obliged to subject his adjoining territories to demarcation. In view of very strained relations between Lahore and the new State of Jammu and Kashmir, Captain Abbott was entrusted the task of laying down the limits of Hazara. This left the boundary of Chamba and Spiti to be determined, of the latter with Ladakh and Tibet, or, as a boundary commissioner soon after explained, the trijunction of Ladakh–Tibet and Spiti (British India) to be fixed. There was, therefore, no basis for delimitation of the whole boundary in Kashmir. Article II of the treaty of Amritsar explains the scope of boundary delimitation. "The eastern boundary of the tract, transferred by the forgoing article, of Maharaja Golab Singh shall be laid down by commissioners appointed by the British Government and Maharaja Golab

* For text see appendix III.

Singh respectively for that purpose and shall be defined in a separate engagement after survey."[75] No party other than the British Government and Maharaja Golab Singh was involved in the exercise of demarcation which was limited to settling the trijunction point. Having come into possession of Spiti the Himalaya ceased to be the coveted boundary for the British.

Article IV of the treaty barred Maharaja Golab Singh from changing the limits of the territories of which the State of Jammu and Kashmir was constituted. The prohibition implied that no addition to or surrender from these territories could be made without British concurrence. The intent was to confine Maharaja Golab Singh within his British recognised territories and not to allow him to venture into Tibet again, or into Yarkand which the British had credited Wazir Zorawar Singh with, or the Pamirs. At the same time, it must be noted, that no clause of the treaty empowered England to change the frontier of the State which they eventually set about to achieve.

There is no mention of the seizure of Spiti in British records. It has been suggested that Maharaja Golab Singh was compensated for its loss with transfer to him of some other territory.[76] Of this too there is no record. The only explanation under the circumstances, therefore, is that Spiti had political and strategic importance for England which was articulated a little later thus : "The trans-Sutlej division...juts out like a promontory into the sea of Himalayan mountains, and enables us form British soil to stand and survey at a comparatively close distance all that goes on between Kashmir on one side and China on the other, with foreign countries spread before us."[77] In command of Spiti the British prevented any approximation between Kashmir and Nepal which, with Sikhs, had been "fraught with danger and inconvenience" to them. Their presence in Spiti blocked one of the two routes leading to the plains of India from Tibet and Ladakh (Central Asia).

References

1. A Third Journey of Exploration in Central Asia. Address to the Royal Geographical Society on 5th June 1916 by Sir Aurel Stein. Geographical Journal for August and September 1916. Also Indian Historical Quarterly (IHQ) Vol. XIII. No. 3. p. 406.
2. Italian Expedition to the Himalaya, Karakoram and Eastern Turkistan. By Filippo De Filippi. p. 381.
3. A Study of the Chronicles of Ladakh. By Dr. Luciano Petech, 1939, p. 100.
4. Gates of India. By Colonel Sir Thomas Holdich, 1910, p. 172.
5. Visits to High Tartary, Yarkand and Kashgar. By Robert Shaw, p. 23.
6. Tarikh-i-Rashidi of Mirza Mohammad Haidar Dughlat. Tr. by Denison Ross. Commentary by Ney Elias, p. 385.
7. Rajatarangini, Kalhan's Tr. By Sir Aurel Stein. Vol. I. Book IV. Verse 168. Also Chronicles of Ladakh, p. 101.
8. A Study of the Chronicles of Ladakh. By Dr. Luciano Petech 1939, p. 158.
9. White Paper. Notes And Letters. 1954-1959. Ministry of External Affairs. Government of India, p. 26.
10. 14th May 1891. Foreign. PC. No. 101 of 14th May 1891. Moorcroft's Persian Correspondence.
11. Undated. Foreign. PC. English translation of Persian letters received. January 1822 to June 1822. Register No. 70 Part I, No. 131. (6A+B) Moorcroft's Persian Correspondence.
12. 30th July 1821. Foreign. PC. Register No. 70, Part I, January 1822 to June 1822. No. 131 (6A+B) Moorcroft's Persian correspondence.
13. 19th July 1821. Foreign. PC. Register No. 70, Part I. No. 131 (6A+B). January 1822 to June 1822. Moorcroft's Persian correspondence.
14. 15th August 1821. Foreign. Miscellaneous. PC. No. 63, of 20th September 1822 Moorcroft's Persian correspondence.
15. 18th April 1822. Foreign. PC. No. 76 of 20th September 1822. Moorcroft's Persian correspondence.
16. Asiatic Researches. A Journey to Lake Mansarovar. By William Moorcroft, p. 448.
17. Pamphlet Series. No. 27, Foreign Department. Travels in Central Asia by Mir Izzatullah. p. 20.
18. Geographical, Statistical And Historical Description of Hindustan. By Walter Hamilton. 1820. Vol. II, p. 573 and 599.
19. An Account of Koonawur In The Himalaya. By Captain Alexander Gerard, p. 96.
20. 29th September 1820. Foreign. PC. No. 21 of 10th October 1820. Moorcroft's Persian correspondence.
21. 15th April 1821 Foreign. PC. No. 35 of 10th October 1823. Moorcroft's Persian correspondence.
22. *Ibid.*

23. *Ibid.*
24. 15th August 1821. Foreign. Miscellaneous. PC. No. 63 of 20th September 1821. Moorcroft's Persian correspondence.
25. *Ibid.*
26. *Ibid.*
27. *Ibid.*
28. Himalayan Battleground. By Margaret Fisher, Leo Rose and Robert Huttenback. p. 43.
29. Tibet. A Political History. By Tsepon W.D. Shakabpa, 1967, p. 135.
30. 17th December 1921. Foreign. PC. No. 66 to 20th September 1822. Moorcroft's Persian correspondence.
31. Southern Tibet. By Sven Hedin. Vol. III. p. 38.
32. 17th December 1821. Foreign. PC. No. 66 of 20th September 1822. Moorcroft's Persian correspondence.
33. Antiquities of Indian Tibet. Archaeological Survey of India. New Imperial Series. By Dr. A.H. Francke. Vol. L. Part II, p. 250.
34. Travels in Hindustan. By W. Moorcroft. Vol. I, p. 220.
35. Ladakh. By Alexander Cunningham, p. 326.
36. Undated. Foreign. PC. No. 53-A of 5th October 1835.
37. Travels in Kashmir, Ladakh, Skardo. By G.T. Vigne. Vol. II, p. 343.
38. 28th June 1837. Foreign. PC. No. 31 of 11th September 1837.
39. Ist February 1838 Foreign. SC. No. 15 of 1th August 1838.
40. Undated. Foreign. SC. No. 180 of 28th August 1841.
41. 22nd September 1840. Foreign. SC. No. 139 of 26th October 1840.
42. 5th July 1841. Foreign. SC. No. 29 to 30th August 1841.
43. 15th July 1841. Foreign. SC. No. 34 to 16th August 1841.
44. 21st July 1841. Foreign. SC. No. 36 to 16th August 1841.
45. 17th July 1841. Foreign. SC. No. 27 to 30th August 1841.
46. 20th September 1841. Foreign. SC. No. 66 to 20th September 1841.
47. 23rd September 1841. Foreign. SC. No. 67 to 18th October 1841.
48. 27th December 1841. Foreign. SC. No. 75 to 7th February 1842.
49. 11th January 1842. Foreign. SC. No. 61 to 24th January 1842.
50. 11th January 1842. Foreign. SC. No. 61 to 24th January 1842.
51. 24th January 1842. Foreign. SC. No. 62 to 24th January 1842.
52. 2nd February 1842. Foreign. SC. No. 101 to 30th March 1842.
53. 25th February 1842. Foreign. SC. No. 74 to 21st March 1842.
54. 21st March 1842. Foreign. SC. No. 85 to 21st March 1842.
55. 23rd March 1842. Foreign. SC. No. 38 to 8th June 1842.
56. 27th March 1842. Foreign. SC. No. 1 to 30th March 1842.
57. 7th March 1842. Foreign. SC. No. 134 to 29th June 1842.
58. Journal of Asiatic Society of Bengal. Vol. X. Part II. 1841. Abstract Journal of Routes.
59. 27th April 1842. Foreign. SC. No. 25 to 1st June 1842.
60. 2nd May 1842. Foreign. SC. No. 41 to 6th July 1842.

61. 3rd May 1842. Foreign. SC. No. 42 to 6th July 1842.
62. 11th May 1842. Foreign. SC. No. 24 to 22nd June 1842.
63. 27th May 1842. Foreign. SC. No. 29 to 3rd August 1842.
64. 27th May 1842. Foreign. SC. No. 29 to 3rd August 1842.
65. Governor General's despatch to the Secret Committee. No. 15 of 8th June 1842.
66. 13th June 1842. Foreign. SC. No. 29 to 3rd August 1842.
67. 15th August 1842. Foreign. SC. No. 95 to 26th October 1842.
68. Founding of the Kashmir State. By K.M. Panikkar. p. 84.
69. Ibid. Text of the treaties. p. 85.
70. Undated. Foreign. SC. No. 62 of 24th May 1843.
71. 28th August 1842. Foreign. SC. No. 84 to 12th October 1842.
72. 28th October 1842. Foreign. SC. No. 64 to 21st December 1842.
73. Tibet. A Political History. By Tsepon W.D. Shekabpa. p. 179.
74. Text of the treaty of Lahore-relevant clause.
75. Text of the Treaty of Amritsar, 1846. Appendix III.
76. Himalayan Frontiers. By Dorothy Woodman. 1969, p. 38.
77. 1st August 1866. Foreign Pol A. No. 51 of September 1866.

Chapter 2
Attempts To Pull Back Boundary

The boundary commission, envisaged in the treaty of Amritsar, had a lame start. The British named P.A. Vance Agnew and Captain Alexander Cunningham as their nominees on it and invited Maharaja Golab Singh to appoint, not boundary commissioners but, two "intelligent" men to "*attend*" on British commissioners. The commission was thus reduced in status from a joint to a British commission. England also voiced demand for Spiti district of Ladakh. The two developments and, even more, a subsequent British move to altogether change the scope of the commission, persuaded Golab Singh to tacitly refrain from participating in the commission's proceedings. Worse was to follow, Tibet too kept aloof. Initially a brief for the British commissioners, well within the parameters of the treaty of Amritsar, was laid down by Colonel H.M. Lawrence, Agent, Governor General, NWF, and Resident in Lahore. The brief strikingly reveals the fears the British then entertained about Golab Singh and obliquely disclose the reasons for their claim to Spiti. The Maharaja, it was anticipated, would make another sally into Tibet. Colonel Lawrence pretended not to be certain whether whole of Spiti was to be included in the British territories.[1] Evidently the Maharaja had resisted the British demand for the Ladakh district. The commissioners were to limit themselves to such demarcation "as will give a clear and well defined boundary and will prevent the possibility of future disputes." To Agnew, the senior British commissioner, Colonel Lawrence elaborated this point. "Bear in mind that it is not a strip, more or less, barren or even productive territory that we want, but a clear and well defined boundary in a quarter likely to come little under observation."[2] The commissioners were enjoined"...You will remember that it is an object to prevent Jammu troops, traders and people turning our flank to the northward (Tibet)."[3] The demand for Spiti's incorporation into British India admirably served this purpose, deny as it did to the Dogra rulers of Jammu and Kashmir some of the principal routes to Tibet–the Lahaul and Sutlej lines. So also did it ensure that British flank in north India was not turned by a link up between Kashmir and Nepal, as had almost come off on the Sikh entry into Tibet in 1841. Eastward the boundary was to run to such a point of territory "as is clearly beyond the Maharajas influence and both the Jammu and Tibet authorities were to be distinctly informed that no encroachment by any party or pretence will be permitted."[4] When the two British commissioners were in agreement as to the proper boundary line they were to lay it down, presumably ignoring any differences the Maharaja's or Tibetan commissioners might entertain. The delimitation was thus to be an exercise in coercion. Keeping the British boundary objectives in view and avoiding as much as possible, all cause of offence to Maharaja Golab Singh and his people, or to Tibetan authorities, the commissioners were to quietly and unostentatiously make enquiries as to the lines of trade between Central Asia and the Punjab. They were to explain to any Chinese or Tibetan authorities that they might fall in with, as also any traders they might meet, that no duty would be levied on shawl wool or other commodities that might be brought into the British territory. While this promotional work was desirable from British Government's view, the boundary commissioners were not to enter into any engagements regarding trade. 'Pashm' wool persisted as a factor in the determination of the boundary with Tibet. Again no trade in 'pasham' could have been possible without the routes running through Lahaul and Spiti under British control.

The Governor General, now Lord Hardinge, virtually overturned Colonel Lawrence's guidelines and laid down a brief for the commissioners that was well beyond the treaty of Amritsar and clearly in the long term British imperial interests. He thus truly laid the foundation of the present boundary dispute. The boundary commissioners were directed by the Governor General to bear in mind that by the treaty of Lahore of 9th March 1846,"all rights and interests of the Lahore Government in the Chinese frontier" were transferred to the British Government.[5] Here was another demand, after Spiti, on Maharaja Golab Singh, pregnant with portentious possibilities, for there is no mention of any such similar rights and interests "in the Chinese frontier" in the treaty of Lahore. Presumably Hardinge sought to base British rights and interests "in the Chinese frontier" on article IV of the treaty of Lahore under which Maharaja Dilip Singh of Lahore ceded to the East India Company "in perpetual sovereignty...all his forts, territories, rights and interests, in the hill countries which are situated between the rivers Beas and Indus, including the provinces of Kashmir and Hazara." There is no mention of "Chinese frontier" in the treaty and the reference to the Indus is in the context of Hazara and not Ladakh as is explained later. Even so Maharaja Golab Singh was not a signatory to the treaty of Lahore between the Sikh and the British. Its provisions could not bind the Maharaja. The treaty of Amritsar, which Golab Singh signed, made no such claims as Hardinge now aired, and laid no limits on the frontier with China. In the event, Hardinge's directions to Henry Lawrence were only a hint, an after thought, to widen the scope of the boundary commission with regard to Tibet and eventually to Chinese Turkistan. This departure from the treaty of Amritsar was brought about by the censure of Lord Hardinge by the Secret Committee of the Board of Directors of the John Company, for transferring Kashmir to Golab Singh.

Consequently delimitation of the boundary was now no more limited to ceded districts. To give effect to Hardinge's directions, Colonel Lawrence sought a letter from Government to Lhasa authorities "informing them of the alteration of affairs since their treaty (of 1842) with Lahore was concluded." The abrupt change in policy left no time for the boundary commissioners to embark on the enlarged mission. The season was too far advanced then to enable them to do more than lay down the boundary between the British and Jammu and Kashmir territories in the district of Spiti and establish clearly the point at which the two meet the Tibet frontier. In the following season it was considered admissible that the two officers "should proceed along and map the whole *northern* and *western* borders of Maharaja Golab Singh's principality."[6] Here was British policy being formulated to include the northern boundary (Kuen Lun) and western frontier (Gilgit-Yasin) for delimitation. Even on commerce, the Governor General reference to "frontier trade" was enlarged by Colonel Lawrence into "Central Asian trade" and earlier correspondence recalled virtually to once again seek an end to the Ladakh-Kashmir 'pashm' monopoly. Revenue, apparently, having been collected in Spiti for 1846, the Maharaja was coerced to issue a "purwana" to his officials disclaiming "all interference in regard to that district."[7]

Notwithstanding England regarding Tibet as Chinese Tartary, it was Lhasa, and not Beijing, that Lord Hardinge, to begin with, chose to approach for cooperation in the delimitation of the eastern boundary. In this England was being practical. China then did not count in Tibet. A letter from the Governor General, despatched via Gartok, to the Wazir ('Kalon') of Lhasa conveyed that the British Government deemed it expedient to "settle definitely the boundaries to the east of the countries ceded to.... Maharaja Golab Singh, in order that hereafter no question or dispute may arise concerning their exact limits."[8] As the territories of the empire of China adjoined those of the British Government and of Maharaja Golab Singh, Hardinge proposed to Lhasa to depute confidential agents "to point out... the exact limits of the Chinese frontiers in order that no interference may through ignorance be exercised" with the territories of Tibet. Further, among the rights the British considered to have inherited from the Sikhs, the Governor General laid claim to commercial privileges and on the score sought amendment of the 3rd article of the treaty of 1842 (British version) to provide free transit to trade or, rather, allow free flow of 'pashm'. But Hardinge tilted at windmills. His communication to the Lhasa Wazir remained unopened at Gartok. Tibet then forbade any contacts with Europeans.

That the entire eastern boundary–and not the trijunction–and the northern boundary as well was to be laid down by Vance Agnew and Captain Alexander Cunningham was again conveyed to Colonel Lawrence.[9] British saw justification for this enlargement of the commission's scope in the treaty of Amritsar. Article IV of this treaty laid down that the limits of Jammu and Kashmir would not be changed at any time while article IX enjoined on the British to "aid" Maharaja Golab Singh in protecting his territories. An insight into British predilections on the boundary issue is provided in an Indian Foreign Department memo for the Military Department.[10] Marking the boundary was found "expedient with the view of preventing encroachments on the Chinese (Tibetan) frontier and of obviating all causes of dispute on this account..." The British appear to have remained apprehensive of Maharaja Golab Singh undertaking another expedition against Tibet were another disruption of 'pashm' or tea trade to occur. Delimitation seemingly was to be of existing boundary so as to bind all the three parties to it as laid down on the ground. Later developments do not, however, bear this out.

It was only after Hardinge failed to receive any response from Tibet that contact was made with China, through the British plenipotentiary at Hong Kong, Sir John Davis, to further the prospects of boundary delimitation.[11] Events leading to the constitution of the boundary commission and objects set out for it were detailed to Sir John Davis for communication to the Chinese minister, Keying, at Canton. Playing upon the well known contemporary Chinese fears of encroachment, Keying was assured that the British Government, as a "friend and ally of China," could prevent dependent States, that is Jammu and Kashmir, and her own subjects "from transgressing the laws of mutual friendship." But to do that effectually it was found necessary to ascertain the exact boundaries "which divide the Tibetan territory from that pertaining to Great Bretain and from that also which has been conferred on Golab Singh."[12] Here again it appears what was sought was the determination of the trijunction. Keying's negative response is well known.[13] British clarification[14] to Keying did not carry any weight. Keying insisted "since, however, (the) territory has its ancient frontier, it was needless to establish any other."[15] China, still smarting under the blows she had received in the opium war with England, could have hardly been seduced so soon. But in the succeeding years England bend over backwards to win the confidence of China to make it a willing tool of its foreign policy and military objectives in Central Asia.

Under the circumstances the boundary commissioners, Vance Agnew and Captain Alexander Cunningham, reached the Ladakh-British India-Tibet border and by themselves alone demarcated the boundary between the territories of Maharaja Golab Singh and British.[16] That the British intention was not to ascertain old boundary but to lay down a new one that suited their interest again becomes clear from what the two boundary commissioners proceeded to do. Selecting a plan that would completely preclude any possibility of future dispute, they "adopted as a boundary" such mountain ranges as form watershed lines between the drainage of different rivers.[17] They thus introduced a foreign, a European, concept of boundary making in India. The boundary between the British district of Lahaul and Zanskar in Ladakh was, therefore, the snowy range called "Paralassa" (Baralacha) by Gerard. Beyond the Baralacha pass (16,500 ft.) to the eastward there was an old, well known, boundary stone called "Phalangdanda" which marked the limit between Lahaul and Ladakh. This stone had also been noticed by Moorcroft and stands in the midst of an open plain on the right bank of the Yunam river.[18] There being no recognised boundary mark on the other side of the stream, the commissioners "selected" a "remarkable" cream coloured peak called Turam (?) as the northern limit of British India. As it "appeared" that the country eastward of the "Phalangdanda" belonged to Spiti, they determined that the boundary between Spiti and Ladakh on the westward should be the Yunam river as far as the junction of Cherpa or Cherep river, both upper waters of the Sutlej. Almost due northeast from this junction a square rock, fortlike in resemblance, called Lanka, was selected as another fixed point in the boundary from the Cherpa river. Beyond this to the eastward, the boundary commissioners, adhering to the principle which they had first laid down, determined that the whole of the Cherpa valley with its tributaries belonged to the British Government. The snowy range to its right bank which feeds all the north affluents of the Cherpa river, they decided, should be the northern boundary between Ladakh and the British district of Spiti. This same range extends towards the east, past the southern end of the Tsomorreri, where it was declared to form "the well known boundary between Ladakh and the Chinese territory." The boundary commissioners, therefore, determined that the boundary between Ladakh and Spiti should continue from the head of the Cherpa along the same range to the Chinese boundary, thus including within Spiti all the streams which water that district, they gave to Ladakh all the streams which water its southern district of Rupshu.[19] The range referred to here is the one that later came to be called as the Ladakh chain.

Plainly the British boundary was advanced northwards. Not only had Spiti been sliced away from Jammu and Kashmir but several hundred miles of Ladakh territory right up to the very shores of the Tsomorreri, was under British delimitation, recommended to be incorporated into Spiti. The object was to deprive Jammu and Kashmir not only of this vast area but even more of access to Tibet in the region for several routes lead from Rupshu to Lahaul and Spiti and plains of north India and to Tibet. The errors noticed earlier to the Tsomorreri having an exist are thus explained. All this was sought to be justified under the western concept of watershed. This was not all. Far more damaging was the projection of Vance Agnew, the senior boundary commissioner. According to the information he then had, the only doubtful points on the boundary were its two extremities–the southeastern and the northwestern.[20] Interestingly enough these two extremities also led into the plains of India, the southeastern one besides, into Tibet, and northwestern into Afghanistan as well. One termini Agnew himself identified with Demchok, some distance from the Tsomorreri. The situation of Demchok struck Agnew to be such as would "interfere with intercourse" between Rudok and Gartok by the valley of the Indus." The other extremity Agnew did not clearly mark out at all, but his references to Nagar and Hunza, as he notionally drew the boundary of Jammu and Kashmir, imply it to be Gilgit. The right to roads and passes was "nowhere dubious except near Demchok." This little hamlet on the Indus was one of the three routes of advance into Tibet of Wazir Zorawar Singh's troops in 1841. Vance Agnew admitted Demchok was claimed for Maharaja Golab Singh but added "and may be so by the Chinese also." This suggests that at some point of time there had been written or verbal exchanges on the boundary issue in which the claim to Demchok was made in response to British queries. The British commissioners, certainly Vance Agnew is on record to have, met Maharaja Golab Singh at Srinagar. As for the Chinese they had made no such claim. The village was then and has thereafter beden in the possession of Ladakh administration. Vance Agnew, therefore, obfuscated and the reasons for this obfuscation was that Demchok would "interfere with intercourse" between Rudok and Gartok, near the source of the Sutlej. It was to cut off these two important western Tibetan towns that Wazir Zorawar Singh had sent a column of his troops through Demchok in 1841. Demchok thus commands the Indus Valley and to prevent its dominance by the Dogras Colonel Lawrence was persuaded to urge on his boundary commissioners that it was an object "to prevent Jammu troops, traders and people turning our flank northeastward."

In his memo on the boundary in Lahaul–Spiti, Captain Alexander Cunningham did not pin point the trijunction of the territories of Maharaja Golab Singh, the British and the Tibetans. He just suggested a boundary line. Vance Agnew went further and pronounced that "the exact point where the boundary of Spiti, Ladakh and Changthang (Tibet) meet does not, I believe, at present exist." He argued "As rivers are lost in the desert the three boundaries become unidentified in the uninhabitable mountains south of a line drawn from the southern extremity of the Tsomorreri to the monastery of Hanle." By obfuscating on the trijunction point, Vance Agnew sought to provide for British intervention in the boundary north of Spiti to Demchok and beyond to the Pangong-tso. In describing the mountains as "uninhabitable" military significance was sought to be lent which gained wide currency in subsequent British documents relating to the boundary issue towards the north as well. The Chinese (Tibetans) boundary, Vance Agnew explained, touched Spiti (British) frontier on the Para river, a Sutlej tributary, near Akehe. Thence it followed the crest of the inaccessible ridges round the end of the valley of Handla (?) and ran down on the river near the hamlet of Demchok. In Demchok, according to Vance Agnew, the boundary crossed the Indus and ascending the opposite mountains ran along the ridge "so that the pass to Rudok or Haralla (?) road via Chibra is in the hands of Chinese (Tibetans)." The road referred to here is the line from Lahaul via Chibra to Rudok. Chibra itself is almost half way between Demchok and Leh and is the junction of the roads from Gartok and Rudok.

The boundary Vance Agnew drew continued along the top of the ridge so as to leave to Ladakh the little rivulet running by Rahrong–(The Rhari or Lha-ri stream?)–and leading upto the pass called Baka-la as also

Chushul rivulet running down the other side into the Pangong lake. Thence the boundary Vance Agnew traced ran along the Pangong lake and the ridge forming the eastern boundary of the river Durqualeh till it falls into the Indus feeder, Shyok. There from the ridge bounding the valley of the Shyok on the east was considered by Agnew to be the boundary upto the Karakoram mountains. Here again by the Karakoram mountains is meant the Karakoram pass for the whole range continued to have no separate name, being part of the Kuen Lun system. Beyond the Pangong-tso the most important claim of Agnew relating to the boundary was that the Karakoram ridge formed the dividing line between Yarkand and Nubra in Ladakh, the States of Little Tibet (Baltistan) and the independent tribes farther west. Where the Karakoram ceased to be Maharaja Golab Singh's boundary it would be "when an independent tribe, Nagar or Hunza, interposed" between Little Tibet and that chain. Hunza and Nagar, whom Vance Agnew calls "independent tribe" had acknowledged, as has been noticed, supremacy of the Sikhs and were among the dependencies of Kashmir transferred to Jammu and Kashmir under the treaty of Amritsar.

Vance Agnew's personal explorations and survey of the boundary were limited to a small strip of Lahaul-Spiti Ladakh frontier. Neither he nor Captain Alexander Cunningham went to any part of the Karakoram, not even in the neighbourhood of the Pangong lake. The boundary that Vance Agnew laid down was largely the one the British conceived in Calcutta. Clearly, therefore, the British disregarded the historical boundary that Maharaja Golab Singh had inherited in pursuit of what they fancied ought to be the northern and eastern limits of his territories. That the boundary commissioners had not covered the ground along the boundary is admitted by the senior Commissioner himself. He had, he reveals, defined the boundary "on reference to the maps and after comprehending the ground natural characteristics of the boundary above detailed." The vast territories to the north of the Karakoram ridge Vance Agnew dismissed with the remark that there was nothing else to acquire nearer than Yarkand, Rudok and Gartok, a remark that caught on in later years. But the inference is justified that Maharaja Golab Singh categorically asserted his territorial limits right upto the Kuen Lun in response to which Vance Agnew seems to make this remark in his memo. The objection to proceeding to the great intermediate distance in Vance Agnews boundary line–between the two termini–was, as he himself put it, "solely the delay and expense to Government, in compassing an object to all intents and purposes already attained..." This is a facile argument. Lot of time, treasure and human effort later went into physically laying down the northern boundary of Afghanistan and the Pamirs, the latter directly related to the northern limits of Jammu and Kashmir. Maharaja Golab Singh was fully aware of the British designs. By not nominating his deputies to the boundary commission, he impliedly questioned British Government's right to wrest Spiti from him and lay down the boundary of his State. The British were then hardly prepared for a collision.

As to the lines of commerce between the Punjab and Central Asia that the boundary commission was enjoined by Colonel Lawrence to find out, Vance Agnew drew attention to the Yarkand road, east of the Shyok river, to Rudok, but that it was "prohibited by the Chinese Government." He, therefore, recommended "that a road for the Turkistan trade be, if profitable, secured from Yarkand to Rudok and Gartok, east of the Shyok river, as also a road from Gartok (besides that by the Nitighat) to Lahaul be opened from the vicinity of Akehe on the Pusa (?Para) river to the Baralacha pass via Phirsi (?) and Cherpa river."[21] The road to Yarkand, east of the Skyok, was the line starting from the Indian boundary pass of the Lanak la, traversing the eastern part of Aksai Chin and ending at Polur, the use of which the Gyalpo of Ladakh, and not the Chinese, had proscribed as was noted by Moorcroft. A variation of this route, noticed earlier, let to Rudok. Trade between India and Central Asia via Ladakh was paltry to require a specially developed road. The anxiety of Vance Agnew to cultivate this commerce through such an exclusive line of traffic was in the interests of the British as reflected in Colonel Lawrence's instructions to the boundary commissioners. A regular traffic, big or small, on the route was by itself a guard against any military surprises at, or near, the boundary of Jammu and Kashmir, Tibet and British India in Spiti. Attention of Government was also drawn by Vance Agnew to the Leh-Yarkand road, over the Karakoram ridge being open in the depth of winter because of paucity of moisture in the Ladakh climate. As a result there is hardly any snow on the hills and rivers and torrents en route remain frozen. The implication of this in military terms was that an invasion from north by this line was possible in winter.

Vance Agnew led boundary commission failed to lay down the boundary of Jammu and Kashmir principally because of the non-association of commissioners of Maharaja Golab Singh and Tibet or China. Their abstention must be attributed to doubts the British move raised in Jammu and fears it excited at Lhasa or Beijing. Tibet was hermetically sealed to Europeans while China had just then felt the full weight of British power in the course of the opium war. The boundary both with Tibet and Chinese Turkistan was too old and too well observed to have readily been assented to any change by the principal States involved–Jammu and Kashmir and Tibet. China then fully recognised the Kuen Lun as the boundary between Eastern Turkistan and Ladakh. The boundary changes might well have been marginal had the brief for the boundary commissioners been limited to the one laid down by Colonel Lawrence. Spiti's seizure would seem to have been also prompted by the advice of Captain Alexander Cunningham while engaged in the cis-Himalaya surveys. He saw its annexation vital for a British share in 'pashm' trade. For a while the Governor General toyed with the idea of giving up the "immediate intention" of "inspecting the whole border" but did not. A new commission was decided to be appointed. Regardless of this uncertainty, Colonel Lawrence had sent up Vance Agnew to Gilgit. Without even reaching Gilgit, Vance Agnew declared that Maharaja Golab Singh had "no hold" over it.[22] This grossly inaccurate statement Colonel Lawrence glossed over, calling it an "error". He was credibly informed, Colonel Lawrence wrote to H.M. Elliot, Secretary with the Governor General, that some years ago a Sikh "Thana" (border post) was established in Gilgit. Understandably it was desirable that doubts were set at rest and Government put in possession of distinct information as to Maharaja Golab Singh's boundary.

The new, or the second, boundary commission was to carry out the objects which from "unavoidable causes" were not accomplished by the commission deputed in the preceding year. The commission was to comprise: (i) Captain A. Cunningham, senior commissioner, (ii) Dr. Thomas Thomson and (iii) Lieutenant A. Strachey, who had, in the previous year, 1846, when Vance Agnew and Captain Alexander Cunningham were engaged in demarcation of the Ladakh-Spiti-Lahaul boundary, travelled incognito in Tibet and explored the adjoining Mnah-ris-skor-gsum.[23] No direct reference was made to the eastern or northern boundary of the State. But Colonel Lawrence was advised to write to Maharaja Golab Singh urging upon him to depute "competent officers" for a similar purpose to his frontier.

Generally the commission's original and main object was, with least possible delay, to define and record "such a decided and unmistakable boundary as will prevent the possibility of future dispute..." To this object all others were to be made subservient. Boundary marks, which during the proceedings of the first commission had become prominent, were neither required nor found probably possible. Instead there were plenty of mountains ready to the commission's hand. These "natural pillars" were not only to be carefully mapped for registry with the British Indian Government but their appearance and bearings were to be "fully and distinctly recorded in writing and a copy furnished to the representatives of the three contracting parties." The absence of pillars on the frontier in Jammu and Kashmir, at least on the Kuen Lun, is thus no argument as is now made out, that the boundary is not delimited. The commission was to submit its report to Government from the neighbourhood of Gilgit when the Governor General was to judge the propriety of the commissioners returning or resuming their exploration via Hunza-Nagar range. This range–the British were not apparently sure of its name–the commissioners were particularly told "would seem to form with the Karakoram the natural boundary sought."[24] That, however, Colonel Lawrence hastened to add, was "more a conjecture on his part from the study of the map and it was for the commission to inquire without reference to preconceived notions of any kind." The unnamed range referred to here is, of course, the Hindu Kush. What is of significance is that without consideration for the historical boundary and regardless of the lack of previous exploration, survey and delimitation work, the British had decided on these mountain ridges to be the rampart of the British empire. Demographic, including ethnographic, factor, which later influenced British thinking on the boundary, was to be examined and Strachery was directed to acquire informations as to population and religion of the little known countries which were to be the scene of the commission's labours.

Its mission the commission was to complete in two years.[25] Vance Agnew's argument about delay and expense was thus dismissed. Population factor was again stressed, probably in the context of uninhabited Aksai Chin. To gain geographical knowledge the Governor General desired the commissioners to winter beyond the Karakoram ridge. Were the commissioners to be permitted by the Chinese to proceed to Yarkand or even to Khotan nothing, Elliot underscored, could be more satisfactory. But if the commissioners were "unable to pass the Karakoram to the north" then Rudok, on the borders of the "great desert," where then all was unknown, was suggested by Elliot to be the next best resting place for the Englishmen. The great "great desert" is a reference to Aksai Chin plateaux, for Europeans, the British including, had then hardly any information about them or similar plains to their east in Tibet. That the Karakoram ridge was to be the northern limit of India is indicated by Elliot to the commissioners. They did not need any permission to cross the Karakoram. Wintering in trans-Karakoram was suggested to enable the Commissioners to have a hard look at the Yarkand valley and Aksai Chin, approaches to which are also in Yarkand, Khotan and Rudok.

Without even waiting for the boundary commission to proceed to Ladakh, Hardinge commended to the Secret Committee the Karakoram ridge boundary line to strengthen the impression that British empire's northern limit in Jammu and Kashmir was conceived at Calcutta. The greater part of the boundary between Ladakh and Tibet, the Governor General argued,[26] was "laid down by nature, the Chibra hills, the Pangong Lake and the Karakoram mountain forming the line of demarcation and.... Scarcely any portion except the two termini can admit of dispute..." By declaring the two termini open to dispute, the British left to themselves the choice of a frontier around Demchok in southeast Ladakh and Hunza-Nagar in the Gilgit region, northwest part of Jammu and Kashmir. There was subdued optimism about "Chinese" participation in the demarcation work. Reports had reached the British of the arrival of some officials in Gartok. But it was not improbable that these officials had arrived as much to prevent British commissioners crossing the boundary as for delimiting it.

Chinese sensibilities very much required England provide a strong enough basis for seeking her cooperation in delimitation of the boundary. But all that Hardinge or Sir John Davis could think of was to repeat the assurance that the frontier sought to be determined was Ladakh's "old" boundary[27] with Tibet. For the accomplishment of this task Keying was urged to depute Chinese commissioners to the boundary with Ladakh. Intriguingly once again the boundary of Ladakh to be ascertained was with Tibet and not also the one with Chinese Turkistan. If England shied away from forthwith delimiting the frontier with Eastern Turkistan as was clearly conceived, the reason could only be to avoid arousing too many suspicions in China. Also England was obsessed with Golab Singh's intentions against Tibet. The issue of Chinese cooperation in the delimitation work was referred to the "Resident Great Minister,"[28] a dignitary who was just about tolerated at Lhasa. Though Sir John Davis was hopeful of satisfactory accomplishment of Lord Hardinge's purpose,[29] plainly the Chinese once again aborted the British effort.

The second boundary commission too, therefore, started as *ab initio* a failure. But unlike the first commission, if this one could not lay down the British conceived limit of Ladakh and Tibet, it was a thumping success in causing to know what was the true boundary between the two territories. When the British commissioners arrived at the Tibetan boundary village of Khyuri, on the right bank of the Para, in Spiti, from

Bashahr, they were given to understand that Tibetan officials had, indeed, reached Gartok not, however, for settlement of the boundary but for adjustment of revenue. This report was confirmed by the chief men of the Tibetan villages of Shaktolb and Chooret, who met the British commissioners "on the boundary" to "prevent" them from entering their territory. Thus in Spiti, it is clear, that the boundary ran along the villages of Khyuri, Shaktolb and Chooret. The British commissioners claimed it was their intention to proceed by the direct route to the Tsomorreri and Hanle in Ladakh, where Maharaja Golab Singh "agents" were expected to meet them. Here again British interest in the Tsomorreri is further confirmed by the direct road from Tibet to the lake through which also a highway passed from Lahaul to Leh. But Tibetan farmers, led by their headmen, firmly held to their boundary and compelled the British boundary commissioners to proceed by the "circuitous route" across Spiti, via Dankur and the Parang pass to the Tsomorreri and Hanle. The commission did not consider it justifiable to "force" its way through Tibet.[30] The real purpose of the commissioners to proceed through Tibet was to reach not the Tsomorreri but Gartok for direct contact with the Tibetan authorities. Though Captain Alexander Cunningham does not explicitly say it, evidently the British Commissioners were disuaded from this course by a hostile demonstration by Tibetan villagers on the boundary line. This demonstration was not to be the last but this and similar disapprovals by the Tibetans along the boundary line upwards to Demchok, the first of the "disputed termini," fully established how well known the ancient boundary of Ladakh was, British obfuscation notwitstanding. Of the Tibetan hostile demonstration against the British boundary commissioners the Garpon (Governor) of Gartok was informed. Having been checkmated from entering Tibet and operating from its soil, the commissioners did the next best thing. They proposed to the Garpon to depute the Tibetan "Sardars" if they had arrived from Lhasa, to Hanle "for the purpose of pointing out the ancient boundary."[31] The boundary commissioners made another important "discovery," that of the trijunction of Spiti (Ladakh) Bashahur (British) and Chumurti (Tibetan) at Zangsum, so named after a hot spring. Zang seemed to the boundary commissioners to mean "three boundaries," in allusion to the frontier of Spiti, Bashahr and Chumurti. So a trijunction existed and was not lost in the desert as Agnew had canvassed. The boundary between Spiti and Chumurti, the commissioners found, was formed by the river Gyu, which joins the Spiti river.

The non appearance of the "Chinese" or Tibetan, commissioners was announced to Government by Colonel Lawrence.[32] Captain Alexander Cunningham virtually rung down the curtain on the second boundary commission reporting the failure of Maharaja Golab Singh's "agents" also to reach Hanle. There was no information available even on their whereabouts. That was most galling for, as Captain Alexander Cunningham remarked, "Had there been any 'Chinese' commissioners on the frontier, the absence of the Maharaja's agents would have prevented us from settling any portion of the boundary during this season."[33] The Maharaja appears to have appointed Mian Jowahir Singh, his nephew, and Mehta Basti Ram, Governor, or Commandant of Ladakh, as his deputies on the boundary commission. The two deputies were scheduled to have reached Hanle by 10th September 1847, but had not arrived by even the 15th. Too evidently the Maharaja had designedly withheld his cooperation. With the collapse of the boundary part of the agenda, the commission fell back upon the other part of its brief, to acquire geographical, political and demographic information.

If Captain Alexander Cunningham's report to Colonel Lawrence was terse on the Ladakh Tibet frontier in Spiti, that of Strachey was comparatively uninhibited. He was stopped at the boundary around the southern point of the Parang (Para) river's course in the northwest corner of the Karab Bargyab district, the westernmost part of Tibet, on 29th August 1847. His proceedings help in locating another boundary village, Tsurup, where, after Shaktolb, he was prevented from going ahead. Taking an alternative route by the Temba Chen pass, Strachey crossed the valley pointed out to him as the boundary, three days journey above Akehe hamlet, the highest inhabited place. The Parang river by Strachey's account appears to intermittently pass through Spiti and Karab Bargyab district. The Tibetans, it appears from Strachey's communications, were so much exercised by the presence of Englishmen near the boundary that a battalion of troops was mustered at Gartok which daily held "exercises." The two ranking officers, whom the British were made to believe to be entrusted with revenue work, had been really sent mainly, if not wholly, in consequence of the Governor General's letter to the Tibetan Minister, in the previous year. The purpose, Strachey surmised, was of preventing communications, desired by the British Government, by every artifice and such "show of force as they can and dare oppose to purely peaceable advances on the part of the British."[34] To prevent these "peaceable advances" of England, the high Tibetan official had, on confirmation of the arrival of the boundary commissioners on the frontier, despatched horsemen to guard every pass of their western frontier from Shipki on the Sutlej to Demchok on the Indus, which appeared to Strachey "is the Lhasan frontier point upon the left bank of the Indus."[35] Strachey thus below up Vance Agnew's fanciful one of the two doubtful termini. Another boundary point that emerges from Strachey's despatches is the Setting pass in Chumurti district of Tibet from where Tibetans expected the Englishmen to infiltrate.

The boundary commission having broken up by about the end of August 1847, Maharaja Golab Singh's "agents" joined Captain Alexander Cunningham, Mian Jawahar Singh on 22nd September at Puga, far to the north of the fixed rendezvous at Hanle, and Mehta Basti Ram, on 27th September at Gya, near Leh. Mian Jawahar Singh had stayed 22 days at Leh which Captain Cunningham underscored to argue that the two "agent" of Maharaja Golab Singh had "ample time" to have met the British officers at Hanle.[36] The failure of the Chinese deputies to reach the boundary was with regrets conveyed by Hardinge to Sir John Davis at Hong Kong. Not only had they failed to appear but that the British officers had met with "opposition" from Tibetan people on attempting to cross the boundary.[37] Golab Singh too had ignored summons to his commissioners to join the Commission though these were repeated.[38] Coupled with their absence on the frontier in 1847 with non-attendance by any duly appointed agent in the previous season, when Vance Agnew and Captain Alexander Cunningham were in Ladakh, Captain Alexander Cunningham was "induced to believe that the absence of the Maharaja's commissioners on the frontier is not the result of accident but of a designed plan to delay as long as possible, if not absolutely to thwart altogether, the final settlement of the boundary." He even went further to infer that "...the Maharaja himself is unwilling to have his eastern boundary finally determined."[39] Why was Maharaja Golab Singh unwilling to have his boundary finally determined if it was not that the limits British sought to impose on him were to his territorial and strategic disadvantage?

From the movement of the British Commission along the frontier, as also other indications, Golab Singh became painfully aware of what kind of boundary the British had in view to replace the ancient limits of Ladakh. The first commission, had determined that the boundary between Ladakh and Spiti should run from Lingti boundary stone to the Lanka Hill and from that along the mountain range on the northern bank of the Cherpa river, "as far as the southern end of the Tsomorreri from which point we understood that the Chinese territory commenced."[40] British objective to extend their territorial limits to the very shores of the Tsomorreri, far to the north, was consistently pursued by them and explorations and surveys for the purpose were conducted even before the formation of the State of Jammu and Kashmir. But extension of the Tibetan or, as the British called them, "Chinese" territories was astonishing. The purpose behind the move is best understood from an earlier despatch of Strachey to Colonel Lawrence in which he noted "Hanle occupies that part of the southeast Ladakh...abutting upon Karab Bargyab, Chumurti and Tashigang...the western frontier districts of Lhasan Mnah-ris-skor-gsum, between the Sutlej and Indus."[41] The apprehension of a fresh attack on Tibet, by the Dogras of Jammu, and of being outflanked continued to influence England's policy to seek a changed northern boundary. That such a boundary amounted to loss of Hanle and Rupshu districts of Ladakh to the British and Tibetans, even though an unpopulated desert, was, apparently, of no import to England. Indeed, Captain Alexander Cunningham saw the loss really of but one village, Chumur. The other loss of territory along the proposed Ladakh-Tibet boundary was of Chibra. Rupshu is the only district of Ladakh which produces 'pashm' wool.

The other reason for the proposed dismemberment of Hanle and Rupshu from Ladakh was 'pashm'. The Lahaul-Gartok line, by which countraband 'pashm' trade was carried on with British India, partly passed through Rupshu district. On the seizure of Spiti, which Captain Alexander Cunningham admits was to secure access to 'pashm'[42] a custom house was built on the north bank of the Parang river, a month or two before the arrival there of the second boundary commission. Inquiries by the commissioners revealed the building was constructed on Rupshu district land. The custom house blocked the road by which Noorpur and Ludhiana in the Punjab were chiefly supplied with wool. It thus on the one hand prevented contraband trade and on the other indicated the territorial limits of Jammu and Kashmir in the region. It was this route which Captain Alexander Cunningham had, in his report of 1846, pointed out to the British Government "...as the best as well as the most direct from Kulu and Lahaul to Gartok and Rudok."[43] The British had consistently encouraged contraband 'pashm' trade by this road. Such trade consequently posed a threat of invasion of Tibet, now by Dogras of Jammu. To keep the entire road in British India, Captain Alexander Cunningham had proposed surrender of Chumur hamlet, possessing but two houses and nineteen inhabitants. He, of course, did not refer to the sacrifice of the entire Rupshu district that would be involved in the transfer of the hamlet. If the boundary proposed by him was not found acceptable, Captain Alexander Cunningham had an alternative proposal. He proposed the chain of mountains connecting the Baralacha, Parang and Ganskil passes as the boundary. This boundary being far to the south, involved sacrifice of 'pashm' trade, unless on the next occasion of any differences with the Chinese "...cession of the two shawl wool producing districts of Rudok and Gartok, both of which are more accessible to (British) subjects," was secured.[44]

Whether the Maharaja took up the boundary issue with Colonel Lawrence, in the light of the proceedings of the boundary commissioners, is not evident from British records. Perhaps he did, for the British had to climb down from their untenable position. This is evident from Colonel Lawrence's communications to Elliot. In the absence of his nominees from the boundary commissions, Colonel Lawrence observed, maharaja Golab Singh could not be "bound" by the decisions of the British officers with regard to the boundary.[45] He was unhappy with the boundary commissioners for not following his brief and remarked the boundary was not to secure wool trade or any other traffic or any particular line of road "to the prejudice of our neighbours"–Tibet and Jammu and Kashmir." If we are fairly entitled to the northern line (Tsomorreri), proposed by Captain Cunningham, well and good, if not the southern one by Baralacha, Parang and Ganskil passes will, I conceive, be equally acceptable, or nearly so," Colonel Lawrence conveyed to Elliot. This part of the boundary was between Ladakh and Spiti and was not linked with the northern boundary. One last effort was made by Colonel Lawrence to resurrect the second boundary commission. He proposed to Elliot to address Golab Singh and request that the Maharaja and Captain Alexander Cunningham should, if possible, settle the northern boundary to their mutual satisfaction, and if not, decide on such preliminaries as would enable them to have it adjusted on the spot. Nothing like that happened. Golab Singh would have hardly been in a happy frame of mind after the not hidden British designs on the eastern boundary districts, as to agree to any propositions on the northern frontier.

When he reached Demchok on 10th October 1847, Strachey saw for himself that a rivulet (Rha-ri), "constitutes the boundary in this particular quarter between Mnah-ris-skor-gsum and Ladakh."[46] Reaching it from Hanle, Strachey found Demchok a hamlet of half a dozen huts, not permanently inhabited, divided into two, one Ladakhi and the other Tibetan, by the rivulet Rha-ri, which enters the left bank of the Indus. The Tibetan part of the hamlet, Strachey noticed, was full of people engaged in agricultural labour, but "all ready with the usual prohibition against the advance of strangers..." His advance to Mnah-ris-skor-gsum frontier had excited "alarm" at Gartok. A small guard of Dogra troops had accompanied Strachey whose presence he mentions only on reaching Chushul later. The presence of these troops was mistaken for British movement on the frontier causing "consternation in Gartok." A "chain of messengers" was posted all the way from Tashigang to Demchok, "so numerous that," according to the figurative expression, "...they were joining hands."[47] All this clearly establishes that Demchok was an Indian frontier village on the boundary with Tibet. Also apparent is that the boundary all along, from Spiti northwards, was very well known on both sides for, wherever the boundary commissioners had attempted to step into Tibet they were thwarted.

Extensive exploration was also undertaken by Strachey of the Nubra-Shyok valley, including a part of the winter route to Yarkand. He turned east to head for the Pangong-tso. The boundary on the north side of the lake, he found, lay "half way in the northern shore," on the south side of the lake, it ran across a valley traversed by the high road between Ladakh and Rudok, the Junglam. Over a small margin of flat bank along the western half of the south side were a few hamlets of the highest limit of agriculture. The narrow valley runs parallel to the Pangong lake and opens to the east side of the Chushul valley, opposite the village. The boundary, Strachey found, was four or five miles from Chushul.[48] The Dogra troops that accompanied him Strachey left behind at Chushul village and himself travelled in the narrow, uninhabited valley for 25 miles without hindrance, passing through the Tsarul, a lake similar to the Pangong-tso but smaller in size. Half way between Chushul and Rudok, he was met by Tibetans and allowed to make another march on the promise that he would not enter Rudok or any inhabited place. That brought him to the east end of the Tso Shaldat, a third lake, still smaller than the Tsarul, only 12 or 13 miles from Rudok. Strachey was there "on the Rudok frontier," visited by the Zimskang, the Tibetan official in charge of Rudok, to whom he explained the circumstances which had given rise to the presence of British agents on the Lhasa frontier. Both the lake valleys to within 9 to 10 miles of Rudok were claimed by the shepherds of Kargyan in Ladakh. But Strachey argued in favour of Rudok people, who had "exclusive possession" without a "practical dispute for many years past."[49] The claim, he found, had never been "formally adjudicated." Strachey, however, acknowledged larger part of the country to the north of the Pangong-tso belonged to Ladakh. He ascertained that it comprised four pastoral valleys of some extent, separated by high mountains.

A last attempt to inform Gartok and Lhasa officials of the circumstances and objects of the visit to the Ladakh-Tibet boundary by British boundary commissioners was made by Strachey through the "Lapchak" mission sent triennially from Leh to Lhasa. The "Lapchak", or the "ambassador," as Strachey called the head of the mission, was instructed to verbally communicate with the Tibetan officials. These official were advised to open up communication with Strachey before he left Leh.[50] But this endeavour of Strachey was no more successful than the earlier British efforts to involve Tibet in the boundary demarcation. That was the end of the British boundary commissions. Instead of boundary delimitation, advancement of virtually non-existent British trade through Ladakh with Central Asia became the instrument of British policy. By controlling the trade, or, at least, having a say in its management, the British objective was to keep the lines of trade of Ladakh with Central Asia under their close observation for these could well be the routes of invasion. Given Ladakh's large extent and sparse population, reports about an invasion by any of these lines would have taken months to reach Simla and even more to Calcutta. This had been foreseen in 1846. Another cause for concern to England on trade and trade lines was that most of this Central Asian trade was then cornered by Russia.

Largely geographical were the explorations of the third boundary commissioner, Dr. Thomas Thomson, in the context of Jammu and Kashmir's boundary. His findings are crucial both in regard to Ladakh's geography as well as boundary. He followed Wazir Zorawar Singh's Ladakh invasion route, via Kishtwar into Zanskar and thence to Leh. While en route to the Karakoram pass, the valleys of Nubra and Shyok were explored by him. From Sasser, not more than three or four miles of the upward course of the Shyok river, he was in sight of three glaciers. Dr. Thomson does not name them but these are now known as Rimo, Siachin and Bilafond. Rimo was later found to be the common source of the Shyok that flows southward of the Karakoram, and Yarkand river which runs northward.[51] This has relevance in the context of the watershed concept of boundary, which Dr. Thomson himself applied while attempting to determine the boundary of Ladakh, or western Tibet as he called it.

On 19th August 1848, Dr. Thomson reached the limit of his journey northward, the Karakoram pass.[52] Setting the Karakoram pass as the limit of his exploration was a broad hint to Maharaja Golab Singh as to the extent of his State for Dr. Thomson went to the Karakoram as a boundary commissioner. Contrary to his instructions, he surveyed the northern face of the pass for a distance of some 500 yards beyond which a small stream occupied the middle of a very gently sloping valley. The stream described by Dr. Thomson is one of the headwaters of the Yarkand river.

Far from endorsing Vance Agnew's line of Ladakh's northern boundary, Dr. Thomson dilated on the difficulties encountered in this exercise. Greater part of the surface of the country, he notes, is transversed in all directions by ranges of mountains

> "in every respect similar to the Himalaya of which in fact those south of the Indus are ramifications while those on the north are branches of the snowy chain of the Kuen Lun.[53]

Generally running from southeast to northwest, these chains of mountains had no separate names as Dr. Thomson clearly suggests but were collectively called the Himalaya southward and Kuen Lun northward. Their unity was not limited to only common nomenclature. This common nomenclature came, however, to be changed at the instance of and, indeed, by the British. Thus the chain immediately to the south of the Indus was named by Sir Sydney Burrard of the Survey of India as the Kailash, starting in the neighbourhood of Mansarovar and reaching Hunza over which towers the Rakaposhi peak. North of the Indus, another ridge came to be christened the Karakoram by the Schlagintweit brothers in 1850s. So artificial has been this name that a conference had to be called in the early decades of the 20th century to consider the issue. But by bifurcating this range of mountains from the Kuen Lun range, the British shifted the boundary from northernmost ridge to the southern ridge of the Kuen Lun, the Karakoram, to exclude Aksai Chin and Yarkand Valley from Ladakh.

Dr. Thomson considered the northern boundary of Tibet to be formed by the range with the name of the Kuen Lun. Of not more than four places was Dr. Thomson aware in which passes exist across the range. The most westerly of these passes is the Muztagh, near Skardo, Alibransa, the Karakoram and the most easterly pass, which Dr. Thomson did not name but which he indicates connected Rudok and Khotan. By the present nomenclature of the Ladakh mountain chains, it is evident that the first three passes mentioned by Dr. Thomson are on the Karakoram and the fourth, which is, perhaps, Hedin's Keria la, on the Kuen Lun. From Dr. Thomson's notices, it can be safely concluded that the present day Kuen Lun and Karakoram were but one mountain system until the middle of the 19th century. Between the chain, now called, the Karakoram and Kuen Lun, Dr. Thomson further notes, "is situated a tract of country of unknown extent which seems to be made up of a number of isolated lake basins quite unconnected not only with one another but with the general drainage of the countries by which they are surrounded."[54] This most evidently is Aksai Chin though, again, Dr. Thomson does not so name it. Aksai Chin name was not current then, as noticed.

Development of trade being part of the boundary commissioners brief, Strachey invited Yarkand merchants at Leh to directly trade with British India through Bashahr. But such trade with British India was unacceptable to the Governor of Ladakh and, surprisingly, to Bashahr itself. The Governor, understandably, saw in this direct trade loss of Leh's centrical position, besides leading to the opening of new routes. The consent of the Governor was necessary as without it passports would not have been issued at Leh to Central Asian traders intending to go to British India.[55] To watch the Central Asian trade lines leading into Ladakh, the British Indian Government proposed these be thrown open by affording sufficient protection to traders, imposing moderate and fixed rate of duty and by abolishing all "vexatious exactions."[56] The Yarkand traders sought, or were induced by Strachey to seek, for themselves, their marchandize and generally for traders using these roads "safe conduct,"[57] through the territories of Maharaja Golab Singh. A got up affair of looting of the Yarkand merchants by the officials of the Maharaja persuaded the merchants to pray for "interference"[58] of British officers. Such interference for due protection of English commercial interests and for securing the rights of traders was seen possible were a "British agent stationed in Ladakh which from its central position, must be the emporium of commerce between Hindustan, Tibet and the countries of northwestern China."[59] These commercial considerations were all a facade. What England sought was a European officer posted in Ladakh togather military and political intelligence and to project her power in Central Asia. The proposal was not immediately pressed, probably because of the involvement of Strachey in the Yarkand merchants' "protest."

In a painstaking study[60] of Ladakh's trade, Strachey traced out the lines of commerce leading to Leh from Yarkand, Tibet, Kashmir, Bashahr, Chamba and Lahaul. On the Changchenmo route, via Western Aksai Chin, Strachey is silent. His silence is to be construed to mean that no trade then passed over it. The lines of trade he refers to give an idea about the frontier areas or posts of Ladakh-Tibet and Ladakh-Kashgaria boundary. He also deals with articles of trade of which, at least one, soda, commonly called "phul" in Ladakh, Baltistan and Kashmir, was exported to these regions. This "phul" came from the Soda Plain of Aksai Chin and was used then–as indeed now-notably in decoction of tea. Of the routes, the one from Leh to Rudok, the Ladakh part of the Junglam, was negotiable in all seasons but frequent only during the warm half of the year. The road to Yarkand from Leh went over the Karakoram. The summer branch of the road was 33 days long journey. In winter, as the Saser la was impassable, traders preferred going via Agam and Shyok, the Shyok being fordable or sometimes passable on ice. This road, 4 days journey longer, led via Kukyar and Karghalik to Yarkand. The summer route ascended either the Kilian or Sanju dawan over the Kuen Lun. Kilian and Sanju were the first permanent habitations at the north foot of the mountains, small Turkish villages, sites of custom houses where 'Rahdaris' (passports) were checked and custom duties paid, or, as Strachey obliquely put it, "where travellers have to give an account of themselves."[61] The winter highway coincided with the summer lines as far as Elalik Shap. It then entered a river bed to Chiragsaldi, a Kashmir frontier pass, to head for Kokyar. Strachey described Kokyar as "a small village and Chinese outpost," similar and similarly situated to Kilian,[62] of the summer route.

All these routes did not, however, appeal to Strachey. Were all countries civilised and well governed, trade from southeast Turkland to India would, he was certain, take one route altogether west of Baltistan and Kashmir, entering northwest India by the gorge of the Indus. Another line he favoured, was the Polur-Keria la-Lanak la-Rudok road over eastern Aksai Chin and Mnah-ris-skor-gsum to the Gangetic provinces via the gorge of the Karnali river, leaving Ladakh, Kashmir and Kinnaur to be frequented only to the extent of their domestic requirements. But the first route of his preference Strachey found closed by "the predatory habits of the people of Chitral, Kanjut and others." The second route of his choice was no less shut out by "the incubus of the Chinese Government." Strachey's now and Vigne's in 1830s were the earliest attempts by Englishmen to exclude Aksai Chin from Jammu and Kashmir and in Strachey's case reflect official British opinion, at least in a section of Government. Of the road through Mnah-ris-skor-gsum to the Gangetic plains, Moorcroft had made British aware of. Strachey in his report made them acquainted with the Chitral-Indus valley route to doubly enhance the strategic importance of Gilgit, from where one line reached Kashmir valley and another, through Chilas, down the Indus river to the Punjab.

The findings of the boundary commission, geographical, scientific and statistical, rather than the report on delimitation of boundary on the east and north of Jammu and Kashmir, were commended to the Board of Directors of the John Company by the Governor General, Lord Dalhousie. Strachey was praised for his survey of the country from Leh to the scene of his former researches near the Mansarovar lake. The result of Strachey's geographical researches was shown in a much elaborated map, one of the many adduced in evidence before the Chinese during negotiations on the boundary with India. The boundary commission or the "Tibet mission," was declared a failure. Yet the findings of the British boundary commissioners indicated :

> "....there is nothing which requires adjustment, and that we may safely leave matters as they are, under their present indefinite form, without fear of aggression on either side. That this was also the opinion of the Chinese, before the mission started, is shown in the High Imperial Commissioner Keying's letter to Sir John Davis, dated 13th January 1847."[63]

That was the farthest the eastern boundary of Ladakh came afresh to be identified. The focus after the second boundary commission shifted to the northern limits of Jammu and Kashmir. In the absence of the officials of Maharaja Golab Singh and Tibet, no delimitation of the frontier had been possible though Dalhousie blamed "the stubborn jealously of the Chinese" for the failure. Yet British commissioners, Vance Agnew in particular, did project a boundary line, but the British Indian Government was unable to win acceptance for it. Some findings, as of Strachey, would have been acceptable both to Jammu and Kashmir and Tibet for such indeed, was the boundary :

> Half way in the northern shore of the Pangong lake, on the south side of the lake across a valley traversed by a high road between Ladakh and Rudok, across the narrow valley running parallel to the lake divided therefrom by a narrow line of mountains and opening into the eastern side of the Chushul valley, 5 miles opposite Chushul village, Lake Tsarul, 12 or 13 miles from Rudok, southward to Demchok and Shipki la.

One error Strachey made was to place Pal in Rudok whereas the boundary was at Pal.[64] North of the Pangong-tso large part of the country was assigned by Strachey to Ladakh. In this part are found two important passes, the Lanak la and the Kongha la, both seized by China in 1950s. Strachey found out the near true boundary of Jammu and Kashmir which the Tibetans confirmed through their hostile demonstrations against the Englishmen. But it is one thing to find the boundary and another to accept it. British military and political interests were not served by such a boundary, one reason Aksai Chin was left out from the boundary commissions.

British direct intervention in Jammu and Kashmir on the frontier or any other pretext also ended, for a while, with the second boundary commission. But British obfuscation on the boundary issue was extensively purveyed by British citizens and military officers who, in large members travelled in the State for sport and recreation which really were a facade for intelligence gathering. Earliest among these was Mrs. Harvey who visited Jammu and Kashmir in early 1850s. In her travelogue, full of invective against Maharaja Golab Singh, Mrs. Harvey declared the Karakoram as the northern limit of Ladakh[65], like Vigue, Vance Agnew and Strachey.

References

1. 23rd July 1846. Foreign. Sc. No. 1332 of 26th December 1846.
2. 23rd July 1846. Foreign. Sc. No. 1331 of 26th December 1846.
3. 23rd July 1846. Foreign. Sc. No. 1332 of 26th December.
4. *Ibid.*
5. 25th July 1846. Foreign. 1846. No. 1333 of 26th December 1846.
6. 31th July 1846. Foreign. Sc. No. 1334 of 26th December 1846.
7. 31th July 1846. Foreign. Sc. No. 1335 of 26th December 1846.
8. 4th August 1846. Foreign. Sc. No. 1336 of 26th December 1846.
9. 4th August 1846. Foreign. Sc. No. 1337 of 26th December 1846.
10. 27th August 1846. Foreign. Sc. No. 1343 of 26th December 1846.
11. 29th August 1846. Foreign. Sc. No. 1338 of 26th December 1846.
12. 18th November 1846. Foreign. Sc. No. 140 of 28th August 1847.
13. 13th January 1847. Foreign. Sc. No. 145 of 28th August 1847.
14. 21th January 1847. Foreign. Sc. No. 146 of 20th August 1847.
15. 26th January 1847. Foreign. Sc. No. 148 of 28th August 1847.
16. 10th May 1847. Foreign. Sc. No. 701 of 30th December 1848.
17. Undated. Foreign. Pol. No. 703 of 30th December 1848.
18. W. Moorcroft. Travels. Vol. I, p. 220.
19. Undated. Foreign. Pol. No. 703 of 30th December 1848.
20. 13th May 1847. Foreign. Sc. No. 154 of 28th August 1847.
21. *Ibid.*
22. 20th May 1847. Foreign. Sc. No. 153 of 28th August 1847.
23. 10th July 1847. Foreign. Sc. No. 156 of 27th August 1847.
24. 16th July 1847. Foreign. Sc. No. 181 of 28th August 1847.
25. 27th May 1847. Foreign. Sc. No. 162 of 28th August 1847.

26. Governor General's despatch to the Secret Committee of 28th July 1947. No. 48 of 1847.
27. 1st August 1847. Foreign. Sc. No. 27 of 30th October 1847.
28. 8th August 1847. Foreign. Sc. No. 28 of 30th October 1847.
29. 12th August 1847. Foreign. Sc. No. 26 of 30th October 1847.
30. 29th August 1847. Foreign. Sc. No. 23 of 27th November 1847.
31. 29th August 1847. Foreign. Sc. No. 23 of 27th November 1847.
32. 14th September 1847. Foreign. Sc. No. 22 of 27th November 1847.
33. 15th September 1847. Foreign. Sc. No. 26 of 27th November 1847.
34. 20th September 1847. Foreign. Sc. No. 130 of 31st December 1847.
35. *Ibid.*
36. 27th September 1847. Foreign. Sc. No. 136 of 31st December 1847.
37. 4th October 1847. Foreign. Sc. No. 24 of 27th November 1847.
38. 18th October 1847. Foreign. Sc. No. 25 of 27th November 1847.
39. 20th October 1847. Foreign. Sc. No. 131 of 31st December 1847.
40. 20th October 1847. Foreign. Sc. No. 134 of 31st December 1847.
41. 20th October 1847. Foreign. Sc. No. 130 of 31st December 1847.
42. Ladakh. By Alexander Cunningham. P 13.
43. 20th October 1847. Foreign. Sc. No. 134 of 31st December 1847.
44. *Ibid.*
45. 23th November 1847. Foreign. Sc. No. 129 of 31st December 1847.
46. 15th November 1847. Foreign. Sc. No. 68 of 27th May 1848.
47. 26th January 1848. Foreign. Sc. No. 73 of 27th May 1848.
48. 18th June 1848. Foreign. Sc. No. 8 of 7th October 1848.
49. *Ibid.*
50. 1st July 1848. Foreign. Sc. No. 10 of 7th October 1848.
51. Explorations In The Eastern Karakoram and Upper Yarkand Valley. Survey of India with Dr. Filippo De Filippi Scientific Expedition. 1914. Published by the Survey of India. 1922.
52. Undated of 1848. Foreign. Fc. No. 208 of 27th October 1849.
53. 10th October 1849. Foreign. Fc. No. 332 of 29th December 1849.
54. *Ibid.*
55. 2nd April 1848. Foreign. Sc. No. 7 of 7th October 1848.
56. Undated. Foreign. Sc. No. 181 of 28th August 1847.
57. 25th August 1848. Foreign. Sc. No. 38 of 27th October 1849.
58. Undated Foreign. Sc. No. 40 of 27th October 1849.
59. 17th August 1848. Foreign. Sc. No. 37 of 27th October 1849.
60. 5th July 1851. Foreign. Fc. No. 156 of 12th September. 1851.
61. *Ibid.*
62. *Ibid.*
63. Governor General's Political despatch No. 50 of 31st July 1851.
64. Himalayan Frontiers. By Dorothy Woodman. p. 60.
65. Adventures of A Lady In Tartary, Tibet, China and Kashmir. By Mrs. Harvey. Vol. I, p. 190.

Chapter 3
Search For New Boundary

British records, such as Edward Thornton's "A Gazetteer of the Countries Adjacent To India," set at rest doubts that the "Muztagh and Karakoram" is but the Kuen Lun.[1] Nothing was then known about the Angartaksia, its position, height and direction.[2] This range is put by the Gazetteer as the northern limit of Skardo, separating it from Chinese Turkistan.[3] Ladakh's eastern boundary, Moorcroft's findings notwithstanding, is placed at 79°36' and not 82°E longitude, bounded by Khotan! and Changthang in the east.[4] Such a boundary knocked out east Aksai Chin from Ladakh, obviously to shut out of it the Lanak la-Keria la-Polur highway and its variation, through Rudok, to the British provinces via the Niti pass. Because of this road, China now claims Niti area in the central sector of the northern boundary. The Gazetteer lent official credibility to Vigne's exclusion of Changthang, later Aksai Chin, from Ladakh. The policy had clearly firmed up to keep out of British empire such borderlands of Ladakh or Gilgit over which travesed trade routes originating in Central Asia. This was seen as a strategic compulsion for England to protect the British empire in India. In pursuit of this policy the Gazetteer saw Ladakh to its north vaguely bounded by the unexplored Yarkand valley and not the Kuen Lun as revealed, beyond all doubt, by Mirza Haidar. The Gazetteer was published in 1844, two years before the formation of the State of Jammu and Kashmir. British knowledge then about the region's geography appears to have been limited to Mir Izzatullah's observations and explorations of Lieutenant Wood, Leech and Lord in the Hindu Kush. But that was not a constraint. Wood explored the upper Oxus branch that springs from the Sirikul lake. His explorations established there are plateaux at the either end of the parallel chains of mountains, Aksai Chin (Changthang) to the southeast and the Pamirs to the northwest. The British in pursuit of a strategic, in contradistinction to the natural and historical, boundary undertook studies and surveys to acquire a thorough hydrological, orographic and hypsometric knowledge to decide on the strategic advantages and disadvantages of the two plateaux to them.

The first systematic survey of Jammu and Kashmir was carried out by Captain T.G Montgomerie of the Survey of India, beginning 1855.[5] More important, was however, the extensive scientific exploration of Baltistan, Ladakh, Tibet and Eastern Turkistan "entrusted" by the British Indian Government to Schlagintweit brothers, Herman, Adolphe and Robert. Accompanied by the surveyors of the Survey of India, they carried out explorations in 1856 and 1857. Their progress was not without unexpected difficulties, ending in the murder of Adolphe in Kashgar in 1857. These explorations provide the earliest geographical knowledge about Aksai Chin and other areas north of the Muztagh-Karakoram ridge before British interest revived on the northern boundary. Secondly these yield crucial information about the northern limits of Jammu and Kashmir. The added merit of their findings is the Schlagintweits not being Englishmen, though professed agents of the East India Company.

His explorations in Skardo led Adolphe to the largest group of glaciers, the Rimo, Siachin, Urdok, Bilafond, Kondus, Baltoro, Gasherbrum and the rest, many now of military significance. He most carefully examined the western part of the Karakoram range. But his attempts to cross it by the Muztagh were frustrated by the "predatory tribes" infesting its northern foot in the Yarkand valley. The "predatory tribes" could only be the people of Hunza. So early were the Kanjutis in control of a part of Yarkand Valley. The two other brothers, Herman and Robert, were the first Europeans to cross both the Karakoram and Kuen Lun chains and "cleared" the British "mix up" over the two. On the basis of their "observations" they declared the Karakoram ridge as the watershed between India and Central Asia as against the Kuen Lun hitherto "mistaken" as the water-parting.[6] This and some other findings of Schlagintweits proved to be misleading, as will be noticed. Their success the Germans owed to their guide, Mohammad Amin, who led them from the Karakoram pass by the unfrequented and prohibited route through western Aksai Chin to the Kuen Lun and across it by the Hindustash pass as far as Bushia on its northern face in Khotan. The Hindustash pass, overlooking Aksai Chin, was thus the boundary pass. Sven Hedin towards the end of the 19th century and Flippo De Flippi in the early years of the 20th century took this very line for their explorations-Panamik, the last northward village in Nubra, Daulatbeg Uldi, Karakoram pass, Kiul Kiol Salt Lake, Sikandar Mokam, Karakash valley, Sumgol, Ilchi or

Brinjga pass. Stein calls it Brinjak pass (16000 ft.). Schlagintweits christened the entire Muztagh-Karakoram ridge as the Karakoram or Black Mountain range[7], in sharp contrast with the snow-clad white Himalaya. Credit for naming the Karakoram was later given by British geographers to Moorcroft and Hayward.

Of the secondary trade lines detailed by Schlagintweits, the one that ran through Lingzithang to the Hindutash and across it to Bushia had a fort at Sikandar Mokam on the flank of the pass. It was not permanently occupied, not being easy to victual. A more important line, starting from Leh, which later came to be named as the Changchenmo road, was marked with stones by Adolphe, in the Aksai Chin desert. This route, Schlagintweits say, was not a commercial line[8]. There was another fort, or fortified site, on the bank of the Karakash river[9], along the road, a little before Sogat was reached. Whose forts were these if not of Ladakh? These were to the south of the Kuen Lun while the Chinese had their fortified posts or forts at Sanju, Kilian and Kukyar to its north. In Yarkand valley the Germans noticed the Pakpho village beyond which, they mention, lay Ak Masjid, a Chinese boundary and custom post with Chinese soldiers and officials[10]. A lesser reason for the British preference for the Karakoram as Ladakh's northern boundary becomes evident from the findings of Schlagintweits. A comparative study they made revealed that though the mean height of the Himalaya peaks exceeds that of the peaks of the Karakoram, yet the mean elevation of the crests and passes "is decidedly greater for the latter." In the case of the Kuen Lun it is less than the Himalaya. The mean elevation of the three chains is : the Karakoram 18,700, Himalaya 17,800 and Kuen Lun 17,000 feet.

No less importantly, the Schlagintweit mission helps establish criminal jurisdiction of the Maharaja of Jammu and Kashmir north of the Karakoram in the Yarkand Valley. Adolphe Schlagintweit, completing his surveys in Aksai Chin, headed for Kashgar. When he reached Sogat or its neighbourhood at the head of Aksai Chin, some six miles short of Shahidulla, his camp was looted by his attendants. They carried the booty towards Kukyar[11]. Some three years later while in Ladakh, Lt. Colonel Irby, a British officer, urged the "Thanadar" (governor) of Ladakh, "to use his exertions to recover... (Adolphe's) property... in the possession of some persons in Sanju."[12] Such exertions would have been possible only on the ground that the plunder had taken place on Ladakh soil at Sogat. Implied, therefore, in the request of Colonel Irby is the jurisdiction of the State, north of the Karakoram. This criminal jurisdiction of Jammu and Kashmir in the Yarkand valley is distinctly established in a murder case later.

Montigomerie's surveyors fixed numerous peaks in the Karakoram-Muztagh range along which it was claimed the northern boundary ran[13]. In 1862 "stations were fixed on the Chinese frontier from which a number of peaks in Tartary were determined." The Chinese frontier here referred to is the Kuen Lun and this is confirmed by the General Report, Great Trigonometrical Survey for 1865-66. The claim that the Karakoram is the northern boundary in Ladakh is thus obfuscation. The observations from the Kuen Lun were materially to aid in the construction of maps of districts "into which surveyors will probably be unable to penetrate," that is the districts of Khotan[14]. These and related surveys also became the basis of the map of Jammu and Kashmir's northern boundary by W.H. Johnson, which like Strachey's map, was produced by India during the earlier negotiations with China on the frontier.

In the southern Pangong lake region, an eastern eminence, Tuggu Nuggu, had been a fortified post which Captain Godwin Austin, in the course of his surveys in 1863, estimated to be a work of the time of Qosot Mongol invasion of Ladakh, 1681-83. Over a mile beyond it low spurs about on the lake and the way leads to a bay, Phursak, which forms the boundary with Tibet[15]. On the northern side of the lake the plain of Pal was, Godwin Austin says, a disputed ground. But this site the Zimskang of Rudok chose for his camp on the bank of a stream, to prevent Godwin Austin trespassing into Tibet, a clear indication of the boundary. Strachey was thus wrong in placing Pal in Tibet. Northwest of Pal, the road led to the Changchenmo valley. The boundary with Ladakh was Kiung Gang la (17,259 ft.). At this pass were stationed, throughout the summer months, a guard of Rudok men. Further north Johnson surveyed Lingzithang or Aksai Chin for two seasons ending 1864, reaching them from the Changchenmo valley by the Lumkang pass, probably Changlung la (19,280 ft.). He was assisted by a Ladakhi guide, whom he euphemistically alludes to as "shikari" (hunter), who identified places and passes for him. Johnson's surveys were almost contemporaneous with the overthrow of Chinese power in Eastern Turkistan in 1864.

There was no awareness in Khotan that roads from there ran into Ladakh. When on the collapse of Chinese power in Eastern Turkistan, a Mohammad Habibullah assumed power in Khotan as "Badshah," men were commissioned to explore a direct route to Ladakh. Such a line of communication was shown to the Khotanese by Mohammad Alam[16] who, with Mohammad Amin, had guided Schlagintweits through Aksai Chin and Herman and Robert to Bushia in Khotan. As Habibullah's envoy Juma Khan was guided by Mohammad Alam to Leh by the Yangi dawan to the Karakash valley. The Badshah's "communication was tendered to the officers of Maharaja Ranbir Singh at Leh. The British too had, a little earlier, deputed a native surveyor, Abdul Hamid, to explore the proscribed Polur-Keria la-Rudok-Kulu line. Abdul Hamid mysteriously died over the Karakoram road. While engaged in making his observations from the Kuen Lun summit stations, Johnson was invited by Habibullah to visit Ilchi. "...to pass beyond the frontier of Ladakh," that is the Kuen Lun, his work site then, Johnson did not have Government's permission.[17] The invitation was, nevertheless accepted by Johnson on the condition that the "Badshah" sent his son or minister to receive him "at the first village on the northern side of the Kuen Lun range of mountains."[18]

From accounts of natives, Johnson gathered that the Kuen Lun stretches in an easterly direction for a distance of 100 miles from the sources of the Karakash and then terminates on an extensive plain communicating with the Changthang plateaux of Tibet. By skirting the Kuen Lun range "wheeled conveyances might be easily taken from Ilchi to the Changchenmo valley near Leh," with water, grass and wood obtainable along the road[19]. This was an exaggeration. The only obstacle Johnson foresaw to the opening of this line was the certain opposition of shepherds of Rudok in the portion which passed over Tibetan Changthang. Quite evidently Johnson was referring to the Lanak la-Keria la-Polur road. The extensive plain was the eastern part of Lingzithang or Aksai Chin over which the route ran. Himself Johnson travelled to Khotan by the Yangi dawn route, the one taken by Juma Khan, earlier, which also ran over Aksia Chin, to the west of the Lanak la-Keria la-Polur line, and Changchenmo valley to the south. Of the Leh-Yarkand line also, especially its winter variation, Johnson took note of. He suggested the Maharaja should despatch "guards of adequate strength to occupy the ground within his boundary in the vicinity of the plain called Kirghiz Jungle on the Kukyar (winter) route and at Shahidulla and Ilnagar on the Sanju (summer) routes."[20] Kirghiz Jungle pass and Ilnagar were thus Jammu and Kashmir State's outposts overlooking the Yarkand valley with Shahidulla a little to the south. Johnson called Shahidulla "Maharaja's guardhouse" with "a guard of 25 sepoys and 50 Tartars" in 1865 to protect the "kafilas" or caravans, from the Kanjuti and Kirghiz robbers. It is evident from Johnson's account that Shahidulla was not a fort and troops garrisoned there were not for purposes of defence but to "escort caravans" over dangerous ground. Johnson's details about the

Maharaja's garrison are again significant in that Tartars were also in his service. These Tartars most likely were the Kirghiz who very lately had overflowed into the Karakash valley (Shahidulla) from Sanju and Sirikul.

Of the other territory related to the boundary issue that Johnson mentions is the Minsar enclave, a village beyond Rudok and Gartok in Tibet, latitude 31°10' longitude 80°50' "from which the Maharaja receives a revenue of Rs. 500 per annum." On his return from Khotan to Ladakh via Sanju, Johnson found the last portion of the Changchenmo-Shahidulla route as particularly pleasant, being the whole way up the "wide and even" Karakash valley. He noticed numerous extensive plateaux, near the river, covered with wood and long grass. "These being within the territory of Maharaja of Kashmir could easily be brought under cultivation by Ladakhis and others if they could be induced and encouraged to do so by Kashmir Government."[21] Johnson thus categorically states that the Karakash valley was "within the territory of the Maharaja of Kashmir." Its colonisation that he suggested was largely for military considerations. Being almost on the boundary line, a productive Karakash valley would have been a source of supply to a chain of border outposts such as Shahidulla, Kirghiz Jungle and Ilnagar which otherwise, were too far away to be victualled from Nubra or Tanksi. Besides the habitations would have relayed information about any hostile force approaching Ladakh. The absence of any habitations north of the Karakoram ridge materially influenced British military thinking. Agriculture would not have been new in the Karakash valley. Johnson himself noted that Oibuk on the left bank of the Karakash had been under cultivation until the beginning of the 19th century.[22]

From Johnson's report and map, the boundary clearly ran across the Pangong lake, larger part of it in Ladakh, climbed northwards, west of Karnak, Kiungla, Kepsang pass, turned northeast, keeping well within Ladakh the sources of the Keria river, far to the east of longitude 81°, thence westward to the Yangi dawan, Hindutash dawan, south of Nissa, north of Ilnagar, Zokongra, Walaghat, perhaps, the Indian name of the Sanju pass, Chadartash and Katai Tam. This boundary puts entire Aksai Chin inside Ladakh and Shahidulla four marches within Jammu and Kashmir and not on the boundary line itself as is generally assumed in British records. Oddly, however, Johnson's map shows Ladakh's eastern limit only 80°30' and not 82°E longitude. His map was entirely recast by Colonel Walker of the Survey of India. From Shahidulla the road threaded along the Karakash to Oibuk, Pilatagosh, Mirza Abubakar, Bostan and Sanju pass. The Maharaja's guardhouses, or "forts," were also located at Bostan and Ilnagar. The Chinese post in this region, noticed by Johnson, was at Kilian where the "Karaul" (boundary post) was garrisoned by 50 men "to prevent strangers from entering the country..." Sanju, crossing which Johnson entered Ladakh, was another "Karaul" though the post then appears to have been located farther north at Karamlak Jilga.[23] The third post was at Kukyar.

The surveys, studies and subsequent journey of Johnson to Ilchi induced an admission from the British that the Angartaksia, or the Kuen Lun, was the "boundary between the territories of the Maharaja and the province of Khotan."[24] Such a conclusion was possible as these surveys and studies either preceded or coincided with the eviction of China from Eastern Turkistan. The advent of Yakub Beg Kushbegi, later Atalik Ghazi and Amir, of Kashgaria, activated the boundary issue. The Changchenmo line, and not the Lanak la-Keria la-Polur highway, became the centre of British attention as a commercial and military road. England pretended it was the shortest and easiest way to project her political and commercial interests in Central Asia. It was evidently intended to keep the Lanak la-Keria la-Polur route and, therefore east Aksai Chin out of Ladakh. T.D. Forsyth, Commissioners of Jallandhar division, which then included the Sutlej Hill States, took "considerable interest" in the revival of the Central Asian trade. Khotan being anxious to establish friendly relations with the British Government, it was suddenly realised that the direct route to it did not lay through Leh. "...it can be reached by the shortest, easiest and pleasantest route...by Puga, the Pangong lake, Changchenmo and thence over a level plain to Khotan." The level plain referred to is, of course, Lingzithang or Aksai Chin. Only a small portion of Kashmir territory, it was reckoned, would be crossed by the Changchenmo line.[25] The small portion of Kashmir territory did not include Aksai Chin or the "level palin." The alternative route avoiding Changchenmo was considered slightly circuitous, skirting on Rudok territory from where it would have crossed into Aksai Chin by the Lanak la. Maharaja Ranbir Singh was not, however, inclined to open the proscribed Aksai Chin road (western part), even though both Khotan and Yarkand were "favourable to an alliance (with England)," and feared to fall into the jaws of Russia. But greater than all-far more imminent, Forsyth felt, "is the danger they dread falling into the hands of Kashmir." Contrary to his treaty obligations, the Maharaja was credited with the intention of undertaking "a foreign incursion," for which supplies had been collected at Leh. Forsyth recalled the visit of the Lieutenant Governor of the Punjab to Jammu when the Maharaja had made no secret of his intention to extend his territory towards the north.[26]

The truth was that as many as ten trading caravans had been attacked by the Kanjutis in the latter half of 1865 and the beginning of 1866, "an alarming increase of depredations never before withnessed on this route."[27] Though Shahidulla was garrisoned by the Maharaja's troops for some years to afford protection to trading caravans against Kanjuti raids, it was not easy to provision it. Early in 1866 heavy snowfall blocked the Leh road. Consequently the garrison of Shahidulla guardhouse, then comprising 10 soldiers, was obliged to cross over to Khotan territory. "The king (Habibullah) supplied them with what was necessary and after providing them with road expenses has had them escorted back to their country,"[28] an eminently friendly treatment. Again it was ignorance rather than sheer obfuscation that a British agent, Pandit Manphool, credited the Maharaja having a "guard of 25 men stationed at Sogat *within Yarkand* territory"[29] in 1865. Evidently the Pandit mistook Sogat for Shahidulla. In 1866 troops from Leh itself accompanied trading caravans to Shahidulla and beyond.[30] This implies that withdrawal of garrison from Shahidulla was voluntary and for considerations of logistics.

But Hunza depredations persuaded Yakub Beg Kushbegi to depute an envoy to the court of his "neighbour," Maharaja Ranbir Singh, to seek an alliance and to convey his decision to destroy the Kanjuti robbers who were "great obstacle to the increase of trade..."[31] Towards the attainment of this objective he had already brought Sirikul, a dependency of Hunza, under his subjection. No supremacy or any other rights were claimed by Yakub Beg over Hunza in his communication to the Maharaja. The Kanjutis were also warned by the Kushbegi through the ruler of Sirikul, "not to plunder on the road."[32] Naturally Maharaja Ranbir Singh was influenced by Kashgaria's intention to attack his vassal, Hunza. To pre-empt Kashgaria, a Kashmir attack was to be led from the north and supplies for the troops were, therefore, laid.[33] It were these supplies that Forsyth conjured were to be used in the "foreign incursion" by the Maharaja. The attack from the north was intended to warn the Kushbegi to keep off Hunza and signal to the British the Maharaja's resolve to assert his rights in the Yarkand valley. Already Kashgaria had trespassed into Sirikul where earlier the Chinese had no rights. The incursion would appear to have been prompted by consideration to forestall Russia building a cantonment at Tashkurgan[34] than to punish Hunza. Nevertheless Ranbir Singh was expected to depute a strong force to the Gilgit-Hunza boundary "to overawe and chastise the Kjanjutis, the Maharaja's force to act in cooperation with the one which the ruler of

Yarkand will appoint on his side."[35]

The Kashmir Government was advised to regarrison Shahidulla, preferably with a larger body of troops, with supplies and stores sent in advance.[36] This advice was tendered by its own political agent, deputed to Central Asia, to anticipate the Kushbegi in Hunza. The situation became curiouser with a Yarkand official, Kadir Mirab, in-charge of villages Minkhfo and Sanakshu, in the vicinity of Kokyar, proposing to tender feality to Maharaja Ranbir Singh to whom he submitted a petition.[37] That feality was offered underscores that Jammu and Kashmir's boundary ran beyond Kirghiz Jungle to Kulanuldi to be contiguous with Kashgaria in Kukyar. Of the trade issues to be sorted out between Kashmir and Kashgar was imposition of duties at Shahidulla and in Nubra. This reveals presence of civilians officials, besides troops, at Shahidulla.[38] These customs officials had continued to function at Shahidulla until November 1866 when they too were obliged to leave.[39] With their departure, Kashmir was never allowed to reoccupy Shahidulla though, for practical purposes, it continued to be its boundary point.

The sharp turn in Central Asian affairs brought about a slow but discernible shift in British policy on the boundary issue. A strong necessity was felt for the protection of British commercial and political interests in Central Asia. On the pretext of exactions of Kashmir officials on British trade in Ladakh, an Assistant Commissioner was proposed to be posted at Leh during the hot season of 1867 "notwithstanding the distastefulness of such an arrangement to the Maharaja."[40] To assuage the fealings of Maharaja Ranbir Singh, the Indian Foreign Department felt posting of a medical officer might, perhaps, best meet the exigencies of the case.[41] Besides acquiring some knowledge of "passing political events in Chinese Turkistan," the officer was to enlighten Government on "the present value and capacity for future expansion of the trade between India and Central Asia,"[42] through Ladakh, a trade which the Viceroy, Sir John Lawrence, thought was already "a good deal over-estimated."[43] Deputation of a British officer was finally sanctioned and Dr. Henry Cayley came to be posted at Leh on "an experimental basis."[44]

Forsyth, unlike Sir John Lawrence, saw India's trade with Central Asia "well nigh extinct." But he found hope for its revival in the opening of the trade line that "skirts the Kuen Lun range to the east, passing Changchenmo, Pangong lake, Puga, cutting across an angle of Ladakh territory and coming down by the Baralacha to Lahaul and Spiti to Rampur..." This, of course, was the Changchenmo route, bypassing Leh, beginning in the north in the Karakash valley, for he says it "skirts the

Kuen Lun..." Though this line ran through Changchenmo valley, Pangong lake and Puga, Forsyth saw it cutting across only an "angle" that evidently was Hanle. What of the other extensive areas through which the route passed in the north? Forsyth's description of the Changchenmo road seems to approximate to Hardinge's boundary line! To open the road to commerce, the British Indian Government was advised to "enter into some arrangement," not with the Kashmir Government but, "with Yarkand and the authorities of those parts."[45] Other routes to Turkistan from India were also noticed by Forsyth, the most direct of which was the western line from Chitral down the Indus valley. But this line was then unsafe and, therefore, ruled out by him. The most eastern road noticed by Forsyth was Moorcroft's Moghal line, "an old and really good road with wood, water and provisions at every station, and paved in the time of the Moghal emperors, practicable for wheeled carriages throughout the year, and which leads through a pass in the Kuen Lun chain, far to the *east of Kashmir*, straight down to the North West Provinces (modern UP)..." It was claimed to run through Tibet and all progress through it was "jealously watched and prohibited." Though Forsyth ran this line far to the east, he quite evidently refers to the Lanak la-Keria la-Polur highway that passed through Rudok, Gartok, Niti to Najibabad in Uttar Pradesh. This line was not far to the east of Kashmir but bulk of it ran over east Aksai Chin. This, significantly, is confirmed by the Punjab Government. It saw what it called the "Changchenmo" line, or, really, the Rudok-Keria la-Polur variation of the main Lanak la-Keria la-Polur highway, as the most direct route between Lahaul and Yarkand and elaborated that it traversed "a small corner only of the Maharaja's territory..." and then ran for "three or four stages" in the Rudok province of Tibet.[46] The acknowledgment by the Punjab Government that this road partly passed through Ladakh decisively help's in determining the northeastern limits of Aksai Chin. There was another road, the real Changchenmo route that also the Punjab Government considered for trade. It also, similarly, passed through "a corner only of Ladakh territory," and would have been in general use "but that the Maharaja of Kashmir has prohibited is adoption..." The corner only of Ladakh territory would again appear to be Hanle. The British had before them the surveys of the Survey of India and the report of Johnson. Yet Forsyth was vague on the line of British commerce with Central Asia. Selection of a line, therefore, became the first priority with Dr. Cayley.

Part of the Changchenmo line—Lahaul, Rupshu, Puga—Dr. Cayley had himself passed over on his way up to Leh. But in his first report to the Punjab Government, he traced the whole road. He readily admits the route was since long closed "by the Ladakh officials." From Puga the Changchenmo line passed the head, or the western extremity of the Pangong lake, or else left the Leh road at Upshi on the Indus and crossed by an easy pass to Tanksi and the Pangong-tso. The road then ascended the Changchenmo valley and crossed in Changlung pass, which is very easy and free of snow. Thereafter it lay for several marches over wide undulating plains and crossed an easy pass into the Karakash river valley and followed the stream for six marches to Sogat, at the foot of the Sogat pass. The passes were all low and free of snow and there were no rivers to cross and over wide plains, which Dr. Cayley identifies as Aksai Chin, grass and fuel were plentiful. Unlike Forsyth, Dr. Cayley again truthfully admits "the road lies entirely in Kashmir territory and leaves the Chinese frontier far to the east."[47] Except making the road pleasant and full of grass and fuel, which it was not, this was a faithful description of the Changchenmo line.

But Dr. Cayley did not altogether eschew obfuscation. He imagined that the Kushbegi was "offended with Kashmir Government for having formed an alliance with Khotan and also for establishing a military post at Shahidulla, which is nearly three marches north of the Karakoram pass and consequently in Yarkand territory..." The "depot at Shahidulla," he claimed, "(was) destroyed,"[48] presumably by the Kashgarians. Yakub Beg Kushbegi had himself sought an alliance with the Maharaja. But that apart, what is evident from Dr. Cayley's report is that the boundary touched the Karakoram pass, ran northeast to Sogat and thence stretched along the Kuen Lun to leave the Karakash valley and Aksai Chin in Ladakh, or nearly the same as is now erroneously claimed by the Government of India. However, he proposed the Punjab Government to urge the Maharaja to open the Changchenmo line and also improve, if possible, the other lines of traffic through his territory.[49] The endorsement of Dr. Cayleys suggestion that the Maharaja should undertake repair of the Karakash and the Leh-Yarkand trade lines was an acknowledgement by the Punjab Government that these regions formed part of Jammu and Kashmir State. Within months of his arrival in Ladakh, Dr. Cayley undertook exploration of the Changchenmo line in the Pangong-Karakash river head region, going over the drainage of the Indus and the Tarim basins, Tarim basin partly in Ladakh and largely in Eastern Turkistan. The purpose of these explorations was to find a short cut to the traditional Changchenmo road, as Dr. Cayley himself indicates. The shorter route had water at every stage, the longest interval being 20 miles, an optimistic account again.

At Jallandhar Forsyth exulted that a trifling cost of £500-Rs. 5,500 had rendered passable the Kulu-Ladakh road for laden animals, even as the Changchenmo line was declared fit for the passage of loaded camels. In a build up for the opening of the road to traffic, Forsyth made claims which were either totally false, based on imperfect knowledge, or inspired by political and military considerations. Once astride Changchenmo-Lingzithang-Karakash valley and with a political agent at Leh, the British could press forward with their trade and, no less, with their political influence into Central Asia. Such an influence was seen to lend a measure of stability to the Kushbegi without which all trade would be unavailing and which alone could secure the British against Russian moves to establish a cantonment at Guma,[50] at the head of the road to Karakoram and Changchenmo, with right of way. Such a demand was claimed to have been made on China in 1859 or 1860. The Chinese, according to a story, evidently apocryphal, placed it before 'Aksakals' or consular agents, of different trading countries for an opinion. As the Russians, the 'Aksakals' suggested, did not ask to come within the line of forts along Chinese boundary and as the road they asked for–over the Yarkand valley–did not belong to China, the Russians had better consult, not the Maharaja of Kashmir but, Kokand and Badakshan.

All that Russia, however, got was some ground at Panjtilik, three miles west of Kashgar, on the road to Kokand, where they ultimately set up their consulate. The fictitious report on Guma cantonment gained immense credibility with Englishmen, among them Sir Richard Temple, then a member of the Viceroy's Council. Forsyth played on British fears of being outflanked. Whilst so eagerly watching "the front"–the northwest frontier–he cautioned, "it is just as well to see whether our rear is so perfectly secure from all approach..."[51] It was not, Forsyth warned, for "an exceedingly easy road exists by the Changchenmo valley by which land camels can pass from Yarkand to Leh, and where camels can go, armies may follow." Another factor seen by Forsyth in the situation was the long season of severe winter all over the Himalaya, which prevented any move on the south side and hindered obtaining intelligence from the trans-Himalayan countries. But action and motion were not so entirely impeded by the winter in Turkistan. If then Russia obtained mastery over Turkistan what was to hinder her, in case of a war with England, from moving their forces to Guma, their coveted cantonment, so as to block trade, or to make an advance upon Leh at a time when England would be unable to send any force to oppose them? Were a

Russian force to enter Eastern Turkistan it would, it was visualised, become necessary either to have a political agent in Yarkand or Kashgar to watch and give timely notice of their movements or to have a British force at Srinagar or Leh to guard against sudden attack.[52] "...in real sober truth," Forsyth aruged, in another paper on Central Asia, "India is more vulnerable by Russia on the north than on any other side."[53] Though this view was alarmist, Russian factor increasingly influenced British thinking on the northern boundary after the exit of Sir John Lawrence. Even on trade he had remained convinced that not much could spring up between India and Eastern Turkistan however much it was fostered for one reason "The route appears too long and the obstacles too many for such a result to come to pass."[54]

Russia alone was not a disturbing factor for the British. Kashmir's opposition to their tampering with the historical limits of the State was no less a cause for worry to them. That Maharaja Golab Singh defeated British designs to delimit the northern boundary, as suited their strategic interests, has already been noticed. His successor, Maharaja Ranbir Singh did not hide his opposition to the British Indian Government pressuring him to reopen the proscribed Changchenmo road to traffic. Nor did the Maharaja see eye to eye with the British on trade with Central Asia. With the Punjab having gone under the British and the Afghans having finally withdrawn from India, Kashmir's opposition was mostly covert as becomes evident. The Kushbegi's envoy having agreed, on British persuasion, to return home by the Changchenmo line, "suddenly" changed his avowed intention and chose to travel by the "inhospitable Karakoram" highway.[55] His decision was attributed to the influence of Kashmir officials. Again, Ranbir Singh was extremely unhappy with the British decision to post an agent, Dr. Ceyley, at Leh. Of his unhappiness the Maharaja never made a secret. So much so that Forsyth suggested to his Government it might be "wise and politic" to accede to the Maharaja's request and withdraw the agent from Leh subject to abolition of transit duty and opening of the Changchenmo line. In that event Central Asian traders could take the Tsomorreri to Lahaul route to the Punjab. This argument Forsyth himself pressed on Ranbir Singh who then suddenly gave up his opposition to reopening the Changchenmo line. The only condition he setforth was to levy tolls in the event of his having to construct roads and bridges over the line.[56] Such duties would have asserted his sovereignty over the territories the route passed through.

To link up the Lahaul-Tsomorreri road with the Changchenmo line, so as to altogether bypass Leh, Roberts Shaw was sent up to explore and survey a short cut higher up the course of the Indus river. In the Karakash valley Shaw found "a group of stone huts, all signs that this road was once in use."[57] The huts might as well have been a guardhouse, noticed earlier by Schlagintweits, military barracks, or even human habitations. Shaw was quick to claim that the Chinese used to visit the Karakash valley for quarrying jade which abounds in the Kuen Lun. Some other false claims are made by Shaw. He described the Shahidulla guardhouse, a fort, which the Kashmir Government later declared to be a cantonment, and went on to claim that four years earlier, in 1864, "when troubles were still going on the Turkistan" the Maharaja of Jammu and Kashmir sent a few soldiers and workmen across the Karakoram "(his real boundary)" and built the fort. Shaw implies the Maharaja took advantage of disturbed conditions in Kashgaria, built the so-called fort and so advanced his frontier from the Karakoram to Shahidulla. No less false was his statement that the Maharaja's troops occupied the fort for two seasons 1865 and 1866, but they gave it up "when matters become settled and the whole country united under the king of Yarkand." The worst falsehood of Shaw was his assertions that "in reality the Maharaja has no more right to Shahidulla than I have. He has never had any real rights on a river which flows northward through Turkistan, nor over the pastures of the Kirghiz, who pay taxes to Yarkand." Maharaja Ranbir Singh's right to Shahidulla was acknowledged by the British themselves. As to the Kirghiz they paid no tax to China and their status is discussed elsewhere. Shaw alludes to "recent maps." These, presumably, included a Turkistan map, issued in 1868, which showed Jammu and Kashmir boundary to run over the crest of the Kuen Lun. Though Shaw's credibility is to suspect to permit any reliance being put on his claim, yet he lived among Turkistan troops of Kashgaria at Shahidulla. These troops, as Shaw himself later clarified, had rebelled against the Atalik Ghazi and crossed the boundary into Shahidulla. It is inconceivable that the Kushbegi would have trespassed into Shahidulla let alone posted troops there to prevent Shaw's entry into Yarkand as he claims. The same could have been achieved at Sanju or Kilian, without any expense or contretemps. The Kuen Lun was correctly described as the southern limit of Kashgaria by Shaw. But having at the same time confined Jammu and Kashmir to the Karakoram, he remains silent about the huge tract of territory between these two chains. British policy was yet to evolve on this tract.

It is evident from Shaw that Kashgarians looked upon the

Changchenmo route, by which he, and earlier to him, the envoy, Nazar Mohammad, travelled to Yarkand, with trepidation, apprehensive that it might be used as a road of invasion rather than a line of commerce. Such a view the Kashgarian envoy had possibly gathered at Jammu or Leh. It was not, therefore, without reason that Shaw assured the Kashgarians that British had "no wish to cross the Himalaya and her interest lies in the existence of a strong and a friendly power on the north of these mountains." But the occupation earlier of Shahidulla by the Maharaja's troops would appear to have been well received by the Atalik and his officials, so also the construction of "thanas" and forts on the Changchenmo road. Shaw was told the Atalik would be delighted were these forts continued down the line to the Yarkand river valley. Such simple statements were twisted by Shaw who took pains repeatedly to suggest to the Kushbegi's officials that Shahidulla fort was an encroachment on the Turkish boundary and "when Lord Sahib (the Viceroy) hears of such an encroachment on the Turkistan boundary, he will be angry." Such and similar suggestions, especially on the actual boundary, were increasingly to emanate from Englishmen, particularly after the return of China to Eastern Turkistan.

British interest in Changchenmo road and trade with Eastern Turkistan caused anxiety and apprehension in Russia also. A Russian officer, Captain Reinthal, was despatched to Kashgar, along with several Russian traders and an escort of Cossaks.[58] A Russian paper claimed that Reinthal was sent to Kashgar to negotiate with the Atalik,[59] the negotiation being, presumably, a sequel to the certain opening of the Changchenmo road. Shaw's visit to Kashgaria was, therefore, a counter move by England to neutralise Reinthal's presence there. England suspected Reinthal had demanded a site for a Russian commercial factory or a consulate at Kashgar, under a treaty signed ten years earlier with China.[60] As then these fears of England were groundless. Evidently Russia felt no less threatened by British moves in Kashmir. This was the beginning of the Anglo Russian political and military rivalry in Central Asia that later became known as the "great game." Shaw was met by Turki officials on crossing the Sanju boundary pass the same officials later escorted him back to Sanju pass on his return journey, providing him there with provisions for his journey to Leh. That Kashgar officials did not venture beyond Sanju boundary pass and chose to load him there with supplies discredits Shaw's claim that Shahidulla fort was occupied by the Kashgarian army.[61] In that event all the formalities would have been gone through at Shahidulla. That the Atalik received Reinthal well is acknowledged by Shaw, who himself was held incommunicado, being prevented even from meeting Hayward. The latter had followed Shaw into Lingzithang to trace the source of the Karakash river to determine the water parting and also explore an upper stream of the Yarkand river and the Uprang or Shaksgam valley at the foot of the Aghil range, an offshoot of the Karakoram. In Kashgaria Hayward was suspected of looking for new roads and was allowed no opportunity to survey. Notwithstanding this debilitating factor, Hayward saw enough of Kashgaria and its neighbourhood to split up, contrary to Asian belief, the Bolortagh into two parallel chains eastern and western, which became known as Kashgar (eastern) and Sirikul (western) chains. The eastern ridge he named as Kizil Art.[62] The split, subsequent developments show, helped China to advance, with British connivance, and occupy Sirikul and some of the Pamirs.

The Russians, like the English earlier to Schlagintweit brothers, knew the Karakoram and the Kuen Lun ranges to be one with Karakoram a pass by which Eastern Turkistan communicated with Tibet. The Russians placed India's northern boundary along the Hindu Kush-Kuen Lun. So also did they identify Eastern Turkistan's boundary along the Bolor, or the Kashgar ridge, in the west and Kuen Lun in the south.[63] Reference to Sanju and Kilian villages being in the Kuen Lun clears up any doubt. The Yarkand river valley to the south was fairly well defined by Albert Verchere, a geologist, as extending "from the Karakoram...pass to Taskurgan. The valley of the Yarkand river and Aksai Chin are separated, one from the other, by a low ridge of mountains..."[64] Hayward, who had prepared a condensed map, based on his explorations in and around Kashgaria, brought down Ladakh's boundary in it from the Kuen Lun to Karakoram. To the Viceroy's office also, Hayward obliquely conveyed this cartographic change observing that the Atalik's territory "extends from the northern frontier beyond Kashgar to the Karakoram range to the south."[65] But in a memo on trade Hayward acknowledges that the Changchenmo road was proscribed for use by the Maharaja.[66] Hayward radically differed with Shaw on the northern boundary of Jammu and Kashmir. The huge expanse of Aksai Chin and the Yarkand valley were clearly placed by Hayward in Kashgaria. Shaw had left them in an undetermined state in line with the thinking of many in the British Indian Government. His reasons for the Karakoram boundary Hayward hinted at. One was that Panamik, the last habitation met with in the Maharaja's territory, "its at the head of the Nubra valley in Ladakh," in short demographic factor. The other was the possible seizure of Kashgaria by

Russia. Once in possession of Kashgaria, Russia "would virtually hold the whole country up to the Karakoram" range, for there is nothing that could prevent immediate occupation of the country...," Hayward argued, revealing, for the first time, the strategic considerations British saw involved in the northern boundary.

Hayward favoured the Changchenmo line to take off from the Niti pass, rather than Bashahr, and in the north run across the Yarkand valley to Kukyar. In the itinerary for the route, Hayward described Shahidulla stop "A fort on the Turkistan frontier garrisoned by a guard of Turki sepoys. Permission must be obtained to enter Turkistan." The Karakoram here ceased to be the boundary of the Atalik. As to the permission for entry into Kashgaria "Rahdaris," or passports, were issued at Leh where arrivals and departures were noted down in a register. These were checked at Shahidulla where, as noted, civilian officials of the Maharaja were also posted. The Chinese and, after them, Atalik's officials, checked passports at Sanju and Kilian "karauls." At Kukyar, Hayward notes, "No one is allowed to proceed onwards without permission of the Turkistan ruler."[67] On the Kukyar route, Hayward noticed the ruins of huts. He does not say these once were a border outpost of Ladakh. Both Hayward and Shaw lent the weight of their experience in support of the Changchenmo road as the British line of commerce with Central Asia. The Kukyar entrance was considered fit for wheeled carriages. It was closed following Kanjuti raids and, perhaps, also from fear of invasion. For the supplies en route the Lingzithang plateaux, Shaw favoured Lukung hamlet some distance away from the Pangong-tso, as supply depot. Precise route across the Lingzithang plain Shaws opined, depended upon the fullness or drying up of several pools of fresh water, which again varied according to the time of the year. Hence the need for trustworthy guides. He himself, and the Yarkand envoy before him, were "misled" by the Ladakhi guides provided by the Wazir of Ladakh.[68] As a result most of their horses had died and the rest had to return to Leh. The guides familiar with Aksai Chin were Ladakhis. Mohammad Amin was an exception, perhaps, because he was, allegedly, a highway robber. That the Ladakhi guides misled Shaw as well as the Yarkand envoy reflects the opposition of the Maharaja to the opening of the Changchenmo line. To overcome likely opposition of the Atalik to the opening of Kukyar to commercial traffic, Shaw proposed he could be invited to build a fort at Kirghiz Jungle,[69] ostensibly to protect Kashgaria from invasion but really to advance the boundary. From Shaw's suggestion it can be inferred that Kirghiz Jungle was Ladakh's outpost. Hayward endorsed the suggestion but favoured

Kulanuldi as the site of the fort.[70] Suggestions to change the boundary were spurned by the Atalik and, on their return to Eastern Turkistan, by the Chinese for a while. Though to the British Indian Government Maharaja Ranbir Singh had agreed to permit use of the Changchenmo road, the "covert opposition"[71] of the Kashmir authorities to it had persisted as is implied by Dr. Cayley. The opposition of Kashmir was not groundless Ranbir Singh anticipated diversion of trade from Leh and feared exclusion of Aksia Chin from his territories. One indication for exclusion of Aksai Chin from Ladakh was the choice of Lukung as the supply depot for the road. Lukung, like Panamik on the Leh-Yarkand road, is the last habitation on the Changchenmo line. Again like Panamik, Lukung is south of the Karakoram range.

Military implications of the Changchenmo line are explained by Shaw in the context of a paper on Russian advance in Central Asia, prepared by the War Office, London, Shaw appears to have been officially directed to tender his opinion on it in the light of his explorations in Lingzithang and travel in Eastern Turkistan. One obstacle Shaw saw to a Russian advance in to Kashgaria was the Terek pass over the Tianshan. Once across it the Russians were supposed to face no difficulties in reducing the whole plain country of Eastern Turkistan, including the fortresses of Kashgar, Yangihissar and Yarkand "which lie on the route to India." But Terek pass route did not worry England. The Osh-Kizil Art pass-Sirikul road became their concern. It bypassed China altogether and descended down the Yarkand valley without let or hindrance. Russia's boundary as successor State in Kashgaria, Shaw assumed, would be "the Karakoram watershed and the high plains north of Changchenmo...,"[72] Aksai Chin plateaux. In this region the Kuen Lun range had first to be crossed before the high plateaux could be reached. The Kuen Lun range Shaw compared with the letter Y placed horizontally. One route led across its double part, and another across its single part. Both the passes of the former route were difficult and one of them impassable for laden horses. This was the Shahidulla route which left the plains of Eastern Turkistan at Sanju or Kilian. The other the single pass, road left the plains of Kashgaria at Kukyar, crossed the tail of "Y" by a singular depression and at a most easy gradient. This road was partly closed on account of robbers, "but it is evidently the line that would be taken by an invading army." Grass, wood and water were plentiful right up to near the Karakoram range and artillery could be brought the whole way without being dismantled.

Having crossed the Kuen Lun chain by the most western road, an army, Shaw expatiated, would next choose the most eastern line over the Karakoram watershed for all its streams drain south and west into the Indus. Hence by keeping to the east, it would get into the high open country near their sources instead of the deep gorges. "This gives preference to the Changchenmo route over the Karakoram pass route. For though the passes are equally high, yet there are fewer of them and they hardly rise above the level of the table-land, so high is the latter."[73] During this part of the route, Shaw acknowledged, it would be necessary to carry all supplies, even fodder for cattle. The road was considered extremely well suited for camels which had often made their way to Kashmir even by the more difficult Karakoram pass line. He dismissed the argument in regard to scarcity of supplies for, he pointed out, Changchenmo offered no obstacles. The high altitude factor is altogether ignored by Shaw. This line of argument was reasonably correct as to the passage of the Kuen Lun but facile with regard to the crossing of Lingzithang desert as the Forsyth expedition to Yarkand of 1870 was soon to prove. The rest was question of expense. The Changchenmo route bifurcated at Nischu on the southern edge of Lingzithang over the watershed "which forms the northern boundary of the Indus basin and, therefore, the natural limits of the British dependencies"–Jammu and Kashmir. One road went in an easterly direction and was taken by Johnson. The other route went past certain hot springs and was followed by Dr. Cayley in the preceding year. This then was the Changchenmo military road that the British assiduously projected as a trade line. The prospect was seen to change were a British army interposed between these deserts and fertile Ladakh, and defending the passes leading into it with supplied close at hand and open roads of communication along its rear. South of Leh the outer Himalayan ranges became snow-bound during the winter to block passage to all but a few foot passengers. It was, therefore not impossible for Russia, if ready to make sufficient sacrifices of men and money, to place a small army with artillery in Kashmir.

Shaw, expectedly, was read with much interest by the Governor General-in-Council and negotiations on a treaty on the Changchenmo road with the Kashmir Government were ordered. Two issues, raised during negotiations, often acerbic, deserve mention : one concession demanded of the Maharaja was that the Changchenmo line should be superintended by two joint commissioners appointed by the Kashmir and the British Indian Government.[74] The second it was considered desirable by the British that no official of the "Darbar" should be allowed to reside or exercise power of any kind within the limits to which the jurisdiction of joint commissioners might extend which should be a certain line from the general course of the road.[75] This in effect would have sundered all the eastern parts of Ladakh from Jammu and Kashmir and resurrected Hastinge's boundary line. Maharaja Ranbir Singh proposed to construct a town, Ranbirnagar, "in the middle of the Changchenmo route,"[76] to prevent any part of the unpopulated eastern Ladakh being alienated from his State. The actual site would have depended upon where the Changchenmo line started. The British would have insisted it started at Lingti while Kashmir Government would have claimed it began at the western end of the Pangong-tso. Captain Grey, British political agent, who conducted the negotiations with the Lieutenant Governor of the Punjab, in a memo admits "...suspicions of our intentions and a desire to establish his claim to (Changchenmo) district beyond chance of question" led Ranbir Singh to propose to establish the town.[77] But Changchenmo, south of the Karakoram, was not in dispute. Aksai Chin was made disputable and Ranbir Singh was too well aware of it. This awareness was one reason why Dewan Kripa Ram, Prime Minister, told Grey that British engineers deputed to mark the road "should either have nothing to say to territorial boundaries or should accept those pointed out by the Kashmir officials, i.e., that the non-interference on their part, stipulated for, should not extend to allowing engineers to assume what boundaries they pleased."[78] The business of the engineers, Captain Grey agreed, "would lie with demarcating the road, not boundaries...and carry it only to the head of Changchenmo valley..." The inference is clear that so far as the Maharaja was involved, his boundary ended in the Changchenmo valley, north of which is the Karakoram. Captain Grey elaborated "Government would determine on their definite settlement at an early date," and that whatever the Jammu and Kashmir Government might itself claim he personally had no doubt that "we should only recognise such as the Maharaja could himself maintain, or we support him in," which Grey conceived could not "be farther north than the southern slopes of the Karakoram range."[79]

As worded, Grey's memo on the Changchenmo negotiations does not indicate that Maharaja Ranbir Singh had, *per se*, sought British recognition of his boundary. Apart from several references, already noticed, it would appear Dewan Kirpa Ram had "cunningly" laid down boundaries, not of jurisdiction along the Changchenmo road, but "the boundaries of the Kashmir dominions."[80] This appears to suggest that a paper indicating the course of the Changchenmo line along with the boundary of Ladakh was given by the Dewan to Grey. That is why C.U.

Aitchison, Secretary, Indian Foreign Department, argued "the Maharaja's boundaries in that direction have never been defined." In 1863 Sir Richard Montgomery (Lieutenant Governor of the Punjab) reported that the Maharaja considered his frontier to the north to extend "as far as his troops can penetrate." This does not appear to be a statement truthfully attributed to the Maharaja because it does not agree with what Ranbir Singh told Grey viz., Shahidulla was his boundary. If the Maharaja made the statement attribute to him then it must refer to Jammu and Kashmir's boundary in the north-west-Hunza, Yasin and Chitral, and other doubtful termini of Vance Agnew's boundary line. As to Grey's assertion that the State's boundary could not be farther than the southern slopes of the Karakoram, Aitchison expressed his doubt to the Viceroy–

> "...if it is prudent, in the present state of our information, to indicate any definite line, even 'the southern slopes of the Karakoram range' as his frontier."[81]

The matter, Aitchison counselled, should be entirely left indefinite. Evidently an admission so early on the boundary, when the British had not fully grasped the geography of the frontier region and settled political and commercial issues with Kashmir and Kashgar, was fraught with complications. It is, however, clear enough that it were the British, and not the Chinese or the Atalik Ghazi, who questioned Kashmir's territorial limits and sought to tamper with them.

The southern section of the Changchenmo line was no less a matter of dispute. A boundary cairn erected by the State at the head of the Lingti plain, which brought the whole of the plain and one of the principal passes into Ladakh within Jammu and Kashmir territories, was declared "an encroachment" on British territory. The compulsion for this falsehood was the Punjab Government's proposal to throw a bridge across the Tsarap river so as to open out the road from British India, "via the Panjbo-la to the south of the Tsomorreri as far as our boundary." This route was favoured by Forsyth whereas negotiations with the Kashmir Government were based on Shaw's line. The British boundary never really extended as far as the neighbourhood of the Tsomorreri. But the road along this lake, Rupshu and beyond to the Pangong-tso or Tibet the British had coveted since 1847. The Changchenmo line really began only at the northwest end of the Pangong lake, as Forsyth acknowledged and the Kashmir Government asserted. But it was the British object to mark out the best route from the British frontier of Lahaul to Yarkand via the Changchenmo valley.[82] As Forsyth believed the route via the Panjbo-la as the better one than that of Shaw, he considered it a matter of great importance that not a yard of British territory was "surrendered" to the Maharaja. By "maintaining" British boundaries the British hoped to push the road to within a few miles of the Tsomorreri. This was precisely what was sought to have been achieved in 1847.

When the Changchenmo accord was finally reached between the British Government and Maharaja Ranbir Singh his fears about the territorial integrity of his state remained unassuaged. In Kashgar the Changchenmo road range alarm bells. The belief that it could be an invasion route had not rubbed off, Shaw's explanation notwithstanding. The Atalik's new envoy, Mirza Shadi, at his audience with the Viceroy, Lord Mayo, in March 1870, sought in the first instance, a statement of objects which the British Indian Government had in view in opening up the route.[83] The "sole object," the Viceroy replied, was to afford greater facilities for the protection, freedom and encouragement of trade. Evidently to allay the fears of the Atalik, the envoy urged, in the name of his sovereign, that a British officer should accompany him to Kashgaria on a friendly visit. Lord Mayo concurred, suggesting it would probably be best that a British envoy should join Mirza Shadi in Ladakh.[84] For this mission to Kashgaria, Lord Mayo chose T.D. Forsyth, who had a little earlier been to St. Petersburg and held discussions with Russian ministers on Central Asian trade. He was to join Mirza Shadi at Leh and travel by the Changchenmo road as the Kashgarian envoy was credited with having expressed "a particular desire to return by that road" and promised to submit a special report to the Atalik on its advantages as a trade line. Forsyth's visit, Aitchison clarified, was not a mission and had no "political object."[85] He was to return by the Changchenmo route. Commerce was only a facade for the Forsyth expedition. The real reasons were much later disclosed by the Viceroy.[86] The expedition was inspired by reports the British Indian Government had received early in 1870 of a hostile movement on the part of the Amir of Bokhara upon Afghanistan and of a contemplated attack on the territories of the Atalik Ghazi by the Khan of Kokand. Both Bokhara and Kokand were then dependencies of Russia. In Russia itself the Changchenmo treaty was seen to establish English influence in Yarkand and Kashgar. "The dominions of Yakub Beg," the Asiatic of June 22, 1870, reproduced by the Turkistan Gazette, noted, "are not so rich as to make it worth the while of the English Government to take upon itself the trouble of opening a transit road (980 to 1100 miles long) from India to Kashgar and monopolising the markets of Altyshahr."

References

1. A Gazetteer of The Countries Adjacent To India. By Edward Thornton. 1844. Vol. II, p. 1.
2. Calcutta Review. Vol. LX IV. No. CXXVI. 1877, p. 156.
3. A Gazetter of The Countries Adjacent To India. By Edward Thornton. 1844. Vol. 1, p. 119.
4. *Ibid.* Vol. II, p. 1.
5. Memoir on Indian Surveys. By C.R. Markham. Her Majesty's Stationery Office. London. p. 113.
6. Scientific Mission to India And High Asia. By Herman, Adolphe and Robert De Schlagintweit. 1861. Vol. I, pp. 259 and 271.
7. *Ibid.* Vol. I p. 259.
8. *Ibid.* Vol. III. p. 32.
9. *Ibid.* Vol. 1. p. 63.
10. *Ibid.* Vol. III. p. 113.
11. 22nd September 1860. Foreign. Part A. No. 293 of November 1860.
12. 12th December 1860. Foreign. Part A. No. 407 of June 1861.
13. Journal of the Asiatic Society. No. 1. 1860–Memorandum on Survey of Kashmir under Captain Montgomerie.
14. Journal of the Asiatic Society. No. CCX Vl. No. IV of 1864.
15. Journal of the Asiatic Society. Part II. No. I. 1868. Notes on the Pangong Lake by Captain H.H. Godwin Austin. p. 88.
16. Undated. Governor General's despatch to Secretary of State No. 126 of 20th September 1865. Enclosure No. III. Also Foreign, Pol A. No. 137 of June 1868.
17. General Report Great Trigonometrical Survey of India. 1865-1866. By Lt. Colonel J.T. Walker. Printed by G.T. Survey.
18. 22nd April 1866. Foreign Pol A. No. 136 of June 1868.
19. *Ibid.*
20. *Ibid.*
21. *Ibid.*
22. Undated. Foreign. Pol A. No. 137 of June 1868.
23. *Ibid.*
24. 23rd May 1866. Foreign. Pol A. No. 135 of June 1866.
25. 18th July 1866. Foreign. Part A. No. 50 of September 1866.
26. Ibid.
27. Undated enclosure. Political despatch of Governor General No. 121 of 9th July 1867.
28. 24th July 1866. Foreign. Part A. No. 187-189 of March 1867.

29. Governor General's Political despatch. No. 121 of 9th July 1867. Enclosure.
30. 31st July 1866. Foreign. Pol A. No. 187-189 of March 1867.
31. 18th July 1866. Governor General's Political despatch No. 195 of 8th December 1866. Enclosure.
32. 26th August 1866. Foreign. Pol A. No. 187-189 of March 1867.
33. *Ibid.*
34. *Ibid.* 19th September 1866.
35. *Ibid.* 25th September 1866.
36. Undated. 4th October 1866. Foreign. Pol A. No. 53 of October 1866.
37. *Ibid.*
38. 13th October 1866. Foreign. Pol A. No. 187-189 of March 1866.
39. *Ibid.* 4th November 1866.
40. 13th December 1866. Governor General's Political despatch No. 40 of 23rd February 1867. Enclosure.
41. 2nd January 1867. Foreign. Pol A. No. 126 of January 1867.
42. 6th January 1867. Foreign. Pol A. No. 126 of January 1867.
43. 9th January 1867. Foreign. Pol A. No. 126 of January 1867.
44. Governor General's Political despatch No. 40 of 23rd February 1867.
45. Undated. Foreign. General A. No. 2 of March 1868.
46. 4th January 1868. Foreign. General A No. 1 of March 1868.
47. 13th January 1868. Foreign Pol A. No. 7 of March 1868.
48. *Ibid.*
49. 27th January 1868. Foreign. Pol A. No. 6 of March 1868.
50. Undated of September 1868. Foreign. Pol A. No. 2 of November 1868.
51. *Ibid.*
52. *Ibid.*
53. 7th October 1868. Foreign. Pol A. No. 3 of November 1868.
54. 28th October 1868. Foreign. Pol A. No. 4 of November 1868.
55. 27th November 1868. Foreign. Pol A. No. 352 of January 1869.
56. 1 Poh. 1925 (mid-December 1868) Foreign. Pol A. No. 369 of January 1871.
57. Visits to High Tartary, Yarkand And Kashgar. By Robert Shaw 1871, p. 98
58. Kashmir and Kashgar. A Narrative of the Journey of the Embassy to Kashgar. By H.W. Bellew. 1875. p. XVI.
59. Exchange Gazette of Russia. 30th April-12th May 1869. Foreign. S.H. No. 65 of 1869.
60. 11th June 1869. Foreign. SI. No. 49-57 of 1869.
61. *Ibid.* Also Visits To High Tartary. 1871. p. 109.
62. A Sketch of The Geography And Geology of the Himalaya Mountains And Tibet. By Colonel S.G. Burrard And H.H. Hayden. Govt. of India

publication. 1907-08.

63. Russians in Central Asia. By Captain Valikhanof and Others. Tr. By John and Robert Michell. London. 1865. p. 109.
64. Journal of Asiatic Society of Bengal Vol. XXXVI. Part II. Nos. I to III 1867. p. 50.
65. 27th August 1869. Foreign. Pol A. No. 288 of February 1870.
66. 11th October 1869. Foreign. Pol A. No. 296 of February 1870.
67. Undated. Foreign. Pol A. No. 297 of February 1870.
68. 18th September 1869. Foreign. Pol A. No. 73 of July 1870.
69. *Ibid.*
70. Undated (of 11th October 1869). Foreign. Pol A. No. 296 of February 1870.
71. 20th September 1869. Foreign. SI. No. 184 of 1869.
72. 30th September 1869. Foreign. SI. No. 152 of 1869.
73. *Ibid.*
74. 6th October 1869. Foreign. Pol A. No. 74 of July 1870.
75. 19th October 1869. Foreign. Pol A. No. 83 of July 1870.
76. 27th November 1868. Foreign. Pol A. No. 90 of July 1870.
77. 4th December 1869. Foreign. Pol A. No. 92 of July 1870.
78. 4th December 1869. Foreign. Pol A. No. 95 of July 1870.
79. *Ibid.*
80. 21st December 1869. Foreign. Pol A. No. 91 of July 1870.
81. *Ibid.*
82. 19th January 1870. Foreign. Pol A. No. 92 of July 1870.
83. 28th March 1870. Foreign. Pol A. No. 215 of June 1870.
84. 4th April 1870. Foreign. Pol A. No. 216 of June 1870.
85. 14th April 1870. Foreign. Pol A. No. 219 of July 1870.
86. 30th June 1873. Foreign. Secret. No. 366 of June 1873.

Chapter 4
Gilgit Section of Boundary

England anticipated but was helpless to prevent the Sikhs or, as Clerk conveyed to Maddock in 1840,[1] the "Jammu Rajas" schemes "for the extension of their dominion on the north-west of their present possessions and to their designs upon Gilgit and Kashgar"–Kashkar or Chitral, as it was variously called. Hostility of the British in Clerk's communication is unmistakable to the Sikhs acquiring Gilgit, north of which the boundary ran westward. Again a year later Raja Golab Singh was seen taking advantage of internal family dissensions prevailing "between the small Mohammadan States...to extend their dominion or influence to Gilgit and towards Chitral."[2] *Towards* Chitral could only be Yasin or Warshgam, which opens out on the Pamirs to the west and is contiguous to Chitral to the south-west. Vance Agnew gave greater importance to Gilgit, the boundary of which, he proposed, should be laid down by the commission, leaving the Ladakh doubtful termini to be fixed by the officer in charge of Spiti.[3] With roads running from Kokand, Eastern Turkistan, Wakhan and Badakshan to Hunza, Yasin, Chitral and Gilgit and thence to the plains of India, reaction of Englishmen to the incorporation of the region into the newly carved out Jammu and Kashmir State was to declare the Indus as its boundary. That altogether excluded the Gilgit region from the new State. Either towards the realisation of this objective or, at least, to inspect the boundary in the region, Colonel Lawrence sent Vance Agnew to Gilgit in July or August 1847.

In the Gilgit region Hunza was the most important chiefship. It had a running boundary with Chinese Turkistan beyond the Taghdumbash Pamir and Sirikul. Naturally there was a relationship between the two. But this relationship was not one of a vassal and a suzerain, as the British pretended. The earliest contact between the two, of which there is any record, was in 1828 when after Jahangir Khoja, the Sultan of

Kashgaria, was evicted by China and took refuge in Sirikul. A communication from Yank Khaba Amban and Ukhba Ambans urged the Raja of Hunza :

> "As the district of Tashkurgan is *connected* with yours, you will do your utmost to capture Jehangir and send him to me. I shall obtain for you the rank of wonk from the Khan-e-Kalean (emperor of China) and also a reward..."[4]

The communication clearly places the Taghdumbash Pamir in Hunza and acknowledges its suzerain powers over Sirikul. When China reasserted its sovereignty over Eastern Turkistan in 1850, some service was rendered by the Raja of Hunza for which he was given a piece of cultivable land or 'jagir,' as he later asserted, outside Yarkand. No suzerainty was claimed by the Ambans over Hunza. Another cause for contact between Hunza and China arose over the maintenance and protection of roads of commerce for which the Kanjutis along with the Sirikulis, Shighnis and Wakhis were each paid annually a subsidy by China of 4, 6, 10 and 3 'Yambos'* respectively.[5] Contact also came to be establish, much earlier, as much of Hunza's food and other needs were met by Eastern Turkistan for one reason it had a perennially adversarial relationship with the Nagar principality to its south to be safely supplied from Gilgit. There are other early references to Hunza-China relationship in letters and papers seized by the British from the fort of Baltit, Hunza's capital city, after the little war of 1890. Most of these papers are undated. Many relate to exchange of presents between Hunza and China, Hunza sending "tila," or gold dust, annually varying from ten 'miskals'[6] to one 'sar'[V] and five 'miskals.' Of this "tila" the quantity sent to the "Khan-e-Kalan" also differed from four[7] to 15 "miskals."[8] "Tila" was besides, sent to Chinese ambans also.[9] No quantity of "tila" was specifically allocated for the Chinese "Khakan," or emperor, by the Raja himself. In return, the Raja and his officials received costly presents which suggests these were a source of income to him. On, at least, one occasion gold dust was twice sent in one year, the second time the present was seven "miskals." The Raja was thereupon advised to despatch "tila" only once in a year. "Tila" was described by the Chinese ambans as "peshkash"[10] (present or an offering). Later these came to be described as "tribute,"[11]

---

* Lumps of silver, each worth Rs. 170 then.

= Approximately one ounce.

v One Sar = Rs. 3 in weight.

probably in translation by the British, as the Chinese consistently called them "tila" or "presents." Tribute is a fixed quantity or value. It does not vary from year to year.

That Hunza-China relationship was not one between a vassal and a suzerain is established by several incidents. In 1850s Raja Ghazanfar Khan's move to restore order in Dafdar, the limit of the Taghduinbash Pamir with Sirikul, was objected to by the Ambans, who argued it was distant from Hunza.[12] Raja Ghazanfar Khan ignored the Chinese and restored order in Dafdar. Hunza, or Kanjut, went a step further and plundered Sirikul itself. The shocked amban asked "How is it that your men have plundered the Sirikul people? I thought that you and we are friends."[13] Evidently Hunza was not prepared to accept Chinese pre-eminence in Sirikul. China, indeed, did not even have a presence in Sirikul then. This is established by another incident. When Sirikul was attacked by "Kiokandi robbers," as the Sola Amban called the Kokandi invaders, Raja Ghazanfar Khan's brother, Abdulla Beg, with the assistance of local people, repelled the attack.[14] Again, as if in a demonstration of its independence, Hunza attacked and plundered Pakhpo village, north of the Yarkand valley. The village was claimed by both Hunza and China. In retaliation China sent Mohammadan troops to Sirikul which had aided Hunza in the attack on the Pakhpo village.[15] Despatch of "tila" was suspended by both Hunza and Sirikul in 1863,[16] by the latter very likely at the instance of Hunza. In the past too "tila" had not been sent in 1850 and some years later the Kanjut Raja threatened "not to send (it) any longer."[17] The Baltit papers do not, therefore, at all establish Chinese paramountcy over Hunza, which the British clearly assumed on the basis of despatch of "tila." Was "tila" a goodwill gesture or was it related to payments accruing to China for the "jagir" of the Hunza Raja near Yarkand?

In his Gilgit diaries Vance Agnew makes several reference to the boundaries that he thought were those of Jammu and Kashmir with or of neighbouring principalities tributary to it including Hunza whose Raja he called "banditti chief." Gujal. Vance Agnew described as "the first chiefdom across the pass to China." Gujal is the upper part of Hunza, therefore, neither a chiefdom nor across the pass to China. Roads from Hunza northward lay across the Hindu Kush passes, several in numbers, from west to east, Irshad, Mintaka, Kilik, Khanjerab, the last three led to the Taghdumbash and Sirikul, the first to Little Pamir. China as then was still to cross the Kashgar chain to reach these. The other major pass over the Hindu Kush is the Shangshal that led to the Yarkand valley over which to the east ran the Leh-Yarkand trade route. The boundary between Hunza and Nagar was the Hunza river, with "Hunza on the north and towards the grand chain which forms the Chinese frontier."[18] The grand chain is quite evidently the Hindu Kush. The Chinese frontier over the chain was fanciful as it excluded Taghdumbash and Sirikul from Hunza. Here again it is evident that the British had a predetermined boundary in mind.

Vance Agnew noted from a geo-political point of view the frontier region between the Indus and Oxus as of much space. Yet, he remarked, "it is hardly possible to conceive one more thinly inhabited."[19] Hunza-Nagar together had 7000 houses shut up in snowy hills with one outlet to Gilgit, one for a few days to Skardo and one or two into China. Here again population factor weighed in British calculations on the boundary as it had in regard to Ladakh. Vance Agnew's visit caused "alarm" in Gilgit region leading to disturbances which prevented another boundary commissioner, Dr. Thomson, visiting the region.[20] Maharaja Golab Singh was warned that he was bound by articles IV and V of the treaty of Amritsar to refer to them for adjudication disputes with his neighbours. The British pretended the Maharaja sought to alter his boundary in Gilgit by force. The disturbances were not the result of any expansionist designs of the Maharaja but due to an uprising of his feudatories, Hunza and Yasin, which opened out on the trough leading to Kokand and the Little Pamir, a configuration of which the British felt uneasy. As Golab Singh's right to Gilgit was apparently questioned, the Maharaja conveyed to the British by a letter dated 30th June 1849 that the region was taken possession of and included within the boundary of Kashmir by the Sikh Governor, Sheikh Mohiuddin. By sending troops into Gilgit he clarified, he did not intend to advance beyond his own territory. In the succeeding years Gilgit was as often lost as it was held by the Dogras. When in their possession the Maharaja's authority was felt in Chitral, Yasin, Hunza, Nagar and in the Indus valley. In June-July 1860, Colonel Devi Singh's campaign for the final recovery of Gilgit and seizure of Yasin brought to notice the negotiability of the glacier covered route through Shigar (Skardo) to Hunza and Nagar to threaten Gilgit, which later caused concern to England in the context of the northern boundary. Yasin was to have been annexed to Gilgit by Maharaja Ranbir Singh.[21] But the Lieutenant Governor of the Punjab prevailed upon him to withdraw for no apparent reason than that Yasin opens out on the Pamirs. At the "darbars" of the Maharaja, men from Chitral, Dir, Swat, Kholi and Palus, in the Indus valley, were "in attendance as well as from Chilas, Nagar and Hunza, who have been constant attendants for some years,"[22] so noticed captain

Montgomerie to underscore the tributary status of Chitral, Yasin, Hunza and Nagar.[23] But the British chose to ignore this subordinate relationship of these petty States to Jammu and Kashmir.

British opposition to Kashmir's territorial consolidation was based on fear of Russia. Russia had advanced into Kokand by 1864. From Bokhara Russia had sought in 1865 ground for commercial settlements at Charjui and Termez on the Oxus and assistance for the establishment of a Russian firm in Balkh. To the east of Kokand rebellion by Tunganis of Eastern Turkistan led Yakub Beg Kushbegi to carve out Kashgaria as a kingdom for himself. To evaluate these development so near to India, the British Indian Government sent a secret mission to Central Asia headed by Pandit Manphool, in 1865. For the British in India Russian subjugation of Kokand had significant implications. It became a question of interest to England to ascertain how far south the territory of Kokand extended and what would be the "pretensions" which Russia might put forward, having acquired the country. Absorption of Kokand into the Russian empire would have enabled the Imperial Government "to lay claim to other important territories approaching our Indian frontier," such as the left (south) bank of the Oxus and that branch of the river that flows from the Karakul lake in the Pamirs. Possession of the Bolortagh would have extended Russian frontier to the south-east beyond the Sirikul lake while that of Shignan would have brought the dominance of Russia within a short distance of the Indus.[24] Besides, Russia could, through the large number of Kokandians in Kashgar, exercise authority over it. British fears over Russian territorial claims were not baseless. Captain Valikhanof, a Russian political agent, obliquely laid claims to Tashkurgan in Sirikul.[25]

England had yet to devote attention to the cis and trans-Oxus territories of Badakshan and Wakhan, which were independent of Afghanistan then. Pandit Manphool thought of Badakshn as a power by itself to which Chitral, he claimed, was "subject" while Hunza looked to the Mir as "superior."[26] This was a simplistic view. England then was in need of precise knowledge about the two districts. Except for Wood's explorations in the Sirikul lake and its outlet, the Panja stream, England had no knowledge about the upper Oxus waters, Murghabi, Aktash, Aksu, Akbaital Kara-Su, Kokcha, Panja and Surkhab. A political settlement that strengthened British Indian empire's security in the Gilgit region was conceivable once the hydrology and the state and nature of communications in Badakshan (Great Pamir) and Wakhan (Alichur Pamir), west of Yarkand and Kashgar, southward to Peshawar and Jallalabad, were ascertained. Exploration of Badakshan and Wakhan was, therefore, part of the brief laid down for Hayward by Sir Henry Rawlinson, principal exponent of the forward policy that broadly advocated advance of Afghanistan's and British India's north-west frontier to the Hindu Kush and beyond to the Oxus. England having projected the Karakoram-Hindu Kush as India's northern boundary in Jammu and Kashmir, Russia hastened to assert that the limits of her Bokhara protectorate also extended to the Hindu Kush.[27] Russian thus, so early, revealed her intention to be conterminous with the British empire, a prospect England resisted. Contemporaneously with British surveys of the Hindu Kush region, the Russians began, with the assistance of Bokhara, surveys of the Oxus.[28] Navigation of the Oxus, Valikhanoff asserted, would lead to the occupation of its banks by Russia or her entry into Afghanistan[29] by the left (southern) bank through, evidently, Badakshan. Through these probes, both England and Russia jockeyed for strategic advantages before Afghanistan's northern boundary with the Czar's dominion came to be finalised in 1872-1873.

Hayward's explorations, brought to a violent end as would be presently noticed, do not help in unravelling the territorial limits of the countries opening on the Pamirs. His testimony that the Kashgaria territory extended "...from eastern crest of the Pamir range to near Ili,"[30] is misleading. There is no Pamir range. Presumably he calls the Bolor chains by the name of the Pamir range. As the Kushbegi had nominally occupied Sirikul, the "eastern crest of the Pamir range" would be the Sirikul chain, and not the Kashgar ridge, eastern face of which was the true limit of Eastern Turkistan. To reach the Karakul lake, then supposed to be the main source of the Oxus, was Hayward's "great object."[31] But in his imperialist zeal Hayward struck a deal with Raja Mir Wali of Yasin over transfer to him of Gilgit, through British intercession, which ended in the Englishman's murder and exposure of the Government of India in manipulating the boundary as will be noticed. He, therefore, failed to reach the Karakul or even establish the road-worthiness of the Chitral-Peshawar line. An earlier effort by Hayward to reach the Pamirs from Yarkand had also come to nought,[32] following the refusal of permission by the Kushbegi. Hayward accused Maharaja Ranbir Singh in the Anglo-Indian press of committing genocide in Yasin. The Maharaja was also credited by him with designs to advance from Gilgit to Badakshan and to Yarkand via Hunza with whose chief, Hayward was certain, Jammu and Kashmir officials conspired for passage. Curiously at this time the Mehtar of Chitral repeated his request, first made some years earlier, for "assistance of the British Government in recovering Gilgit and Yasin..."[33]

That Yasin, or part of it, was then under the Maharaja, or under his vassalage, the Punjab Government made clear to the Foreign Department in an official communication.[34] Yet Hayward did not fancy that farther than Gilgit the Maharaja could be said to have acquired permanent authority.[35] This was familiar tactics, first used by Forsyth about Aksai Chin. Hayward was convinced possession of Gilgit by the Maharaja was an infringement of the treaty of 1846 inasmuch as the Indus was the boundary fixed for Jammu and Kashmir by it.

The British, Vance Agnew onwards, had rejected that the Maharaja held Yasin. But one of their principal native agents, "F.B."–Faiz Baksh–unambiguously placed it or, at least, a part of it, within the limits of Jammu and Kashmir. In an account of Badakshan as a member of the secret mission, "F.B." noted it was "surrounded by upper and lower Chitral and Gilgit possessions of the Maharaja of Jammu in upper Chitral (Yasin)..." This suggests that part of Yasin was directly held by Maharaja Ranbir Singh. Maharaja Golab Singh had maintained correspondence with Mir Shah, the chief of Badakshan. After the annexation of Gilgit, the forts of Payal (Punyal), Yasin and Mastuj in upper Chitral, or Yasin, were invested by the Jammu and Kashmir troops against which, according to "F.B." the Mir remonstrated. An engagement was concluded between Maharaja Golab Singh and Mir Shah by which, "F.B." claimed, Jammu and Kashmir refrained from "all interference in the affairs of upper Chitral and confined its operations in that territory to the capture of Gauhar Aman," its chief. In 1867 Maharaja Ranbir Singh having once again taken possession of the forts of Mastuj, Punyal and Yasin the Mir, Jahandar Shah, remonstrated against these proceedings. In response the Maharaja recalled to the Mir the friendship that subsisted between the two States since the time of Maharaja Golab Singh and Mir Shah. The latter,

> "had entered sincerely into alliance with the Maharaja's Government. During the Mir (Shah's)... life-time the generals of Maharaja took possession of (Punyal) and Yasin and afterwards delivered them to the chiefs of those countries who acknowledged fealty to the Maharaja. The Mir's late father, on receiving information of the occupation of these territories as above stated, wisely executed a treaty, stipulating that from the date of execution thereof there should exist friendship between the contracting parties, and that the Mir engaged to be friend of friends and the enemy of enemies of the Maharaja's Government."[36]

Ranbir Singh's letter to the Mir of Badakshan nowhere refers to non-interference by the Maharaja in Yasin, as claimed by "F.B." Besides would not the Maharaja's efforts directly to capture Gauhar Aman have amounted to more than interference in the affairs of Yasin? Badakshan was drawn towards Maharaja Ranbir Singh against the annexationist policy of the Amir of Afghanistan. Not only Hayward but many British officials in India suspected the Maharaja intended to incorporate Badakshan as a vassal State into Jammu and Kashmir and so change the boundary of his territories. The Viceroy, Lord Mayo, recalled the treaty of Amritsar and argued it provided "that the limits of the territories of Kashmir shall not be changed without the concurrence of the British Government and that the Maharaja shall leave any disputes or questions that may arise between himself and the neighbouring States to be settled by the British Government."[37] At the "private" interview between the Viceroy and the Maharaja, Ranbir Singh was advised "carefully to abstain from all interference in the political affairs and quarrels of States beyond his frontier, that he should commit no aggression on his neighbours and make no attempt to extend his authority beyond the limits of the territories which had been conferred on his father, Maharaja Golab Singh."[38] Not only was he not to extend his territories, the Maharaja was not even to extend his authority, such as, evidently, over Yasin. Mayo was impelled to make these observations in the light of Hayward's attack on Ranbir Singh in the Pioneer, accusing him of killing women and children.

Hayward's attack on Maharaja Ranbir Singh did not go unchallenged. The Maharaja sent a personally signed memorandum to the British Indian Government while the Jammu and Kashmir Government tendered a note on the history of the occupation of Gilgit, evidently in the expectation that these, or, at least, the memorandum would be published by it. Hayward's claim that the Indus formed the boundary of Jammu and Kashmir and that Ladakh and Baltisan were annexed by the Maharaja in contravention of the treaty of Amritsar, was dismissed by Ranbir Singh. The Indus, he pointed out with reference to the first article of the treaty, was the boundary of Jammu and Kashmir specifically in the Hazara district. In the treaty the Indus was not mentioned "as being the boundary generally everywhere." The territories of Ladakh and Skardo, the British were reminded, came into the possession of Maharaja Golab Singh in 1832-33, during the reign of Maharaja Ranjit Singh, and nearly 15 years before the treaty of Amritsar was signed. The argument that the boundary of Jammu and Kashmir was changed, without British concurrence, was no less refuted. Gillgit during the Sikh rule, it was explained, comprised Gilgit, Yasin, Punyal, Hunza and Nagar and that Gilgit was then a dependency of Kashmir and as such came to be transferred to Maharaja Golab Singh in 1846. "If at any time the people of any of those territories rose up in rebellion, and troops were sent to coerce them, such coercion cannot be held to constitute any alteration of the limits of the Maharaja's territories."[39]

From an examination of the State documents, it becomes clear that Gauhar Aman, the ruler of Yasin, used to pay tribute to Kashmir and his brother, Khalil Aman, resided as a hostage in Kashmir and annual tribute was paid through him. Apart from tribute Gauhar Aman provisioned the Gilgit garrison with supplies from Yasin.[40] Several documents were annexed to the note in substantiation of statements made therein, including a letter of Gauhar Aman to Nathe Shah, commandant of Gilgit. In this letter Gauhar Aman described himself as the "obedient servant" of the Sikh Governor of Kashmir, Sheikh Mohiuddin.[41] The British Indian Government declined to publish even the Maharaja's memorandum on its behalf. Clearly British manipulation of the boundary was exposed. They could neither deny the Maharaja's statements nor accept them, for the publication of the memorandum would have bound the British Indian Government to its contents. This Aitchison underscored to the Viceroy, remarking he considered it "undesirable" that the "authority of Government should be given to the statements" made in the memorandum. All the defence that Aitchison could imagine for the British action was "his (Maharaja's) boundary is so ill defined in that quarter that we can hardly say what is or is not included in his territories."[42] Aitchison's defence is specious in the light of Vance Agnew's diaries, which clearly spelt out Gilgit's boundary, Hunza's relationship with Kashmir, Faiz Buksh's memo on the status of Yasin, besides other reports alluded to by Aitchison. The truth was the British panicked at Ranbir Singh reaching the Pamirs, reaching out to Varshdi or Tashkurgan from Yasin or Warshgam, where too the Russian bear was heading for then. Sirikul was directly reached from Hunza by the Kilik or Mintaka. This was good enough reason for the British Indian Government to question the Maharaja's supremacy over Hunza.

On 17th July 1870, Hayward was murdered at Darkot village at the foot of the Baroghil pass.[43] The issue involved in the murder of Hayward was succinctly setforth by the Lieutenant Governor of the Punjab, Sir Henry Durand, in his official letter of 27th August 1870, to the Government of India. The murder having been committed in Yasin territory, did the Viceroy, he asked, consider "Yasin as within the Maharaja's territory and subject to his authority," whether, in short, it was in the discretion of the Maharaja to treat this offence "as one in which, from his sovereignty over Yasin, the punishment of the offender vests in his will and pleasure."[44] Sir Henry Durand clearly recognised the *de jure* rights of the Maharaja in consequence of Yasin's vassal State status, and so favoured permitting "Kashmir to conquer Yasin (as proposed by Ranbir Singh), and this, while punishing Mir Wali, giving Government some means of curbing the quadrangle of wild tribes between the Chitral-Kunar and Gilgit-Indus rivers,"[45] A not so honest reply, dated 21st September 1870, was returned by Lord Mayo to Sir Henry Durand. As far as the Viceroy could gather from information available, "Yasin (is) part of Chitral."[46] Mayo considered it "undesirable" to permit Kashmir to conquer and annex it:

(1) Because the grant such permission would involve an obligation to help Kashmir to maintain its hold there.

(2) Because it would give Chitral chief reason to doubt the sincerity of the British Government in making, or its power to enforce, the assurance given that the Maharaja of Kashmir had been warned not to endeavour to extend his dominions beyond those conferred on Golab Singh.

(3) Because the occupation of Yasin by Kashmir would be a menace to the neighbouring valleys.

(4) Because there were certain advantages in the existence of a belt of independent territory between Kashmir and Wakhan and Badakshan. If this disappeared it would be difficult to control the diplomatic action of the Maharaja in the countries beyond.

England presumed Kashmir's occupation of Yasin would commit her to render material assistance to the Maharaja. Captain John Biddulph, later British Agent, Gilgit, elaborates this issue but not convincingly. Ranbir Singh himself at no time foresaw such a need arising when he bitterly spoke about the British twice coercing him to withdraw from Yasin after twice having conquered it. As to British assurances to Chitral, the Mehter himself acknowledged the Maharaja's right over Yasin. The main reason was, therefore, Maharaja's dominion becoming contiguous to Wakhan and Badakshan and his gaining access to the Pamirs and Russia. In his communications to the British or even to his own officials, as were likely to be seen by the British, Ranbir Singh described Yasin as an "independent" territory. But there is no doubt that he not only considered Yasin as his own territory, but strove to incorporate it in

Gilgit. In Hayward's murder he saw an excuse to attack Yasin to punish a refractory vassal and ensure surrender of Mir Wali.[47] An attack from Gilgit was, indeed, anticipated by the Mehtar, Aman-ul-Mulk, even earlier than Hayward's murder. The Mehtar described himself a subject of the Maharaja and therefore, addressed him as "Sarkar." To Mir Wali Ranbir Singh was "Sarkar-e-aali"–the highest authority–the Maharaja–to whom he offered to surrender himself.[48] This prospect worried the British and Aitchison advised Charles Girdlestone, then officer-on-special-duty (O.S.D.) in Kashmir, "Lord Mayo does not wish that the 'Darbar' should execute him but that they should surrender him to us."[49] Even more the Viceroy did not wish the Kashmir "Darbar" to know that Lord Mayo had a "strong preference" for this course. Why did the British want to prevent Ranbir Singh from executing Mir Wali? Any such punishment would have been awarded after a fair trial. The only inference that can be drawn from the extraordinary course the British wanted to pursue is that such a trial would have been seen as an assertion of Jammu and Kashmir's right over Yasin and a setback for British interference in Yagistan, or the tribal belt.

Faiz Buksh rightly described Hayward as a "political character," whose rambles in the Maharaja's dominions and the circumstance of his contracting friendship with some of the chiefs of the Maharaja's border were "extremely distasteful to His Highmess." In line with British views, Faiz Buksh claimed that Hayward was "suspected" of communicating to Nagar, Hunza and Yasin that, under the treaty of 1846, these chiefships were excluded from the limits of Jammu and Kashmir. They, therefore, did not owe it allegiance and that in the event of the Maharaja exercising any interference, the British Government of India had the power of restraining him.[50] Such almost were also the expostulations of Lord Mayo with Maharaja Ranbir Singh. But Hayward would appear to have attempted to incite rebellion against the Maharaja. Faiz Buksh also confirms that Maharaja Golab Singh was interdicted by the British from occupying Yasin. Inasmuch as such annexation was, in the British view, against articles 4 and 5 of the treaty of Amritsar, Faiz Buksh notes occupation of forts of Gakuch and Shagal after the campaign of 1866, the last that Ranbit Singh's Government launched. The Maharaja's right to Yasin was acknowledged by the Mehtar Aman-ul-Mulk, who also considered that Darel and Tangir, south of Gilgit, belonged to Jammu and Kashmir.[51] This was admitted by Mohammad Karim, Dewan Begi, or Chief Minister, of Chitral, in course of long conversations with Girdlestone. But the Dewan Begi's assertion that Aman-ul-Mulk then stood "in the relation of paramount power to Yasin and Mastuj" is rejected by Girdlestone.[52] To a combination of circumstances Girdlestone attributed the Mehtar acquiring a voice in the affairs of Yasin. He goes on to recall Yasin's emasculation by Jammu and Kashmir. The other circumstance, which Girdlestone does not at all mention, was the undermining of Ranbir Singh's authority by the British in Yasin. The Trigonometrical Survey of India, however, concurred with Mohammad Karim. Walker asserted that Yasin and the valleys of upper sources of the river of Gilgit are, at present, subject, if at all, to Chitral rather than to Kashmir."[53]

The Mehtar, then under pressure of Kabul, was in quest of "an intimate friendship" with Ranbir Singh and, in pursuit of it, had sent his Dewan Begi to wait on him, contrary though this was to the advice of Mir Mohammad Shah of Badakshan to tender his submission to the Amir of Afghanistan.[54] Ghulam Mohiuddin, alias Pehalwan Bahadur, who had succeeded Mir Wali as the Raja of Yasin, sought 2000 troops from the Maharaja to catch the murderer of Hayward. To an emissary of Ranbir Singh, Aziz Munshi, sent to Chitral to secure the custody of Mir Wali, the Mehtar proposed to conclude a secret treaty between Jammu and Kashmir and Chitral. Towards the realization of this objective Aman-ul-Mulk offered to go for hunting to Ishkoman, or Ashkwan, his "boundary," and suggested that Bakshi Radha Krishan, Governor of Gilgit, should visit Gakuch, the limit of Maharaja's direct rule and one march away from Ishkoman. "...we will get together, make a treaty according as the Maharaja may direct to last for ever. In whatever way the Maharaja may fix my condition, according to that I will carry things on."[55] As to surrendering Mir Wali, the wily Mehtar placed himself "under the orders of the Maharaja." The British saw no advantage for themselves from Pehalwan Bahadur's proposal which they realised, would be acceptable to Ranbir Singh.[56] In any case Mayo insisted, "we cannot permit the Maharaja to go to war with Chitral."[57] There was no cause for war. Mayo was not unaware of secret negotiations proposed by Aman-ul-Mulk. The British Indian Government appears to have preferred to pocket the injury to their prestige rather than allow Ranbir Singh to occupy Yasin.

On the neighbouring Badakshan, Pandit Manphool's line only raised doubts. Not that the Pandit has misjudged British mood and intentions on Badakshan through which also routes ran to Afghanistan and India from Central Asia. The Amir would and, indeed, did not accept exclusion of Badakshan from his dominions. But equally importantly, Russia pointed out Kabul "had no right whatever to the possession of Badakshan and that it was very doubtful whether Badakshan had any rights over

Wakhan."[58] If an Anglo-Russian agreement on the northern boundary of Afghanistan, 1872-73, was still reached, it was, as a Russian official put it, under threat of "war." Wakhan is largely elevated Pamirs where are located some of the chief sources of the Oxus. Control of the head-waters of the Oxus was, according to contemporary European thinking, vital for launching or preventing an invasion of India.[59] The Russian territory of Ferghana in Kokand was separated from the valley of the Indus by the Pamir tableland and the most practicable route from the Pamirs into the basin of the Indus had just then been ascertained and examined. The Pamirs with the Alai plateau to the north in Kokand, are not a steppe to be marched across in any direction but a series of broad valleys along which different routes ran. There are no deep gorges or difficult passes. By the Kunar river another road was equally practicable, across the Punjkora, into the Swat valley and down to Peshawar. In dismay the British realised,

> "Here then is the new highway to India from the Pamir, which is geographically the knot, between the basins of the Oxus and the Indus, between Russian and British rule. It is down the Chitral valley leading direct to Jallalabad and Peshawar... The Chitral valley is' then, the high road to India from the Pamir steppe, and the gate to it is the Baroghil pass," over the Hindu Kush.[60]

In the mountain tract between Kabul and Skardo, bounded on the north by the Hindu Kush and the south by the Indus the position of Chitral, with its roads, therefore assumed strategic importance for the defence of the British empire.[61] The exploration also established what was claimed to be the water parting between Wakhan and Eastern Turkistan. The passes over the Hindu Kush, the Nuksan and Dora, leading from Badakshan to Chitral, were found to be lofty and difficult, the first, besides, was covered with immense mass of ice. The overthrow of Jahandar Shah, the Mir of Badakshan, by Mahmood Shah, with the assistance of Amir Sher Ali of Kabul, persuaded the British to dispel the belief that Chitral was subservient to Badakshan. England was not prepared to trust its vassal, Afghanistan, with control over Chitral routes. This political situation was made curiouser by the appearance in the neighbourhood of Yasin, of Pachino, a Russian explorer, in 1873. Though loud in claiming Badakshan and Wakhan, the Afghans were altogether ignorant about the region.[62] An Afghan envoy, on a visit to India on the eve of the departure of the Forsyth mission to Kashgaria in 1873, also acknowledged that Chitral and Kafiristan were "rebellious" and paid no tribute. It was not so very many years ago "that Chitral ruler did pay tribute to Badakshan." The envoy was asked how far the boundary of Yarkand was from Afghanistan. It was Faiz Buksh, and not the envoy, who explained, "Yarkand boundary extends as far as the Shinde pass," over the Sirikul chain of the Bolortagh. Yet only a year ago, in 1872, Faiz Baksh had, in a report, referred to Sirikul district to the east as the boundary of Eastern Turkistan. Faiz Buksh went on the explain to the envoy that between the Shinde pass–the western limit of the Taghdumbash Pamir–and Sirikul or the Victoria lake, "there is the table-land of the Pamir extending for five days journey." When the envoy asked how far the Anglo-Russian agreement carried the boundary and on being told as far as the Victoria lake, Syed Noor Mohammad, the envoy, remarked :

> "Then there is a wide plain of five days journey in breadth which is open to dispute and gives a road to Russia to Chitral and Kashmir."[63]

The reference is to the Aktash valley, Little and Alichur Pamirs. East of these begins the Sirikul valley, Tagharma and further north Kizil Art or Uzbel pass and the Alai plain in Kokand. All these together formed a "gap" in the mountain chains and between the territories of Afghanistan and Eastern Turkistan to permit north-south movement of men and beasts, as of the Kirghiz tribesmen and their flocks, from the Alai plain to the Hindu Kush. It was through this "gap" that Colonel Yonoff, towards the end of the 19th century, was to march his Russian troops to the Hindu Kush passes. The existence of the "gap" quite naturally influenced British strategic thinking and hence their equivocation on the northern boundary of Jammu and Kashmir. Afghanistan and Kashgaria, later Chinese Turkistan, were to be encouraged to push forward their limits to the Sirikul chain to close the "gap" and shut out the Russians to the north of Kizil Art pass. This objective England relentlessly pursued in the succeeding years, one reason why. Aitchison wished "this (boundary) matter to be left open."[64]

References

1. 23rd September 1841. Foreign. Sc. No. 67 of 18th October 1841.
2. 21st June 1842. Foreign. Sc. No. 28 of 5th October 1842.
3. 13th May 1847. Foreign. Sc. No. 154 of 28th August 1847.
4. Undated. Foreign, Sc. No. 403 of September 1892.
5. Report of A Mission To Yarkand in 1873. Historical and Geographical.

Foreign Department Press. 1875, p. 281.

6. 22nd July 1850. Foreign. Sec. F. No. 428 of September 1892.
7. Undated Foreign. Sec. F. No. 431 of September 1892.
8. Undated Foreign. Sec. F. No. 430 of September 1892.
9. *Ibid.*
10. 22nd July 1850 Foreign. Sec. F. No. 428 of September 1892.
11. Undated Foreign. Sec. F. No. 430 of September 1892.
12. Undated Foreign. Sec. F. No. 432 of September 1892.
13. Undated Foreign. Sec. F. No. 434 of September 1892.
14. Undated Foreign. Sec. F. No. 450 of September 1892.
15. Undated Foreign. Sec. F. No. 459 of September 1892.
16. Undated Foreign. Sec. F. No. 406 of September 1892.
17. Undated Foreign. Sec. F. No. 460 of September 1892.
18. 8th to 14th August 1847. Foreign. Sc. No. 139 of 30th October 1847.
19. 12th to 18th September 1847. Foreign. Sc. No. 63 of 27th November 1847.
20. 1st December 1847. Foreign. Sc. No. 54 of 28th January 1848.
21. 30th May 1863. Foreign. Pol A. No. 74 of July 1863.
22. Journal of The Asiatic Society. Vol. XXX. nos. I to IV 1861. Observations of Captain T.G Montgomerie.
23. *Ibid.*
24. 15th June 1867. Foreign. Sc. No. 163 of August 1873.
25. The Russians in Central Asia. By Captain Valikhanof, M. Veniukof and other Russian travellers. Tr. By John and Robert Michell. 1865, p. 216.
26. Undated, enclosure B. and narrative. Governor General's political despatch. No. 121 of 9th July 1867.
27. 5th June 1869. Foreign. SI. No. 49-57 of 1869.
28. 24th November 1869. Foreign. SI. No. 49 of 1869.
29. The Russians In Central Asia. By Captain Valikhanof, M. Veniukof and other Russian travellers. Tr. By. John and Robert Michell. 1865, p. 403.
30. 27th August 1869. Foreign. Pol A. No. 288 of February 1870.
31. *Ibid.*
32. 2nd October 1869. Foreign. Pol A. No. 293 of February 1870.
33. 27th January 1870. Foreign. SI. No. 191 of 1871.
34. 8th February 1870. Foreign. SI. No. 193 of 1870.
35. 7th March 1870. Foreign. SI. No. 199 of 1870.
36. 16th March 1870. Foreign. SI. No. KW. 191-200 of 1870.
37. 30th March 1870. Foreign. SI. No. KW. 191-200 of 1870.
38. 3rd May 1870. Foreign. SI. No. KW. 191-200 of 1870.
39. 21st July 1870. Foreign. SI. No. KW. 191-200 of 1870.
40. Undated. Foreign. SI. No. KW. 191-200 of 1870.

41. Undated. Foreign. SI. No. KW. 191-200 of 1870.
42. 18th August 1870. Foreign. SI. No. KW. 191-200 of 1870.
43. 29th October 1870. Foreign. Pol A. No. 559 of December 1872.
44. 7th October 1870. Foreign. Pol A. No. Nil of December 1872.
45. *Ibid.* 5th September 1870.
46. *Ibid.* 21st September 1870.
47. 12th December 1870. Foreign. Pol A. No. 555 of December 1872.
48. Undated. Foreign Pol A. No. 607 of December 1872.
49. 4th June 1871. Foreign. Pol A. No. 542 of December 1872.
50. Undated. Foreign Pol A. No. 593 of December 1872.
51. Undated. Foreign Pol A. No. 645 of December 1872.
52. Memorandum on Kashmir and Adjacent Countries. By Charles Girdlestone. p. 59.
53. Report of the Great Trigonometrical Survey of India. 1872. Para 14.
54. 6th July 1871. Foreign. Secret. No. 22 of August 1871.
55. Undated. Foreign. Pol A. No. 615 of December 1872.
56. 21st August 1871. Foreign. Pol A. No. 618 of December 1872.
57. 4th September 1871. Foreign. Pol A. No. Nil of December 1872.
58. 27st March 1873. Foreign. Secret. No. 22 of September 1873.
59. 5th June 1873. Foreign. Secret. No. 18 of December 1873.
60. Extract from Pall Mall Budget. Undated. Foreign. Secret No. 19 of July 1877.
61. Memoir on Indian Surveys. By C.R. Markham. p. 156.
62. 8st July 1873. Foreign. Secret. No. KW. 74-76 of January 1874.
63. *Ibid.*
64. *Ibid.* Undated.

Chapter 5
Awesome Aksai Chin Road, Desert

The Forsyth expedition to Yarkand, 1870, was really a trial run by a large body of men and beasts over the desert Lingzithang, or Aksai Chin, with supplies laid on in advance, so as to have a first hand assessment if an invasion of India, big or small, could be launched from the north. The expedition almost perished in the desert even after its guard of Kashmir troops and British gift of artillery guns to the Atalik Ghazi, to which Forsyth euphemistically refers to as heavy baggage, were left behind in the Changchenmo valley. To Forsyth's horror, the Changchenmo road proved to be neither "exceedingly easy" nor, as Dr. Cayley had vouched, "pleasant," the crap that they and other Englishmen had fed the British Indian Government with. Though the road built by the Kashmir Government was found to be a "good" one, the expedition suffered a heavy loss of baggage animals which, it was feared, would lend the line "an evil reputation from which it may not readily recover."[1] Dr. Cayley referred to carcasses of hundreds of animals on the way,"[2] while Major Montgomerie put the number at 300[3]. Of these a third had died in soda* dust and snow storms but largely unable to withstand the rigours of the journey through the elevated Lingzithang desert. Forsyth alludes to tolls levied by the Kashmir Government at passes, over which the road wound over, in full view of the Atalik's envoy, whose large camp formed part of the caravan. At the end of their journey in Jammu and Kashmir territories, the expedition was made the guests of Yakub Beg, not at the foot of the Changlung pass (19,000 ft.), over the Karakoram, but far to its north, at Balakchi[4], near Shahidulla. Evidently Kashgaria regarded the entire Aksai Chin and the Yarkand valley, to its west, as Jammu and Kashmir territory.

But in his report to the British Indian Government, Forsyth considered

---

* Part of Lingzithang comprises Soda plain and, as the name suggests, is covered with soda. Hence soda dust storms.

Gogra in the Changchenmo valley "the farthest point to which the Maharaja has extended any sign of his authority," Ranbir Singh having, at British request, built the road, "serais" and small store houses for grain. All traces of Buddhist religion in the erection of the "manis," or cairns, with mystical words "Om mane padme om" carved on them, Forsyth claimed, ceased at the south side of the Marsimik pass[5] (18,420 ft.) at the entrance to the Changchenmo valley. Existence of the Buddhist relic in Aksai Chin and Yarkand valley have already been noticed. Having confined the Maharaja's authority to Gogra, Forsyth did not hesitate to requisition the services of Ladakh Wazir "to lay out supplies of gram, grass and fuel along the road *beyond* the Changchenmo," which the Wazir would not have provided had Gogra been the limit of Jammu and Kashmir territory. En route to Balakchi, Forsyth noticed the "celebrated jade quarries" at Gulbashahr and remarked these had supplied the Chinese in former days with the precious stone. But after their expulsion from Eastern Turkistan, the quarries had remained closed. He, however, hastened to admit "the Chinese never claimed any property in the Karakash valley, though they are supposed to have first discovered the quarries..." The expedition found Shahidulla fort "entirely deserted," nailing thus Shaw's false report of its occupation by Atalik's troops. Shahidulla and the Kuen Lun running east Forsyth described as "the boundary of Yarkand territory" and not of Jammu and Kashmir with Kashgaria. Another boundary point of Kashgaria mentioned by Forsyth is the northern watershed of the Karakoram, as had Dr. Cayley earlier. To the west, Forsyth set the limit of Eastern Turkistan along the Bolortagh. Together with his assertion that the Maharaja's authority extended only up to Gogra, Forsyth put a big question mark over Aksai Chin as well as the Yarkand valley. A similar view was earlier expressed by Dr. Cayley but Forsyth's report is the first articulation of British policy on the northern boundary in Jammu and Kashmir.

At Balakchi the Forsyth expedition was aborted by the Amir of Kashgaria's long absence from Kashgar. Relations between Forsyth and the envoy's camp had been soured by the controversy over the Changchenmo line. Traders issued passports by the 'Dadkhwah,' or the governor, of Yarkand to travel to Leh by the Changchenmo highway were persuaded by the envoy, Mirza Shadi, to take the Karakoram route instead. If the British had questioned Ladakh's ownership of Aksai Chin, Kashgaria acknowledged it by issuing passports for travel through it. Return to Leh from Balakchi, across the Aksai Chin desert or even by Karakoram road, was impossible for the expedition without first being refitted at Yarkand. In the event of their having to fly away and as a measure of abundant precaution, some eight or nine ponies and a quantity of grain were purchased at high prices. The grain was caused to be buried near the Karakash river, hidden from the Kashgarians[6]. This act of the British fairly well establishes as to whom Aksai Chin belonged. For, in case of their flight from Yarkand, the Kashgarians would not have, in hot pursuit, trespassed into Shahidulla. So, at least, Forsyth appears to have been certain.

The only success of Forsyth expedition achieved was to allay British apprehensions of an invasion from the north by the Changchenmo line. The large scale destruction of its baggage animals was more than a military lesson. Nearly a hundred had died of high altitude effects, a point on which Forsyth also dwells, at some length, in relation to human beings. Though "no wall of mountains, totally impassable," existed still, Forsyth observes, "the passage of even 100 horsemen over the high desert plains, unless proper arrangements are made, is difficult and might be rendered impossible if a hostile force were ready to receive the invaders, as they arrived weary and worn out. Aksai Chin is thus projected as a great physical barrier which an invading or defending army, had to overcome. Defending Aksai Chin in the event of an invasion was, therefore, a tall order.

British declarations of Aksai Chin being outside the territorial limits of Ladakh, did not, however, prevent the Indian Government to start extending the Changchenmo line from Gogra to Shahidulla, contradictory though the two were. Construction of the road, 'serais' and store houses amounted to virtual "annexation" of Aksai Chin. Dr. Cayley found a bypass from Gogra to Malikshah, south of Shahidulla, which ran only 15 miles through a corner of Lingzithang. The new route, Dr. Cayley reported to Government, was the second, other than the traditional, line to "Shahidulla in Yarkand."[7] While such references came increasingly to be made in British official papers, the ground situation remained unaltered–Shahidulla continued to be the boundary point of Ladakh. W.H. Reynolds of the Survey of India followed Dr. Cayley into Aksai Chin in August 1870 and discovered that the valley of Karakash opens out into Lingzithang and the Changchenmo range is not connected with the lofty, precipitous, snowy peaks at the head of the Karakash, the Kuen Lun, "but is separated from them by a considerable ravine and, running in a western direction, finds an exit into the Shyok river."[8] This had a bearing on the watershed between the Indus and Tarim basins and ought to have to set at rest the British belief that Lingzithang is part of the Tarim basin.

An explanation for as to why the Maharaja's authority was not seen extended to Aksai Chin is to be found in Montgomerie's findings on the Changchenmo road. Construction of new 'serais' between the Changchenmo and Karakash "will be a difficult matter, and so will be the marking out of the route," not because of any territorial dispute or doubt but because, "...that part of the country is subject both to soda dust storms and snow storms, the latter even in summer, during which it is difficult to see even a hundred yards."[9] For a supply depot, visualised in the Changchenmo line scheme of things, Montgomerie, therefore, favoured the "Maharaja's guardhouse" in the Karakash valley, the Sikandar Mokam "fort."[10] He was, however, quick to point out that the Maharaja had "abandoned" the guardhouse. Montgomerie could not see how it could be done. A depot in the Karakash valley would have committed the British to accepting the State boundary. His predilection Montgomerie himself revealed. Shahidulla at the end of the Karakash valley, he suggested, would be "the proper place for it," but then remarked that it was "*now* considered to be Yarkand side..." The British resolve to pull back the boundary line from the crest of the Kuen Lun soon enough broke out into a controversy over a new map incorporating these arbitrary changes.

The Changchenmo road precipitated the great game between England and Russia in Central Asia. Russia deputed Colonel Baron Kaulbar to Kashgar in 1872. A treaty of commerce was concluded by Kaulbar with the Atalik Ghazi which was, however, observed more in breach. The British saw the treaty afforded the Russians "the pretext of going to war," if they desired to extend their Central Asian possessions "further to the south towards Kashmir, or to the east towards China."[11] Indeed, the British envoy to China, T.F. Wade, considered a Russian invasion of Kashgaria "at any moment possible."[12] The Russians no less saw through the "cherished dreams" of English politicians, namely, "the erection of a barrier of neutral States between India and the dominions of Russia in Central Asia."[13] These certainly had emerged as British and Russian policy objectives in Central Asia obliquely admitted by Wade for England. He wrote to the British. Foreign office, "...there will be between (the Indian frontier) and Eastern Turkistan, to speak generally, the Kuen Lun Mountains and the Himalaya, to say nothing of the large wild country of Mohammadan cities just now ruled over by Yakub Beg..."[14] That was for England the relevance of the Amir Yakub Beg and, after him, the Chinese.

As a countervailing step to the Kaulbar mission and to restrain Russia, the Atalik deputed an envoy, Yakub Khan Torah, to India. The Amir of Kashgar was seen to be under Russian pressure to cede territory, notably Sirikul, to them.[15] Sirikul was claimed by the envoy to belong to

Kashgaria and the Kaulbar mission had not sought any territory or location of any posts in the Yarkand territory. It was, however, generally understood that Russia coveted possession of Sirikul. During negotiations on the commercial treaty, the Russians had continually alluded to Sirikul.[16] Yakub Khan Torah was asked to point out, on a British map, the limits of Kashgaria. These the envoy terminated in the northeast at Urumtchi. The northern boundary was identified by him with the Tianshan mountains, the northwestern the Narayn river. No western limit was specifically mentioned by the envoy other than Sirikul in a different context, which was claimed to be within Atalik's dominion. As to the southern boundary there, understandably, is no recorded mention. With the second Turkistan map under preparation, the policy was to show the northern boundary of Jammu and Kashmir undefined.

Russia's interest in Sirikul persuaded the British to examine the practicability for the passage of artillery and scope for logistics over several commercial lines that then passed through this stategically placed district, generally 11,000 feet above the sea. Montgomerie discussed these issues in a memorandum to the British Indian Government.[17] The road leading to Kokand from Sirikul (through the "gap") ran over easy slopes but for fifteen days in a desolate tract. The line to Kashgar involved a high pass while that to Yarkand was hardly ever used. Easiest route between India and Yarkand in Montgomerie's view was the line that led from Peshawar to Chitral, across the Hindu Kush to Wakhan and thence over the Pamir Steppe–the Taghdumbash–to Sirikul. The Baroghil pass over the Hindu Kush he considered to be a formidable obstacle from its altitude of 12,400 feet though later British military experts did not consider the pass such an obstacle. The routes from Sirikul towards Gilgit, Hunza and Baltistan were dismissed as utterly impracticable for regular traffic. Strategically also Montgomerie did not see Sirikul to be important. No force that was likely to make the slightest impression on India, as then held by the British could possibly advance by Sirikul. Nor would its occupation by a hostile force in any way endanger British in India. Was Sirikul, like the Changchenmo line earlier, overrated as the junction of Central Asian trade lines? The report on Ladakh trade lines for 1872 revealed that "no traders departed from or arrived at Leh via the Changchenmo route." The whole trade was carried, as ever, over the Karakoram road. The Changchenmo line was altogether forsaken with "the exception of the guides, sent by the Joint Commissioner, to meet the coming caravans from Yarkand, which they did at Shahidulla."[18] In the succeeding year too, until March, no one had gone over the line.

British manipulation of the northern boundary was rather

inadvertenty exposed by Russia. A Russian map, published contemporaneously with the second edition of the Turkistan map of the Great Trigonometrical Survey of India, showed the northern boundary of Jammu and Kashmir over the Kuen Lun whereas the British map had it pulled back from the crest of that mountain to the Karakoram. This caused enormous embarrassment to the British Indian Government with potential for future injury. Earlier maps had shown the boundary to rest on the edge of the Changchenmo valley and the Karakoram ridge. This alignment was changed, after Johnson's surveys, and the boundary was run over the crest of the Kuen Lun mountains in the first edition of the Turkistan map. When the second edition of the map was being prepared under Colonel Walker, Forsyth had "remonstrated... very strongly on the inaccuracy of the first edition of (the) Turkistan map in carrying the boundary up to the Kuen Lun and said that it should be brought back to the Changchenmo valley and the Karakoram where, indeed, it used to be..."[19] The boundary line was consequently pulled back. That, perhaps, would have been the end of the controversy but for the appearance of the Russian map which put Yasin and the "high plateau northeast of Karakoram (Aksai Chin) into Kashmir."[20] The map also put Faizabad out of Badakshan and all the passes leading into Chitral from the north and northeast into "no man's land." The British and Russian maps disagreed thus.

Forsyth argued that on the basis of contemporary knowledge, presumably British, it would be "very unsafe" to define the boundary of Kashmir in the direction of the Karakoram and if it must be put down at all, "it should run as near the lower Karakash river as possible."[21] He went on to apply another western concept in Asia to fill a void in British policy on the boundary issue. Englishmen, like Shaw, had identified the Kuen Lun as the southern limit of Eastern Turkistan, even as they had insisted the Karakoram was the northern boundary of Jammu and Kashmir. They had thus left Aksai Chin as derelict. For the first time it was argued by Forsyth, "Between the Karakoram and Karakash the high plateau is, perhaps, rightly described as rather a no man's land, but I should say with a tendency to become Kashmir property." There was another reason for leaving the northern boundary undefined as Forsyth elaborated, "It might prove hereafter very inconvenient to put the Kashmir boundary on the Karakoram ridge and thus exclude us altogether from any benefit which might arise from having the high plateaux under our control."[22] Forsyth's *faux pas* was explained away by Aitchison to the Viceroy. For Lord Northbrook he noted, "the boundary cannot be accepted as an authoritative one."[23] The Viceroy agreed that the boundary "is not laid down authoritatively" and desired "we should not do so without communicating to the Maharaja of Kashmir."[24] Consequently, "It was considered desirable to place on record officially that the northern boundary of Kashmir, as shown in Colonel Walker's new map, cannot be accepted as authoritative."[25] In other words, the northern boundary was neither the Kuen Lun, Karakash nor Karakoram. It was undefined.

The Forsyth mission to Yarkand, 1873, provided England with a god-send to explore and survey the territories abutting on Jammu and Kashmir's northern boundary. The mission had the brief to explore the route of the Pamir and Badakshan and in consultation with the Amir of Kashgaria, to return to India by that road. In that event the mission was to procure all the information it could having a bearing "on the various unsettled questions of geographical and scientific interest relating to the Pamir and also regarding the boundaries of Yarkand and Afghanistan in that direction, the strategical value of the Sirikul territory, etc[26]..." The unsettled questions were none other than the ownership of the Pamirs and the Russian claim to them. Forsyth was also directed to "inspect and report specifically upon the recently settled boundary of Afghanistan to the north," under the Granville-Gortschakoff agreement of 1872-1873. This boundary the British later manipulated to their Imperial advantage but to the disadvantage of Jammu and Kashmir.

Three of the mission members, Captains J. Biddulph, H. Trotter and Dr. Ferdinand Stoliczka, a geologist, comprehensively surveyed and mapped the Aksai Chin plateaux[27]. Nain Singh and Kishen Singh, two of the "Pundits" trained by Montgomerie, surveyed the eastern (Tibetan) part of the Pangong lake[28] and the Lanak la-Keria la-Polur line[29] respectively. Colonel T.E. Gordon, deputy mission leader, claimed that the road was proscribed to keep Khotan isolated on account of its goldfields[30]. But the most celebrated and prodigious gold mine was the Thokjalong mine, near Rudok in Tibet. Biddulph attributed their successful journey across Lingzithang to the Maharaja's officials[31]. Changchenmo road, the whole way from Leh, Biddulph found practicable for loaded camels but wheeled carriages were ruled out by him[32]. All through 1873 also the road had not been preferred by traders. In the event the British by coercing Maharaja Ranbir Singh to open the route to traffic had only succeeded in exciting alarm in Russia. It was admitted in Russia that if the British feared a Russian attack by way of Kashgar, "we certainly have equal, if not greater, reasons for being apprehensive of an invasion from india..."[33] Russian writer, M.A. Terentyef, recalled Forsyth's first journey to Yarkand in 1870 by the Changchenmo route, noted cold in Karakoram was less severe than "in the Himalaya" and remarked "the road is suitable for camels and consequently baggage." Sooner or later, Terentyef felt, the "British will avail themselves of the road by Yarkand if we do not anticipate them at this point." British protests that the road was unsuitable for military operations were dismissed by Russians. Such inferences could hardly be drawn from the conveyance to Atalik Ghazi of such cumbersome gifts as pieces of artillery[34].

Two factors appear to have influenced mission members, Biddulph and Dr. Stoliczka, to explore the Gulbashahr jade mines near Shahidulla. Firstly, oblique suggestions had been made that the mines were Chinese owned or, at least, Chinese worked. Secondly, Gulbashahr, in the lower Karakash valley, into which far eastward to Sora[35], the Kirghiz of Sanju and Shahidulla then roamed, had inspired claims that they were Chinese subjects and, by implications, the lower Karakash valley was Chinese. The jade at Gulbashahr was found to occur in large masses but the veins generally only one or two inches in thickness and very irregular in extent. To Dr. Stoliczka, it appeared "almost incredible that all the good jade of Chinese commerce should have come from this place." His doubts were set at rest by Johnson, now governor of Ladakh. All the best jade, at any rate that which furnished large pieces, was obtained by the Chinese further east on the same Kuen Lun range on the road to Khotan[36].

The "fort" at Shahidulla the mission found "deserted."[37] From this boundary post of Jammu and Kashmir, Forsyth, as the envoy of Her Majesty's Government, wrote to Maharaja Ranbir Singh to express the complete satisfaction which all members of his mission felt and wished to express at the admirable arrangements made for their comfort.

> "during the march through your Highness' territory from the time of our arrival at Kohala (entry point from British India, now under Pakistan's occupation) till our reaching this place (Shahidulla)."[38]

Was this an unequivocal acknowledgement of Shahidulla being in Jammu and Kashmir or was it double talk after the controversy with Colonel Walker? Shahidulla being then in Jammu and Kashmir inevitably made the crest of the Kuen Lun as the boundary of the Maharaja's territories, leaving both Sogat and Aktagh, astride the routes to Yarkand from Leh, to the south. This is, though in a different context, acknowledged by Dr. Stoliczka. In his diary for October 22, 1873, he referred to Sarekia, at the southern foot of the Sanju, or Grim, over the Kuen Lun as "this side of the Yarkand frontier..." The Kashgarian envoy, Syed Yakub Khan, too joined Forsyth at Shahidulla. In his journey from Leh to Shahidulla, the Syed was accompanied by the Kalon[39], then in the service of the Maharaja. The mission was seen off at Shahidulla by the

Kalon, Johnson, the Wazir of Ladakh, and its highest official then, and Mehta Sher Singh, the Wazir of Anantnag district in the Kashmir valley[40]. Dr. Bellew, a mission member, refers to the army of Ladakhi porters[41]. Shahidulla being the last post of Jammu and Kashmir near the boundary, all commissariat and beasts of burden for the journey northward to Kashgaria were supplied by the Atalik's Government. On the mission crossing the boundary pass of Sanju, over the Kuen Lun, and on reaching the Sanju village "karaul" at the northern foot of the pass, it was formally served the letter of welcome from Amir Yakub Beg, Atalik Ghazi[42].

During negotiations on a treaty of commerce, Forsyth would appear to have succeeded in persuading the Atalik to lift restriction on the Kokyar road[43] and the bulk of the mission returned to India by this route[44]. The English, to promote trade with Kashgaria and beyond, set up the Central Asian Trading Company[45] which conclusively helps in establishing the criminal jurisdiction of the Maharaja north of the Karakoram chain. To investigate the strategic importance of Sirikul, as indeed the military consequences of Kashgaria going under Russia, the mission split up. A group under Colonel Gordon explored some of the Pamirs to learn about the routes that traversed them and the low passes that have historically offered facilities to invading armies. These together underscored the importance of Kashgar in the context of a hostile advance upon India from the north. Kashgaria in the possession of Russia could produce a vast supply of food and carriage and all that was required for the manufacture of war materials. Kashgar, Maral Bashi, Aksu, Yangi Hissar, Yarkand and Khotan were seen as a strong base for supplying an army passing through Kokand via Osh, over the grassy plains and valleys of the Alai, the Kizil Art, to the north of Sirikul, the Pamirs, and across easy passes at no great height, to Sarhad in Wakhan and Chitral.

> "Sirikul is itself a place of importance, as in it converge roads from Karghalik, Yarkand, Yangi Hissar and Kashgar, average distance from each being 120 miles. From Sirikul the road leads by the Little Pamir to the Baroghil pass in eight marches. The whole of this road, about 370 miles in length, is so good that only about 25 miles near Sirikul and the same extent near Sarhad, require any preparation for the passage of guns."[46]

Guns had, indeed, been taken over the Baroghil (Chitral) and Ishkoman (Yasin) a few years before the mission. By the former route the British frontier was reached in 13 marches via Mastuj, Chitral and Panjkora valleys. By the latter, Torbella on the Indus was reached in the same time via Gilgit, Chilas and the Indus valley. The latter of the two routes was "the best and the nearest road to India." The importance of Kashgar on the flank of such an advance was, therefore, apparent. As long as Kashgar remained in hands friendly to England, no such advance could be made without the certain risk of communications being cut off from the Terek pass, the Gez dawan and Sirikul while aid in arms and money could be sent with perfect safety across the Karakoram. From what had been learnt by their journeys over the Karakoram, the Changchenmo and the ordinary trade routes, Gordon was convinced that "no serious attempt" could be made in that quarter except by very small bodies of men. In the event of Kashgar being in unfriendly hands, and so being liable to be used as a base of operations against India, "the occupation of Gilgit and Ishkoman pass would appear sufficient to check an attack from the direction of the Pamirs." No hostile force, he argued, could cross Baroghil pass in the face of one holding the Ishkoman. In such case, Gordon assumed, "Kashmir would become practically British territory."[47] Such a view only persuaded the Russians to see the Forsyth mission as "chiefly military."[48]

On Sirikul falling to the Atalik, Gordon claims, the Taghdumbash Pamir was "annexed" to Kashgaria and its Kirghiz inhabitants once again pastured their flocks there[49]. In the Yarkand mission report, both the Little and Great Pamirs are assigned to Wakhan and hence to Afghanistan. Aksu or Aktash river, one of the many upper streams of the Oxus, is declared as "forming the well recognised boundary between Kashgaria and Wakhan." But neither Kashgaria, later Chinese Turkistan, nor Wakhan or Afghanistan, as will be seen, were anywhere, even a decade later, near the Aksu. Alichur Pamir is described "nominally" to belong to Wakhan but "practically" to Shignan which also receives its waters. Gordon and his two English explorers, Captains Biddulph and Trotter, projected the same claims, but little more forcefully remarking that the Amirs of Afghanistan and Kashgaria together ruled from Herat in the west to Urumtchi and Turfan in the east. The effect of such a territorial disposal was to shut out Russia to the north of Sirikul, to the Alai plain. Russian writer, Fedjenko, dismissed the claim, remarking "this breathes a good deal of preconceived theory, and I cannot attach to it any serious importance."[50] Gordon virtually endorses the Wakhan Mir's claim to the western half of the Taghdumbash Pamir, from the watershed and the Aktash valley to the west (left bank) of the Aktash river as far as its junction with the Murghab, crediting Kashgaria with the ownership of the eastern half of the Taghdumbash, the eastern side of the Aktash valley, and the Kizil Art plain up to the Alai[51], which was the Russian boundary then. Such a disposal of the Taghdumbash Pamir put out of

India the important trade line from Hunza via Mintaka, the Paik col over the Sirikul ridge, to Tashkurgan and Kashgaria. This road later became the postal communication line between Gilgit and Kashgar. That the territorial claims were at best "preconceived" becomes evident from the diary of Dr. Stoliczka. On the Taghdumbash Pamir Dr. Stoliczka contradicts Gordon which, he notes, "mostly belongs to Kanjut." Mostly only because of the invasion of Sirikul by the Atalik. The Taghdumbash Pamir is but the southern extension of the Sirikul valley. About the ownership of the other three Pamirs–Little, Great and Alichur–he concurred in with Gordon.

The Chinese had built their protective fortification over the hills facing Kashgar "to defend themselves against the incursions of the Kirghiz invaders from the Pamirs and the Alia."[52] They thus had left themselves out of the Pamirs. The first such fortification was "khat" (lower) "karaul." Two miles further up was the "kichik" (small) "karaul" where a road led via Opat to Kashgar and a Kirghiz footpath along the ravine led to Yarkand. Sirikul, over which partly occurred the "gap," was thoroughly explored by Gordon and his English explorers. On their return journey from the Pamirs, Gordon ascended the ridge that separates the Sirikul valley from that of Tagharma to its north, to lay down the borders of the northern plain with considerable accuracy. The Tagharma plain is separated from the Kizil Art plain by a low rounded ridge formed by the projecting spurs from the opposite mountain ranges, the Nezatash, or the Sirikul ridge of the Bolortagh mountains, and the Tagharma to the east. The ridge forms the watershed between the two. The Kizil Art plain, 130 miles long, extends up to the Alai, farther north. It is similar in character to the Tagharma plain. Both are well watered, populated and abound in grass and fuel. The drainage of the Sirikul-Tagharma plains passes into the Sirikul river, which farther southward becomes the Taghdumbash, Tiznaf and finally Yarkand river. The "preconceived" boundary had the merit of closing down the passage from Kokand through the Alai, Kizil Art, Tagharma and Sirikul to the Hindu Kush passes in Hunza, Yasin and Chitral and eastward to Leh.

His explorations in Ladakh and cis-Hindu Kush made it apparent to Biddulph that routes from Central Asia, which converged at Leh, lay for many marches "through one of the most bleak and desolate countries in the world," and though in old times raids had been made by small undisciplined bands at favourable seasons across the Karakoram, "the passage of an army able to threaten our supremacy in India" was out of question. But the Hindu Kush passes, to the west, the Baroghil and Ishkoman Biddulph found were easy. Baroghil in particular he found had so gentle a slope that in summer, when it is free of snow, "a horse can gallop without checking from Baroghil-Ailak (summer village) to Darband at the foot of the pass in Chitral." Southeast of Baroghil-Ailak, a track led up the hillside to the Ishkoman pass. Crossing the pass three roads diverged to Hunza, Gilgit and Yasin. On the Gilgit road the village of Emit in Yasin was reached on the first day, "so that there is absolutely but little more than one day's march between Wakhan and Kashmir territory."[53] From the north, access to the Hindu Kush, was easy. From Osh on the Russian frontier in Kokand it was clear from the Yarkand mission's explorations in the Pamirs, "there is nothing to prevent rapid advance of an army fully equipped to within a few miles of Sarhad (Wakhan). From Sarhad to the top of the either pass, not above a mile and a half of road needed to be prepared for the passage of field guns. Once over the passes an advancing army had a choice of routes to follow by the Mastuj stream to Chitral whence to threaten both Jallalabad and Peshawar, or by the Ishkoman reach Gilgit in three marches and from thence to threaten the Punjab, either by Kashmir or Torbella in the Indus valley. For this consideration Biddulph favoured Maharaja of Kashmir occupying the Yasin valley from Gakuch, the limit of his directly ruled territories, to the Ishkoman pass. Biddulph went a step further even to suggest annexation of entire Yasin and Chitral by Jammu and Kashmir,[54] a course of action Sir Henry Durand had already proposed and the Viceroy, Lord Mayo, had rejected. Two other Hindu Kush passes, the Mintaka and Kilik, eastward, then awaited to be probed.

Forsyth fancied the Amir of Kashgaria, most extraordinarily, was not certain as to the limits of his dominions. But in Forsyth's judgment the Kuen Lun range was not the boundary between Ladakh and the Yarkand valley and Eastern Turkistan but it "is and always has been in Yarkand territory, and as the jade quarries in the lower Karakash valley have been worked by the Chinese for the last 150 years we may assume that the valley forms the boundary."[55] This was precisely the boundary that Forsyth had approved of after his cartographic row with Walker and before leaving for Yarkand with his mission. In his report on the Yarkand expedition in 1870, Forsyth had acknowledged that China had never claimed any property in the Karakash valley. H.W. Bellew, a mission member, significantly observes that the jade quarries showed "no traces of anything more than superficial excavation."[56] These quarries had not, therefore, been commercial source of jade to China. Both in regard to the Kuen Lun being within Kashgaria as well as in regard to jade mines, the "facts" presented to the British Indian Government by Forsyth were, therefore, no facts as ascertained in Kashgar or Kashmir but was his obfuscation in Simla like Shaw's obfuscation, earlier, over the Shahidulla fort having been occupied by the Atalik's troops, which British official papers, including the mission report, *ad nauseam* repeated. Forsyth's purpose was to pull back the boundary from the crest of the Kuen Lun, advertise such a pull back through British maps or some other means and, at an appropriate time, lay it over the Karakoram, as, indeed, was done.

Inevitably Forsyth takes recourse to linguistic and archaeological factors in support of his views on Ladakh's northern boundary. In his confidential report to Government, Forsyth remarks "To judge from names of places, Turki words are used to designate halting places up to the Sasser pass and on the left bank of the Shyok river there are still remains of a wall and fortification erected more than two centuries ago by the Raja of Ladakh to check the invasion of the Turks. Daulatbeg Uldi, Karakoram, Brangsa are Turki names..." Forsyth, like many other Englishmen, is less than truthful. Archaeological remains of a religious structure have already been noticed, so also the rationale for Ladakh defence works to the south of the Karakoram, near the Sasser pass. Forsyth sets store by the prevalence of Turki names of camping sites and other places. But Bellew, point out, when the mission in its onward journey to Kashgar reached Changlung hamlet at the foot of the "Karaul" dawn, the *ultima Thule* of inhabitation on the Karakoram highway, he became fully aware of the first Turki name they had come across. He called it an "empty memorial" of the Yarkand invasion by Sultan Said, the memory of which was unwittingly perpetuated by the merchants from that country,

> "for the Bhots (Ladakhis) here, as elsewhere on this route, have their own names for the several localities, and call this spot Hlasgya...57"

Aksai Chin name was unknown until the middle of the 19th century British officials and explorers appear to have deliberately introduced Turki names and excluded Ladakhi names for camping sites, streams, mountains and passes to provide a linguistic justification for exclusion of trans-Karakoram region from Jammu and Kashmir.

For "convenience sake," Forsyth set the southern boundary of Kashgaria along Aktagh and, in laying supplies for his mission's return, he practically made it, and not Shahidulla to the north, Ladakh's limit which, hitherto had served that purpose. He ran the Kashgarian boundary line,

> "from the eastern corner of the Kuen Lun, longitude 81°E, down the Karakash river to Sogat, across that

pass to Aktagh longitude 78°.5' (approximate), latitude, 35°59', thence down the Yarkand river to Kanjut."

In placing the Kashgarian boundary at 81°E. longitude he was really referring to Ladakh's northeastern limit, which Montgomerie in his trans-frontier map depicted, as will be seen, a little farther east, nearly 82°E longitude. Forsyth thus "improved" upon 80°5' E longitude limit of Khotan that Hayward had set in his letter of October 2, 1869 to Major Burnes, Secretary to the Viceroy. The map attached to Forsyth mission report, 1875, provides confirmation, obliquely albeit, of the accuracy of Montgomerie's map. The mission map leaves to the north, in Khotan, the Hindutash, the boundary pass by which Schlagintweits had crossed over to Bushia in Khotan. Eastern part of Aksai Chin is shown as a blank. But had it been Tibetan or Khotanese territory, the mission could not have shown it as a blank or no man's land, which it was not for the Polur-Keria la-Lanak la road and its bypass to Rudok largely ran over it. The Polur-Keria la-Lanak la main line is now rightly shown linked to the Changchenmo route, the meeting point being to the east of the Amtogor lake near the present Ladakh boundary 80°3'E longitude. The two routes were but one.

About Hunza Forsyth merely declared, "Kanjut is beyond Yarkand territory" and ran the Kashgarian boundary "somewhere along the northern slope of the great Himalaya chain through Taghdumbash... to Aktash on the Pamir and thence by the Taghdumbash plain to Kizil Art."[58] The significance of this boundary line is that it was run north of the Karakoram-Hindu Kush chain, it confined Russia to the north of the Kizil Art pass and denied her the road through Aktash to India and Afghanistan. But to Russia such a line was seemingly unacceptable. Coloned A.N. Kuropatkin, heading the Russian embassy, that followed the Forsyth mission to Kashgaria, declared the Kuen Lun as Eastern Turkistan's southern boundary. His boundary thus excluded Aktash, Sirikul and Kizil Art from the limits of Kashgaria. Tashkurgan was described by Kuropatkin as the "frontier advanced post of the Khanate of Kokand."[59] Russia thus not only left the "gap" open but by calling Tashkurgan an advanced post of Kokand virtually assured herself of access to the Hindu Kush and Yarkand valley.

Westward, in Afghanistan, too England faced the prospect of Russia forcing herself to the Hindu Kush by extension of the route through the "gap." Under the Graville-Gortschakoff accord of 1872-1873, the northern limit of Afghanistan was fixed along the south bank of the Oxus. But in Shignan and Roshan, Afghan territories stretched to the north of the river, beyond the left bank. Forsyth rightly anticipated that north of the river Afghan territories would inevitably come to be absorbed in the Russian dominion once the accord was strictly executed. When that happened it would become easy for Russia to push her claim to Little Pamir and "thus insert a very narrow wedge of actual Russian territory between Afghanistan and Kashgar." It then only remained for Russia to strike across the low pass of Ishkoman to be in Yasin and down to the Indus. Kashmir already was within 40 or 50 miles of the Pamirs from Emit village. As long as the Pamirs were considered impassable for troops, Forsyth argued, it mattered little how far Kashmir penetrated in that direction or who held the petty principalities of the Hindu Kush. "But as the mists of ignorance are gradually dissipated, we are brought face to face with facts and are compelled to acknowledge danger from a quarter whence we have a right to expect loyal assistance."[60] From these "facts" as well as from the outspoken words of warning given to him in Kashgar, Forsyth apprehended considerable trouble, if not danger, unless steps were taken to command that route. British influence, he suggested, ought to be made "paramount" in the direction of Badakshan and Bulkh, to begin with, by "establishing an agent at Gilgit."[61]

Outright annexation, of Kokand placed Russia at almost the same distance from the Baroghil pass as the nearest British military station at Abbotabad in Hazara. Indeed, it was realised, a Russian force starting from Kokand frontier would reach the Baroghil first. It prompted a reappraisal of the Hindu Kush passes. In a fresh memo, Gordon emphasised that Ishkoman in Yasin, with the Oxus valley before it, "is a point of greatest strategical importance, checking the advance from the direction of the Pamirs, holding the Baroghil pass, commanding Chitral and the tribes between that and the northern side of the Peshawar valley, threatening Jallalabad (240 miles), Kabul (315 miles), Balkh (390 miles) and the Oxus line of communications..."[62] Biddulph was directed to carry out exploration of the Ishkoman pass and its immediate neighbourhood on the road from the Kashmir frontier to Sarhad in Wakhan, giving full details as to its capabilities for the passage of troops.[63] The pass was found by him to be blocked by a glacier, "practically of no importance but liable from physical changes to become important for a time..."[64] Another Hindu Kush pass, Darkot, leading direct to Yasin, Biddulph found "permanently impassable for artillery," again on account of a glacier. Only Baroghil, giving way to Chitral, Kunar and Panjkora, was practicable for artillery for ten months in a year but closed on the south (Chitral) side by an easily defensible gorge. To the Ishkoman there were four alternative passes, Mintaka, Kilik, Khanjerab and Shangshal, all in Hunza, linking it with Sirikul. But the British had as then no control over its Raja.

From Osh in Ferghana, to within 35 miles of Sarhad, Biddulph found no road making whatever was required and a very trifling amount of labour would make the whole distance practicable for artillery. Control of the passes was, therefore, a matter of considerable importance to India and "the establishment of a Russian garrison at Sirikul would, under the present circumstances, place the passes at the mercy of that power."

Political response of the British Indian Government was however, uncertain. On the one hand an entente cordiale was sought to be built between Kashgar and Beijing, in pursuit of preserving Kashgaria as a neutral, or buffer, State that would block Russia reaching Indian frontier and yet, on the other, it hesitated to post an envoy at Kashgar, as envisaged in the commercial treaty, fearing for his safety. The Home Government's response to the diplomatic exchange was all but pleasant[65]. British commercial interests were too small while, from a political point of view, it was belatedly realised that such a relationship was not "without embarrassment." China having recovered all the territory in the northwest, uncharacteristically assured British diplomats that they were disposed to treat with the Atalik on most liberal terms. Even more, in the rivalry between Russia and England in Central Asia, China saw herself as an ally of the latter. Britain's and China's interests in the east were considered by high Chinese officials to be "identical" and

> "that the more powerful China grew the better it was for England : both had a common enemy to dread and that was Russia..."[66]

Such sentiments, whether they were meant at all, came ultimately to be exploited by the British on the boundary issue.

Kashgar embassy was still-born. But an important mission of the embassy was entrusted to one of its members, Ney Elias. He was to explore, from time to time, (i) Tibet with the object of penetrating for to the south and east towards India and Nepal frontiers, (ii) the southern and western portions of the Pamirs, including passes leading towards Yasin and Hunza and (iii) the northern and western Pamirs with the upper Oxus and passes leading from the new Russian possessions in Kokand. Of these Elias considered the second the most important[67]. The principal concern of the envoy-designate, Robert Shaw, was to prevent its falling into the hands or under the influence of Russia. But before the embassy could leave for Kashgar, The Atalik was assassinated in May 1877 and China once again seized Eastern Turkistan. The British suspected Russia had aided China to recover Kashgaria. Biddulph apprehended Russia would demand Sirikul "in return for the aid" rendered[68]. Once in possession of Sirikul Russian would be well placed to dominate the

Hindu Kush passes and control the great trade route between east and west Central Asia, giving it military advantages. In the negotiations leading to the Granville-Gortschakoff accord the boundary line of Afghanistan was not drawn further east than the Sirikul lake. Later it became known that "the most direct route from Russian territory to the Punjab lay over the debatable land" between the Sirikul district and Sirikul lake, or the "gap."

Having seized Eastern Turkistan without firing a shot, the first act of China was to close the trade routes and get rid of 17000 foreign traders, waiting for permission to proceed to Yarkand and elsewhere. A small force was also sent to Sirikul where the "Dadkhwah" of Yarkand, under the Atalik, had taken refuge with its chief, Alif Beg. Tashkurgan was seized but no troops were left behind. Even so China had made a token appearance in Sirikul. After Alif Beg's death by Chinese torture, his brother was recognised as the new chief[69]. Elias as the British joint commissioner, along with the Kashmir joint commissioner jointly wrote to the Chinese authorities at Kashgar urging the trade lines be thrown open as per old custom[70]. The British would never have allowed the Maharaja's joint commissioner to sign the letters were Elias not certain that his letters alone would not be entertained. Privately the "Hakim" (chief) Niaz Beg advised Elias to send "a few hundred or a thousand men to Shahidulla" and inform him in advance of their coming. "I will within one day have every Chinese in the nine towns, of which I am "Hakim," put to death, make myself master of the country and become tributary to the British Government." Significantly the troops were to be sent to Shahidulla which suggests whatever notions on the boundary the British had planted in Kashgaria during the Atalik's rule these had not been entertained, for. Niaz Beg was one of his top officials. Also, it is evident that, regardless of British machinations, Shahidulla continued to be boundary post of Jammu and Kashmir State.

Either because of the instability of Chinese rule in Eastern Turkistan after the collapse of Kashgeria, or, more probably, with the intention of reoccupying Shahidulla, Maharaja Ranbir Singh sought British advice on the defence of Ladakh. Elias' memo on the issue was tendered to the Maharaja only in extracts as the joint commissioner had gone into the boundary question, "a point on which (British) Government has not made up its mind," F. Henvey, officer-on-special-duty in Kashmir, conveyed to the British Indian Foreign Secretary, A.C. Lyall. Himslf Henvey saw that "a very effective limit is drawn by the terrible stretch of mountain ridges between the last habitable spot within the jurisdiction of Ladakh and the first settlement in East Turkistan..." It would be extravagant to dream of any real extension of Kashmir power beyond the water parting of the Karakoram mountains, Henvey expatiated, as it would be equally vain to suppose that the Chinese or Andijanis or Turkistanis would attempt to push their outposts even as far as the higher northern slopes of those mountains much less into Ladakh. As to why trans-Karakoram could not be Kashmir territory Henvey explains and brings out the real issue involved for the British in the northern boundary. The region between the head of the Nubra valley and the post of Shahidulla he regarded "as a kind of no man's land, only frequented by passing traders, peopled by the skeletons of men and horses and as real a boundary between the Indian empire and its northern neighbours as would be a vast and waterless desert."[71]

It is evident the British *per se* did not dispute the Kuen Lun boundary of Ladakh but feared the intermediate desert between it and the Karakoram chain through which military operations were then considered well nigh impossible. Another school of thought, whose proponents included Colonel Bell of the Quarter Master General, Captain Ramsay, Elias' successor at Leh and, later, General Sir John Ardagh, favoured precisely this kind of boundary. The Russians were still to arrive in Kashgaria, but even if they had, Henvey doubted they would have ventured on the flag planting business on the southern side of the water parting. He could not resist the temptation, which British imperialist zealots often indulged in, to obfuscate on the boundary. "...it may be," he remarked, "harmless vanity on the part of the Kashmir ruler to carry his eye, in imagination, beyond the mountains up to the limit of the habitable East Turkistan and dream of subjection of these tracts to Dogra sway. Why should we dispel such innocent imaginings and seek to demarcate by pillars or piles of stones a line which nature has already defined?" This was a retreat from Forsyth's Karakash valley boundary, even though it was still in the realm of loud thinking among highly placed British officials. In pulling the boundary from the crest of the Kuen Lun, Forsyth had foreseen an orderly withdrawal to the Karakoram.

Elias in his memorandum on Ladakh's defences admits that a body of Jammu and Kashmir held the "fort" of Shahidulla "*previous* to the retreat of the Chinese from Eastern Turkistan in 1864..."[72] He thus contradicts Shaw's version followed by other Englishmen. But Elias fell into error when he further notes that "the border on the main line of the road to Yarkand was considered to be marked by the fort itself." Shahidulla, at the foot of the Kuen Lun, only commanded the roads to Leh via the Karakoram pass, by the Karakash and Changchenmo valleys and to Sirikul by Yarkand valley. The real boundary was the crest of the

Kuen Lun astride of which were the boundary passes of Sanju or Walaghat, Kilian, Yangi dawan (Yarkand valley), Kokyar and Kulanuldi and many others. The Chinese and the Atlik had their "karauls" at Sanju, Kilian and Kokyar villages on the northern foot of the Kuen Lun. Elias' claim that when inter-communication began to take place with the Kashgar Government of the Atalik, "the fort was found to be held by the Kashgar troops and to be looked upon by them as their frontier post," stands fully exposed by Forsyth's letter to Maharaja Ranbir Singh, datelined Shahidulla, clearly stating it to be the State's frontier. Elias himself had never been to Shahidulla but he understood "it was never a position of any strength, and that it is now in such a state of disrepair that it may be considered entirely useless from the point of view of border defence." Elias obfuscates. Shahidulla was not a fort, was not conceived in terms of Ladakh's defence but to oversee trading caravans negotiate several lines of communications and serve custom and other boundary post purposes. As a bastion of defence, Shahidulla was inconceivable. It involved transport of supplies over 275 miles of barren country. Also it was entirely cut off from Leh for several months on account of heavy snowfall in winter. Elias, expectedly, saw :

> "no advantage in the Maharaja reoccupying Shahidulla either as a defensive post or as a demarcation of the border..."

Instead, he suggested, a line should be drawn as nearly as possible along the most inaccessible range of mountains, and that it be marked off distinctly on the various roads leading from Ladakh to Turkistan at the points where these cross the passes over that range. "Such a boundary would be found on the whole to follow the natural water-parting between the two countries, it would not exclude a single inhabitant of the Maharaja's present dominion, or an acre of habitable ground, while it would, by placing a natural barrier between his people and those of a possible enemy, diminish the chance of trouble arising, and place his troops in Ladakh and Skardo in a better position to defend their provinces than if the border were beyond this barrier and at a greater distance from their bases of supplies, etc." So Elias argued, disclosing the demographic and military factors in the boundary issue. In such a region of snowy mountains and glaciers he admitted it would neither be practicable nor necessary to survey the whole boundary line for demarcation, but merely that marks should be set up at a few points such as those where it was crossed by lines of road or reached by the heads of inhabited valleys such as Nubra. Thus beginning in the west

> "the crest of the Muztagh, or Baltoro, pass might be

> demarcated as the first point; the summit of the glacier at the head of the Nubra valley (formerly a practicable pass) as the second; the summit of the glacier at the head of the Shyok valley as the third; the crest of the Karakoram pass, where the main road to Yarkand crosses, as the fourth; the crests of the two Changlung passes at the crossing points of the alternative routes via Changchenmo as the fifth and sixth; and finally some point on the present Chinese-Tibetan boundary to be afterwards decided on."[73]

Except the undecided last point, the rest of the boundary marks are all over the Karakoram chain. The difficulties Elias observes as to actual demarcation of boundary were also the impediments to delimitation of Ladakh's boundary over the Kuen Lun. Yet the boundary was clearly noted by prominent landmarks. The British knew them as much as the Tibetans and Turks.

On his first visit to Eastern Turkistan in 1879 Elias mentions the Chinese "border village of the Kilian." The "karaul chowki" he found to be a small enclosure with high mud walls having something the appearance of a fort from outside but without guns or any kind of arrangement for defence by infantry. Evidently it was like Jammu and Kashmir Government's Shahidulla post with room for 30 to 40 men to guard the road to Ladakh, entirely free of Chinese officials. A Beg (head) was "responsible that nobody should pass across the border, inwards or outwards, without a written order from the provincial authorities at Yarkand..."[74] The entry and exit were thus regulated by passports. When he called on the Amban of Yarkand, Elias was to show his passport but he had none. To his chief assistant first and then to the Amban himself, Elias was, with the aid of a map, able to make them understand tolerably clearly the situation of the English in India, British relations with Jammu and Kashmir, Afghanistan and Russia and of the relations of the Russians with countries surrounding their borders. The Amban recognised that both English and Chinese frontiers were open to Russian advances from Kokand. Here was an opening for Anglo-Chinese entente. His ready references to maps and his long harangues became Elias' standard tactics during his numerous visits to Yarkand and Kashgar, to prepare the Chinese for the British moves to pull back Jammu and Kashmir's northern boundary southward to the Karakoram mountain range. To the credit of the Chinese, it must be conceded that, to begin with, they spurned British promptings on the boundary. It was during this visit in 1879 that Elias was referred to by the Governor of Kashgar as "Her Britannic Majesty's consul at Ladakh, the frontier between (Yarkand) the Chinese and the British Indian empires (Hindustan)..."[75] No "no man's land" is mentioned to separate the two empires.

In May 1880 Elias reappeared at Yarkand and was struck by Chinese preoccupation with Russian relations and Russian frontier affairs, notably those relating to the Ili province, then under Russia, which they desperately sought back. In contrast there was awareness that the boundary with India gave the Chinese no anxiety. An issue of some import to India was reopening of the Sanju route. The Amban questioned Elias about roads to Ladakh. Evidently the Chinese knew nothing south of the Kuen Lun, about the roads from Khotan to Ladakh, one of which 70 years hence they were surreptitiously to use to claim Aksai Chin. One road from Ladakh Elias did mention but explained it was then seldom used. The line Elias alluded to was the Lanak la-Keria la-Polur road. In Kashgar Elias conducted his discussions with the Governor or the Resident with the aid of a map to explain the "connection between India and Kashmir." Hunza appeared to the Governor as about equal in power and importance to India. Again it is evident that the Chinese had hardly any knowledge about the countries south of the Kuen Lun. No superior relationship was, however, claimed with Hunza. Some "unimportant conversation," as Elias characteristically remarked, also took place "...about the Kuen Lun and Karakoram mountains and the course of rivers springing from them[76]...More explicit Elias could not have been. The discussion had obviously related to the Karakoram watershed.

References

1. 30th July 1870. Foreign. Pol A. No. 357 of January 1871.
2. 26th August 1870. Foreign. Pol A. No. 472 of December 1870.
3. 6th April 1871. Foreign. Pol A. No. 584 of June 1871.
4. 4th August 1870. Foreign. Pol A. No. 363 of January 1871.
5. 2nd December 1870. Foreign. Pol A. No. 382 of January 1871.
6. Undated. Foreign. Secret. No. 70 of August 1872.
7. 20th October 1870. Foreign. Pol A. No. 572 of June 1871.
8. 26th January 1871. Foreign. Pol A. No. 573 of June 1871.
9. 20th March 1871. Foreign. Pol A. No. 585 of June 1871.
10. *Ibid.*
11. Kashgaria. By A.N. Kuropatkin. Tr. by Walter E. Gowan. 1882. P. 62.
12. 28th June 1872. Foreign. Secret. No. 79-106A of August 1872.
13. 21st July 1872. Foreign. Secret. No. 207 of September 1872.
14. 1st October 1872. Foreign. Secret. No. 40 of February 1873.

15. 11th February 1873. Foreign. Secret. No. KW. 19-29 of March 1875.
16. 27th February 1873. Foreign. Secret. No. 229 of March 1873.
17. 18th February 1873. Foreign. Secret. No. 30 April 1873.
18. 4th March 1873. Foreign. Pol A. of 216 of August 1873.
19. 26th June 1873. Foreign. Pol A. No. 452-453 of July 1873.
20. 2nd July 1873. Foreign. Pol A. No. 132-136 of July 1873.
21. 1st July 1873. Foreign. Pol A. No. 452 of July 1873.
22. *Ibid.*
23. 11th July 1873. Foreign. Pol A. No. 452-53 of July 1873.
24. *Ibid.* 12th July 1873.
25. 22nd August 1873. Foreign. Pol A. No. KW. 304-308 of September 1873.
26. 18th August 1873. Foreign. Secret. No. 71 of January 1874.
27. Report of A Mission To Yarkand in 1873. Historical And Geographical. Foreign Department Press. 1875, p. 238.
28. *Ibid.* p. 241. Also Memoir on Indian Surveys. p. 162.
29. Indian Explorers of the 19th Century. By Indra Singh Rawat. Publication Division, Ministry of Information and Broadcasting, Govt. of India. 1973. pp. 72-73. Also Report of A Mission To Yarkand, p. 241.
30. Roof of The World. by T.E. Gordon. 1876, p. 25.
31. 19th October 1873. Foreign. Secret. No. 216-217 of January 1874.
32. Undated. Foreign. Secret. No. 217 of January 1874.
33. Russia And England In Central Asia. By M.A. Terentyef. Tr. By F.C. Daukes. Foreign Department Press. 1876. Vol. I, p. 274.
34. *Ibid.* Vol. II, p. 107.
35. September and October 1873. Foreign. Secret. No. 217 of January 1874.
36. Diary of Dr. Ferdinand Stoliczka, member, Yarkan Mission, Government Central Press, p. 16.
37. September and October 1873. Foreign. Secret. No. 217 of Januasry 1874.
38. 20th October 1873. Foreign. Secret No. 178 of January 1874.
39. 3rd November 1873. Foreign. Pol A. No. 124 of December 1873.
40. Kashmir And Kashgar. By H.W. Bellew. 1875, p. 188.
41. *Ibid.*
42. Report of A Mission To Yarkand. Foreign Department Press. 1875 p. 3.
43. 20th February 1874. Foreign. Pol A. No. 38 of May 1874.
44. Report Of A Mission To Yarkand. Foreign Department Press. 1875, p. 243.
45. 30th May 1874. Foreign. Pol A. No. 190-192 of June 1874.
46. 14th July 1874. Foreign. Secret. No. 70 of August 1875.
47. *Ibid.*
48. Golos. A Russian Paper. 30th July 1874. Foreign. Secret. No. 34. of December 1874.

49. Roof of The World. By Colonel T.E. Gordon. 1876, p. 115.
50. From Kashgar To Kila Panja. By O.A. Fedjenko. Government Central Press. 1876, p. 2.
51. 17th August 1874. Foreign. Secret. No. 72 of August 1875.
52. Report Of A Mission To Yarkand. Foreign Department Press. 1875, p. 264.
53. Undated. Foreign. Secret. No. 73 of August 1875.
54. *Ibid.*
55. 21st September 1874. Foreign. Secret. No. 69 of August 1875.
56. Kashmir And Kashgar. By HW. Bellew. 1875. P 182.
57. *Ibid.* P 154.
58. 21st September 1874. Foreign. Secret. No. 69 of August 1875.
59. Kashgaria. By A.N. Kuropatkin. Tr. By Walter E. Gowan 1882, pp. 12 and 21.
60. 21st September 1874. Foreign. Secret. No. 69 of August 1875.
61. *Ibid.*
62. 2nd November 1875. Foreign. Secret. No. 35 of July 1877.
63. 12th April 1876. Foreign. Secret. No. 77 of July 1876.
64. 15th November 1876. Foreign. Secret. No. 37 of July 1877.
65. 5th April 1877. Foreign. Secret. No. 206 of April 1878.
6. 8th May 1877. Foreign. Secret. No. 196 of October 1877.
67. 20th July 1877. Foreign. Secret. No. KW. 1-206-229 of April 1878.
68. 21th March 1878. Foreign. Secret. No. KW. 1-35-37 of March 1879.
69. 1st September 1878. Foreign. Secret. No. 151 of November 1878.
70. 1st to 16th September 1878. Foreign. Pol A. No. 107 of December 1878.
71. 23rd November 1878. Foreign. Secret. No. KW. 2-3 of February 1880.
72. Undated. Foreign. Secret. No. KW 2-3 of February 1880.
73. *Ibid.*
74. 12th September 1879. Foreign. Secret. No. 270 of November 1879.
75. 23rd June 1880. Foreign. Secret. No. KW. 3-144-146 of January 1881.
76. 31st August 1880. Foreign. Secret. No. 133 of January 1881.

Chapter 6
Shaping British Policy

Annexation of Badakshan and Wakhan by the Amir, Sher Ali, made Afghanistan advance deep into the Pamirs north of the Hindu Kush, and, south of it coterminous with Chitral. Though violative of the Granville-Gortschakoff accord, Afghan presence in the Pamirs was one policy objective of England together with a similar advance westward of Kashgaria, later Chinese Turkistan. Such a double movement, when complete, sealed the "gap," ensured Russia stayed well to the north of the Hindu Kush and did not become contiguous to India at any point on the northern boundary to cause political or military problems. From the Mehtar, Aman-ul-Mulk, the Amir sought tribute, on the ground he was a vassal of Badakshan, and reinstatement in Yasin of Raja Mir Wali[1], the murderer of Hayward. South of the Hindu Kush, establishment of British influence, to begin with, followed by British presence, was another objective of British policy. Accomplishment of this objective was not possible without a serious clash with Maharaja of Jammu and Kashmir. Nevertheless the British pressed on as they had in Ladakh earlier.

The arrival of the Afghans on the Chitral frontier was followed by that of Captain Biddulph in Gilgit, initially for a political assessment. Both eventually had a destabilishing influence on Yagistan. Biddulph became the first European to enter Hunza and Nagar. The strategic fort of Chaprot, commanding Gilgit, from which a year earlier, Hunza had been ejected, was, Biddulph realised, a point of discord between Kanjut and Kashmir. The Raja sought British intervention for the return of the fort to him. From Hunza he found Wakhan was reached in seven days following the course of the Hunza river, which originates in the Hindu Kush close to Langar in Wakhan. After three marches from Hunza, a road across the Hindu Kush, branched off eastward by which on the sixth day the large Kunjuti village of Shangshal was reached. Beyond Shangshal there was no population. The country above Hunza, which

Biddulph did not visit, he was told, opened out into undulating pasture lands. This country was the Taghdumbash Pamir. Both Hunza and Nagar, Biddulph proposed, should be "openly" claimed as British territory "on the strength of tribute they pay to the Maharaja..."[2] That would rein in Hunza which had a running boundary with China. With Yasin, then inaccessible to the British, Biddulph proposed to deal differently, extending only England's influence there to render the passes secure from the possibility of a sudden attack. "Biddulph had no doubt Ranbir Singh would have little difficulty in subduing Yasin. But he did not believe the Maharaja would be able to maintain himself permanently there. Even supposing the Maharaja's troops to be equal to the task, Biddulph claimed "the drain on the Kashmir treasury would become greater than it could stand, and a subsidy from the British Government would certainly be demanded."[3] A yearly payment of money appeared likely to reconcile both chiefs to declaring themselves feudatories of British Government. But from a military point of view that alone was of no great advantage. The only alternative then that presented itself to Biddulph was to make such arrangements as to secure the command of the passes by a military force at short notice. This appeared possible by a secret understanding with the Maharaja, strengthening the force stationed at Gilgit by the supply of good arms, and the establishment of a British officer permanently at Gilgit.[4]

As long as Badakshan was free, Chitral's relations with it had often bordered on vassalage. After its annexation by Afghanistan, Aman-ul-Mulk had temporised with the Amir. Sometime late in 1876, the Mehtar made several moves to restore his relations with Maharaja Ranbir Singh. In a letter to him, the Mehtar remembered "interchanging envoys and letters and of union and allegiance was customary" between his father and Maharaja Golab Singh. "...Year by year hawks and horses were despatched from this side as *nazrana* (tribute)."[5] The shifty Mehtar blamed the conduct of the sons of Gauhar Amar–Mulk Aman, Mir Wali and Pahlwan Bahadur–for the lapse of this practice. "And now," recalling the practice of his father, "I elect the friendship of and submission to the Maharaja, for the friend of Your Highness is my friend, and the evil disposed to Your Highness is my enemy." Amir Sher Ali, having taken possession of Badakshan, planted a cantonment and stationed troops at Zebak, only two days journey from Chitral. To the Mehtar the Amir's presence, certainly, and of some other unidentified powers constituted "the congregation of great and powerful chiefs... encamping in these mountain regions."[6] In another communication to Ranbir Singh, the

Mehtar offered exchange of resident confidential agents posted at Gilgit. Jammu, Srinagar and in Chitral.[7] Were the Maharaja to so desire, Aman-ul-Mulk offered to send his eldest son, Nizam-ul-Mulk, to the Roshan fort on the frontier of Yasin or to Gakuch in Punyal, with Pahlwan Bahadur, to meet Bhai Ganga Singh, the governor of Gilgit. This defection of the Mehtar stirred the Amir to remark, "...God knows whether the Maharaja has adopted this line of conduct (of taking Chitral under his protection) of his own accord."[8]

That Aman-ul-Mulk made these overtures to the Maharaja of Jammu and Kashmir with British concurrence is not unlikely, for the Viceroy, Lord Lytton, about this time proposed to Ranbir Singh that "such States as Chitral and Yasin should come under the control of a friend and ally of the British Government, like His Highness, rather than be absorbed in the course of events by powers inimical to Kashmir..."[9] The power inimical to Kashmir was Afghanistan in the irredentist sense, Kashmir having been an appendage of Kabul. Lytton's proposition was made in the broader, context of Russia. The desirability of Ranbir Singh taking Chitral and Yasin under his wings, Lytton himself explained, "...became the more necessary from there being certain passes through the mountain range bounding these territories...for the passage of troops."[10] As then, with the Indus valley still ruled by independent Pathan tribal chiefs, the British had no access to Chitral and Yasin, except through Jammu and Kashmir. They had, therefore, no option but to rely on the Maharaja. Having communicated to Ranbir Singh his views on the peaceful absorption of Chitral and Yasin, which Lytton believed "to be a subject near to the Maharaja's heart," there was one additional measure which the Government of India thought it necessary to carry out for the further security of Kashmir frontier and the transmission of regular and reliable information regarding the condition of that frontier, viz., "to station a British officer at Gilgit who would be specially charged with these duties." It was explained that the duties of this officer would be confined to "external frontier relations, and that he would exercise no interference in the internal administration of Kashmir." Additionally, the Viceroy expatiated, he wished "to refrain from exercising any direct control over the States adjacent to the frontier but would prefer in all cases that the influence of the Maharaja's Government should be directly brought to bear on them."

Lytton found the need for a British agent at Gilgit had already arisen in consequence of the annexation of Kokand by Russia and the attitude of the Amir of Afghanistan towards Chitral. Some years later the Mehtar revealed Biddulph was sent to Gilgit following Russia reaching an understanding with Amir Sher Ali. The Maharaja consented to the appointment subject to several conditions that sought to limit the British official to specific duties visualised by the Viceroy as also to some others that Ranbir Singh spelt out in a 'kharita'* to the Viceroy.[11] A 'sanad,'= incorporating all these assurances, was sought by the Maharaja and duly conveyed to him by Lytton in a 'kharita' dated 22nd December, 1877.[12] Expectedly Bhai Ganga Singh was informed that, Nizam-ul-Mulk, would, as desired by the Maharaja, meet him in the vicinity of Summa, one march from Gakuch as well as Yasin, in order that a "treaty" might be contracted by Jammu and Kashmir Government with Chitral. An inconsequential sum was advanced to the Mehtar on the pretext of his assistance to Biddulph during the latter's visit to Yasin, so as to keep him attracted towards the Maharaja, while substantial pecuniary aid was to follow the conclusion of a "formal agreement" between Jammu and Kashmir and Chitral.[13] Having tied up the Chitral end, the Viceroy directed the commissioner of Peshawar division, Sir B. Pollock, to caution the Amir, Sher Ali, against "endeavouring to assume sovereignty," besides Bajaur, Swat and Dir, over Chitral.[14]

To the Secretary of State Lytton detailed the steps taken to secure "an efficient control over the passes of the Hindu Kush between the eastern confines of Afghanistan and the north-western frontier of Jammu and Kashmir," notably the Karambar, Darkot and Baroghil. All these passes lead from Sarhad, in Wakhan, in the valley of the Oxus, Afghanistan, the first to the head of the Ishkoman valley and thence to Gilgit, the second to Darkot village at the head of Yasin valley, besides Yasin over the Tawi, Tagawi or Shandur, passes to Mastuj and the valley of Chitral, the third, of course, to the head of Chitral valley. Fair prospect was seen in the Kashmir ruler, supported as he was by the power and prestige of the British Government, being able to acquire such influence and control over Chitral and Yasin as would enable British India, in course of time, to make such political and military arrangements as would "effectually command the passes of the Hindu Kush."[15]

At the meeting between Bhai Ganga Singh and Nizam-ul-Mulk and Pahlwan Bahadur no formal accord was signed. Yet the suzerainty of the Maharaja of Jammu and Kashmir was once again established over both Chitral and Yasin. Like the Mehtar, Pahlwan Bahadur offered to receive

* A formal letter.
= A legal document.

an agent of the Maharaja at Yasin, and send hawks and horses in tribute. He had been disinclined to meet the governor of Gilgit fearing that Jammu and Kashmir troops would be stationed in Yasin.[16] Maharaja Ranbir Singh was willing to provide, in a measure, the Mehtar with the means to resist Kabul. But not so with regard to material, a view shared by Major P.D. Henderson, then officer-on-special-duty in Kashmir. Any gift of arms "seems to (be) out of the question..." Even money gift was, to begin with, to be restricted to the smallest amount which should suffice to ensure Aman-ul-mulk looked "in this direction," that is towards the Maharaja.[17] When Henderson called on the Maharaja, Ranbir Singh remarked with regrets of his "having twice gained possession of Yasin whence he had retired only at the desire of Government."[18] If the Maharaja was still drawn into the Chitral developments, it was at the persuasion of the Viceroy. He had, perhaps, no illusions about the ultimate British objectives.

Lytton agreed that it would be well to secure the allegiance of the Chitral ruler by the promise of a yearly payment of "such amount as Your Highness may consider suitable and that, for the present at any rate, no arms should be supplied to him."[19] As regards the conditions of allegiance, the Viceroy again concurred with Ranbir Singh that they should be as brief and as little onerous as possible, consistent with the main object to be secured. Although immediately it appeared unnecessary and even undesirable to send troops into Chitral, Lytton wanted Ranbir Singh "to cause a careful examination to be made of the passes leading to Chitral and full information to be collected as to the character of the roads, the supplies available and other matters likely to be of use, in the event of military operations in those parts becoming unavoidable." It was possible to send a few (troops) but with the consent and accord of its ruler.[20] The road was long and the main constraint was want of supplies. The Maharaja found it necessary to subsidise, Pahlwan Bahadur also, Yasin falling en route to Chitral. A draft treaty, elaborating Lytton's views, conveyed earlier, was sent to the Mehtar for signature and seal. An annual "mawajib" (subsidy) of Rs. 12,000 was fixed for Aman-ul-Mulk, including Rs. 2000 for his son, Nizam-ul-Mulk, were he to reside at Srinagar as Chitral agent.[21] The Mehtar was assured by the Maharaja that "such arrangement shall be made for the defence and protection of Chitral as you wish and our friendship and alliance require."

If the Afghan factor had induced the Mehtar to accept British suzerainty via Kashmir, no such consideration weighed with Hunza. Indeed, British disinclination to assist him to recover Chaprot made Raja

Ghazan Khan see danger, a feeling accentuated by the formal appointment of Biddulph as officer-on-special-duty or, really, Political Agent, in September 1877, entrusted with gathering of political and topographical information about the Hindu Kush region.[22] The recovery of Kashgaria by China was, it would appear, calculatedly brought to the notice of the governor of Gilgit by the Raja–calculatedly because of the arrival of the British. It implied Hunza was looking northward rather than southward. This is further evident from Ghazan Khan's claim that he had despatched "the customary tribute to the Great Khakan," or the emperor of China, and expected to receive "the 'shank' agreed upon in former times."[23] The 'shank' appears to be presents or subsidy given by China to Hunza. The Chinese commander-in-chief in Kashgar, Zunk Tunk Daubaklao, had called upon Ghazan Khan to declare whether he was "willing to submit and serve the emperor" under whose rule, the Chinese claimed, he had formerly been.[24] Biddulph saw no fault in the Raja having sent tribute to the Chinese prior to their exit from Kashgaria. But for eight and a half years (since 1869) the Raja had "eaten the salt of the Maharaja and whoever is a dependant of the Maharaja is *ipso facto* a dependant of the English Government."[25] It was an erroneous statement made by Biddulph for Hunza's vassalage to Jammu and Kashmir was anterior to 1869 and dated to 1840, after the capture of Skardo by Wazir Zorawar Singh. This is the British, however, did not as then know. Therefore, subsequent political changes, the exit of Chinese, the advent of the Atalik and re-emergence of China in Eastern Turkistan, had no bearing on Hunza's relations with Jammu and Kashmir. Significantly no Chinese envoy had descended on Hunza after the recapture of Kashgaria. But an envoy had gone to Sirikul "to summon Alif Beg to Yarkand." Ghazan Khan would appear to have merely acted "on a message transmitted by Alif Beg."[26]

This raises a legitimate doubt about Ghazan Khan's claim of vassalage to China to which Biddulph took exception, though for a different reason. A strong inducement might have been the prospect of restoration of a jagir in Yarkand, seized earlier by the Atalik. Hunza was promised increased subsidy for the aid given to Alif Beg. The Kanjutis themselves considered Sirikul their dependency. Sirikul to the Chinese, Biddulph opined, was of no importance. It thrust a wedge between Afghans and Kashgar. But in the hands of a "strong power"–evidently Russia would be "a constant menace to the Chitral passes."[27] Yet another development related to Chinese come-back to Eastern Turkistan was the return of Kirghiz to Taghdumbash and Little Pamir. Hunza made no secret of its intention to "resume the system of raids" on the Kirghiz for what Biddulph called blackmail but what to Hunza legitimately was tax.[28] Whether it was, blackmailk or tax, it implied ownership of both Taghdumbash and Little Pamir, of the latter, at least, after the Kanjutis defeated their chief, Bozai, at Bozai Gumbaz. Himself Ghazan Khan clarified the issue of his vassalage to China, raised by Biddulph with him :

> "I am not a dependant and tributary of the Khakan of China as I am on the bestower of dignities, the Sarkar (Maharaja)."[29]

His father, Raja Ghazanfur Khan, Ghazan Khan explained, had gone to Yarkand and had a large jagir appointed to himself, which he had bought. Also a "trustworthy" Kanjut, Mullah Muqim, being in Kashgaria during the Chinese war against the Khojas, descendants of earlier rulers, had performed service to the Chinese and the Khakan had, in recognition, "increased the fixed 'shank,' and rewards and dignities." Therefore, Ghazan Khan concluded, "I am sending tokens of friendship to the Amban." Sending vakils, or agents, to which also Biddulph had taken exception, the Raja considered unobjectionable. Ghazan Khan's explanation was not accepted by Biddulph. He insisted Hunza's relations with China prior to 1869 were those of a "feudatory." Therefore, if Hunza agents took to the Amban as "presents, the things formerly agreed upon, and receives from him a fixed shank," what difference was there from former arrangements? As to the purchase of a jagir by his father, Biddulph remarked, "Jagirs are not bought and sold." The service rendered by Ghazanfar Khan and Mullah Muqim to the Chinese, Biddulph argued, were "as feudatories at the time to the Khakan of China..."[30] Spiritedly Ghazan Khan controverted the British Agent. He wrote to Biddulph :

> "I am (at all times) ready to carry out any orders of the exalted Government.* Of course I send my agents everywhere, viz., I have friendly relations with Wakhan, Badakshan, Shighnan, Chitral, Yasin, etc. But I owe allegiance only to the exalted Government in whose pay I am, and who is the source of munificence. I sincerely value the friendship of Government and have of my own accord tendered allegiance to and become a well wisher of that Government. I do not acknowledge the authority of any one in the same way as I do that of the generous Government. I do not deny having

* Evidently the Maharaja's Government

> sent an agent but have not done it from any bad feelings or an ill-disposition towards Government. There is no harm, according to the custom (prevalent) among kings, in sending an agent anywhere..."[31]

This unambiguous declaration of Ghazan Khan made Biddulph to admit that the Raja "acknowledges his allegiance to the Maharaja and his relations with other rulers to be only those of friendship."[32] To Biddulph it appeared "the first time" he had formally acknowledged it. Together the two letters of Ghazan Khan fully establish not only his being a feudatory of Jammu and Kashmir but also that his relations with China were not on a similar footing and were limited, as with Sirikul, Wakhan and Shighnan, to payment of subsidy by China for a variety of services. This is a clear distinction drawn by Ghazan Khan himself in his first letter to Biddulph. British ignorance of Hunza having tendered allegiance to the Sikhs as early as 1840 is also revealed by Alfred Lyall, Secretary, Foreign Department. On Biddulph's Gilgit diary for 13th April 1878, he noted, Hunza was "recently taken under Kashmir protectorate." Lyall opined "Chinese occupation of Kashgar territory" is becoming felt at Hunza, which lies *just north* of Gilgit." Consequently the "petty chief" of Hunza had sent "customary tribute" to China. It was feared that Chinese advance south-west to the unoccupied (politically) and debatable lands about Tashkurgan and Sirikul "will introduce a new complication if they do press forward."[33] Only complication to be expected was Hunza's expected resistance. Sirikul's importance had again caught on. But the Chinese, instead of pushing forward, "assigned" the Kirghiz of Tak, Shakshu, Pakpho, Taghdumbash Pamir and Aktash (Alichur) Pamir to Hunza, numbering 4,000 tents but much less according to Biddulph's estimate. Hunza also sought Biddulph's permission to attack caravans between Yarkand and Leh (Shaihidulla) on the plea that the Chinese were not friends of the British but really "to counterbalance the loss of Chinese subsidy."[34] Such attacks, had these been undertaken, would have been a challenge to the Chinese who had taken upon themselves to protect commercial routes in the neighbourhood of Hunza. Yet Biddulph went on insisting that Chinese looked upon Ghazan Khan as owing obedience to them.

But it was Sirikul that worried the British. Were the Chinese, it was realised, to cede Sirikul to Russia as a *quid pro quo* for her assistance in the recovery of Kashgaria then "their political frontier will at last touch ours, or would, at most, be separated only by a thin strip of debatable land," Lyall noted for the Viceroy. "Debatable land" was, of course, the

Taghdumbash Pamir. He thought it advisable to consider and settle definitely the precise line that might be taken as demarcating the country which should be included within the sphere of political subordination to India. Petty chiefs of the country between Sirikul on the north, Kabul on the west and Kashmir on the south, were seen as much perplexed "tendering allegiance and tribute to all three powers–China, Kabul and Kashmir–alternately." In the north-west extremity of Kashmir were Hunza, Nagar, Yasin and Chitral of whom the first three Lyall considered as "politically subordinate to Kashmir," while Chitral had lately tendered allegiance to the Maharaja and received a civil reply. But Hunza, Lyall went on, had just then sent tribute to some Chinese authority at Tashkurgan and although the Chief disavowed any political intentions, yet he was seen as clearly attempting to renew his relations with Chinese in Kashgar, while Chitral was openly trimming between Kabul and Kashmir. Chitral also claimed Yasin. Whenever Sirikul was occupied by a strong Government, either Russian or Chinese, Lyall feared, all the political vacillation of the petty border chiefships would increase, so that it might be time to survey, more closely, the situation in the region, and to consider, if not determine, the limits within which British political supremacy, given in exchange for a guarantee of protection, must not be disputed, either from inside or outside the line. Lyall had no doubt that Hunza, Nagar and Yasin, could be brought within this limit. The question of including Chitral he saw open. "The *natural frontier*" that Lyall, along with Colonel Gordon, saw emerge on a map they put up to the Viceroy was "the main range of the Himalaya from east running north-west, until it joins the Hindu Kush whence the line sweeps round along the Pamir and turns south-west, enclosing the basin of Yasin stream and other southern affluent of the Indus."[35]

The map showed another boundary in blue line. Lyall declared it "the nominal Kashmir boundary which has been extended beyond the Himalayan main range." This was the historical boundary running over the crest of the Kuen Lun-Kashgar ranges. Lyall considered it "doubtful whether the claims of Kashmir to hold territorial jurisdiction up to this line, if disputed from the north, could conveniently be supported by the British Government.[36] He, however, ignored that this was an ancient boundary line and had never been disputed in the past. China with conterminous boundary had not. Russia could not have if only the Maharaja had been allowed to run his boundary, as in the past, to Sirikul which Englishmen like Henvey had speculated upon. But the British did not want Russia to touch India's boundary. That a Jammu and Kashmir boundary very much existed, as Lyall admitted, and was sought to be superseded, revealed British intentions. This boundary was well established and the actual line demarcated at numerous entry and exit points of routes of commerce which points could be crossed with "rahdaris" (passports) alone.

By and large Lord Lytton agreed with Lyall. But in a minute on Sirikul the Viceroy, in effect, laid down British policy to be pursued on the boundary and even indicated an acceptable boundary line. The first principle of this policy was the need felt by Lytton to define how far British indirect influence and authority might be advantageously extended in the direction of Sirikul and at what precise line any further advance of Russian influence and authority should be actively resisted. Beyond the line of active resistance thus fixed there would always remain a zone of quasi-independent territory, within which it might be advisable, indirectly or diplomatically, to oppose, and, if possible, delay the advances of the Russian power. The object of any such indirect opposition was to be postpone, till the latest possible moments, that contact, which Lytton believed to be inevitable, between the Russian and British empires in Central Asia. That contact which, whenever it occurred, would greatly increase British difficulties in India. He went on to observe :

> "I do not believe it to be in our power to prevent the occurrence of this contact, sooner or later, but, as yet it is still in our power to *select* the points, at which it should occur; and in selecting these points, it is essential that we should not commit ourselves to the occupation, whether military or political, of any position, from which we may be afterwards obliged to withdraw."[37]

Sirikul, Lytton decided, clearly belonged to the outer zone above indicated. It was, he considered, part of Kashgar and must always follow the fortunes of the Kashgar Government or dynasty. No one had, of course, proposed a policy based on the ultimate occupation of Kashgaria. To the adoption of such a policy the Viceroy saw obvious and overwhelming objections. He argued :

> "We must, therefore, as wisely suggested by Mr. Lyall, restrict all our efforts to the maintenance of an adequate political control over the States along the southern slopes of the Pamir, which fall within the natural boundary of British influence, formed by the Hindu Kush, and the main range of the Himalaya, running

eastward from its junction with the Hindu Kush."[38]

These States Lytton identified as Hunza, Nagar, Yasin and Chitral. Their territory comprised important passes, through which, if those passes were in hostile hands, an enemy might, perhaps, be able to advance upon Peshwar from a strong base established in Kashgaria.

> "They, moreover, cover the north-western frontiers of Kashmir, and were they in the hands of a strong, independent and hostile power, they might become the bases of operation against Kashmir which we should be bound to defend, under penalty of losing our whole position in India if we either shirked that duty or failed in the performance of it. On the other hand, our control over these States, should it ever be firmly established, will greatly strengthen the hold we are establishing in other directions upon Afghanistan."[39]

Lytton did not consider it desirable to annex these States but thought it expedient to keep in British hands the political control over them and, in his opinion, it was incumbent on the British to prevent at any cost the establishment of a political control over these states by any other power, be that power Russia, Kashgar or Kabul. The only point on which the Viceroy differed with Lyall related to the position of Chitral in the area in which British political supremacy was not to be disputed. Lytton held destiny of Chitral was not open to question. The late Secretary of State for India had "approved and sanctioned" Lytton's decision that Chitral, as well as Hunza, Nagar and Yasin, must be brought indirectly under British control and that this could best be done by extending to those territories the authority of the British vassal, Jammu and Kashmir. While it was desirable that the object in view should be effected gradually and peaceably, still there must be no hesitation to resist, if necessary, by force, all attempts on the part of any other power to establish control over these states. With Lyall and Colonel Gordon the Viceroy agreed :

> "...that our natural frontier along the north-west corner is formed by the Himalaya range and the Hindu Kush."

With regard to the Jammu and Kashmir boundary of the map, Lytton conceived

> "that the blue line, which is really fictitious, should for all practical purposes be regarded as such, and dismissed from consideration."[40]

The boundary that Lyall and Lytton proposed was the Himalaya-Karakoram-Hindu Kush line. The effect of this boundary line was to sunder Aksai Chin, Yarkand valley, Taghdumbash and Sirikul from Jammu and Kashmir and its dependencies. Indeed under it Hunza was reduced to about half, the part lying to the south of the Hindu Kush. The merit of this line lay in its being a *natural boundary*, natural in the sense of being defensible to the British. As against this strategic boundary there was the blue line Kashmir boundary, "nominal" in the view of Lyall and "fictitious" as Lytton saw it. Yet the British had taken note of it and indicated it in their maps. Here again differences on the boundary were between the British, who sought a strategic boundary, and the Maharaja of Jammu and Kashmir, who insisted on the historical boundary. By the latter boundary all of Aksai Chin, Yarkand valley, Taghdumbash Pamir and Sirikul remained in Jammu and Kashmir. The British did not consider the blue line boundary a natural boundary because it was certain to make the British dominions conterminous with the Czarist empire, a contingency they dreaded more for political rather than military considerations. Lytton himself admitted "it would greatly increase British difficulties in India. These difficulties were British fears of uprisings in India were a diversionary Russian force, big or small, to invade India in the north in support of another in the north-west. Of these British fears the Russians were fully cognisant. As early as 1875, M. Venukof, member of the Russian Geographical Society, St. Petersburg, wrote : "...the English themselves recognise the fact that the appearance alone of an external enemy upon the soil of India, or even upon her frontier, would be sufficient to excite (an)... outbreak and to convert into the theatre of war the whole country..."[41]

The British, unlike the Maurayans or the Kushans, were not sons of the soil but colonialists. Military reverses, or even political withdrawal from advanced positions, wanting in logistic support, would have created, a situation many times worse than Jawaharlal Nehru's and Krishna Menon's on holding out the Thagla Ridge, along the McMahon line, northern frontier, in Arunachal Pradesh, nearly a century later, in November 1962 when China attacked India. Theirs was a popular, nationally backed Government. It just about escaped yet with immense political damage. Precisely for a situation like this in mind, Lytton had laid down: "...it is essential that we should not commit ourselves to occupation, whether military or political, of any position from which we may be afterwards obliged to withdraw." The views of Lytton and the British Indian Foreign Department were amplified in military and geographical terms by Colonel Gordon. His interpretation is of importance as it spelt out the boundary the British wanted in India at the Gilgit end. From the north-west to east, the boundary was seen to run over the Baroghil pass, the western Muztagh range (Hindu Kush) forming the watershed and natural boundary between Wakhan, the Taghdumbagh Pamir and Sirikul on one side and Mastuj, Yasin and Hanza on the other, and its continuation, what then had come to be known as the eastern Muztagh or Karakoram range, forming the watershed between the Indus and Yarkand rivers.[42] In order to command and hold Baroghil pass, Gordon considered it absolutely necessary to include upper Mastuj (upper Chitral or Yasin) in the red line (British boundary) for although Ishkoman or Karambar pass commands the Baroghil, yet by reason of being a winter route only, the full advantage of its position could not be obtained. The possession of Mastuj was to secure the pass thoroughly with its communication with Yasin via the easy Shandur pass, which was used throughout the year. That was why Yasin or Warshgam, ultimately came to be annexed to Jammu and Kashmir.

Of these conclusions arrived at by Government, Biddulph was informed by Lyall, who further suggested that "...it would be very advantageous if the Kashgarian districts of Sirikul could be held by the Chinese or by any authority rather than the Russian Government."[43] What, is really important about Lyall's communication to Biddulph is the clear indication it gives of British dependence on China in Central Asia. Sirikul had always great significance for India. Besides the Baroghil pass, Sirikul commands the Oxus valley. From Sirikul pressure could be exerted on Hunza, Nagar and Kashmir itself. For these reasons and no less due to major commercial routes, including an all weather road to Hunza and another via Tagharma and Kizil Art to the Alai in Russian Ferghana, over which artillery could pass, Biddulph did not agree with Lyall's suggestion for ensuring Chinese control over Sirikul. He, instead, argued in favour of "Sirikul being considered as neutral territory by which the line of the Alai would practically remain the Russian frontier."[44]

Biddulph's note on Hunza-Kirghiz relations is significant. He categorically states that the Kirghiz of the Pamirs, and that includes Kirghiz of the Karakash valley, "paid no tribute" to China. That sets at rest such claims, chiefly of Shaw. Tribute by the Kirghiz was also refused to Hunza, which however, claimed it of all on the Taghdumbash Pamir. Occasional raids were made but no regular tribute was exacted till Raja Ghazanfar Khan had sent an expedition against them. Kirghiz under Bozai were completely defeated and Bozai killed in action. Kirghiz were again defeated in Tagharma in Sirikul, where they had erected a fort, and at Surjulgah on the Taghdumbash Pamir. These expeditions, Biddulph says, were undertaken "with the consent and partial aid of the chief of Sirikul, Bawash Beg"[45] and established Hunza's sway over Little Pamir and Taghdumbash. When Yakub Beg Kushbegi established himself at Kashgar, the Kirghiz submitted to him and moved east to the northern slopes of the Kuen Lun and Karakoram. In 1875, after the Kanjutis attacked them on the Taghdumbash Pamir, the governor of Sirikul under the Kushbegi sent a force that sacked the Hunza fort of Misgar. The reoccupation of Kashgar by China saw the Kirghiz migrate back to the Pamirs from the Kuen Lun and Karakoram. The assignment of Tak, Shakshu, Pakhpo, Taghdumbash and Aktash (Alichur) by the Chinese to Hunza was a mere recognition of the hold Hunza had over these and the Little Pamir.

In his secret despatch to the Secretary of State for India, Lytton took pains to detail the views of the British Indian Government on the boundary in the context of advancing Russian influence and Russian presence. He proposed to regard Sirikul "as an open destrict"–nearer to Biddulph's view and farther from his own–giving access to India's frontier, which might at any time fall into unfriendly hands. Same, he held, to be true about Wakhan, which from its geographical situation was as much open to Russian usurpation as Sirikul and occupied an equally commanding position with regard to passes leading to the Indian frontier. If at any time Russia were to endeavour to establish a footing, or, at least, an influence in Wakhan, the result, it was felt, would be to extend Russian predominance close up to the line of the Karakoram-Hindu Kush frontier that was desired to be established and to bring within its range the passes like Kilik, Mintaka, Khorabort and Baroghil leading across that line towards the south. On the other hand the greater part of the territory that interposed between Sirikul and Wakhan and the border of India proper the Yarkand valley and Taghdumbash Pamir, was seen "well within the reach of our effective influence." Lytton, it is clear, did not envisage ceding trans-Karakoram-Hindu Kush territories to China but visualised only effective British influence over them. China had just then returned to Eastern Turkistan after 15 years and had yet to be seduced on the boundary issue. The Viceroy had no doubt that the movement of events "in this quarter, thought, at present, indeterminate and complicated is so far significant that it should place us on our guard." If a strong, independent and hostile power were established to the north, the passes might become "lines of a demonstration against Kashmir, which might, at least, be useful as a diversion to facilitate and support the flank of more serious operations in Afghanistan." If, on the other hand, British influence was extended and by degrees, consolidated over the country and if it was resolved that "no foreign interference can be permitted on this side of the mountains, or within the drainage system of the Indus, we shall have laid down a *natural* line of frontier which is distinct, intelligible and likely to be respected," Lytton argued.[46] Lytton's minute and secret despatch to London left very little to be said. The little left related to Kabul's position in regard to Chitral and the outlying trans-Indus Mohammadan chiefships. Lyall saw Kashmir's engagement with Chitral as good a "red flag as any we can set up just as yet." The preference as then, in the absence of British contiguity to Chitral, was to tack Mehtar on, even nominally, to Kashmir, than to left him to drift towards Kabul, for "it would not answer to let the Amir generally assume the position of a predominant and central power over all those outlying Mohammadan chiefship on our frontier."[47]

The political situation in Gilgit came to a boil, following Biddulph's induction into the region. In Kashgar Elias had reports, which later proved to be inaccurate, that three envoys, or agents, of the Hunza Raja had, one after another, arrived there, the first two in the spring and autumn of 1879 and the third in April 1880. They had called on the Chinese "governor." The first envoy had presented "nazar" (tribute). The third envoy had also tendered "nazar". He had brought a letter stating that an army of nine lakh Hindus, under Ram Kishan, together with nine thousand Englishmen, had asked for a passage through Hunza to Sirikul.[48] This letter also contained the intelligence that the Raja had taken the "karaul" on the border of Hunza and Gilgit-Chaprot-and an assurance that he would continue to hold it "in the interest of the emperor of China." There was no reason for Hunza to compromise its status, as Elias' report suggested, other than the presence of the British in Gilgit. This presence was, however, put to an end by "a general rising of the surrounding tribes." Colonel Tanner, then surveying in the neighbourhood, who had returned to his recess quarters to bring up his mapping and calculations during the summer of 1880, was ordered back to Srinagar to command a body of troops in the service to Ranbir Singh and "under instructions to proceed to Gilgit for the relief of Major Biddulph..."[49]

After his Gilgit fiasco, Biddulph wrote a long memo on the situation on Gilgit frontier which in part, also dealt with Hunza's relations with China. To the north-east, Raja Ghazan Khan, Biddulph wrote :

> "...maintains correspondence with the Chinese Governors of Yarkand, who rather tolerate than encourage his advances. He has an overweening belief

> in the power of the Chinese empire, to whom he desires to render allegiance in return for protection...[50]"

That overtures were made by Hunza to the Chinese is also corroborated by Elias, on this occasion from Leh. With reference to the Kanjut envoys who visited Kashgar in the spring, Elias reported to the Indian Foreign Department :

> ...their object was to induce the Chinese to recognise Kanjut as a vassal by returning to the custom which existed previous to Tungani rebellion (1863), of receiving an envoy once a year and bestowing on him a "khillat" (robe of honour) in the name of the emperor of China. The Resident gave the envoys no definite answer, but promised to refer the matter to Peking for decision."[51]

Elias' biographer, Gerald Morgan explains :

> "About this time the Mir of Hunza sent a deputation to Kashgar saying he was afraid of being annexed by Kashmir and asking to be taken under Chinese rule."[52]

The fort of Chaprot was, indeed, "seized" but jointly by Hunza and Nagar, followed by an abortive invasion of Gilgit by Pahlwan Bahadur of Yasin. In a swift move the Mehtar moved into a defenceless Yasin, in the absence of Pahlwan Bahadur, and annexed it to Chitral.[53] A part of Yasin he gave to one of his sons and another to Mohammad Wali, son of Mir Wali. The Mehtar appears to have held out a promise to the British to allow them to construct a cantonment in Yasin, provided its division as effected by him was recognised.[54]

Biddulph's presence in Gilgit spurred the Russians to open a consulate in Kashgar, ultimately set up in November 1882.[55] So near Gilgit, the consulate, in course of time emerged, as the centre of Russian activities in south Central Asia. In March 1883 a Russian expedition was organised under M. Lessar to survey an ancient channel of the Oxus and in May of that year a scientific expedition, under Colonel Prjevalsky, was announced to explore Central Asia, including Tibet.[56] A group of 25 Russians and some Kirghiz entered Wakhan in September via the Alai. The Wakhis, fled in different directions. The Mir, Ali Mardan Shah, escaped to Yasin, all apparently on account of the advent of the Russians.[57] But Ghazan Khan of Hunza linked their flight to the Afghan demand on the Wakhis to construct a road from Zebak to Yasin for attack on Gilgit.[58] Many Afghan posts were to be set up in Wakhan so as to reach Ishkoman in Yasin, two stages away from Punyal on the

Gilgit frontier.[59] The Russian party, which entered Wakhan, was statedly on its way to Chitral and thence to "Siah Posh" Kafir country. Another group of Russians, probably under Captain Patiata, had been to Shighnan, whose Mir the Afghans thereupon imprisoned.[60] While the Russians had been in Roshan and Shighnan, they had struck a peg "to separate the Russian frontier from the Afghan territory."[61] The Russians thus forcefully pointed out their frontier under the agreement of 1872-73 with Britain.

Russian explorations in the upper Oxus Pamir territories of Wakhan, Shighnan and Roshan persuaded the British to investigate their boundaries. Afghanistan having large parts of these Pamirs under it, Amir Abdul Rahman's opinion was invited. The boundary projections of the Amir reveal on astonishing identity of his views with those of England. That he claimed Chitral and a part of the Little Pamir was to be expected. But more importantly the Amir stretched the southern boundary of Wakhan as far away as the neighbourhood of Yasin and over the Kar Ghazvin pass, an unidentified saddle. Across this pass he assigned the country to Hunza.[62] In the east Wakhan was stated to extend to Langar. Beyond Langar and up to Sirikul, the Little Pamir was said to belong to Kashgaria.[63] Chinese Turkistan was thus notionally advanced from the east face of the Kashgar range over the elevated trough, across the Sirikul chain right up to the Sirikul lake, the shut out the gap. The eastern boundary of Shighman was identified with Shakhdara and Ghund. The country beyond was declared to be China's. The other part of the eastern boundary of Ghund was terminated at Hauz-i-Murghabi or Yeshil Kul* beyond which, again, was considered to be China[64]! The limits of Zebak in Badakshan were set on the crest of the Dora, Agram, Nuksan and Kharteza passes, which all lead into Chitral.[65] Hunza's boundary was put on the Kilik pass. Beyond was pronounced to be Chinese Turkistan.[66] The territorial limits of Yasin were set forth correctly—Iskoman, Darkot and Darband-i-Tamaski.[67] That these boundaries barred Russia from the Pamirs was again not astonishing. What was amazing was that Afghanistan should have halved Hunza by assigning Sirikul, Taghdumbash and Little Pamirs to Chinese Turkistan, besides Alichur Pamir. The Amir was not anticipating England. He was, as China was soon to be, privy to British designs. The ground situation in the region is revealed by Elias' explorations.

---

* There is another Yeshil Kul to the east along which the Polur-Lanak la route traversed.

Russia's own activities in the Pamirs were seen by the British as objectionable. The great Alai plateau, through which flows Surkhab, or Vakhsh, she claimed her own territory in virtue of its forming the pasture lands of her Kirghiz subjects. Russia also took formal possession of Lake Karakul by hoisting the Russian flag there. Southern Pamir districts, including the head waters of the Murghabi and other Oxus feeders, she had surveyed and mapped, avowedly in the exclusive interests of science, but possibly with ulterior political objects. Russian officers had not only thoroughly explored Alichur and Sarez Pamirs, thus coming into contact with "Afghan" districts of Shighnan and Shakhdara, but had penetrated to the "Chinese frontier" on the east and had taken observations on the margin of the Sirikul lake at the head of Wakhan valley. They were, to the discomfort of the British, getting into perilous proximity to the passes leading into Gilgit as well as into Chitral. Further movements of Russia in this direction, it appeared to the British, required to be watched. That was one aspect of the issue. There was yet another factor that struck the British. Before a boundary settlement was reached, it had to be considered that if the trans-Oxus territory was detached from Afghanistan, it could not be left as a derelict, at the mercy of the wandering Kirghiz of the Pamir. The sheltered lands in the river valleys running down to the Panja would assuredly be peopled by refugees from the neighbouring Tajik and Uzbek States. These communities would assuredly place themselves under the protection of Russia, which had displayed the greatest energy for several years past in surveying the Pamirs and extending her name and influence up to the very sources of the Oxus. That these sheltered lands ought to become Russian, under the 1873 Agreement that limited British influence to the upper Oxus, was ruled out. The expeditions, which were in the previous year, 1883, launched from Ferghana base, were directed to include Wakhan and eastern Badakshan in their operations, and even to cross the great range of the Hindu Kush into the valley of Chitral and it was only owing to the energy of Amir Abdul Rehman, who barred their way in Roshan and Shighnan, that the grand design of tapping the Anglo-Indian frontier failed. From the southern skirts of the Pamirs, Russia, the British grasped, could keep up communication in one direction with her military stations of Kokand and Samarkand, while to the east Russia could hold in check the Chinese of Kashgar. To the south Russia could command access by the easy Baroghil pass, both to Kashmir and Kabul through the open valleys of Gilgit and Chitral.[68]

Anglo-Russian relations deteriorated and in 1885. There was talk of war breaking out between the two nations. In such an eventuality the British feared Russian agents would not only haunt the steppes to the north of the Hindu Kush and raise the Badakshis, Wakhis and others against them and the Afghans, but that they would intrigue among the tribes to the south of the water-parting. "It is impossible to believe that they will refrain from bringing pressure to bear on such chiefs as those of Yasin, Chitral, Kafiristan, Hunza, etc..."[69] The establishment of the Russian consulate at Kashgar only strengthened British suspicions. Russian commerce and Russian residence in Kashgaria were seen to give Russian Government agents opportunities to influence Chinese policy along the frontier of Jammu and Kashmir and small States lying between Kashmir and Afghanistan. Elias suggested to the British Indian Foreign Secretary, Mortimer Durand, later Sir Mortimer, temporary deputation, of a British agent to Kashgar to counter the Russians. Mortimer Durand agreed but instead of an agent favoured despatch of a special mission to Eastern Turkistan, until the issue of setting up a British consulate in Kashgaria was sorted out with the Chinese.[70] The Viceroy[71] and the Secretary of State for India concurred.[72]

A thinly disguised military mission was also decided to be sent up to the Hindu Kush region under Colonel W.S.A. Lockhart to establish friendly relations with Chitral and Kafiristan, report on the routes and passes, resources and inhabitants of this region, and, if the venture could be made without undue risk, to cross at one or more points on the Hindu Kush into Badakshan, returning at once to the Kafir territory.[73] Mortimer Durand wished the despatch of the mission to be a quiet affair for if the Afghans heard of the mission going to Kafiristan or Kashmir and Chitral came to know of it before-hand, "(Lockhart) may find all sorts of difficulties thrown in his way and trouble may ensure..."[74] The Military Department considered the mission a matter of the first importance for the British to obtain full information regarding the routes and resources of the country lying between Chitral and Faizabad (Badakshan) and of the possibility or otherwise of military operations being undertaken on that line.[75] In the event of war, Russia was expected to make a diversion in that direction and it was essential to know what strength of force could be sent and how it was to be maintained. While the establishment of a British agency, or consulate, at Kashgar or Yarkand was taken up by the Indian Foreign Department with the British Charge d'Affaires at Beijing,[76] the special mission, headed by Ney Elias, was to explore the Afghan districts on the upper Oxus. Elias was to visit Wakhan, Shighnan and Badakshan and ascertain, as nearly as possible, "the recognised boundaries between these districts and the Russian and Chinese possessions on and near the upper waters of the Oxus."[77]

Notwithstanding British precautions, it does not appear that the appointment of either of the two missions remained a secret. First, Jammu and Kashmir and, soon after, Hunza took initiatives which had a bearing on their respective boundaries. The Wazir of Ladakh sought to reoccupy Shahidulla[78] while Hunza constructed a fort south of Tashkurgan on the Taghdumbash Pamir.[79] Elias, en route to Kashgar then, claimed that the fort was attacked and demolished by the Sirikulis, vassals of Hunza.[80] Nor were British fears about "all sorts of difficulties" arising for the Lockhart mission groundless. Reports trickled into Peshwar about the governor of Gilgit, Bakshi Mulraj, exciting Aman-ul-Mulk's fears. The Mehtar was told that the Lockhart mission intended building military cantonments in Gilgit and Yasin "where some of his country would be taken up."[81] In Chitral the Lockhart mission discussed the British perceived threat to India from both Wakhan and Badakshan side. Aman-ul-Mulk was asked what assistance might be expected from him. The Mehtar's response appears to have been a tricky one. Lockhart was advised "to get hold of Gilgit as soon as possible and garrison and store it..."[82] That, of course, was the role that Gilgit had historically played before and after Kao's invasion of Bolor in the 8th century. Had the Mehtar then anticipated the British? Himself Aman-ul-Mulk undertook to guard all approaches from the Baroghil to Dora until the arrival of the British troops. Lockhart planned to go upto the Dora pass which opens on Kafiristan. He did go to the eastern fringe of Kafiristan and signed an agreement with the Kafir tribes of Bashgal to aid Great Britain in the event of an enemy approaching their frontier.[83] The Mehtar and Lockhart also signed an accord the contents of which were confidentially conveyed to the Indian Foreign Department. The accord committed to writing the terms and conditions for Chitral's aid. A later modification of the agreement threw open all routes to the British, importantly the Indus valley road.

That Taghdumbash Pamir belonged to Hunza is confirmed by Lockhart himself. In a conversation with Bahram Khan, Jammu and Kashmir representative at Chitral, Lockhart described it as "Kashmir (Pamir?)," which he intended to visit via Hunza and thence go to Shighnan.[84] Taghdumbash lies to the north of the Hindu Kush and was linked to Hunza by the Kilik and Mintaka passes. Lockhart later went to Taghdumbash by the Kilik. Aman-ul-Mulk's parting advice to Lockhart once again was, "Get hold of Gilgit at once. Make Gakuch and Sher Kila also your own, or let me hold the two latter, or if not the two latter, then

Sher Kila only for you. They have nothing to do with Kashmir these two..."[85] Lockhart was struck by the "sense" in Aman-ul-Mulk's advice but lamented it was "unseasonable, if not unreasonable." In Calcutta nothing for the Viceroy, Mortimer Durand underscored the Mehtar had agreed to afford passage to British troops in case of need. Consequently the British Indian Government felt "the whole question of the future status of Chitral and the neighbouring tracts" would have to be considered. That was seen to involve recasting of the arrangement of 1877–the treaty relations between Jammu and Kashmir and Chitral-and, more ominously, reinstallation of "an English officer on the northern Kashmir frontier with direct charge of our relations with Chitral and possibly other duties."[86] Quite obviously that was intended to be the first step towards seizing Gilgit.

The main objects in taking over of Gilgit were spelt out by Lockhart in a memo addressed to Mortimer Durand. "...Gilgit would secure for us the continued loyalty of Chitral, carrying with it our right of way through the Mehtar's dominions and his active cooperation in time of need."[87] That ensured the safety of the Hindu Kush. Once acquisition of Gilgit was accomplished. Lockhart had no doubt that pressure could be brought to bear on the independent Pathan tribes of the Indus valley by which a military road could run up from Peshawar to Chitral and Dora. A British garrison of Gilgit was to be raised as to derive from its elements both political and military efficiency. It was to compose of a carrier battery, i.e., a battery of mountain guns carried by men, on the principle of the Kashmir "Kahar" batteries, the carriers to be Baltis, and gunners Punjabi Muslims from the Salt Range. The infantry was to be four companies again of the Punjabi Muslims, eight companies raised one each in Gilgit, Hunza, Nagar, Darel, Tangir and independent Kafiristan and two in Chitral. Lockhart dismissed the prospect of any civilised army being able to march through Hunza, "Yet a horde a Chinese could manage it. Reason the more for our getting hold of Gilgit," he remarked.[88]

The Wazir of Hunza, then on a visit to Gilgit, was asked by Lockhart about the Chinese connection. The Wazir said :

> "Chinamen came into Hunza from Yarkand every year generally but that there was no political connection between the countries. No tribute (was) ever claimed."[89]

From a military point of view the Lockhart Mission also established, on secondary but unquestionable evidence, that Russia had three feasible lines of approach to India, viz.,

(a) Through Badakshan to Zebak, and thence over the Hindu Kush by the Dora,

(b) from Osh by the Pamir to Kila Panja (Wakhan), and thence over the watershed by either the Khankhon (Yur), Baroghil, or Sawar Shui routes,

(c) from Osh to Kanjut by the Kilik pass.

Between (B) and (C) there is the Ishkoman pass leading from the east of Wakhan to Gakuch, but as this, on account of an accentric glacier, could never be relied on from one year to another, and as it might at any time become totally impracticable, no prudent enemy would lay his plans for an advance by so unreliable a route.

From Zebak there were four possible passes, viz..., (a) the Dora, (b) the Agram, (c) the Nuksan, (d) the Kharteza. Of these Dora was the only route practicable for the passage of an army. By it 'kafilas' of laden mules and ponies frequently passed for five or six months of the year. There was, therefore, no question that by it invasion was feasible. Nevertheless it was a route by which a large force would be compelled to march in echelons for a variety of reasons, Captain E.T. Barrow, mission member, affirmed in a memorandum.[90] This single factor exposed an invading force to the prospect of very high casualties. Besides, forage, firewood and supplies were all scarce so that an army would not be justified in attempting the passage. The question, therefore, arose would the Russians deem it worthwhile to detach any force to operate by the Dora road. The answer in the view of the mission was that even a brigade would produce an effect out of all proportion to the effort involved. In the first place a Russian force appearing in Chitral would inevitably be the signal for a rising of all the wild tribes lying between it and Peshawar– a result which would compel the British to add considerably to their garrisons in Peshawar and the Khaibar, while were British troops anywhere in advance of Jallalabad, their line of communications would be in a very critical position. A small Russian force might, therefore, hope to accomplish much while, if defeated, it would at the worst, only risk its own destruction.[91]

British Indian "military authorities" pronounced "occupation of Gilgit" as "undesirable." Lockhart's entry into Hunza turned out to be a near trap. Raja Ghazan Khan attempted to impede the mission's progress towards the Kilik pass and beyond. He was civil but firm in his interview with Lockhart to whom he, for the first time, claimed, he was "the subject of the king of China and could acknowledge no other masters."[93] The British factor had finally changed Hunza's political equations. Ghazan Khan's Chinese connection had been superficial. But it was now exaggerated by Ali Gauhar, headman of Gulmit, en route to the Kilik as

Lockhart's guide. An "elchi"-envoy-went every year to Yarkand with "a nominal tribute" and brought back valuable presents "for G.K. (Ghazan Khan)."[94] Also, every three or four years, an official came to Hunza. On Lockhart's visit to Hunza, Ghazan Khan had bluffed the Chinese he had allowed the mission to pass "in consideration of a grant of land." That Hunza's submission to China were the result of British interference is established by a Foreign Department note by Assistant Secretary, E.R. Thomson. He blamed Major Biddulph's action in advising the Kashmir Government "to withhold the Hunza subsidy (which) seems to have driven Ghazan Khan into the hands of the Chinese."[95] Under Secretary J.A. Crawford dismissed the connection as "some vague intercourse or intrigues with the Chinese authorities."[96] The British view of the four decades old Hunza-Nagar-Kashmir relations was reiterated, yet Crawford appeared distinctly to play them down. He did not consider these States were "in alliance with the Maharaja of Kashmir," and went on to note "the Government of India have not formally recognised their position in this respect, but have asserted the right to take a material interest in all the Kashmir Darbar's relations with any of the States on... (the) frontier." To have adverted to these issues thus there was reason. The change in British policy on Gilgit revived their differences with the State. More importantly significant developments had then taken place in the Anglo-Dogra relations. On Maharaja Ranbir Singh's death in August 1885, the British, in total violation of the treaty of 1846, foisted a Resident on his successor, Maharaja Pratap Singh, and so put an end to the independent status of Jammu and Kashmir. Consequently, thereafter, Kashmir's relations with the tribal chiefs and Rajas and countries, such as Tibet, which the Maharaja had personally conducted until then, often in a manner opposed to British interests, were, thereafter, run by the British Indian Foreign Department in Imperial interests.

Lockhart's proposal for the take-over of Gilgit was tantamount to virtual annexation of Gilgit. Having just drastically altered Jammu and Kashmir's status, it was, perhaps, feared such a move might cause embarrassment disproportionate then to any political or military gain. No less importantly, how were the tribes, along the Indus, already in ferment on account of Lockhart's visit, to view such a take-over? Mortimer Durand, therefore, sought to be prudent, not so much about the proposal itself as much as to the timing of its implementation. He was not convinced that the necessity for a British Agency at Gilgit was established or that occasional visits by an English officer would not serve all purposes. Nor did he fancy sending up British troops. An efficient contingent of

Kashmir troops could be raised and their efficiency insisted upon. But were it from a military point of view necessary to get a firm foothold at Gilgit, he believed it could be done without serious difficulty. The effectual cooperation of Jammu and Kashmir he wrote to the Viceroy, Lord Dufferin, must be insisted upon "and she will not like it, but I do not think her feelings in the matter need be considered."[97]

The ferment among the Indus tribes boiled over. Mulk Aman, ex-Raja of Yasin, overran whole of Yasin.[98] Chitral too was in danger of an attack from Dir in the Indus valley. Embarrassed on account of the presence of the mission in the region, the Mehtar became anxious for Lockhart's departure. Another fall out of the Lockhart mission was the murder of Raja Ghazan Khan by his son and successor, Safdar Ali Khan, sometime in August 1886.[99] Intimation about the murder and succession and, more importantly, of the "intimate friendship" between Hunza and Nagar, the new Raja and Jafr Khan of Nagar, separately conveyed to the Governor of Gilgit. Safdar Ali promised to "present ourselves jointly in the service of the Sarkar" (Maharaja). Jafr Khan explained, "we will now send our vakils jointly to kiss the feet of the Sarkar," a reference to the despatch of tribute.[100] Quite evidently Safdar Ali, strongly differed with his father' letting Lockhart into Hunza. The Foreign Department acknowledged, "...that Safdar Ali Khan is well disposed towards the Darbar and that Hunza and Nagar are apparently reconciled..."[101] after their long feud. Both these shifts in Hunza's policy increasingly became evident in the following years.

Hunza having become tributary to China was first noticed in the official Peking Gazette of only 3rd March 1885, just before Raja Ghazan Khan confided in Lockhart. Based on a Chinese official report from the Taotai, civil governor, of Kashgar, a memorial from the governor of the Chinese Turkistan was published in the Gazette of 13th November 1886. It once again claimed that "the head of the Kanchuti State to the south of Selekuerh had presented his annual tribute offering of an ounce and a half of gold dust and had been given in return two pieces of satin in the name of the Emperor of China."[102] The British Minister in Peking, Sir John Walsham, identified K'anchut with Kanjut and Serekurerh with Sirikul but did not lend much credence to the report. The Gazette notice is, however, significant in another way. The Chinese, by virtue of this report, officially recognised that territories south of Sirikul, notably Taghdumbash Pamir, comprised Hunza. Also, China, for the first time claimed suzerainty over Hunza in only 1885. Therefore, the Chinese claim was as then a recent event, contrary to British obfuscation, which pushed it back to mid-18th century. A little earlier than the Peking Gazette notice, the Journal de St. Petersburg, 3-15th September 1886, reported the arrival in Hunza of the Russian explorer, Lieutenant Grombtchevsky.

The affairs with regard to the Mehtar of Chitral were no less curiouser. The Amir stepped up pressure on Aman-ul-Mulk, seeking his submission and, as a threat, let loose his rebellius brother, Sher Afzal, in the adjoining Afghan province of Badakshan. At the same time Afghan troops were appointed to be sent against Kafiristan over which Chitral claimed sway. An expedition into Kafiristan, the Mehtar wailed, virtually meant an expedition to Chitral, so closely are the two geographically linked.[103] To the Maharaja, Aman-ul-Mulk repeated the request that a strong garrison be posted to Sher Kila on the border of Yasin and the Gilgit garrison strengthened to keep off the Afghans from Chitral.[104]

References

1. Undated. Foreign. Secret. No. 83 of August 1875.
2. Undated. Foreign. Secret. No. 36 of July 1877.
3. 15th November 1876. Foreign. Secret. No. 37 of July 1877.
4. *Ibid.*
5. Undated. Foreign. Secret. No. 42 of July 1877.
6. Undated. Foreign. Secret. No. 36 of July 1877.
7. Undated. Foreign. Secret. No. 43 of July 1877.
8. Undated. Foreign. Secret. No. 36 of July 1877.
9. 17th-18th November 1876. Foreign. Secret. No. 38 of July 1877.
10. *Ibid.*
11. 26th November 1876. Foreign. Secret. No. 39 of July 1877.
12. 22nd December 1876. Foreign. Secret. No. 40 of July 1877.
13. 28th March 1877. Foreign. Secret. No. 51 of July 1877.
14. 30th March 1877. Foreign. Secret. No. 49 of July 1877.
15. Secret despatch to the Secretary of State for India. 11th June 1877, No. 17 of 1877.
16. 12th June 1877. Foreign. Secret. No. KWI. 60-79 of November 1877.
17. 6th July 1877. Foreign. Secret. No. 69 of November 1877.
18. 7th July 1877. Foreign. Secret. No. 70 of November 1877.
19. 2nd August 1877. Foreign. Secret. No. 73 of November 1877.
20. 19th August 1877. Foreign. Secret. No. KW. 4-60-79 of November 1877.
21. 29th August 1877. Foreign. Secret. No. 76 of November 1877.
22. 22nd September 1877. Foreign. Secret. No. 1 of February 1878.
23. Undated. Foreign. Secret. No. 80 of July 1878.
24. Undated. Foreign. Secret. F. No. 409 of September 1892.
25. 12th April 1878. Foreign. Secret. No. 80 of July 1878.

26. 13th April 1878. Foreign. Secret. No. 80 of July 1878.
27. 13th April 1878. Foreign. Secret. No. KW. 1-35-37 of March 1879.
28. 21st to 28th April 1878. Foreign. Secret. No. 85 of July 1878.
29. Undated. Foreign. Secret. No. 85 of July 1878.
30. 24th April 1878. Foreign. Secret. No. 85 of July 1878.
31. Undated. Foreign. Secret. No. 89 of July 1879.
32. 4th to 13th May 1878. Foreign. Secret. No. 89 of July 1878.
33. 8th May 1878. Foreign. Secret. No. KW. 1-35-37 of March 1879.
34. 21st to 28th May 1878. Foreign. Secret. No. 92 of July 1878.
35. 23rd May 1878. Foreign. Secret. No. KW. 1-35-37 of March 1879.
36. *Ibid.*
37. 12th June 1878. Foreign. Secret. No. KW. 1-35-37 of March 1879.
38. *Ibid.*
39. *Ibid.*
40. *Ibid.*
41. A Brief Sketch of the English Dominions in Asia. By M. Venukof. Tr. F.C. Daukes. Simla. 1876, p. 4.
42. 22nd July 1878. Foreign. Secret. No. KW-2-35-37 of March 1879.
43. 22nd July 1878. Foreign. Secret. No. KW-2-35-37 of March 1879.
44. 20th August 1878. Foreign. Secret. No. KW-2-35-37 of March 1879.
45. 20th August 1878. Foreign. Secret. No. KW-2-35-37 of March 1879.
46. Secret despatch to the Secretary of State for India No. 49 of 28th February 1879.
47. 15th May 1879. Foreign. Secret. No. KW-1-39 of January 1880.
48. May to August 1880. Foreign. Secret. No. 133 of January 1881.
49. A Memoir on The Indian Surveys, 1875-1890. By Charles Black. Printed and published by Secretary of State for India. London. 1891, p. 144.
50. 31st March 1881. Foreign. Secret. No. KW-314-399 of July 1881.
51. 1st-15th October 1881. Foreign. Pol. A. No. 9 of February 1882.
52. Ney Elias-Explorer and Envoy Extraordinary in High Asia. By Gerald Morgan, p. 135.
53. Undated. Gen. and Pol. File No. 170/69A. Year 1909. (Jammu Archives).
54. Undated (1882) Foreign. A. Pol. E. No. 193 of September 1882.
55. 26th January 1883. Foreign. Secret. E. No. 64 of March 1883.
56. 28th January 1883. Foreign. Secret. E. No. 164 of August 1883.
57. 12th September 1883. Foreign. Secret E. No. 160. of December 1883.
58. Undated. Foreign. Secret E. No. 174 of December, 1883.
59. 18th September 1883. Foreign. Secret. E. No. 173 of December 1883.
60. 23rd September 1883. Foreign. Secret. E. No. 168 of December 1883.
61. 13th November 1883. Foreign. Secret. E. No. 169 of March 1884.
62. 16th November 1883. Foreign. Secret. E. No. 170-A of March 1884.
63. 16th November 1883. Foreign. Secret. E. No. 171 of March 1884.
64. 16th November 1883. Foreign. Secret. E. No. 172 of March 1884.

65. 16th November 1883. Foreign. Secret. E. No. 173 of March 1884.
66. 16th November 1883. Foreign. Secret. E. No. 177 of March 1884.
67. 16th November 1883. Foreign. Secret. E. No. 179 of March 1884.
68. 8th August 1884. Foreign. Secret. F. No. 62 of November 1884.
69. 6th March 1885. Foreign. Secret. F. No. KW-570B-639 of July 1885.
70. 9th March 1885. Foreign. Secret. F. No. KW-570B-639 of July 1885.
71. 10th March 1885. Foreign. Secret F. No. 570 of July 1885.
72. 18th March 1885. Foreign. Secret F. No. 571 of July 1885.
73. 16th May 1885. Foreign. Secret F. No. 15 of August 1885.
74. 17th May 1885. Foreign. Secret F. No. KW-12-81 of August 1885.
75. 18th May 1885. Foreign. Secret F. No. KW-12-81 of August 1885.
76. 18th May 1885. Foreign. Secret F. No. 591 of July 1885.
77. 26th May 1885. Foreign. Secret F. No. 597 of July 1885.
78. 26th July 1885. Foreign. Secret F. No. 12 of November 1885.
79. 21st August 1885. Foreign. Secret F. No. KW-775-795 of October 1885.
80. 22nd August 1885. Foreign. Secret F. No. KW-775-795 of October 1885.
81. 5th September 1885. Foreign. Secret F. No. 12 of December 1885.
82. 14th September 1885. Foreign. Secret F. No. 380 of March 1886.
83. 1st October 1885. Foreign. Secret. F. No. 391 of March 1886. Also 21st January 1886. Foreign Sec. F. N. KW. 379-522 of March 1886.
84. 13th November 1885. Foreign. Secret F. No. 194 of June 1886.
85. 17th November 1885. Foreign. Secret F. No. 417 of March 1886.
86. 27th January 1886. Foreign. Secret F. No. KW-379-522 of March 1886.
87. 27th February 1886. Foreign. Secret F. No. 213 of May 1886.
88. 3rd March 1886. Foreign. Secret F. No. 208 of July 1886.
89. *Ibid.*
90. 8th March 1886. Foreign. Secret F. No. 460 of July 1886.
91. *Ibid.*
92. 24th April 1886. Foreign. Secret F. No. 455 of July 1886.
93. *Ibid.*
94. 30th April 1886. Foreign. Secret F. No. 461 of July 1886.
95. 15th May 1886. Foreign. Secret F. No. KW-450-551 of July 1886.
96. 29th May 1886. Foreign. Secret F. No. KW-115-118 of January 1888.
97. 13th June 1886. Foreign. Secret F. No. KW-115-118 of January 1888.
98. 7th July 1886. Foreign. Secret F. No. 167 of September 1886.
99. Undated. Foreign. Secret F. No. 1051 of October 1886.
100. Undated. Foreign. Secret F. No. 1053 of October 1886.
101. 13th August 1886. Foreign. Secret. F. No. KW-1-987-1056 of October 1886.
102. 22nd November 1886. Foreign. Secret. F. No. 150 of February 1887.
103. 26th February 1887. Foreign. Secret. F. No. 585 of June 1887.
104. 12th March 1887. Foreign. Secret. F. No. 640 of June 1887.

Chapter 7
Contending British, Russian, Chinese Interests

Elias' Kashgar mission turned out to be one to determine, rather than to find out, the nationality of the Pamirs. By mid-1880s Russia was seen by England set to annex them and ride down the Hindu Kush to threaten the British empire in India. The countries opening on the Pamirs then were Afghanistan through Badakshan, Wakhan and Shighnan, Russia along Kokand and China over nominally British allotted Hunza Pamirs of the Taghdumbash and Little Pamir. The Russians had preceded Elias in the Pamirs by two years having explored them under Dr. Regel in 1883. Russian exploration and mapping Elias found to be "very correct." Thus the frontier between the country claimed by the Chinese on the one hand, and Shighnan and Wakhan on the other, Elias found "nearly correctly given there as Aksu-Murghabi." The upper section of the Murghabi down nearly to the Akbaital confluence was declared by Elias to "constitute the boundary between Wakhan and the Chinese territory." Even this frontier Elias did not consider "natural", not because it was a bad boundary but because it left a strip of "unowned land," or the "gap," some 60 miles in width, between the Afghan and Chinese territory. "Any such strip would lead directly towards the passes in Chitral" and, Elias feared, "might be occupied at any time by Bokhara or some of the family of the Badakshi Mirs in Russian interest." The existence of the "gap," now established by Elias, became the decisive factor for redrawing the northern boundary in Kashmir. By Afghanistan and China closing up from the Russian frontier to the north to the Chitral boundary to the south, Elias suggested, "all chances of...a wedge being driven in, would be obviated."[1] Enquiries made locally both Elias pointed out that the Russian boundary lay over the Kizil Art pass on the range running east and west. Such a boundary excluded by Karakul and Kizil Jik areas from

Russia. The region was too far to the north from the heads of Chitral passes to affect their safety and, as long as a band of conterminuous Afghan and Chinese territory was stretched across farther to the south, the matter was not one of great importance. The Chinese practically making upper Oxus Murghabi as their frontier was just where such a band of neutral territory was most required by the British. His own opinion Elias ventured to offer : "...it is a situation that should be taken advantage of by our Government, and the Afghans should be encouraged, with out delay, to take formal possession of the left bank of the Murghabi from about the Kara-su confluence upwards[2]." Such an act would have obliged the Chinese to do the same on their side. The point north of the Murghabi, where this frontier line should begin, and the point on the Hunza side where it might end, Elias argued, could be settled afterwards on the spot. This manipulation of the boundary Elias did not consider "a great affair" and felt it could best be settled"if done perfectly quietly and without ostentation." No expensive boundary commission and no elaborate survey would be needed, he argued and remarked, "if it can be accomplished, Russia and Russian partisans will be shut out from the passes leading to Kashmir as long as Afghanistan and China remain friendly to England." To Sir West Ridgeway, then heading the Afghan boundary commission, Elias conveyed the caution if the Afghans did not advance, "the Russians would be sure to step in and take the 'non-Chinese Pamirs' up to the head of the Baroghil pass."[3] Yet when Elias had left Yarkand for the Pamirs, he had found the Chinese authority existed only up to Ighiz Yar border village of Yangi Hissar district of Kashgaria. Nor did he come across any evidence of a Chinese outpost at Rangkul as the Yarkand Amban had claimed to Elias. The connection of the Rangkul Kirghiz, he found, was of the "loosest description."[4]

Elias' explorations evoked the Viceroy's "approval and satisfaction." His suggestion that the Afghans should push forward to the Murghabi to meet the "Chinese boundary" did not, however, find immediate favour at Calcutta. Having in the past urged the Amir to withdraw from the trans-Oxus Wakhan and Shighnan, it would have appeared inconsistent to have advised him to advance. But the matter was not dropped and the gap was, thereafter, to be closed "in one way or another,"[5] including Elias' way. The Afghans themselves were dissatisfied with "the weakness and dangerous nature of the frontier as formed by the river Oxus."[6] The frontier claimed by the Amir ran to the north of Roshan and the Murghabi river along with Aksu to the Nezatash pass[7] on the Sirikul chain. That this boundary was claimed with implied British support is evident in

Ridgeway's effort to limit the Chinese to the east of the Nezatash pass[8]. Part, at least, of this country, that between the Mughabi and Karakul watershed, was also claimed by Bokhara[9]. Elias' settlement of the Afghan-Chinese boundary was virtually the award of the Pamir Commission a decade later, in 1895.

How was the Afghan boundary to the north to be shown in a new map then under preparation at the instance of the Viceroy and the President of the Royal Geographical Society? Dufferin desired the map to contain bulk of the topographical information lately acquired in Chitral and in the course of the delimitation of the north western boundary of Afghanistan. The map, under preparation, showed Jammu and Kashmir, for the first time, within the British empire. The decision of Colonel Thuillier of the Survey of India on Kashmir was approved by W.J. Cunningham, acting Foreign Secretary, and later by Mortimer Durand. On the upper Oxus the boundary recognised by England and Russia was the one described in the agreement of 1872-1873. This boundary ended at Sirikul Lake and was undefined eastward in Little Pamir and Aksu valley, largely the "gap." The British refused to admit Hunza claim to them but contested that Afghanistan had no rights east of the lake. These rights, they believed, were only indefinite[10]. Another uncertainly related to the inclusion of Chitral, Yasin and Mastuj, all tributaries of Jammu and Kashmir, within the British empire their future status was, presumably, linked to the final contours of the northern boundary. Mortimer Durand was agreeable to the inclusion of Gilgit, which he thus recognised as Kashmir territory, but left out its feudatories[11]. The proof map, as circulated within the Foreign and Military Departments, showed the northern boundary ending in the Indus, four or five miles south of Gor, leaving the limits of Gilgit undefined[12]. No unanimity of views would, therefore, appear to have existed within the two Departments, or with the Survey of India, on the issue of the northern boundary or, precisely, on the upper Oxus and Gilgit–the "gap." From the Quarter Master General's office or, rather, the Military Intelligence wing, Colonel M.S. Bell urged any new map of Afghanistan should "truthfully show present boundaries settled by commissioners; and where not so settled revised boundaries on the best information obtainable by those qualified to give..." Of these qualified persons Colonel Bell cited Elias for the upper Oxus, General Lockhart on Kashmir (Gilgit) and Residents in Kashmir and Leh between Kashmir (Ladakh) and China. For instance, Bell went on :

> "I should say that the evidence would give some authority for drawing Kashmir's boundary with China

> to the north of that shown on the (Thuillier's) map, i.e., to the north of Aktagh along the Kilian Rud or the ridge, (Kuen Lun) or watershed to the north of it. Also Russian frontier towards the Pamir should be shown as roughly determined by evidence of Mr. Ney Elias. The boundaries should, in my opinion, distinctly indicate those that we think we or our dependencies are entitled to. Anything vague will certainly lead to difficulties in the future."[13]

Bell's view was distinctly opposed to that of the Foreign and Military Departments. He reveals where actually the northern boundary of, at least, Ladakh lay-over the Kuen Lun, by the Walaghat (Sanju), Kilian and Kukyar and beyond to Sirikul, though over the latter he erroneously relied on Elias. In the new map, the boundary in the upper Oxus, i.e., east of Sirikul lake, was to be shown, as in the 1883 map, indefinite. But the boundary was not to end indefinitely on reaching the Indus near Gor. It was to be prolonged "around the south, west and north of Gilgit till it returns to the longitude 75^0," where the map ended, thus including within the British border Gilgit, but not the feudatory States of Jammu and Kashmir-Hunza. Yasin and Chitral[14]. But the Quarter Master General's office was not satisfied. From a military point of view it sought the inclusion of the Jammu and Kashmir tributaries within the British boundaries[15].

Take over of Gilgit, earlier turned down, was soon, though not surprisingly, reopened. Discussions for months, including with military authorities, left Mortimer Durand no better enlightened. On the one hand there was no doubt from a military point of view that England should hold the country lying under the northern end of the Hindu Kush, for one reason Russia before long would be busy at this extremity next to Afghanistan and, in the event of war or confusion, would cause trouble by establishing herself, or her influence, in Chitral. The British had, therefore, to be prepared before hand. Chitral and the tribes surrounding it needed to be brought under control. Some British military force was seen necessary in the neighbourhood to prevent any demonstration such as Russians would find it easy and profitable to make if the field were clear. It was also considered useful to known what was going on in the direction of Wakhan and Shignan, across the Chitral passes, to which British military authorities attached considerable importance. On the other hand there was a great deal to be said against establishment of British officers beyond the Kashmir border. The posting of Biddulph had involved the British in disputes with small principalities about Gilgit. He was unable to procure much information or establish British political influence. At such a distance, as of Gilgit from British India, he could not be protected without great expense and other inconvenience, the Kashmir Darbar, which had always secretly resented his presence, had shown "no great disposition or capacity" to protect him. Eventually he was placed in a dangerous and undignified position by a tribal rising and was withdrawn.

Yet all these objections appeared to the British to be no objections at all. The issue really was if the British pushed forward in Gilgit, they would have to reverse the policy followed for the past decade, terminate the Maharaja-Mehtar agreement of 1877, oust Kashmir influence altogether, assume practical control of the relations of Jammu and Kashmir with the neighbouring States, and hold power to deal with populations in the region so as to watch and defend this strategic frontier. The Darbar would certainly not like that and there was bound to be some difficulty in securing their cooperation. Again such a forward thrust would arouse the jealousy of the Amir who had shown himself sensitive about British dealings with Chitral. Troublesome complications could no less arise, in pursuit of such a policy, with regard to Chinese "claims" over Hunza. The proposal was not one which British Indian Government could, therefore, accept with unmixed satisfaction. It would cost money and it could land the British Indian Government in embarrassment. Nevertheless even Mortimer Durand, contrary to his earlier view, was inclined to the opinion that on the whole it was better to face the risk and expense and start at least, to re-establish the British Political Agency in Gilgit" this time on a really strong footing." That embarrassment and risk visualised was clearly in regard to Jammu and Kashmir is evident in Mortimer Durand's remark on the altered Anglo-Dogra relations :

> "We have put an end to the assumption of independence which characterised the rule of the late chief (Ranbir Singh), and we have to deal with a weak and timid ruler whom I believe we shall be able to control and carry with us. It will, I think, be possible to bring our influence to bear upon him in such a manner that we shall get a good and trustworthy Kashmir force in Gilgit, and that in other respects he and his officials will cooperate with usufficiently for practical purposes."[16]

That Mortimer Durand's optimism was altogether misplaced is a future development. Having recommended establishment of the British Agency in Gilgit, Mortimer Durand had other suggestions to make. No British troops were to be sent up to Gilgit, as proposed by Lockhart, but the Maharaja's offer to contribute to Imperial defence was to be accepted and he was to be asked to provide a Dogra regiment to be trained and armed by the British with the latest contemporary weapons. This regiment was to be stationed at Gilgit and to be commanded practically by the British Agent, Gilgit. A corps of Mohammadans was to be raised from the neighbouring tribes as recommended by Lockhart. The Agent in Gilgit was not directly to take over management of Gilgit but it was considered inevitable he should exert complete control over the Gilgit governor. To this line of approach the first Resident in Kashmir, Sir Oliver St. John, was opposed. Mortimer Durand alludes to this, so also Sir Aukland Colvin, Member, Viceroy's Council. The proposal was held over in the face of spirited opposition in the Viceroy's Council by Sir Aukland Colvin and C.P. Irwin, another member. Irwin saw no ground for apprehending any serious attack upon India through the country between Bamian pass and Baltisan. To start the Agency, Irwin opined, would alienate the Kashmir Darbar[17]. Sir Aukland relied on Sir Oliver St. John's view that the goodwill of Kashmir was not likely to be secured by the arbitrary termination of the agreement entered into in 1877 between the Government of India and the Maharaja and by ousting of the latter from his position vis-a-vis his subordinate, Chitral[18]. That opposition to the Gilgit Agency was truly formidable is also obvious from the circumstantial evidence of Borrow modifying his memo on the strategical aspects of Chitral and the Hindu Kush region with Lockhart's concurrence. His "further insight into the Dard character" made him doubtful about value of the corps of Guides proposed to be locally raised. "The Scheme", he noted, evidently in the light of attack on it, "would perhaps, deeply incense the Kashmir Darbar" and considering it had given ready assistance to the Lockhart mission, "we owe it some consideration in his matter." No less was Barrow convinced, after what he had seen of Kashmir troops at Jammu and elsewhere, "that a body of picked men from that army would be very efficient and valuable force if properly trained." He, therefore, proposed that the force in Gilgit" should remain a Kashmiri one."[19] But Barrow stuck to the mission recommendation that the British Agent should hold both military and civil charge of Gilgit.

The Viceroy's Council having undergone a marked change in its composition, once again Mortimer Durand raised the Gilgit issue in a memo, now in a wider perspective, "the present situation in Central Asia."

The same forward policy that he had earlier commended in relation to Gilgit, he now ventured to suggest, should be followed with regard to the mountain belt of independent territory, which stretched along the British frontier from the most northerly passes of the Hindu Kush to Baluchistan. In Gilgit he wished to start the Agency and have there under an English officer, or more than one, a good corps of Dogras raised from Kashmir with some levies raised from the small Mohammadan chiefships of the neighbourhood, regardless of the susceptibilities of Jammu and Kashmir. From Gilgit further efforts could be made to gain the friendship of the Kafirs, who held "an important position" and were claimed to be "well disposed," and southward, of the Khans of Dir, Bajaur, Swat and Buner. Eventually, Mortimer Durand hoped, thedirect route to Chitral via Dir would be opened. This was the shortest road from British territories to Chitral which might be required to support the Mehtar in resisting a Russian demonstration[20]. The precise position of the British Agent in relation to the subordinate chiefships and their "nominal suzerain Kashmir" was a somewhat difficult point. But Mortimer Durand had "little doubt that in the present temper of the Kashmir Darbar," he could, if authorised, arrange through Mr. Plowden (Resident), some fairly satisfactory scheme."[21] A month later, Lord Dufferin sanctioned the scheme directing "steps can now be taken to carry the proposed arrangements into effect."[22] The virtual annexation of Gilgit, the Viceroy was "anxious", should be brought about, "if possible, with the consent and cooperation of the Kashmir Darbar..."[23] Lord Dufferin must have had basis for his anxiety.

Far from consenting to the annexation of Gilgit the Maharaja set himself on a collision course with the British. The Maharaja's garrisons were about early January 1888, ejected from the forts of Chaport and Chalt on the boundary between Gilgit and Hunza and Nagar. Raja Jafr Khan justified the ejection of the garrisons on the ground of "suspicions" against Kashmir troops[24]. The expulsion was a smooth affair, conducted in a "friendly manner," for not a shot was fired for offensive or defensive purposes, which made the British suspicious. The ejected troops were "safely" sent away, communications from Nagar were not discontinued nor were Hunza-Nagar troops masse on the boundary[25]. The Chaprot disturbance was in reaction to the British forward thrust towards Gilgit but to the Resident it appeared to be "a serious collapse of the Darbar policy" and testified to the "inefficiency and weakness of its frontier administration..." He questioned whether the conclusion accepted by the Government of India for the protection of the northwest frontier of

Kashmir could be carried into effect except by arrangements which were complete in themselves and went on to suggest :

> "As in Baluchistan the Imperial Government has found it necessary to supersede the Khan of Kalat in carrying out the Imperial scheme of frontier defence in that direction, so also in the Gilgit direction, it will be necessary, while making use of the name of the Kashmir Darbar, to take care that the actual working of the scheme is in all essentials British."[26]

Even further Plowden went. He suggested stationing British troops in Kashmir and proposed Political Agent replacing the governor of Gilgit. What Plowden euphemistically called supersession of the Khan of Kalat was deposition. Evidently the decision to establish Gilgit Agency had made no headway, one reason for the Viceroy's anxiety. Plowden, as he elsewhere revealed, had broached the Gilgit scheme to the Maharaja and the State Council, which the Resident had "helped" to reconstitute. It is safe to conjecture that, while the reconstituted Council fell in line with his views, the Maharaja himself, however, timid and effete he was, viewed the scheme as amounting to annexation of Gilgit which he was asked to countenance. He, instead, offered to join the Imperial defence scheme. The extraordinary recommendations of Plowden outwardly elicited no support in the Foreign Department, being, perhaps, prematurely made. Crawford did not "see any necessity for openly superseding the Darbar's authority in Gilgit."[27] Mortimer Durand concurred arguing with the Viceroy that British interference ought to be limited to the organisation of a "respectable military force in Gilgit." That far he was confident to carry the Darbar along. But were Gilgit annexed or the political suzerainty of Kashmir over the petty principalities of the neighbourhood put an end to, and, above all, "British troops put into Kashmir just now" we shall run a risk of turning the Darbar against us."[28] As a first step, he suggested sending up temporarily and quietly a selected military officer who should, with the consent and assistance of the Darbar, visit Gilgit and see exactly how things were going on with special reference to the rising on the part of Hunza and Nagar. Lord Dufferin agreed.

The Chinese factor soon enough surfaced over Hunza, Chaprot providing the occasion. First Safdar Ali claimed that a Chinese military officer of Kashgar had visited him[29]. The disclosure would appear to have been made to impress the Gilgit governor with the likely involvement of the Chinese in Chaprot. Then the Tsungli Yamen* complained to the British Minister at Beijing that Yin-ti (Kashmir) tribe within the jurisdiction of Wen-tu-ssu-tan (Hindustan) mustering a full force entered the territory of K'anchuti with the design to seize the district K'e-p'u-lo-to (Chaprot). As per the report of the governor of Chinese Turkistan, it was "*some years* since Kanjut tendered its allegiance to China," the Tsungli Yamen sought to know the reason which led to the invasion[30]. No extravagant claim was made on Hunza's vassalage which was limited to "some years." The Foreign Department too gave up obfuscation. It was pointed out it were Hunza and Nagar that had invaded Chaprot, and that both were regarded as "under the suzerainty of Kashmir though this had not been officially recognised by the Government of India under any arrangement with the Darbar."[31] Safdar Ali Khan of Hunza had, it was recalled, in an undated letter of about September 1886, written to Gilgit authorities, after the murder of his father and his own succession, "what may be regarded as a complete submission to Kashmir." This was a belated British recognition of Kashmir's suzerainty over Hunza.

Mortimer Durand viewed the complaint as "attempted interference of China," an eventuality which he had apprehended and which "is a serious complication." The British had only themselves to blame for it. The late Hunza chief, Ghazan Khan, was accused of double dealing, acknowledging Chinese suzerainty while at the same time professing allegiance to Kashmir. To the Viceroy the importance of Hunza was thus underscored by Mortimer Durand :

> "From it Chinese Turkistan can be reached by a pass or passes, which we have not explored, and immediately to the north, across the Kilik pass, lies the "gap" between Afghanistan and China. By pushing through this "gap" in however insignificant numbers, or by becoming the successors of the Chinese in Kashgar....,the Russian may at any time acquire very inconvenient rights or claims over Hunza..."[32]

Precisely because of these factors had the British in the past steadfastly refused to recognised Jammu and Kashmir's rights over Hunza. But in the changed Anglo-Dogra equation, Mortimer Durand wished Kashmir to break into Hunza and reduce it to complete submission, a proposition which Jammu and Kashmir had often made in the past only to be rejected. While the British had for long sought to fully subdue Hunza, the Chinese connection with it, which they had themselves

* Chinese Foreign Officer.

assiduously cultivated in Imperial interests, had never been critically reviewed. But given the factors involved in shaping the boundary to the north, it was evidently, time to altogether eliminate Chinese influence in Hunza, south of the Hindu Kush. Unambiguously China was to be told that British rights to deal with Hunza as they pleased would be maintained and they would not be hampered by any nominal allegiance tendered to her. Lord Dufferin desired the "whole case" to be privately put before the British Minister at Beijing[33]. The British version of the events at Chaprot was verbally detailed to Tsungli Yamen on 16th June 1888 and later in writing by Sir John Walsham. It was explained Chaprot was not part of Hunza territory but belonged to Jammu and Kashmir. Notices, of Hunza paying tribute of one ounce and a half of gold annually, had appeared in the Peking Gazette of 3rd May 1885 (earlier this date is mentioned as 3rd March 1885), 13th of November 1886, and 27th September 1887. On that ground the governor of Chinese Turkistan spoke of Kanjut owing allegiance to China. Whatever the foundation for the claim, Chinese Government was informed "that the chief of Kanjut has also long been feudatory of Kashmir, receiving a yearly pension and paying tribute."[34] Surely a petty border chief could not justifiably be permitted to create disturbances on Indian soil with impunity and in reliance on his pretension to be tributary State of the Chinese Empire.

Having clarified to China the political status of Hunza, Lord Dufferin hastened to present a facet of the boundary issue to the Secretary of State for India, "We cannot recognise Chinese rights in Hunza." It was imperative, the Viceroy wrote, that "in this quarter we should keep the Chinese and every other power to the north of the barrier formed by the line of the Himalayas and Hindu Kush... we must in practice maintain our right to deal with Hunza direct, notwithstanding its nominal suzerainty to China."[35] For this policy Her Majesty's Government's approval was sought. It confirmed British resolve to pull back India's northern boundary to the Himalaya-Hindu Kush line and, more than that, visualised an end to a virtual dual Anglo-Chinese control over Hunza south of the Hindu Kush, effecting its virtual partition. With the Viceroy's decision the Secretary of State for India, Lord Cross, was fully in accord. The "impolicy of permitting any foreign power to gain a footing on the southern slopes of the Hindu Kush" was duly brought to the notice of the British Foreign Secretary, Lord Salisbury.[36] But such a footing China had, by virtue of her British fostered suzerainty over Hunza, already gained.

British view of the Hindu Kush States turned out to be opposite of the Dogras. The Maharajas gave precedence to Nagar for local advantage to gain access to Hunza and leash it. Captain A. Durand, the officer selected to report on Gilgit, found Hunza from its position and "by reason of its claim to be independent of Kashmir and to be a feudatory of China of far greater importance," than Nagar. Indeed it was second only to Chitral in importance.[37] The other importance Captain Durand noticed of Hunza was geo-political, the roads that led from Gircha to Sirikul and Yarkand, by the Khanjerab, Kilik and the Irshad pass to Wakhan, by the Chiking pass to the Ishkoman valley, and finally the road from Hunza by Chalt to Gilgit. Curiously, while the British had repeatedly expressed fears of Russia becoming active on the north west extremity of Kashmir-Afganistan, no mention is made by Captain Durand of the road from Hunza via Mintaka, Paik pass on Sirikul ridge, to Tashkurghan and Kashgar, a potential invasion route to Russian territories that influenced England on the boundary issue. To the "gap" between Lake Victoria and Aktash, the first Chinese post, lying west of Tashkurghan, that gave access to Hunza, attention was drawn to. That, the Foreign Department was urged, should be remedied at once, otherwise "...Russia will certainly in time push down through this "gap" to the frontier of Hunza and be in an excellent position for making her influence felt." For the realisation of British policy objectives in Gilgit, establishment of the Gilgit Agency was favoured by Captain Durand, the British Agent handling relations with Kashmir's tributary States through the medium of the Resident in consultation with the Maharaja, the local Governor and the Kashmir Government being thus side stepped. The Kashmir troops were to be reorganised and 1200 regular infantry, 100 garrison artillery, I screw battery and 500 irregular troops posted to Gilgit with four British officers, including the Agent and a doctor seconded to them. The Resident, Lt. Colonel R.P. Nisbet, fully agreed with these recommendations of Captain Durand, further suggesting that the Agent should be conferred the post of Gilgit governor by the Maharaja.[38] The British certainly were bent on taking over Gilgit by fair or foul means. Nisbet confided in Sir Mortimer Durand that he had in his hands "a batch of 34 letters in Maharaja's own handwriting..."[39] These showed "that His Highness has been intriguing with Russia and is guilty of other treasonable acts."[40] Pratap Singh was deposed in March 1889, the supposed grounds for deposition were the forgeries, the Maharaja's "offer" to abdicate and "misgovernment."[41] To the Secretary of State establishment of the Gilgit Agency was justified on the ground of "completely changed" state of affairs in Kashmir following the deposition of the Maharaja. With the Maharaja out of the way, the State Council, nominally headed by Pratap Singh's youngest brother, Raja Amar Singh, accepted the British Agency at Gilgit, and proposed to bear the entire cost of the Gilgit scheme.[42]

Hunza raid on the Leh-Yarkand trade line in 1888, induced the British to explore the Shangshal pass over the Hindu Kush. It was from Shangshal that caravan looting was usually launched by the Kanjutis. The exploration was to be undertaken by Captain F.E. Younghusband, via Shahidulla where the Kanjutis had looted the local Kirghiz. Captain, soon to be Lieutenant Colonel, Durand, as British Political Agent at Gilgit, was to offer increased subsidies of Rs. 2000 each per annum to Hunza and Nagar if raiding by Hunza in the Shangshal valley and elsewhere stopped.[43] Nagar had no understanding whatever with Russia or China but that was not true about Hunza[44]. Raja Safdar Ali was said by Captain Durand to have agreed to British demand–to stop raids on the Leh-Yarkand highway, permit British officers to freely transit through Hunza, exclude Russians from his territories and stop Chinese interference[45]. But the British Agent was not convinced. Safdar Ali might "outwardly" conform on the issues raised for the sake of increased subsidy. "From Captain Durand's official communication to the Resident in Kashmir, it is evident that Safdar Ali had only a "connection" with China which he was agreeable to "sever."[46] Interestingly, during his long, angry exchange with the Agent, Safdar Ali claimed to have a treaty with Russia but made no mention of China. The treaty was nothing more than a letter from the Russian explorer, Captain Grombtchevsky seeking permission to visit Hunza in 1888, and promising a Russian subsidy. Safdar Ali was then in great dread of Kashmir. The Maharaja, spurred by the British, had massed his troops for recapture of Chaprot. When Younghusband met him in the Yarkand valley in October 1889, Grombtchevsky showed him letters from Safdar Ali inviting him to Hunza[47]. Younghusband saw in the Shangshal valley a manned military post[48]. To Younghusband Safdar Ali justified his raids on the Leh-Yarkand road on the ground that profits from them were "part of his revenue."[49] If the British wished him to stop the raids, Safdar Ali sought an increase in his subsidy. Renewal of raids by Hunza suggests that the Chinese had suspended the payment of subsidy, perhaps, as a mark of displeasure[50] to which Grombtchevsky later alluded to Sir Donald Mackenzie Wallace, Viceroy's Secretary.

The visits by Captain Durand to Hunza and Younghusband to Yarkand valley also yielded two different accounts of the limits of Hunza. Ahmed Ali, a surveyor, who accompanied Captain Durand, described Hunza to be bounded to the north by the lofty, snow-clad "Barbar range,"[51] or the Hindu Kush. Ahmed Ali divided Hunza into two parts, one part starting from the Hunza river in the south, near Gilgit, to Attabad and Mayun and the second thence onward to the Kilik pass over the Hindu Kush. The first he named Hunza district and the second Gujal. This division, without doubt, is ethnographic, Gujal was then inhabited by Wakhis or people of Wakhan origin. Another account of Hunza's limits can be gleaned from the statement made by Zira Bai, a Kirghiz of Shahidulla, in connection with Younghusband's visit to Shangshal. From her statement, it is clear that there was "awal" (first) Kanjut starting from the Hunza river near Gilgit[52]. "Awal" Hunza, perhaps, stretched to the Hindu Kush, beyond which to the north was "doam" (second) Hunza, comprising the Taghdumbash Pamir, Sirikul and Raskam part of the Yarkand valley where the Kirghiz lived in large numbers. Safdar Ali himself referred to the Hindu Kush passes, Kilik, Mintaka, and Shangshal, as "upper passes."[53] Had these been the limit of his chiefship the reference to them would have been distinctly different. Captain Durand had intended to explore "the Saltoro pass. Saltoro was finally explored by Younghusband. Younghusband's entry into "awal" Hunza by the Mintaka pass, unsuspected to exist by the Lockhart mission, opened the possibility of a lightly equipped Russian force marching over it to the south.

Younghusband's exploration was not limited to Saltoro pass but also covered the mountain tract between the Karakoram in Ladakh and Shangshal in Hunza. He described it as an "immense glacier region." Consequently both the Muztagh and Saltoro were impracticable for all military purposes. West of these glaciers upto the Kilik pass routes led to the Hunza river valley, by the Shangshal, Khanjerab and Mintaka. Younghusband identified three roads for a possible Russian attack on Gilgit, (1) from the Russian frontier near the Tuyuksu pass, by the valley of the Aksu river and Wakhan to the Kilik pass, (2) over the Paik pass on the Taghdumbash Pamir, (3) a difficult line from Kashgar by the Gez defile on to the Taghdumbash Pamir. Besides these there were three other roads from Yarkand to the Taghdumbash Pamir. Of these the one by the Ighiz Yar was considered the best by him. It was therefore, comparatively easy for the Russians, by marching a force by the Tuyuk-su pass, to assemble on the northern boundary of Hunza. To the north beyond Mintaka he had not then gone. Younghusband referred to British traveller, St. George Littledales, for routes to the south of the Tuyuk-su, he having journeyed from Osh to Yasin in 1889. Carts, Littledales thought, could be taken to the Pamir river-Oxus[54]. He only confirmed what the Russian geographer, Kostenko, had said that "the roads on the Pamirs are easy in all parts."[55] To render Gilgit secure from attack Younghusband argued "we must get the Raja of the country (Hunza) well under control..."[56]

The increase in their subsidies had put the Rajas, both of Hunza and Nagar, in good humour and Safdar Ali was even persuaded to remark that whereas formerly he was a "friend with the Chinese (and) Russians....,he has now no friends but the British Government."[57] Yet the lurking danger from the British drove the irreconcilable enemies, Hunza and Nagar, to swear a "defensive alliance."[58] There was "uneasiness" in the Shinaki tribes too, on the periphery of Gilgit. Colonel Durand himself attributed apprehensious of Hunza and Nagar to the construction of the Gilgit-Chalt road. No less could the Shinaki "uneasiness" be traced, as Colonel Durand did in his letter to Nisbet, to "our annexation of Kashmir and the fear that we mean to follow this up by a conquest of the country on both sides of the Indus..."[59] Nevertheless Colonel Durand could not resist the temptation to implicate the deposed Maharaja, Pratap Singh, claiming he had urged Hunza and Nagar "to combine to resist us..."[60] The best way to arrange in future, Colonel Durand suggested to Cunningham in the Foreign Department, "is to let the British Agent be governor."[61] The motive in seeking to set "the whole frontier in a blaze" was seen by him to ensure withdrawal of the British Agency.[62]

Safdar Ali's problems with China too surfaced in the northern part of his chiefship, an off-shoot as these were no less of the overall British designs. Efforts of China, egged on by the British, to take over the Pamirs, Hunza's Taghdumbash including, induced Raja Safdar Ali to send a punitive force to Chadartash, north of the Kilik, in April or May 1890, to punish the Kirghiz, his "subjects"[63] as he called them, for defiance of his authority. Seven Kirghiz, including Kuch Mohammad, the Beg of the Taghdumbash Pamir, and his wife were made "prisoners." A Kashgar trader, a Chinese subject, who happened to be with the Kirghiz, was killed in the "raid", as Colonel Durand from Gilgit and Captain Ramsay from Ladakh, described the action, consistent with British policy not to recognise Taghdumbash as 'doam" Kanjut. Letters from the Chinese officials were altogether ignored by Safdar Ali[64]. The Chinese also despatched an amban to enquire into the incident but this official does not appear to have proceeded beyond Sirikul. Chinese enquiries into the "raid" brought satisfaction to Colonel Durand as these implied "a definite Chinese claim to the Pamirs north of Hunza..." But then these also advanced Chinese claims to suzerainty over Hunza which could and did lead to difference of opinion between England and China.

Safdar Ali's "raid" was seemingly provoked by the Kirghiz of Taghdumbash, besides those of Great, Little and Alichur Pamirs, having paid taxes to the Chinese. The first settlement of the Kirghiz that Khushwakt Khan, a British agent, came across was at Chalab, in the Little Pamir. The Chinese had established a tenuous authority over this Pamir through the local Kirghiz. Kuch Mohammad was also said to have refused to tender the usual "forced offerings of felt and dried apricot" (tribute) so that Safdar Ali sent a party to coerce him[65]. But papers seized from the Baltit fort in Hunza reveal that the tribute or, rather, revenue was voluntarily despatched and included "namda" (felts), "jul" (horse cloth) and "Jamad-do-band" (shirts). Far from forcing Kuch Mohammad to pay, Safdar Ali complained to him in another letter that after collecting the revenue he had withheld it. Kuch Mohammad seems to have sought to subvert Safdar Ali's authority by aligning with the Chinese[66]. He was finally dismissed by Safdar Ali which came to the notice of the Chinese, a third Baltit paper reveals. To the Chinese Safdar Ali explained that the Kirghiz chief had always guided the English and Russian travellers to Hunza. The Amban was satisfied and approved the Raja's action. This version does not agree with that of Captain Ramsay, or even of Colonel Durand's. Another Baltit paper, an undated letter from Kuch Mohammad to Safdar Ali, written before the former's arrest, clearly reveals that Kuch Mohammad was an official of Safdar Ali in the Taghdumbash Pamir. He had then reported to Safdar Ali the movements of the Kirghiz of Sarekia–as the Kirghiz of Shahidulla were really known-accompanying an Englishman-Younghusband-and the arrival of "Tora Sahib"–Grombtchevski–in "our 'karaul' in safety." The punitive action of Safdar Ali would seem to have been viewed by the Gilgit Agency as a trespass if not an act of war. Lieutenant Manners Smith had contemplated military action had only the "condition" of the troops in Gilgit been good. The Gilgit garrison was a detachment of the Jammu and Kashmir troops which, after the deposition of Maharaja Pratap Singh, the British distrusted. But the "most important result" of Khushwakt Khan's journey to the Pamirs was the "discovery" of a "new" pass, Khortabhort, and an easy route over it to the Little Pamir from Ishkoman and Gilgit.

The presence of the Kirghiz at Chalab "paying revenue to China delighted the Indian Foreign Department as "it practically closes the 'gap' on the Little Pamir[67]." Nizam-ul-Mulk, was credited with having joined an "offensive and defensive alliance" with the chiefs of Hunza and Nagar "against any action that may be taken by the British in the direction of building cantonments or forts in Yasin, Chalt or Chaprot."[68]

A fugitive, Raja Mulk Aman, was added to the party. Notwithstanding this reaction to their plans, Captain Tyler was deputed to Chitral, accompanied by Dr. Robertson, bound for Kafiristan, in September 1890, to select sites for forts, one of which was chosen at Shagot, en route to Badakshan. The Amir of Afghanistan became "very angry at the military works" undertaken in Chitral and the presence of British officers there[69]. No less uneasy in his mind was Amal-ul-Mulk, both at the proposed construction of a fort at Shagot and Dr. Robertson's visit to Kafiristan.

When Captain Younghusband was again deputed to the northern frontier in 1890, the Chinese allowed him to freely move about and, indeed, persuaded him to visit the Alichur Pamir where a Chinese inscription, first heard of by Elias, had surfaced then, supposedly indicating the limits of Chinese authority. While he was at Sirikul, Nazim Khan, a brother of Safdar Ali, visited Younghusband. Nazim was on his way to Kashgar with Hunza's gold "tribute" to China and to look after the Raja's jagir in Yarkand. No harm was seen by Younghusband in these embassies which could, arguably, be connected "only" with the Raja's jagir. As long as the British did not definitely raise the question as to who was Hunza's suzerain, Younghusband did not fancy "the Chinese will ever start it of their own accord,"[70] for their supposed rights were British designed. Along with the tribute there was a letter from Safdar Ali for the Chinese Amban. The Raja recalled his request made in the previous year, for imposing a levy on the caravans trading between Leh and Yarkand, impliedly as compensation for stopping raids on them[71]. There were reports that the Chinese were then endeavouring "to obtain a more definite hold on the Hunza Raja." It was then even said that proposals had been made to Safdar Ali "for the establishment of a Chinese post in Kanjut territory" which the Raja and his minister were "seriously considering."[72] In Kashgar the Taotai agreed to increase payment in lieu of the Hunza "levy" on caravans[73].

The making of the road from Gilgit to Noman made both Hunza and Nagar chiefs threaten that any attempt to carry the road beyond Nomal would result in "hostilities."[74] Safdar Ali expected "an attack from Gilgit."[75] The Chinese too anticipated trouble and had received reinforcements, either for despatch to Hunza or to the Pamirs. Fortifications were constructed by Hunza on the Khorabhort, explored in the previous year, 1890, so as to close the road to Ishkoman[76]. The local situation did, suddenly, take a turn for the worse. Uzr Khan, the moving spirit behind the Hunza-Nagar alliance, killed his brothers and made preparations to seize Chalt and Chaprot forts. Colonel Durand forestalled him, reaching the forts first with troops and guns[77]. That was good enough to cow down Hunza and Nagar. But the military movement excited the Russians. Before the flash point was reached Cunningham put on the brakes. In agreement with Younghusband, he favoured "doing nothing strong in the Hunza direction" until the Pamir boundary issue was settled[78]. Sir Mortimer agreed, suggesting to the Viceroy, Lord Landowne, that Colonel Durand might "came down and settle what is to be done this winter."[79] The fall of 1891 was quite apparently chosen for war with Hunza-Nagar. Raja Safdar Ali, however, atleast outwardly, showed himself conciliatory, protesting his loyalty to Government, and reminding the British Agent of the friendship between England and China, which an attack on Hunza would only sour. Were he attacked, Safdar Ali professed to be "strong" enough to resist, "till the armies of the Emperor of China arrive."[80]

The Resident in Kashmir, Colonel W.F. Prideaux, saw the situation had materially changed after the murders in Nagar and the inclination of Safdar Ali "to play off the dependence of Hunza on China as a counter move to the advance of British authority in Gilgit."[81] Urged by the Russian Consul in Kashgar, the Chinese "were inclined strongly to assert their suzerainty over Hunza..."[82] In Kashgar on the one side there was a strong belief that the British were to annex Kanjut and on the other reports were current that the Russian Governor General of Turkisan would bring two or three thousand troops and occupy the Pamirs and Sirikul[83]. Prideaux sought an early decision with regard to any Chinese claims upon Kanjut. The Agent at Gilgit was to ascertain, if possible, "whether any relations existed between Kanjut and China prior to the deputation of Colonel Biddulph to Gilgit."[84] There was implied admission in the query that the British were responsible for Chinese factor in Hunza. Biddulph himself had found that Hunza gave "nominal allegiance" to the Trakhane (Raja) of Gilgit whose rule lasted from the commencement of the 14th century to the Sikh conquest[85]. Hunza then became a tributary to the Sikhs from 1842 and then to the Dogras from 1846 when Gilgit passed on to the Maharaja of Jammu and Kashmir. The first time Hunza Raja tendered his allegiance to the Chinese seemed to have been, as far as the British were aware, after the insurrection of the Seven Khojas in 1847. In these disturbances Hunza had aided the Chinese and the Raja was conferred a jagir in Yarkand and a fixed subsidy. In return Hunza gave a nominal allegiance. But this connection was snapped by the Atalik seizing Khashgaria in 1864. In 1869 the late Raja Ghazan Khan, "definitely" again became tributary to Kashmir,

> "So that if the Chinese pretensions must rest on the payment of tribute since the conquest of the New Dominion in 1878, referred to in the "Peking Gazette" on 23rd April, 1891, or even on the agreement of 1847, ours is the prior claim."[86]

So wrote Colonel Durand to Prideaux. This account of Hunza-China relation is inaccurate, as will be seen. It is also an about-face from the stand the British had earlier taken on Hunza's status in relation to Kashmir.

Of the impending Russian advance on the Pamirs, the Chinese were blissfully ignorant. Sir John Walsham personally, did not rule out such an expedition. He warned Lord Salisburry, "...absolutely nothing can be done by the Chinese Government to counteract such an expedition," and even if the Russian operations eventually extended to the borderland (the lower Yarkand Valley) between Jammu and Kashmir and Chinese Turkistan, Sir John Walsham much doubted whether the Chinese would venture to take any action. For one reason :

> "The (Tsungli) Yamen has always declined, in my discussion with them,.....to admit that China and India are conterminous in this region, holding that there was a belt of Mohammadan tribes which separated them."[87]

This Mohammadan belt comprised the Yarkand valley, Taghdumbash Pamir and Sirikul all south of the Kuen Lun, Peopled, from time to time, by Kanjutis, Pakhpos, Baltis, all of Indian origin and the Kirghiz. On the Russian movement on the Pamirs, Safdar Ali was better informed than the Chinese. To the British Agency at Gilgit, he calculatedly conveyed the presence of 1000 Russians on the Pamir[88]. Some of these Russians had gone to Shighnan via Somatash in the Alichur Pamir. The presence of Russians was confirmed by Ali Mardan Shah. In London the British army intelligence credited the Russians with the intention to declare the country to be their own territory and "make the Hindu Kush their frontier."[89] From Gilgit, Colonel Durand wrote to his brother, Sir Mortimer, whether Russians annexed more of the Pamirs or not, "I think this autumn is the time to establish our hold up to the Hindu Kush..."[90] From the refusal of Kanjutis to meet Younghusband in Kashgar, it was conjectured in Gilgit that messengers sent to Kashgaria by Safdar Ali had sought help both from China and Russia *after* Colonel Durand's march on Chalt[91]. A request for Russian assistance appears to have been made when the Kanjuti envoys called on the Russian Consul in Kashgar.

Russian troops, perhaps, less than 200, finally descended on the Pamirs by the Alai-Akbaital-Aksu route. A Chinese general, Chang Tajen, with 10 troops with him and 20 more on the Alichur was hardly in a position to stop the Russians. One half of them went to the disputed Alichur and the rest came to the Little Pamir. Younghusband had, in anticipation of the arrival of the Russians, left Kashgar and reached the Pamirs. He positioned himself on the Taghdumbash Pamir. To Cunningham, Younghusband wrote,

> "My intention now is to patrol about the upper Taghdumbash Pamir and Bozai Gumbaz and open up communication with Durand and Gilgit by the new pass, Khorabhort..."[92]

Taghdumbash and Bozai Gumbaz were the northern limits of the "doam" Hunza. Younghusband should, in truth, have claimed them as Hunza territory and thus put off the Russians from reaching in the Hindu Kush. But such a claim ran counter to the British policy and more than the policy, the fictitious British maps. A larger Russian force, accompanied by the Governor General of the Russian Turkistan, headed southward for the Alai to back up the little contingent already on the Pamirs to deal with extensive Chinese and Afghan encroachments.

In their southward journey, the Russians reached Paik, a march below the Mintaka pass into Hunza. Local Kirghiz fled on their approach. When asked by the Russians whose subjects they were, the Kirghiz replied they were subject to whoever owned Tashkurgan, underlining the confusion caused by the British backed Chinese claim over Sirikul and Little Pamir. From Paik the Russians went on to explore the Indian frontier in Yasin and Chitral, penetrating to the Darkot pass. Colonel Yonoff, heading the Russian contingent, informed Younghusband that he was deputed by the Governor General of Russian Turkistan "to annex the Pamirs."[93] The Russian Pamirs were to include Rangkul and the Aksu valley. Tashkurgan was left to the Chinese. It was not certain whether the Taghdumbash Pamir was to be annexed by Russia. The Russian frontier was to run by the Wakhijrui pass in Wakhan to the Khorabhort pass, also known as Baikra or Tashkupruk pass, cross the Panja river somewhere below Bozai Gumbaz and then stretch along the watershed of the range dividing the Little from the Great Pamir, and the Great Pamir, as far as Yol Mazar, was to be included in the Russian territory. The Afghan boundary was to run in a straight line from the Sirikul lake to the junction of the Kokcha with Oxus. Such a boundary made Russian territorial limits to touch India. By assigning Tashkurgan to China, Russia denied herself access to the "gap." But she gained a better road that ran through Great Pamir which Badakshan had used to assist the Kashbegi to secure Kashgaria in 1864. The way out the British saw was China occupying the Pamirs. Were the Chinese not to pull the British chestnuts out of the fire, they had no option but to consolidate themselves in the Hindu Kush region. For this, strong measures against the Raja of Hunza were conceived to be necessary. Another reason there was for strong action against Safdar Ali. Hunza had commenced intriguing with Russia.

The great power rivalry in the Pamirs touched off a diplomatic crisis in the Anglo-Russian relations. On 17th August 1891, approaching midnight, Colonel Yonoff with a party of Cossacks, rode to Bozai Gumbaz, where Younghusband was camped. Colonel Yonoff had "orders" from the Governor General of Turkistan "to expel" him "from Russian territory."[94] Were Younghusband to resist, Colonel Yonoff had instructions "to use force." Under "protest," therefore, the Englishman agreed to leave and not to use several passes, listed by the Russian, for his exit from the Pamirs. In a detailed despatch to Cunningham the next day, Younghusband reported he was to have been escorted "out of the Russian territory into Chinese territory."[95] Instead of leaving for Chinese territory, Younghusband stayed about Taghdumbash Pamir, near the foot of the Kilik pass and, through the Khorabhort pass, he opened communications with Gilgit and mounted a watch on Hunza. Manners-Smith, acting for Colonel Durand, despatched Agency Guards to the Ishkoman and Yasin valleys "to watch the Russians in Wakhan." Safdar Alik was warned that "he will be extremely foolish if he allows single Russian into his country..."[96] The deputation of Younghusband to the Pamirs to find out the frontiers of the Chinese and Afghans was rightly seen by Russia as an attempt at joining these boundaries. This was clearly stated to Younghusband by Colonel Yonoff[97]. Russian pronouncement to annex the Pamirs was Yonoff's swagger, for Younghusband saw no signs of a permanent occupation[98].

The "findings" of Younghusband on the frontier between China and Afghanistan in the Pamir region were incorporated into a memorandum and, accompanied by his map of the upper Oxus region, were confidentially communicated to the Chinese Minister in London by Lord Salisbury. The Minister was asked "...whether the frontier thus indicated is recognised by the Chinese Government as correctly describing the limits of Chinese jurisdiction in (the Pamir) direction, in which case Her Majesty's Government on their side, are ready to recognise it and inform the Indian Government of the Agreement which has been arrived at."[99] Elaborating Younghusband's boundary, Elias placed Bash Gumbaz "within the territory claimed by China." Bozai Gumbaz was "just beyond it, and within what we should recognise as Afghan territory." That joined the Afghan boundary with that of the Chinese even though the Afghan disclaimed Bozai Gumbaz. As to Khorabhort pass, the water-parting between Afghanistan and India, in the neighbourhood of Bozai Gumbaz, Elias was uncertain whether it fell within Chitral or under the "Khan" of Hunza. His impression was it lay within Yasin and consequently in Chitral territory.[100] The Chinese were inspired by Younghusband joining their boundary with that of the Afghans. In Yarkand they gave "an iron plate with an inscription in Chinese on it to the Beg at Sirikul, with instructions to secretly bury it in the ground on the summit of the Mintaka pass..." The plate was meant "to represent an old boundary mark," like the Somatash inscription in the Alichur Pamir which the Chinese claimed was their boundary. This Somatash stone was also claimed as their boundary by Russia. To the Afghans, the stone had names engraved in "kafir" (infidel) characters. The names turned out to be Chinese on which the Russians said "...the stone is yours (China's) but the boundary is ours..."[101]

The British Indian Government did not consider the Yonoff Mission "a mere exploring party but an expedition sent to annex the Pamirs upto the border of Hunza." If, as was reported, the Chinese had a general and some troops at the junction of the Akbaital and Aksu rivers, and another official at Somatash, in the Alichur Pamir, the annexation was "a very bold move." The Russian object, Sir Mortimer saw, was "a direct point at Hunza, which will now be coterminous with Russian territory." Were the Russians to take Taghdumbash, "they will command not only the Kilik and Khorabhort passes but also the easy Khanjerab and Mintaka, which is fit for ponies."[102] That was an alarmist, if not a distorted, view of the Russian riposte to constant British provocations and intrigues in the Pamirs. The British could hardly reconcile themselves with the Russian *promenade militaire*, which is what Yonoff mission was. From the Taghdumbash, Younghusband wrote to Gilgit Agency for troops to be stowed away up in a valley even though Taghdumbash was avowedly Chinese. The Gilgit Agency toyed with the idea of forcing on Safdar Ali the presence of a British officer in his territory, with a force sufficient "to prove that Hunza is subject to (the British), until such time as the question of the Pamir frontier is definitely settled... "Should it, however, be necessary to settle the question of the possession of Hunza by force of arms," while Captain Younghusband is still close to the frontier on the *other side of Kanjuit territory*"–"doam" Hunza–, it was considered" quite feasible and a useful move to send a light column round..."[103] to close the passes leading to the Pamirs. Here was an unequivocal admission by England that north of the Hindu Kush, the Taghdumbash Pamir was Hunza.

By asserting that the "other side of Kanjut territory" was Hunza, England could freely send her troops across the Hindu Kush to prevent a Russian advance. But to keep open communications with Gilgit and Yarkand the British needed free access through Hunza. There was an alternative to the Kilik and other Hunza passes in the Bozai Gumbaz road up the valley of the Wakhijrui pass along the Taghdumbash Pamir to detect and, if possible, cut off Russian communications with Hunza.[104] In London Lord Cross proposed that the Chinese Minister, Sieh Tajen, might be informed that "Kanjut, which is *south of the Hindu Kush*, is held to be within the sphere of influence of the British Government."[105] Territories to the north of the Hindu Kush, including the Taghdumbash Pamir and Raskam, were to be outside Hunza, virtually effecting its partition. Sir John Walsham in Beijing was directed by Lord Salisbury to impress upon the Chinese the importance of "effective occupation"[106] of such positions as they claimed on the Pamir plateaux, and especially the Alichur Pamir, these being then traversed by armed Russian parties. Lord Cross considered it of utmost importance that any attempts on the part of Russian armed parties to penetrate into Hunza and Chitral "should be in the last resource resisted by force if all other means fail to induce them to retire." He proposed, with the concurrence of Lord Salisbury, to inform the Viceroy and Governor General of India that "the instructions which have been issued for this purpose are approved by Her Majesty's Government."[107] Expectedly Lord Salisbury concurred.[108]

To take Russia to task over Younghusband's expulsion from Bozai Gambaz, its exact location had first to be ascertained. England was not unaware that Bozai Gumbaz was in Hunza's Little Pamir, one reason, evidently why Younghusband had taken refuge there. Yet the Resident in Kashmir was asked whether Bozai Gumbaz was locally regarded to be in Wakhan.[109] In the event it was, then instrusion by armed Russians was a violation of Afghan territory. Elias argued Russians had entered what British had always understood to be Wakhan.[110] But, Barrow's Gazetteer placed Bozai Gumbaz just above the Little Pamir and outside Wakhan. Besides, Russians themselves had admitted to Younghusband that they had explored the Khorabhort, crossed the Darkot Pass to the Baroghil, descended into Wakhan and forded the Panja opposite Sarhad, "which is well known to be Afghan, and returned to Bozai Gumbaz through Wakhan territory." All this Sir Mortimer proposed to Lansdowne, should be cabled to the Secretary of State for India.[111] What then the Indian Government was in immediate need of, to keep the Russians at an arm's length from the Hindu Kush, was unrestricted transit facilities to the British through Hunza. Messengers had, rather, freely been allowed to transit through Hunza. But when their frequency increased, Safdar Ali represented to Colonel Durand at Gilgit on the issue. Himself in a letter to the Agent, Safdar Ali alluded to his understanding with Colonel Durand and recalled having pleaded that "...owing to the smallness of this country and the wretchedness of the people," he had begged that intercourse with Kashgar, Yarkand and the Pamirs through his territories should be stopped. Further the Raja had said that all persons coming from the Chinese, Russians and Afghans with the object of going towards Gilgit will be sent back. You and we have entered into these promises." In future, the letter went on, "you will not send any one again by this route, because it will break your promises made to me..."[112] The expression "up country" used by Safdar Ali is evidently for the territory to the north or "doam" Hunza.

Other factors were also involved, as Colonel Durand saw, in warding off the Russian threat. British hold on Gilgit needed to be strengthened first by building a strong fort at Chalt on the road to Gilgit from the Hindu Kush and, thereafter, by bringing both Hunza and Nagar effectively under British control. Construction of the fort at Chalt was certain to lead the Gilgit Agency into hostilities with Hunza and Nagar. Such a threat, Colonel Durand proposed in a memorandum on Gilgit, should be met. At the least sign of opposition, a small force could "cross the frontier and subdue both the principalities. How, after the two chiefships came under British control, was Hunza, that had territories north of the Hindu Kush and direct dealings with China, to be dealt with? Colonel Durand dismissed Hunza's rights over the Taghdumbash Pamir and Sirikul as "shadowy."[113] Safdar Ali was declared to be absolutely untrustworthy. He was accused of breaking every stipulation of his agreement with the British Indian Government, a charge refuted by Safdar Ali himself. In return for "blackmail" from Kashgar, he was credited with having abstained from raiding the Leh-Yarkand road. This "blackmail" was the subsidy Hunza was paid under an old agreement with China for protection of routes of commerce. The British were even more irked by Safdar Ali receiving Chinese officials in Hunza and inviting Russians into it. Above all he had sought Russian help against England. Both to meet the Russian threat and Hunza-Nagar contingency, Gilgit, then garrisoned by a brigade of Kashmir army, was proposed to be strengthened with British troops,

British officers and British guns. To permit their deployment in Kashmir, the deposed Maharaja and the State Council were informed. It was explained that this was being done "in fulfilment of (British) obligation to aid Kashmir in protecting its territory."[114] His memorandum certainly perked up the British Indian Government. In a second memorandum, a few days later, Colonel Durand again pressed for "real control of the country to our north up to the crest of the Hindu Kush." This had been recognised in Chitral to the west and lately in Ladakh to the east (where the Karakoram crest was proposed to be boundary) and the establishment of similar control over Hunza was a consistent application of the general principle laid down by the British Indian Government. Colonel Durand noted :

> "Our control over Hunza proper, i.e., that part of the country south of the Hindu Kush, should be a support to the Chinese Government. It will show that we are decisively insisting on the claim which we have always advanced that our frontier is the Hindu Kush, that it thus marches at this point with theirs, here the Taghdumbash Pamir, and we are thus blocking out the Russians from a broken flank in their frontier line."[115]

On the 10th of October 1891, the British Indian Government formally sanctioned Colonel Durand's proposal to move troops across the frontier were Hunza and Nagar to collect forces with a view of preventing the construction of the Chalt fort.[116] Besides China, there was another imponderable factor that had to be weighed before an attack on Hunza was launched. What if Safdar Ali retreated to his trans-Hindu Kush possessions and from there waged war against England south of the chain. Both Russia and China could get involved in such a conflict and make it harder for England to consolidate her hold south of the Hindu Kush. That this eventuality was seriously considered is evident from the British Agent's move to enlist the assistance of the Mehtar of Chitral. A Chitral force could easily reach the Pamirs and the Kilik pass to block Safdar Ali's passage to the Taghdumbash or "doam" Huna.[117] Safdar Ali sought help from China in arms, ammunition and mounts. His pleas evoked only excuses from the Taotai. All that the Taotai was keen on was to instal a Chinese official in Hunza.[118] Left to their own devices, Raja Jafr Khan of Nagar pledged to the British Agent on his own, his son Uzr Khan's and that of Raja Safdar Ali's behalf that they "should not take even one step beyond their own frontier."[119] The British Agent recalled to the Rajas that a Russian force had moved into the Pamirs earlier in the summer, explored the passes of the Hindu Kush leading southward. For the first time Safdar Ali was unequivocally told

> "Your State lies to the south of these mountains which here form the boundary of the Indian empire and is within the borders of British India."[120]

For these reasons it was felt necessary for the protection of Kashmir and of his own State that the troops of the supreme Government should have "free access" to Hunza. By such means alone could the requisite arrangements be made for safeguarding there the frontier of the empire.

The task entrusted by the British to the Mehtar to block the northern exists from "awal" Hunza, Aman-ul-Mulk found beyond his capacity. The journey by the Pamirs to the Kilik extended over 10 days through snow covered mountains. The severity of the December cold would have killed the horses and, in the event of the force being held up en route, there was no possibility of the Mehtar vietualling these troops who, any way, were not equipped to fight in winter. Above all he felt :

> "...it is not impossible that the Kirghiz tribesmen or the inhabitants of Sirikul may rise in support of the ruler of Hunza..."[121]

Whether the Mehtar's explanation was genuine or laboured is of no import. But his observation is. It strongly indicates that the Kirghiz tribesman of the Taghdumbash Pamir, to which the northern exits from the "awal" Hunza lead to, and the inhabitants of Sirikul were subjects of the Raja of Hunza. The principal reason for this war was to sever the Taghdumbash Pamir, Sirikul and Ruskam from Hunza and confine it to the south of the Hindu Kush-Karakoram chains.

Safdar Ali made a last attempt to secure "immediate assistance" from China and Russia as well.[122] The Taotai had evaded the Kanjuti appeals for assistance but now found it hard to do so any longer. The Russian Consul General at Kashgar lent support to Safdar Ali, as the British troops broke into Hunza south of the Hindu Kush, threatening, unless the Chinese could keep Hunza, the Russians would invade Sirikul.[123] Perforce the Taotai agreed to intervene and deputed Changed Tajen to Hunza. But the little war was over on 20th December 1891. Expectedly Safdar Ali, accompanied by Uzr Khan and Wazir Dadu, fled to "doam" Hunza and the Kanjutis, south of the Hindu Kush, made a "complete submission" to the British.[124] Hunza was virtually split into two, Safdar Ali holding only territories north of the Hindu Kush. Had Hunza's defences lasted, the Russians, British writer, E.F. Knight claims, were to have aided Safdar Ali with breech loading guns and a supply of ammunition if not with Cossacks.[125] But Colonel Durand sets at rest such a claim remarking that the Governor General of Russian Turkistan had refused any assistance to the Kanjutis.[126] Another English writer, Colonel Schomberg does not even believe that Russia had any share in instigating the chiefs or the tribesmen to take the offensive.[127] Yet Colonel Durand, writing about the results of the brief war, asserts that a "well known" Russian statesman, whom he does not identify, remarked on the fall of Hunza :

> "Ils nous ont fermes la porte au nez." (they have slammed the door in our faces).[128]

Chinese intervention was face saving. Chang Tajen entered Sirikul with just 160 cavalrymen! Macartney at Kashgar saw through the sham and wrote to Colonel Durand, "the intentions of the Chinese are...most friendly and peaceable and if Chang Tajen does go to Hunza, it will only be for the purpose of making enquiries and endeavouring to enter into pourparlers with you."[129] The Russian Consul, was credited by Macartney with "...daily badgering the Taotai to send troops into Hunza..." In St. Petersburg, Russian Foreign Minister, M.de Giers, protested to the British Minister, Sir Robert Morier, against "Anglo-Indian troops preparing to force the passage of the Khanate of Kanjut with a view of occupying some strategic points on the Pamirs."[130] Russia had her own reasons to make curiouser the "great game." Her protest underscored Russia's fears of British designs on the Pamirs. China, "being aware of the friendship between the two empires," had "not entered into hostility" with the British Indian Government.[131] All she asked of the "Zoondai," or the Viceroy and the Governor General of India, was to know the reason for the British bringing troops into Hunza, whose ruler, significantly, had with a large following or more than 500 retreated to the Taghdumbash, or 'doam' Hunza and not to Kashgaria. The Taotai sought Colonel Durand to keep his troops "within your own limits."[132] In another communication to the "Zoondai," the Taotai claimed Hunza as a "dependency of the Chinese empire." Yet the British had "not notified" to the Chinese the advance of their troops.[133] Neither had a letter been despatched explaining to them what was the origin of this affair. For the British, to the south of the Hindu Kush passes, the presence of Safdar Ali Khan, Wazir Dadu and Uzr Khan of Nagar on the Taghdumbash Pamir "with their well armed followers" offered "a standing menace."[134]

Whatever his purpose, Chang Tajen's visit to "awal" Hunza with or without his troops, was unaccepable to the British, unless he came simply from the Taotai to see Colonel Durand. The British were not prepared to "allow for a moment the Chinese claims over Hunza..."[135] south of the Hindu Kush. Were, therefore, Chang Tajen to come with the idea of enquiring about Hunza, he was not to be let in. Having instigated the Chinese all along, the assertion of their suzerainty over Hunza, south of the Hindu Kush as well, was not unexpected. Colonel Durand felt the way to meet it was, if necessary,

> "tacitly to allow the Chinese suzerainty over the Tham (Raja) of Hunza insofar as his shadowy rights over Taghdumbash extend, but not as regard the country to the south of the Hindu Kush."[136]

This fell short of condominium which China later proposed and England out of hand rejected. Apparently to lend strength to Chinese claims over Hunza, against much older rights of Jammu and Kashmir, the Taotai, of Kashgar, Li Tajen, asserted Kanjut had paid tribute to China since the time of Emperor Chien Lung, 1736-1796.[137] No such claim had earlier been proffered to Sir John Walsham. Was it under pressure China made the claim? Li Tajen conceded there was little possibility of Safdar Ali returning to Hunza. The "shadowy" rights of Hunza over the Taghdumbash, Colonel Durand elaborated, were those "given by striking the road."[138] Even if the British were "only" to stick to "awal" Hunza, Colonel Durand favoured "some arrangement should be come to enabling us to cross the Pamirs without referring to Peking for passports." China thus did not issue passports for the Taghdumbash and Little Pamir, Hunza's rights over these evidently being more than those conferred by "striking the road."

A token protest against the British invasion of Hunza,[139] was duly made in London by the Chinese Minister, Sieh Tajen. The protest was treated lightly and the Minister was assured that Her Majesty's Government had no wish to interfere in any way with the payment of tribute or with any right over Hunza which China might be found to posses.[140] The action which had been taken was simply dictated by the necessity of protecting Indian frontier against Russian encroachments and in this respect the British "were acting equally in the interest of China." The Chinese Minister was not seriously perturbed by the developments in Hunza. He readily assented to the necessity of British interference and finally limited himself to pressing two points : (i) that the Hunza State should not be suppressed out of all existence and (ii) that the customary tribute should be kept up.[141] The Chinese were, indeed, peeved that the British had invaded Hunza without so much as informing them. Were the British to retain possession of Kanjut, and push forward their outposts into the passes leading to the Pamirs, it was conveyed to them in London, that the Tsungli Yamen feared "Russian would not remain inactive, but would see in these acts a reason for returning to the Pamir and that before any arrangement can be concluded between the British and the Chinese Govenments, with respect to the Alichur Pamir, the question of the Pamirs shall have been settled by a Russian occupation of all the Pamir regions."[142] Similar sentiments were also conveyed by the Tsungli Yamen in Beijing to Sir John Walsham. It was hoped that Britain would, in her own interests as well as from her friendship for China, "allow the Chinese Government to have a voice in the settlement of the Kanjut question."[143] Chinese loss of face was, therefore, sought to be offset. China informally favoured Nazim Khan, an illegitimate brother of Safdar Ali, as his successor in Hunza.[144] The British readily agreed with this choice.

From Taghdumbash, Safdar Ali had moved on further north to the more habitable Sirikul. When the Tsungli Yamen Ministers had called on Sir John Walsham in Beijing on the 25th February 1892, to press their claims over Hunza, they had stated "that the Raja of that place.... was in the proximity of the Chinese frontier..."[145] China thus acknowledged Sirikul was not Chinese but Hunza territory. Safdar Ali alleged to the Chinese that he was assailed and expelled from his State by a British force. He, therefore, appealed to China, as a tributary, for aid. Were China to refuse assistance, Safdar Ali threatened to seek it from Russia. The Chinese hastened to clarify they, of course, would not assist Safdar Ali nor prevent him from approaching Russia, being afraid of that power. But their argument they repeated that were Britain to incorporate Hunza in their territories, Russia might make the consent of China to such a procedure with regard to a tributary an excuse for annexing the Pamirs. China was well aware of British anxiety for disposal of the Pamirs in a manner that ensured the safety of their Indian empire. This and their own interests, they felt were best served by constituting the Pamirs into "a neutral ground between the three bordering empires." Only "incidental allusions were made to delimitation" of the Pamirs by the Tsungli Yamen Ministers.

There was little likelihood of Safdar Ali ever returning to Hunza, south of the Hindu Kush and, even if he did, being restored as the Raja. Nor could the British have annexed Hunza. Still Sieh Tajen pressed Lord Salisbury "not to sanction the dethronement of the Hunza Chief or to allow any change in the status of Kanjut without the previous understanding with China[146]." This was not much that China sought from Britain and even this little was plainly under Russian coercion. Lord

Landsdowne readily concurred with the Home Government and an assurance was conveyed to China that annexation of Hunza was not contemplated, and it was intended to maintain in power a member of the ex-chief's family. Beyond these "concessions" the Secretary of State for India was not prepared to go. He did not at all admit the right of China to interfere in the internal administration of Kanjut, nor was the British Government prepared to "suffer a Chinese official to interpose as a court of appeal" in a matter which concerned the Government of India and the rebellious action of one of its subsidised States.[147]

Yet this was what China was keen about, not so much for Hunza, as for herself, to win Russia's approbation. Were Safdar Ali to be replaced, his successor, Tsungli Yamen urged, should not be installed until a Chinese officer from Kashgar came to an understanding with the British officer in command on the spot. When Sieh Tajen, who communicated the proposal, was asked by Lord Salisbury if on the accession of Safdar Ali there had been any such formal participation he, of course, pleaded ignorance.[148] Though the Chinese proposal was incongruous, Lord Salisbury saw "some justice" in the request. Had not the Chinese Government played the British game of their fictitious suzerainty over Hunza? A "forcible change" of rulers ought not to appear to have been effected by the British authorities without any tangible sign of China having been even nominally consulted. But really Lord Salisbury wished it to be impressed upon the Government of India that on the question of the north-west frontier of the British Indian possessions, "it is a matter of serious importance to have the friendship and goodwill of China and of her officers in Kashgar and that it is worthwhile to purchase that friendship and goodwill..."[149] With these views Lord Cross agreed and he commended the Chinese proposal to the Viceroy for acceptance.[150] But the Chinese presence at the installation ceremony was not to form a precedent.

When China finally forsook her "tributary," Safdar Ali sought aid of the Russian Consul General at Kashgar against "the unjust and arbitrary proceedings" of the English in Hunza. He was, Safdar Ali wrote to Petrovski, directed by a British officer, commanding a body of troops, to build roads for their use in making an advance on the Pamirs. Having regard to the importance of maintaining tranquillity on the frontier between China and Russia, the Consul urged the Taotai in a communication, to "lose no time in taking steps for succouring him in his distress and extending sympathy to a neighbouring State."[151] More importantly the Consul recognised that the State of Hunza was incorporated into the

Chinese empire in the 25th Year of the reign of Chien-lung and 45 Years ago Raja Ghazanfur Khan had rendered assistance to China in suppressing the Khoja insurrection. The Hunza chief was, therefore, entitled to Chinese assistance. The intercession of the Consul caused only alarm to the Chinese. Safdar Ali's arrest was contrived. Russia's support to China over Hunza was not so much to lend credence to her fictitious claims. By pressing China over Hunza, Russia sought to create problems for England south of the Hindu Kush as well. British intervention in Hunza proved detrimental to the Kanjut State in another way. China hastened to establish her sway over Hunza territories to the north of the Hindu Kush in the Pamirs, depriving Safdar Ali of them as well. China issued flags to different "karauls" and the flag for Sirikul bore the legend in Chinese and Turkish :

> "Tashkurgan "karaul" subject to the Kalan-Khakan" (the great emperor).[152]

Expectedly Sieh Tajen was formally assured by Lord Salisbury "that the Government of India do not desire to annex the State of Hunza or to make any change in its status..."[153] The cause of military action by the British against Hunza was also explained to China. In response to his letters to the Viceroy, the Taotai was informed by Sir Mortimer :

> "Kanjut is, as you know, on the side towards India of the mountain range which separates India from the Chinese empire."[154]

This brief, yet pregnant, statement must surely have reassured China, officially as it came on behalf of the Viceroy and Governor General of India. It virtually conveyed to China that the Taghdumbash Pamir, Little Pamir, Sirikul and Raskam, all to the north of the Hindu Kush range and comprising "doam" Hunza, were Chinese territories. Sir Mortimer appears to suggest that the military action against Hunza was taken by Kashmir and the cause for it were raids committed by the Kanjutis on the Leh-Yarkand road, which was less than the truth. Chinese susceptibilities were more than met and Sir John Walsham was assured by the Tsungli Yamen that China "would no longer support the (Hunza) Raja" in his attempt to regain his lost position.[155] Such a Chinese posture was vital for England for with his armed followers trans-Hindu Kush Hunza territories were a good launching pad for attacks on the British-held Kanjut to the south of the chain, a conflict which could have conceivably widened by Russian involvement, direct or indirect. England and China, therefore, appear to have acted in concert. Safdar Ali was treacherously handed over by Tolu Bai, "Karaul" Begi of Tashkurgan, to the Chinese "in view to show his good services to the British Government." This placed the Begs of Sirikul "on very hostile terms with Tolu Bai....," and "highly inimical in all matters relating to British Government."[156] With his own people, Safdar Ali appeared to have been highly popular.[157] Given these factors, and to accommodate the Chinese, Colonel Durand proposed "to appoint Muhammad Nazim Khan Raja" in a "darbar" to be held at Gilgit later in March 1892, the title of Nazim Khan was to be changed from Raja to Mir.[158] Nazim Khan, had received a formal letter of appointment from the Taotai but he was not allowed to reply to it,[159] lest it be construed as recognition of the Chinese rights south of the Hindu Kush.

Both the new Mir and Wazir Humayun, whom the British recalled from exile and appointed Nazim Khan's minister, pressed evidence on Kanjuti claim to Taghdumbash.

> "...the whole of Taghdumbash Pamir from Dafdar to Wakhijrui, including Raskam, has belonged to Kanjut from time immemorial....during the reign of Ghazan Khan, a dispute arose between the people of Hunza and Sirikulis, because the former wished, in excess of their rights, to prevent the flocks of the latter from coming to the Taghdumbash for the purpose of grazing there. The dispute was referred to the Chinese governor at Kashgar, where a deputation of several grey-beards (elders) from Hunza was sent to give evidence. After inquiry the claims of the Sirikulis are said to have broken down, and their representatives to have signed an agreement, attested by their seals, acknowledging the superior rights of the Kanjut Mir..."[160]

Other evidence brought forward by the Kanjutis was :

1. The existence of a ruined fort, once occupied by them at Dafdar and of houses, also in ruins, in Raskam.

2. Among the men having signed the agreement on behalf of the Sirikul is were : Yakub Shah Mingbashi and Tolu Beg, "karaul" Begi.

It had been Raja Ghazan Khan's intention to rebuild the fort at Dafdar. In the absence of local wood, gates for the fort had been sent from ("awal") Hunza. But owing to his murder, the project was never carried out.[161] The existence of the agreement between Hunza and Sirikul was confirmed from Tashkurgan by Jan Mohammad, British agent and news-writer.[162] As against all this verifiable evidence, Younghusband, who had extensively explored and mapped Sirikul, termed Hunza's collection of revenue from grazing on the Taghdumbash Pamir as "blackmail" on the Kirghiz and Sirikuli inhabitants. Younghusband also claimed the Mirs of Hunza had "sent raiding parties to the Pakhpo district (in Raskam) almost up the Kukyar (Chinese boundary) to demand a yearly contribution from the villagers under the threat of violence..." Interestingly he, however, admitted that the only spot north of the Hindu Kush to which the Mir of Hunza "has any real claim is the valley leading down from the north side of the Shangshal pass to the Oprang river." There, in 1889, he had found traces of former cultivation and a fortified post, named Darwaza, held by the Kanjutis.[163] Younghusband's admission is too thinly disguised. In the valley leading down from the Shangshal pass to the Oprang the Kanjutis had extensive economic rights which England could not ignore. In another communication to the British Agent at Gilgit, Jan Mohammad again confirmed the conclusion of the agreement on the Taghdumbash Pamir, which had been signed and sealed, among others, not by Tolu Beg himself, but by his father, Mir Baba Arbab. Raskam, extending from Kin to Charaghsaldi on Jammu and Kashmir frontier, four or five marches in length, was then "abad" (inhabited). His enquiries confirmed that Shakshu and Pakhpo, "paid tribute from old times to the Kanjutis."[164] British allegation against Kanjutis levying blackmail on the Taghdumbash, Sirikul and Raskam inhabitants thus stood exposed.

Once installed as the Raja, or Mir, of Hunza, both Nazim Khan and his minister, Humayun, there is reason to believe, pressed the British Indian Government to settle the future of the districts to the north of the Hindu Kush. But the Indian Foreign Department did not favour the boundary issue to be forthwith dealt with.[165] England was hardly then in a position to do so. What boundary would finally suit them, especially in Hunza, they had still to decide. The Chinese also contributed to their uncertainty. Some issues the Tsungli Yamen had conveyed to the Governor of Xinjiang at Urumtchi and the Taotai assumed that Kanjut would "eventually be placed under the joint protectorate of Great Britain and China."[166] True to her tradition, China sought to squeeze maximum advantage for herself from England's political difficulties. Chinese views and, even more, British apprehension that China might, as seemed to them not unlikely, abandon her "claims" to the Pamirs, persuaded Colonel Durand to suggest, "....it might be as well not to let Hunza claims to tribute in (Taghdumbash and Raskam) regions go by default..."[167] But even as a tactics this did not appeal to Government. Other issues still remained. To the communications he had received from the Chinese, it was considered "undesirable" that Mohammad Nazim Khan should send any reply to the Taotai or to any letter he may receive in future."[168] The Chinese delegate chosen to go to Hunza for inauguration of Mir Nazim Khan was Brigadier General Chang Hang Tao.[169] The Chinese Government wished before hand to know what part he would take in the installation of the new Mir. The Viceroy laid down the delegate was to attend as "an honoured spectator...taking no part..."[170] China then conveyed her desire to present a hat to Nazim Khan. The Indian Foreign Department out of hand rejected the request, Lansdowne agreeing minuted, "It would not do after all that has happened to let the Hunza chief accept any present or decoration which would constitute him a subordinate, or officer of the Chinese Government, and I understand that... would be the result of the acceptance of the hat."[171]

References

1. 2nd November 1885. Foreign. Secret. F.No. 247 of March 1886.
2. 25th November 1885. Foreign. Secret. F.No. 251 of March 1886.
3. Ney Elias. Explorer And Envoy Extraordinary In High Asia. By Gerald Morgan, p. 182.
4. 20th December 1885. Foreign. Secret. F.No. 261 of March 1886.
5. 5th February 1886. Foreign. Secret. F.No. 260 of March 1886.
6. 10th March 1886. Foreign. Secret. F.No. 275 of July 1886.
7. 28th April 1886. Foreign. Secret. F.No. 199 of August 1886.
8. 2nd May 1886. Foreign. Secret. F.No. 200 of August 1886.
9. 4th May 1886. Foreign. Secret. F.No. 201 of August 1886.
10. 1st May 1888. Foreign. Secret. F.No. KW. 226-236 of July 1888.
11. 2nd May 1888. Foreign. Secret. F.No. KW. 226-236 of July 1888.
12. 14th May 1888. Foreign. Secret. F.No. KW. 226-236 of July 1888.
13. 13th June 1888. Foreign. Secret. F.No. KW. 226-236 of July 1888.
14. 24th July 1888. Foreign. Secret. F.No. 236 of July 1888.
15. 18th October 1888. Foreign. Secret. F.No. KW. 3-192-197 of August 1889.
16. 17th September 1886. Foreign. Secret. F.No. KW. 115-118 of January 1888.
17. 18th October 1886. Foreign. Secret. F.No. KW. 115-118 of January 1888.
18. 21st October 1886. Foreign. Secret. F.No. KW. 115-118 of January 1888.
19. 21st February 1887. Foreign. Secret. F.No. 721 of June 1887.
20. 21st May 1887. Foreign. Secret. F.No. 286 of October 1887.
21. 9th September 1887. Foreign. Secret. F.No. KW. 115-118 of January 1888.
22. 10th October 1887. Foreign. Secret. F.No. KW. 115-118 of January 1888.
23. 18th October 1887. Foreign. Secret. F.No. KW. 115-118 of January 1888.
24. 28th January 1888. Foreign. Frontier A. No. 181 of May 1888.
25. 2nd February 1888. Foreign. Frontier A. No. 164 of May 1888.
26. 31st March 1888. Foreign. Secret. F.No. 63 of July 1888.

27. 28th April 1888. Foreign. Secret. F.No. KW. 1-63-86 of July 1888.
28. 6th May 1888. Foreign. Secret. F.No. KW. 1-63-86 of July 1888.
29. Undated. Foreign. Secret. F.No. 107 of July 1888.
30. 7th June 1888. Foreign. Secret. F.No. 103 of October 1888.
31. 11th June 1888. Foreign. Secret. F. KW. 1-89-110 of July 1888.
32. 13th June 1888. Foreign. Secret. F. KW. 1-89-110 of July 1888.
33. 14th June 1888. Foreign. Secret. F. KW. 1-89-110 of July 1888.
34. 21st June 1888. Foreign. Secret. F. No. 104 of October 1888.
35. 30th June 1888. Foreign. Secret. F. No. 118 of July 1888.
36. 254th August 1888. Foreign. Secret. F. No. 118 of October 1888. Enclosure.
37. 5th December 1888. Foreign. Secret. F. No. 553 of May 1888.
38. 13th February 1889. Foreign. Secret. F. No. KW. 2-544-559 of May 1889.
39. 27th February 1889. Foreign. Secret. F. No. 80 of April 1889.
40. 3rd March 1889. Foreign. Secret. F. No. KW. 1-80-98 of April 1889.
41. 16th March 1889. Foreign. Secret. F. No. KW. 1-80-98 of April 1889.
42. 1st June 1889. Foreign. Secret. F. No. 47 of July 1889.
43. 5th August 1889. Foreign. Secret. F. No. 108 of October 1889.
44. 21st August 1889. Foreign. Secret. F. No. KW. 2-231-252 of September 1889.
45. 1st September 1889. Foreign. Secret. F. No. KW. 2-231-252 of September 1889.
46. 6th September 1889. Foreign. Secret. F. No. 118 of October 1889.
47. 24th October 1889. Foreign. Secret. F. No. KW. 2-59-84 of February 1890.
48. 20th October 1889. Foreign. Secret. F. No. KW. 2-59-84 of February 1890.
49. 28th October 1889. Foreign. Secret. F. No. KW. 2-59-84 of February 1890.
50. Undated. Foreign. Secret F.No. KW. 2-59-84 of February 1890.
51. Undated. Foreign. Secret F.No. 274 of May 1890.
52. Undated. 1889. General & Pol. File No. 18 of 1889 (Jammu Archives)
53. Undated. Foreign. Secret F.No. 120 of October 1889.
54. Undated. Foreign. Secret F.No. 18 of June 1891.
55. Russian Central Asia. By Henry Lansdell. Vol. 1, p. 492.
56. 30th December 1889. Foreign. Secret F.No. 79 of February 1890.
57. 12th January 1890. Foreign. Secret F.No. 137 of April 1890.
58. 3rd February 1890. Foreign. Secret F.No. KW. 2-351-380 of May 1890.
59. 10th February 1890. Foreign. Secret F.No. KW. 2-351-380 of May 1890.
60. 24th February 1890. Foreign. Secret F.No. KW. 2-351-380 of May 1890.
61. 24th February 1890. Foreign. Secret F.No. KW. 2-351-380 of May 1890.
62. 4th March 1890. Foreign. Secret F.No. KW. 2-351-380 of May 1890.
63. 2nd June 1890. Foreign. Secret F.No. 193 of August 1890.
64. 21st July 1890. Foreign. Secret F.No. 32 of September 1890.
65. 2nd August 1890. Foreign. Secret F.No. 152 of September 1890.
66. Undated. Foreign. Secret. F. Nos. 426, 427, 444, 423 and 399 of September

1892.

67. 30th August 1890. Foreign. Secret F.No. KW. 151-156 of September 1890.
68. 8th September 1890. Foreign. Secret F.No. 44 of September 1890.
69. 21st September 1890. Foreign. Secret F.No. 162-A of March 1891.
70. 30th September 1890. Foreign. Secret F.No. KW. 3-123-148 of March 1891.
71. 13th October 1890. Foreign. Secret F.No. 129 of March 1891.
72. 17th January 1891. Foreign. Secret F.No. 231 of May 1891.
73. 10th February 1891. Foreign. Secret F.No. KW. 2-130-254 of November 1891.
74. 4th April 1891. Foreign. Secret F.No. 167 of July 1891.
75. 23rd April 1891. Foreign. Secret F.No. KW. 2-105-117 of August 1891.
76. 25th April 1891. Foreign. Secret F.No. 172 of July 1891.
77. 27th May 1891. Foreign. Secret F.No. 130 of November 1891.
78. 27th May 1891. Foreign. Secret F.No. KW. 1-128-131 of June 1891.
79. 30th May 1891. Foreign. Secret F.No. KW. 1-128-131 of June 1891.
80. 4th June 1891. Foreign. Secret F.No. 178 of November 1891.
81. 13th June 1891. Foreign. Secret F.No. 234 of July 1891.
82. 25th June 1891. Foreign. Secret F.No. 199 of November 1891.
83. 27th June 1891. Foreign. Secret F.No. KW. 2-130-254 of November 1891.
84. 9th July 1891. Foreign. Secret F.No. 198 of November 1891.
85. Tribes of The Hindu Kush. By Colonel J. Biddulph. pp. 20 and 29.
86. 22nd July 1891. Foreign. Secret. F.No. 207 of November 1891.
87. 23rd July 1891. Foreign. Secret F.No. 96 of December 1891.
88. 25th July 1891. Foreign. Secret F.No. 270 of September 1891.
89. Undated. Foreign. Secret. F.No. 96 of December 1891.
90. 27th July 1891. Foreign. Secret F.No. KW. 2-261-282 of August 1891.
91. 1st August 1891. Foreign. Secret F.No. 272 of September 1891.
92. 4th August 1891. Foreign. Secret F.No. 296 of September 1891.
93. 13th August 1891. Foreign. Secret F.No. 96 of September 1891.
94. 17th August 1891. Foreign. Secret F.No. 114 of September 1891.
95. 18th August 1891. Foreign. Secret F.No. 117 of September 1891.
96. 18th August 1891. Foreign. Secret F.No. 75 of September 1891.
97. 20th August 1891. Foreign. Secret F.No. 287 of September 1891.
98. 22th August 1891. Foreign. Secret F.No. 299 of September 1891.
99. 24th August 1891. Foreign. Secret F.No. 96 of December 1891.
100. 25th August 1891. Foreign. Secret F.No. KW. 1-261-282 of August 1891.
101. 27th August 1891. Foreign. Secret F.No. 232 of December 1891.
102. 28th August 1891. Foreign. Secret F.No. KW. 1-72-126 of September 1891.
103. 29th August 1891. Foreign. Secret F.No. 289 of September 1891.
104. 29th August 1891. Foreign. Secret F.No. 312 of September 1891.
105. 29th August 1891. Foreign. Secret F.No. 264 of October 1891.
106. 30th August 1891. Foreign. Secret F.No. 96 of December 1891.
107. 31st August 1891. Foreign. Secret F.No. 96 of December 1891.

108. 31st August 1891. Foreign. Secret F.No. 96 of December 1891.
109. 2nd September 1891. Foreign. Secret F.No. 105 of September 1891.
110. 4th August 1891. Foreign. Secret F.No. KW. 1-72-126 of September 1891.
111. 6th August 1891. Foreign. Secret F.No. KW. 1-72-126 of September 1891.
112. Undated. Foreign. Secret. F.No. 234 of November 1891.
113. 4th September 1891. Foreign. Secret F.No. KW. 1-130-254 of November 1891.
114. 10th September 1891. Foreign. Secret F.No. 210 of November 1891.
115. 14th September 1891. Foreign. Secret F.No. 230 of November 1891.
116. 10th October 1891. Foreign. Secret F.No. 241 of November 1891.
117. 7th November 1891. Foreign. Secret F.No. 230 of January 1892.
118. 23rd November 1891. Foreign. Secret F.No. 36 of April 1892.
119. Undated. Foreign. Secret. F.No. 90 of April 1892.
120. 29th November 1891. Foreign. Secret F.No. 51 of January 1892.
121. 18th December 1891. Foreign. Secret F.No. 280 of June 1892.
122. 15th December 1891. Foreign. Secret F.No. 39 of April 1892.
123. 19th December 1891. Foreign. Secret F.No. 42 of April 1892.
124. 25th December 1891. Foreign. Frontier A. No. 102 of January 1892.
125. Where Three Empires Meet. By E.F. Knight, p. 381.
126. The Making Of A Frontier. By Colonel Algernon Durand, p. 264.
127. Between Ten Oxus And The Indus. By Colonel R.C.F. Schombert, p. 129.
128. The Making Of A Frontier. By Colonel Algernon Durand, p. 264.
129. 5th January 1892. Foreign. Secret F.No. 68 of April 1892.
130. 6th January 1892. Foreign. Secret F.No. 45 of April 1892.
131. 8th January 1892. Foreign. Secret F.No. 60 of April 1892.
132. Undated. January 1892. Foreign. Secret F.No. 95 of June 1892.
133. 13th January 1892. Foreign. Secret F.No. 65 of April 1892.
134. 20th January 1892. Foreign. Secret F.No. 186 of March 1892.
135. 28th January 1892. Foreign. Secret F.No. 69 of April 1892.
136. 28th January 1892. Foreign. Secret F.No. 64 of April 1892.
137. 31st January 1892. Foreign. Secret F.No. 11 of May 1892.
138. 3rd February 1892. Foreign. Secret F.No. 251 of June 1892.
139. 16th February 1892. Foreign. Secret F.No. 4 of May 1892.
140. 17th February 1892. Foreign. Secret F.No. 5 of May 1892.
141. 18th February 1892. Foreign. Secret F.No. KW. 2-1-91 of April 1892.
142. 22nd February 1892. Foreign. Secret F.No. 37 of May 1892.
143. 22nd February 1892. Foreign. Secret F.No. 151 of July 1892.
144. 23rd February 1892. Foreign. Secret F.No. 125 of July 1892.
145. 25th February 1892. Foreign. Secret F.No. 20 of May 1892.
146. 3rd March 1892. Foreign. Secret F.No. 78 of April 1892.
147. 4th March 1892. Foreign. Secret F.No. 27 of May 1892.
148. 4th March 1892. Foreign. Secret F.No. 29 of May 1892.
149. 5th March 1892. Foreign. Secret F.No. 28 of May 1892.
150. 9th March 1892. Foreign. Secret F.No. 81 of April 1892.
151. 10th March 1892. Foreign. Secret F.No. 154 of July 1892.

152. Undated. Foreign. Secret F.No. 129 of June 1892.
153. 16th March 1892. Foreign. Secret F.No. 161 of June 1892.
154. 17th March 1892. Foreign. Secret F.No. 83 of April 1892.
155. 18th March 1892. Foreign. Secret F.No. 167 of July 1892.
156. 20th March 1892. Foreign. Secret F.No. 140 of June 1892.
157. 22th March 1892. Foreign. Secret F.No. 141 of June 1892.
158. 24th March 1892. Foreign. Secret F.No. 131 of June 1892.
159. 31st March 1892. Foreign. Secret F.No. 139 of June 1892.
160. 4th April 1892. Foreign. Secret F.No. 158 of June 1892.
161. *Ibid.*
162. 19th April 1892. Foreign. Secret F.No. 533 of June 1892.
163. 20th April 1892. Foreign. Secret F.No. 159 of June 1892.
164. 6th May 1892. Foreign. Secret F.No. 163 of August 1892.
165. 7th May 1892. Foreign. Secret F.No. KW. 1-89-203 of June 1892.
166. 10th May 1892. Foreign. Secret F.No. 155 of July 1892.
167. 13th May 1892. Foreign. Secret F.No. 162 of August 1892.
168. 12th May 1892. Foreign. Secret F.No. 168 of June 1892.
169. 25th May 1892. Foreign. Secret F.No. 147 of July 1892.
170. 27th May 1892. Foreign. Secret F.No. KW 1-89-203 of June 1892.
171. 8th June 1892. Foreign. Secret F.No. KW. 1-130-177 of July 1892.

Chapter 8
Chinese Contradictions

A seemingly insignificant development with regard to the northern frontier was the association of young Andrew Dalgleish with the British owned Central Asian Trading Company in 1880. He then went upto Yarkand and followed up this visit with another in 1881. Of this visit Elias, then British Joint Commissioner at Leh, took notice. Though he had no passport Dalgleish was admitted into and allowed free movement in Yarkand. The Amban did not levy even the "usual duties" on his merchandise "as a mark of friendship for the English."[1] To Dalgleish, the Chinese spoke "of the border at Shahidulla as British border."[2] But British officers, like Elias, never accepted Shahidulla as boundary.[3] With a recommendation from none other than A.O. Hume,[4] then a Secretary to the British Indian Government,* Dalgleish appears to have joined the British secret service, ostensibly as a "news-writer" at Yarkand. He, it can further be conjectured, seems to have thus tread on the toes of an Afghan, Dad Mohammad, apparently in a similar but older employment of the Government of India. Dalgleish's tragic end later provides decisive evidence of Jammu and Kashmir's complete jurisdiction over the trans-Karakoram territories, fully acknowledged by China and Russia despite British obfuscation.

On the strength of his frequent journeys to and long stays in Yarkand, Dalgleish drew the attention of the Foreign Department to "the comparatively narrow tract of Chinese territory that intervenes between the Terek pass and Shahidulla...at the present moment entirely at the mercy of Russia."[5] From the Terek the so-called "gap" between Afghanistan and Chinese and Russian empires started southward down to Hunza, Yasin and Chitral or led south-east through the Yarkand valley, to Shahidulla. The territory comprising the "gap," as noticed, was mostly Kanjuti or Ladakhi, not Chinese. A year later, in 1883, Dalgleish conveyed

---

* Hume, later, founded the Indian National Congress.

to the Foreign Department what China considered its western and southern boundary :

> "The western frontier extends to the Bolan (Bolor) Mountains and follows this range in a southerly direction until it meets the northern spur of mountains that springs from the Hindu Kush. This northern spur runs in an east-south-east direction and joins the Kuen Lun range taking in the Yangi dawan (overlooking Yarkand valley) via Kokyar, the Kilian pass via Kilian and the Sanju pass via Sanju, which becomes the southern frontier. The Chinese consider all to the south of Sirikul district and the above named three passes, the territory of their friendly neighbour, the British."[6]

Such a boundary line of Kashgaria almost entirely agrees with the historical boundary of India in the north. Except for Sirikul, which Dalgleish himself reveals he persuaded the Chinese to take under their rule, however nominal, it left Taghdumbash and Raskam to Hunza and the Yarkand valley to Skardo and Ladakh. After his persuasion Dalgleish claimed "the fort of Sirikul (Tashkurgan) flies the Chinese flag and the Begs of Sirikul have received new robes of honour, (as a mark of their subordination to China), from the Amban of Yarkand and have been made to understand that the entire district of Sirikul is now under Chinese rule." In form a take over was, perhaps, effected. But the district and its Begs remained effectively under Hunza. To nullify Kanjuti vassalage of China, Dalgleish advocated the Maharaja taking and holding Hunza for commercial and strategical considerations. Ridgeway, Under Secretary in the Foreign Department, later Sir West, agreed, noting for Charles Grant, Foreign Secretary :

> "The importance...of preserving the supremacy of Kashmir over Kanjut (Hunza) cannot well be exaggerated. Mr. Dalgleish does not appear to know that Hunza's allegiance to Kashmir is unquestionable, and that it can be enforced by Kashmir without any difficulty."[7]

All the doubts the British had about Kashmir's claim to Hunza vanished but only after Russia's threat through the "gap" had loomed large. No more was the Maharaja's hold over Hunza "nominal." It was "unquestionable." England, surely, was intent on intervention in Gilgit, in Kashmir.

When the Kashgar mission headed by Elias, arrived in Leh, Dalgleish was already there. He had been expelled from Yarkand after ten months of unauthorised stay. Dalgleish had left Yarkand by the end of May, followed by the Kashmir Aksakal. Through him, from the Kilian boundary point, Dalgleish sent his compliments to the new Amban with the remark : "...in Central Asia, China has only one friend, England."[8] Dalgleish wished to return to Yarkand. Through the good offices of the Foreign Department, he sought a passport from China for Eastern Turkistan so as to carry on business as a "trader."[9] Should it not be deemed feasible to send a British consul to Yarkand and Kashgar, Dalgleish, offered "to collect news for Government of doings in Central Asia," when he returned to Yarkand. With the concurrence of the Governor-General-in-Council, Dalgleish was once again appointed, initially for a period of one year. Dalgleish set out for Yarkand on 20th March, 1888, from Leh, followed by Dad Mohammad, a Kakar Pathan. He was not destined to reach Yarkand. On 10th April, 1888, he was shot dead by Dad Mohammad" on the other (north) side of the Karakoram in the tent of one Osman Andijani....after making the pass."[10] The report on the murder was brought direct to the Wazir of Ladakh, Dr. Suraj Bal, and not to the British Joint Commissioner or his office, by Dalgleish's servant, Ahmed Jan. A detailed report followed from the Kardar of Tonchi. Dad Mohammad would appear to have had accomplices, including the "Punjabi Faqir" and Osman Andijani. In exercise of his criminal jurisdiction, in this case beyond the Karakoram which the British had repeatedly set as the boundary of Jammu and Kashmir, six Ladakhi guards, regulars and irregulars, accompanied by two "Arghans" (half caste Ladakhis) in charge of a Jemadar, were despatched by Dr. Suraj Bal towards Shahidulla and Yarkand. He sent letters to the Kashmir and Afghan Aksakals at Yarkand together with an "ishtihar" (notice) announcing a reward of Rs. 500 (or about 4000 Tongas) to any one who either secured the murderers or enabled the Wazarat to secure any or all of them.[11] The Aksakals were adviced by the Wazir to put themselves in communication with the Chinese authorities, this being necessary from other factors apart, in the event of Jammu and Kashmir armed guards or police entering Eastern Turkistan. The Wazir apprehended the murderer might have made off from Wahab Jilga, one march further north, from the site of the crime, from where a road then led off to Hunza or Yagistan. The British Joint Commissioner was notified of these proceedings, Dalgleish having been a British national, and invited to suggest any further measures needed to be taken.

Significantly Dad Mohammad sent a message to the Wazir of Ladakh and not to the Amban of Yarkand or the Taotai of Kashgar, through

Mohammad Jan, from Balti Polo or Balti Brangsa, just short of Wahab Jilga, to the north of the Karakoram pass :

> "that he is sorry he cannot write a letter as pen and ink were not handy; that the Bhots (Ladakhi carriers of Dalgleish) would take at least ten days before they could get back with the news to Leh; that another ten days would be required for any search party to come up; that meantime he would be the Lord of the jungle."[12]

Clearly implied in the message is that the Wazir of Ladakh wielded jurisdiction beyond the Karakoram pass. Dad Mohammad was not an ordinary criminal. He had served the British Indian Government and was, otherwise too, a respectable Afghan. It is not correct, as Ramsay suggests, that the murder was committed to rob Dalgleish. The Wazir sent another search party comprising "10 military men with arms etc.," and one 'munshi' (clerk), assisted by two Turki speaking 'Arghans,' towards Yarkand. A fresh notice, issued by the British Joint Commissioner, raised the reward for apprehending Dad Mohammad to Rs. 5000 by the Government of India.[13] Despite acknowledgedly prompt proceedings of Dr. Suraj Bal,[14] the Viceroy cabled Sir John Walsham at Beijing to enlist Chinese assistance for seizing the murderers.[15] This turned a criminal issue into boundary issue. In response to Sir John's queries, the Viceroy telegraphed : "Murder was committed between (the) crest of (the) Karakoram and Wahab Jilga, not in Chinese territory. (I) cannot say whether (the) murderers were Chinese subjects."[16] The Tsungli Yamen was duly informed of the murder of Dalgleish, committed "between the crest of the range of mountains known as the Karakoram, or Tsungling range, and a place in the pass of the former name before it reaches Chinese territory." Arrest of the culprits, two of whom were identified as Andijanis residing at Yarkand, was sought through the Chinese Eastern-Turkistan authorities.[17] The parties, troops and all, despatched by the Wazir of Ladakh, headed towards Shahidulla. They found whole of Dalgleish's property lying at Wahab Jilga. Only a rifle was missing and a box broken. But Ramsay presumed "boxes have been opened and the most valuable things stolen."[18]

The search parties had briefly stayed at Shahidulla. The troops did not proceed beyond.[19] But had the murderers been found "this" (or Indian) side of Shahidulla they had instructions to "seize" them and bring them back to Leh. Three of the first search party, including Eshi, a Ladakhi of the "Bhot" regiment, which served as police, went to Yarkand.

Dad Mohammad had been aided to travel by an unused path so as to avoid the Chinese post at Kilian, where the "Rahdaris" (passports) were checked. The "Punjabi Faqir" had been to Kilian but had left a day or two earlier to the arrival of the Kashmir police party. He was, however, soon arrested by Eshi and others. In Yarkand Dr. Bal's letters were handed over to different Aksakals. They also sought letters from the British Joint Commissioner. The murder was reported to the Amban. Three other accomplices of Dad Mohammad, Gulban, Osman and Khal Mohammad were in Yarkand and the Amban was willing to hand them over to Eshi's party if the Aksakals would be answerable "for their being made over to the Ladakh authorities." When Eshi returned to Kilian en route to Leh, "Punjabi Faqir" was handed over to him to be escorted to Leh. Ramsay sought instructions as to who was to try them, the Wazir by himself or the two Joint Commissioners together? Plowden, then Resident in Kashmir, appeared at one time to have favoured the Wazir by himself conducting the trial, which was also the legal position the site of the murder not being on the Changchenmo route and the accused not being Englishmen.[20]

The Taotai of Kashgar pointed out the crime was committed in "British territory."[21] But to keep up British fiction, Ramsay considered "the murder was perpetrated in the moot territory between the crest of the Karakoram and Shahidulla."[22] Dad Mohammad escaped to Russian territory and the British became dissatisfied with the Chinese authorities for their failure "to take that prompt and vigorous action which the circumstances of the case required."[23] The Chinese seems to have insisted that the surrender of the accomplices of Dad Mohammad would be made over only to a Kashmir officer. Consequently Ramsay asked the Ladakh Wazir, Pandit Radha Krishan Kaul, to depute the "Naib" (deputy) Wazir, Sardar Akbar Khan, to Eastern Turkistan.[24] Though serving Jammu and Kashmir State, Akbar Khan might well have been amenable to British influence. Ramsay's request was referred by the Wazir to the spineless State Council, which, surprisingly, turned it down.[25] Instead the State chose the Munshi of the Ladakh Wazarat, Shamsuddin, and deputed him to Central Asia, in search of Dad Mohammad. Shamsuddin carried letters from the Russian consul general at Kashgar and the British. The latter had depute Lt. Bower but not enjoying a legal status had perforce to sit out the search. Dad Mohammad was finally tracked down to Samakand and, at the instance of Shamsuddin[26] arrested on the order of the Russian Deputy Governor. E.F. Knight in his "Where Three Empires Meet" gives a considerably different account[27] and yet admits that the arrest was effected at the instance of the Kashmir official.

Elias mission, was rightly linked with redrawing of boundaries and Jammu and Kashmir Government made a determined effort to physically occupy Shahidulla. Elias was alarmed and in a communication of which only an extract is available, reported to Sir Mortimer :

> "This very energetic and, rather, over active Wazir (of Ladakh) has also raised another question, which I think the Government ought to take note of. He wants the Maharaja to reoccupy Shahidulla in the Karakash valley. I cannot exactly ascertain from him whether he has recommended the step officially yet or not, but at all events I see indications of his preparing to carry it out, and in my opinion, he should be restrained, or an awakward boundary question may be raised with the Chinese without any compensating advantage. Previous to the rebellion in Eastern Turkistan which broke up Chinese rule there in 1863, the Kashmiris had occupied Shahidulla for nearly 20 years [in a side note: nearly ever since they had Ladakh (1834)]. About 1865 they abandoned it and in 1868 Shaw and Hayward found it occupied by the Andijani (Kokandi) troops of the late Amir Yakub Beg. In 1873-74, Sir D. Forsyth recognised the Amir's ownership and recommended the Maharaja's boundary to be drawn to the north of Karakash valley as shown in the map accompanying the mission's report. This I believe has *never been accepted* by Kashmir, and the boundary has been left an open question."[28]

Elias' reasons why Jammu and Kashmir had better leave Shahidulla alone were : 1. That it was too far away from its base to be held effectively–it was 240 mile from Leh and 170 mile from the farthest outlying village in that direction. Five big passes intervened and it was cut off in winter. 2. The Chinese, though they had never occupied the fort, after their return to Eastern Turkistan (or even earlier) had, Elias, like other Englishmen, claimed, assumed the government of the (Kirghiz) people who lived in the Karakash valley, and had levied taxes on them since 1881. Shahidulla was only 65 miles from the Chinese 'karaul' on the other side and only one pass intervened. 3. The immediate cause of the Wazir's wish to reclaim the place was the discovery in the Karakash valley, somewhere near Shahidulla, of a lapis lazuli mine which, Elias believed, was really discovered by a Bajauri Pathan over whom Kashmir had no jurisdiction. Beside, Elias insisted the mine was almost valueless. Above all he favoured, as heretofore, the Indus watershed as the boundary. He, therefore, sought the Kashmir 'Darbar' to be "restrained." Other than on distance disadvantage, Elias' arguments were misstatements or false statements which trivialised the boundary issue. Elias appears to have held out threats and blandishments to the Wazir, Pandit Radha Krishan Kaul, to abandon physical occupation of Shahidulla.[29] The Foreign Department proposed Colonel Sir O. St. John, the British officer-on-special-duty in Kashmir, should advise "the Darbar not to occupy Shahidulla."[30] The Viceroy agreed.[31] Only extracts[32] of Elias' letter were sent to Colonel Sir O. St. John, full contents would have only further estranged the State. Maharaja Ranbir Singh having passed away and a Resident foisted on his successor, Maharaja Pratap Singh, he was advised "to refrain" from authorising occupation of Shahidulla.[33] Consequently the Resident was assured that Shahidulla "will never be occupied against the wishes of H.E. the Viceroy..."[34] Far from laying claim to Shahidulla, or kicking up a border row, as Elias had imagined, the Chinese had continued to limit themselves to their boundary at Kilian "karaul."

The frontier line between China and Kashmir having been questioned by the British Indian Government, Ramsay from Leh was not certain "where the boundary is between Ladakh and Kashgaria."[35] The sixth edition of the Turkistan map pointed the boundary "at Aktagh," midway between Shahidulla and the Karakoram pass while, according to the Ladakh Gazetteer, "Shahidulla lies on the frontier of Ladakh and Yarkand territories." In the view of Captain, later General, Cunningham, "the Karakoram range is the boundary." To Ramsay the Wazir of Ladakh put Shahidulla as the limit of Jammu and Kashmir. Ordinarily the boundary should be the watershed, Ramsay went on, but pointed out, "the only evidence to the contrary lies in the fact that in 1873 when our mission was going to Yarkand, it was escorted to Shahidulla by Ladakh officials and there met by Yarkand officials."[36] His own view on the boundary issue was different. It might be as well, Ramsay proposed, to get the point settled while Eastern Turkistan was still under China for he "confidently anticipated that before very long Kashgaria will become a Russian province."[37] The boundary issue he raised with the Resident was in the context of construction of the Shyok-Daulatbeg Uldi section of the Leh-Yarkand road, then under active consideration. To its construction Ramsay was opposed. From a purely commercial point of view he found it doubtless necessary, from a military point of view not. From Daulatbeg Uldi to the crest of the Karakoram is just 11 miles. "...the knowledge that such a good road existed to within so short a distance of their frontier might induce the Russians to construct a similar road from Yarkand to the Ladakh border," Ramsay argued. As against 11 miles from Daulatbeg Uldi to the Karakoram crest, the distance between the latter and Shahidulla was 79 miles. It was, in the view of Ramsay,

> "desirable that it should be clearly settled that the Ladakh frontier was at Shahidulla and not at the Karakoram pass. The extra 79 miles of the mountainous country, which could be kept without good roads, would be valuable in itself as barrier against the Russian aggression via the Karakoram and it would also place in our keeping the entrances from the yarkand side to the several Changchenmo routes towards India..."[38]

T.C. Plowden, the Resident in Kashmir, counselled the Foreign Department that it would be "advisable to ascertain the views of the Kashmir Darbar"[39] which, notwithstanding the British then virtually ruling the State, would hardly have consented to rolling back the northern boundary from Shahidulla. With the western end of the northern boundary still unresolved, predictably the Governor General-in-Council did "not desire at present to discuss the boundary between Ladakh and Kashga."[40] Besides the views of Ramsay were at variance with the large group of British officers. For official purposes the British had no option but to continue to regard the Sanju, Kilian and Kukyar passes as China's boundary to the south, one reason for this was collection of duties by China on Eastern Turkistan's import-export trade with India at these frontier posts. A commercial treaty was in 1887 being negotiated by the British with China for India's Central Asian trade and for establishment of a British Indian consulate at Kashgar. The Chinese, it was certain, would continue to collect their duties on this trade at these frontier posts. The boundary could not have been changed for the purposes of the treaty. Younghusband, therefore, proposed Yarkand river as the northern boundary, for one reason Eastern Turkistan then possessed one village in the vicinity of the southern slopes of the range which forms the watershed between the Yarkand and Tisnaf rivers. The Tisnaf rises in Sirikul. Younghusband, when last in the region, was told that the Chinese had measured land for purposes of assessment of revenue, "as far as five miles south of Kukyar..." On account of this village the Turks had conveyed to Younghusband that the Jammu and Kashmir boundary ran" as far down as the Yarkand river." Younghusband suggested to the Foreign Department :

> "On the banks of the Yarkand river there are some stretches of good pasture land, and it would be advantageous that the Kashmir frontier line should include these and should run along the watershed between the Yarkand and Tisnaf rivers."[41]

For trade under article VII of the proposed commercial treaty, Younghusband favoured the following passes should be named as the roads by which goods should be permitted to cross the frontier :

1. Tashkurgan leading to Kukyar.
2. Chiraghsaldi leading to Kukyar.
3. Yangi (Yarkaud valley) leading to Kukyar.
4. Kilik leading to Shekbash.
5. Kilian leading to Kilian.
6. Sanju leading to Sanju.
7. Hindutash leading to Khotan.
8. Yangi (north of Aksai Chin) leading to Khotan.

These were also the passes that marked the genuine boundary between China and Jammu and Kashmir. The British were thus as aware of the northern boundary of the State as they were of its eastern sector. Younghusband wished article VII to be so worded (for instance changing the words "routes" into "places" or "points") that, in the event of Russians ever occupying Chinese Turkistan, it might be possible to fall back on this article,

> "to claim the frontier upto the watershed of the Kuen Lun and keep them out of the Yarkand valley."

The debate on the northern boundary did not die down with the Governor General-in-Council declining to take it up with China. Colonel M.S. Bell, Deputy Quarter Master General, Intelligence Branch, joined issue with the Foreign Department, fear persisting in British military circles of Russia absorbing Eastern Turkistan. But for the British policy pursued, which he viewed critically, Bell was certain "Kashmir's borders would have enveloped Kanjut and China's suzerainty would not be now acknowledged there..." He, indeed, proposed why not the Government of India call upon China "to restore Kanjut to Kashmir and withdraw her protection given to its chief." Before the question of the boundaries of the upper Oxus provinces, Russian Central Asia and Kashmir came to be seriously considered, Bell favoured the presence of a consular agent at

Kashgar. He also considered it important to :

> "demarcate the borders of Sirikul and Kashmir and generally between China and Kashmir which may be taken along what may be termed outer-shed, i.e., the line of passes Yangi, Kilik, Kilian, Sanju, Sangi to south of Polur, etc..."[42]

Bell, therefore, acknowledge that the Kuen Lun was the boundary of Jammu and Kashmir. Even more, he admitted south of Polur was Ladakh, not Tibet. In advocating demarcation of Sirikul-Kashmir boundary, Bell implied Taghdumbash was within Kashmir. Were the commercial treaty to be signed with China, goods were proposed to pass and repass by the cols Younghusband had listed.

The concatenation of circumstances which had earlier led Ramsay to suggest demarcation of the boundary were totally distinct from those which had persuaded Elias to take the opposite view. His principal arguments Ramsay spelt out were : (1) northern boundary had come to assume imperial proportions and it was, therefore, no more the concern of Jammu and Kashmir and its neighbours. (2) British policy ought to confine Russia at as great a distance as possible to the north-west of the Hindu Kush-Muztagh-Karakoram ranges, (3) it was in the interests of both Britain and China that the "no-man's" lands "near our respective *assumed* frontier," should be formally taken possession of by one or the other before Russians came near enough to interfere or share in the appropriation. Whether China retained Eastern Turkistan or not, it was, in the view of Ramsay, in British interest to get the "Chinese border demarcated now." Moreover he saw it was to British advantage "to make China's frontier conterminous with ours for this would give us a neighbour who might resist Russian aggression..."[43] The "wretched savages" then in possession of the "no-man's land" were not fancied to defend it. The allusion is to Hunza which then held part of the Yarkand valley, all of Taghdumbash and Sirikul, which all was part of the so-called "no-man's land." Unless the Government of India had already made up its mind on the question, Plowden felt, it could be examined on the occasion of the Viceroy's approaching visit to Kashmir,[44] evidently in consultation with the State. In the Foreign Department, Cunningham diplomatically remarked, "The Chinese domination of the Karakash is not, perhaps, quite effectual, and one day it may, if convenient and desirable, be easy for Russia to step in; but as it seems to me the position is this that China would certainly oppose the assertion of the Kashmir rights."[45] China had not the remotest control over it, being still confined to her historical boundary, along the Kuen Lun, to the north of the Karakash valley, over the passes of the Sanju, Kilian Kukyar and Yangi. The Chinese were not even aware of the routes leading to the Karakash valley or the Aksai Chin, further east. Sir Mortimer's view was no different from Cunningham's. It did not seem desirable to him "to run the risk of a troublesome controversy with China in order to push a Kashmir post beyond the Karakoram. I would rather let the matter drop."[46] The Viceroy, Lord Dufferin concurred.[47] That still was not the end of the argument.

Once again Ramsay kindled a debate on the northern boundary in Jammu and Kashmir. Another memorandum on the issue he preferred, now at the instance of Sir Mortimer. In this paper Ramsay critically examined the views expressed by Sir Douglas Forsyth in a memo he had sent to the Government of India in July 1873 and of Ney Elias, expressed twelve years later in July 1885. In once again urging Government to settle the northern boundary, he was influenced by Andrew Dalgleish's brief memorandum on the Chinese position in Yarkand. Sir Douglas Forsyth had argued it would be very unsafe to define the boundary of Jammu and Kashmir in the direction of the Karakoram and if it must be put down at all it should be put as near lower Karakash river as possible. What frontier line he would have actually drawn was not clear. But Ramsay believed Forsyth would have "followed the course of the Karakash river, down to a point, not farther south than Shahidulla, where the Karakash first strikes the Karakoram-Yarkand road, and not farther north than the foot of the Sanju pass, where the Karakash turns to the east and flows away in the direction of Khotan." In the view of Ramsay, therefore, Forsyth's recommendation amounted to this, that advantage should be taken of any existing doubt "to now fix our frontier as far north as possible." This is a laboured interpretation because, firstly, between the Karakash and the Kuen Lun, the natural as well as the real boundary, there hardly is any distance. By bringing down the frontier from the crest of the Kuen Lun to the Karakash the intention was to unsettle the boundary line and provide for its eventual pull back to the Karakoram pass. Besides, as Forsyth favoured lower Karakash as the limit of Jammu and Kashmir, what was to be the boundary, east of lower Karakash, for the Aksai Chin plateaux? Forsyth, it appears, deliberately left this boundary unspelt because he considered Aksai Chin a "no-man's land."

As for Elias, Ramsay thought, he had not look at the issue from an Imperial point of view. His view appeared to Ramsay to have been, as it were, prefaced by the words, "so far as the Kashmir Darbar is concerned..." Three and half years had elapsed since Elias had written on the boundary issue. In the interval events had marched apace, so far as the advance and consolidation of Russian power in Turkistan was concerned, and Ramsay believed "time has passed when we can afford to regard the question of the northern frontier of Kashmir as one chiefly concerning the Darbar and its present northern neighbours." What alarmed Ramsay was the Chinese position in Yarkand. Dalgleish had noted that the Chinese were :

> "very unwilling to extend their territory southwestwards, that it was only after frequent and urgend recommendations made by him to the Chinese authorities at Yarkand that they had sent troops to occupy the fort of Sirikul and that he believed that the Chinese now considered their frontier was bounded by a line extending from Sirikul to Kukyar, Kilian and Sanju."[48]

While British manipulation is quite evident, Chinese occupation of Sirikul at this period of time was only notional. Even so as then China was still nowhere in Taghdumbash and Yarkand valley. The Chinese conduct in regard to the murder of Dalgleish also showed to the British that the Eastern Turkistan authorities did not regard the Karakoram passes as their frontier. The land to the north of the Karakoram and Muztagh ranges, Ramsay considered, was of no pecuniary value either to the British or to the Chinese. To the Chinese it could be of no value from any point of view. But with the British, and assuming that the eventual annexation of Kashgaria by Russia was exceedingly probable, "the case is different."

Like other Englishmen Ramsay saw the Hindu Kush and Muztagh ranges "a natural barrier on the north and north-west frontier, the value of which depended chiefly on the extent of its impassability, and the absence of all made roads and bridges. Ramsay argued :

> "So long as and to such extent as these mountains are within our border, no roads will be made, for the cost of construction would be warranted only by military exigency, and it is impossible to imagine circumstances under which we should wish to send soldiers to such a place. In certain places roads can be made, and did the mountains belong in any degree to a hostile power, anxious to take possession, even temporarily, of the northern provinces of Kashmir, such roads might be made as far south as our border, without our having

> any right to object. The nearer this frontier was to the inhabited regions on our side of the mountains, the greater would be the inducement to construct such roads. It follows, therefore, that it is to our interest to include as much as possible of the inhospitable mountain ranges within our own border.
>
> "The most important portion to be fixed would be from the extreme north-western extremity, where the frontiers of Russia, Afghanistan, China and Kashmir would meet and from there eastward to Muztagh range. Till this part of the frontier is delimited, the door remains open through which Russia may come down south-east of the Little Pamir, into the 'no-man's land' at the back of the Kanjut country–a wedge like position between India and Kashgaria which it would not suit us that Russia should occupy."[49]

The Muztagh range being "terribly difficult to cross," it did not, in Ramsay's view, very much matter whether the boundary was at the Indus system watershed or at the northern base of the mountains. The road from Yarkand to Leh, via the Karakoram pass, even in its existing condition, presented no great difficulty and was yearly traversed by merchants with large number of heavily laden ponies. It was open all the years round and as thousands of ponies travelled over the road safely it could not be held to offer any great obstacle to an expedition advancing from Yarkand against Ladakh. Were a good road to exist as far as the Karakoram pass, the mountain barrier would be of little use, "and for this reason, we should endeavour to fix our frontier as far as possible north of the Karakoram pass,"[50] Ramsay argued, in harmony with Ladakh's traditional thinking on defence against invaders from the north. He favoured the boundary east of Shahidulla-Karakoram road should also be settled, especially if the Karakoram pass was to be the frontier. Another argument for demarcating the frontier that Ramsay pressed on Government was this. If the boundary was allowed to remain unsettled, the broad belt of "no-man's land" would also remain unadjusted. The Chinese would do a good deal to avoid coming into conflict with the Russians. "If, therefore, the latter now come down behind the Kanjut country, the Chinese sooner than risk having to fight about it would disavow all claim to the 'no-man's land,' but if the frontier had been formally demarcated, the Chinese could not, without loss of dignity, to which they would not submit, allow the Russians to enter upon that country and at the same time the Russians would be aware of this...In the same way if the Chinese agreed to give over the 'no-man's land' to us, the mere fact of its having been declared to be British territory, would suffice to prevent Russian encroachment..." With the Resident in Kashmir Colonel R.P. Nisbet, Ramsay's views found favour. Nisbet urged Government "that the adjustment of the whole northern and northwestern frontier of Kashmir should not be further postponed."[51] But for this the views of the Kashmir Darbar were needed to be obtained. Nisbet was sure these "would no doubt be favourable." Quite evidently this issue had been subject matter of discussion and friction with the Darbar earlier. The next step to be undertaken seemed to Nisbet to ascertain "what part of the border remains unexplored, "...work out on the spot the best *scientific frontier* to include the most inaccessible portions." It was a development least connected with Ramsay's latest dissertation that hastened British decisions on the northern boundary in Jammu and Kashmir. On the 18th September, 1888, Kanjutis raided "*Kashmir territory*[52] (italics in the original) between Sogat and Shahidulla." Khalchuskan, a 'nullah' between Shahidulla and Sogat, first and Sogat, later were the scenes of the Kanjuti depredations. Four Kirghiz families were looted and several men, women and children sold into slavery. Several caravans being then still in Leh, Jammu and Kashmir irregular troops, 23 strong, were despatched by the Wazir of Ladakh, Pandit Radha Krishan Kaul, on the 9th October 1888 to escort them to Shahidulla.[53] Having originally migrated to the lower Karakash valley from the adjoining Sanju area of Eastern Turkistan, the Kirghiz went in a deputation to Yarkand to seek Chinese protection. It was not given. Months later, in May 1889, before the passes had open after the fall, the Kirghiz sent a representative, Musa, a nephew of their chief, Turdikol, to Leh to offer their submission to the Maharaja of Jammu and Kashmir. The Resident in his weekly diary, containing political intelligence, merely conveyed to Government that Musa has "come to Leh to ask for help against Kanjutis." Their request to the Chinese to protect them against the Kanjutis had been turned down, "on the ground that the Kirghiz paid no taxes to China.[54]" That their allegiance was indeed offered by the Kirghiz to the Maharaja is confirmed by a letter Raja Amar Singh, the Prime Minister, wrote to the Resident on 29th May 1889.[55] In Leh Musa's statement was probably recorded in the presence of the Wazir of Ladakh. Musa then formally tendered the submission on behalf of the Kirghiz of Karakash. "We will consider ourselves your subjects and pay you taxes." The only proviso Musa made in his statement was that the Kirghiz be monetarily assisted in rebuilding the fort of Shahidulla, "which belongs to the Kashmir State," but was in a state of ruin, and that 20 or 30 troops be despatched to aid them to hold the fort. Most significantly it was the Chinese Amban of Yarkand who, Musa disclosed, had advised Turdikol :

> "that he should prefer his applications for help to the authorities in Ladakh from whom, he hoped, he would obtain assistance."[56]

When the Kirghiz had argued with the Amban that they were "Chinese subjects," the Amban had said "that Chinese frontier extended only to the Kilian and Sanju passes." Musa set at rest the British canard, first given currency to by Elias, that the Kirghiz of the Karakash valley paid taxes to the Chinese.

> "We pay taxes to China when we go to the north of the Kilian and Sanju. No Chinese official ever comes to Shahidulla and if we did not leave the latter place, we should pay no taxes to China..."[57]

Musa concluded his statement rather on a belligerent note. Were the Kirghiz not helped by the State, he asserted, "it is our intention to join our relatives, the Sirikuli Kirghiz, who are Russian subjects, and to place ourselves under Russian protection." Musa's statement, or, at least, some amplifications, such as on the issue of payment of taxes, seem to have been made in response to questions put to him, evidently by the Wazir, in order to silence the British on the tax issue. He certainly alarmed and, indeed, embarrassed the British. For the caravans expected in Leh from Yarkand and those proceeding to Kashgaria, Ramsay proposed a small escort[58]. Nevertheless Ramsay was rather uncertain whether to send the escort as that would have negated British posture that Shahidulla was beyond Kashmir. To Mohammad Ali, the Kashmir Aksakal at Yarkand, Raja Safdar Ali clarified that in the past also he had levied taxes on trade on the "road to Ladakh."[59] In a communication to the Amban of Yarkand, Safdar Ali justified his attack on the Kirghiz, the cause for which was stated to be failure of Turdikol to collect tax from the trade.[60] Safdar Ali clearly implies his suzerainty over the Karakash Kirghiz, those being from the same stock as the Kirghiz of Sirikul. Musa's statement, Ramsay suggested to Nisbet, should be considered by Government together with his memorandum on the boundary issue.[61] Were Government to act upon his memorandum and decide to demarcate the boundary, Ramsay suggested "it would be as well to encourage the

Shahidulla Kirghiz by giving them a few hundred rupees for repair of the Shahidulla fort..." Further were the Chinese not to "object" the fort could be occupied and Kirghiz taken under British protection.

Ignoring Chinese declaration on their boundary with Jammu and Kashmir, Sir Mortimer pretended, "Properly speaking the Karakash valley is Chinese territory and Kirghiz are Chinese subjects over whom the Yarkand Amban claims to exercise jurisdiction!"[62] Sir Mortimer's observation was made in the context of Musa's request for aid but it virtually disposed of Ramsay's memorandum. Credence also Sir Mortimer lent to another false British claim, made first by Shaw, that Yakub Beg Kushbegi, the ruler of Eastern Turkistan, had "kept the Kanjutis off the Ladakh road by stationing a mere handful of his Andijanis at Shahidulla..." Immediate British reaction of Kanjuti raid was stern. It was contemplated that an armed party could reach Hunza from Ladakh, as Maharaja Ranbir Singh had attempted in 1860s, and which the British had dissuaded him from undertaking then. Such an armed party while en route, could protect caravans. The Kanjutis could be thus kept quiet. Reports were rife in Yarkand that the Kanjutis intended to close down the Leh-Yarkand road.[63] The Kirghiz proposed to send another deputation of Ladakh. The mission was to be "similar to that of the Kirghiz Musa." British pretension that the Karakash valley was Chinese territory made Ramsay to counter Sir Mortimer's version. He pointed out that the Shahidulla fort was built by Jammu and Kashmir. For some unspecified reasons the State gave up the fort in about 1870. Five years later Amir Yakub Beg sent four or five men from his fort of Bostan or Oibuk, on march north of Shahidulla at the point of junction of the roads leading from Kilian and Sanju to Shahidulla, and took possession of Shahidulla.[64] The Chinese never sent any troops beyond Kilian and Sanju passes.

The considered British response to Kanjuti raid on Shahidulla Kirghiz was to depute Captain F.E. Younghusband "beyond the northern frontiers of the Kashmir State." Younghusband was to get in touch with the Kirghiz, find out their requirements for defending themselves against the Kanjutis and for keeping the trade route between Ladakh and Yarkand open and safe for traders. He was also to ascertain "their degree of dependence on Chinese authorities of Turkistan, in fact collect all information with regard to them." If any intimation was made to him "respecting sovereignty the Kirghiz desire to live under," he was to be "careful to use only the most guarded language in reply."[65] By the end of July 1889, another Kirghiz mission, now under Satiwaldi Kirghiz of Shahidulla, reached Leh. Ramsay this time more truthfully noted, "He has not come here specially to see me..." Musa's deputation to Leh on behalf of the Kirghiz of Shahidulla was confirmed by Satiwaldi, so also the refusal of the Amban of Karghalik to aid the Kirghiz "on the ground that Shahidulla was not Chinese territory." The Yarkand Amban had kept them waiting without giving an answer. Satiwaldi affirmed the Kirghiz of the Karakash valley sought protection and aid of the "Sarkar" against the Kanjutis. The text of the Kirghiz submission, made to the Wazir, was sent to the Resident by Raja Amar Singh and the Resident was asked to convey his views[66], for Pratap Singh had just been deposed on the boundary issue. At Shahidulla the Kashmir troops were to be left behind for a few weeks "as a visible sign to the Kirghiz and others that we can protect the road."[67] Besides locating regular troops there, including for any offensive action, Shahidulla fort was to serve as the post office under a Dastadar (brigadier) of Jammu and Kashmir irregular troops, Sarfaraz Khan, to keep Younghusband in communication with Leh. Beyond Shahidulla Younghusband was to make his own arrangements "as Ladakhis cannot go beyond that place."[68] Quite evidently Shahidulla had remained, for practical purposes, the territorial limit of the State. When he reached Shahidulla, Turdikol, the Kirghiz chief, himself offered to tender allegiance to Younghusband, so he claimed to Sir Mortimer. The offer was formally repeated by all the leading Kirghiz at a meeting at which Younghusband appeared, dressed in full military uniform. This he avoided accepting on the pretext that he had no authority to do so. A sum of Rs. 800 was given to the Kirghiz to rebuild the Shahidulla fort for their protection. Once the Hunza raids were stemmed, Younghusband visualised Raskam, with its productive potential, would be populated again, as it had been before. That, he presumed, "may materially affect the question of the position of the northern boundary of the Kashmir State."[69]

In an official despatch Younghusband discussed the status of the Kirghiz. Like other Englishmen he alleged that the Kirghiz had always paid yearly taxes to the Chinese Amban of Karghalik, a claim that Ramsay in Leh questioned, recalling Musa's categoric statement. In a rare criminal or civil case, the Kirghiz were treated like foreign traders. Before the ouster of Chinese from Eastern Turkistan, the Kirghiz were brought before the Badakshi Aksakal, during the Atalik's rule the governor of Yarkand and, after the return of Chinese to Kashgaria, the Kashmir Aksakal at Yarkand, the Kirghiz having moved into the Karakash valley after 1866. China thus officially recognised at least the Karakash valley Kirghiz to be dependants of Jammu and Kashmir. The Aksakals were appointed by the Chinese and all business of *foreigners* with the Amban was transacted through them. Younghusband's "findings" on the boundary were as fictitious as of any other good Englishman before him. But, interestingly, he was informed by Jan Mohammad that Sadiq Mufti, living at Yarkand, "who had learnt something of maps from the English" and who had in his possession an English map, copied this out in Chinese and showed on it,

> "that from the Karakoram range all the water on one side went to India and all on the other to Chinese Turkistan, and that, therefore, all on the northern side of the Karakoram range belonged to China. This map was sent to the Governor General at Urumtsi, about the time of Mr. Ney Elias' last visit to Yarkand."[70]

Amar Singh's communication to the Resident left Colonel Nisbet little room for manoeuvre. No more could the British obfuscate over Shahidulla being beyond the limits of Jammu and Kashmir when the Kirghiz inhabitants of Karakash valley themselves sought to acknowledge its sovereignty. But to put off Amar Singh, Nisbet reassuringly wrote back to the Raja that Captain Younghusband had "very much in the interest of the Jammu and Kashmir State been deputed by the Government of India to visit the Kirghiz and learn the present situation of affairs..." This he promised to communicate. But more importantly, the Resident advised the Raja, "In the meantime no further action need be taken by the Kashmir officials at Ladakh..."[71] The arrival of Younghusband at Shahidulla, accompanied by an escort, positively alarmed the Chinese. Apprehending Younghusband was actually heading an invading force, supplies from Kashgaria were withheld to him. When a deputation of merchants, presumably at British instigation, sought Chinese protection on the Leh-Yarkand road it was denied, the road being beyond Chinese "karauls"[72] in Jammu and Kashmir territories. One unforeseen development Younghusband fully met. He beat the Russians to winning over the Kirghiz.[73]

From Younghusband's findings, it is evident that cartographic aggression against Jammu and Kashmir first took place way back in mid 1880s, as suspected, through Ney Elias. But Elias clarified he had only given some maps to the Amban of Yarkand about 1880 and a year or two afterwards, when Dalgleish went over there, "the Amban got him to trace one of them while he, the Amban, put in the names in Chinese." This map was in use at the Amban's office in 1885 when Elias was there last. What he remembered was Sadiq had only drawn a map of a part of the Pamirs for him and not for the Chinese. Brazenly Elias insisted, "The information Captain Younghusband gives regarding the Kirghiz (paying taxes to China) is correct, Captain Ramsay's contradiction notwithstanding."[74] The visit in 1885 of a few Chinese, "neither officials nor soldiers," to the jade mines of the Karakash valley was disclosed by Younghusband. It is not unlikely that it was Elias, when he was the Joint Commissioner at Leh, who had himself induced them to undertake the visit for commercial gains. But the Chinese dismissed the mine as of no commercial importance. After this visit the Chinese never again crossed into the Karakash valley, Ramsay once, again, noted, on a Younghusband despatch. That Elias was since long committed to the Karakoram line of boundary he himself reveals. "What I have often suggested–and would again suggest-", he noted, "is that Government should adopt, once for all, the Indus water parting from Hunza in the west to where it cuts the independent Tibet frontier in the east." It was necessary Elias proposed to have this policy :

> "on record, and perhaps, colour the line in our maps to prevent the matter being brought up afresh whenever a new Resident is appointed to Kashmir or a new Political Agent to Ladakh."

This settles the argument that the boundary issue was between the British and the Jammu and Kashmir State which the former, as the paramount power, kicked up so as to change the northern boundary of the State to suit British Imperial interests. Though Viceroys sought the boundary issue to be sorted out with the concurrence of the Maharaja, Elias note reflects the extent the State was coerced.

Lansdowne, agreed with Elias that time had arrived to decide the line which British frontier or British influence should follow. The Viceroy mintued :

> "The agreement (among the British) certainly seems to be in favour of excluding foreign influence from the country south of Karakoram range as far east (approximately) as the 79th parallel. We might, no doubt, if desirable, go further north without virtually encroaching upon any other power, but we should gain nothing by pushing forward to Shahidulla, even if no objections were to be raised on the spot. The country between the Karakoram and Kuen Lun ranges is, I understand, of no value, very inaccessible and not likely to be coveted by Russia. We might, I should think,

> encourage the Chinese to take it, if they showed any inclination to do so. This would be better than leaving a no-man's land between our frontier and that of China. Moreover, the stronger we can make China at this point, and the more we can induce her to hold her own over the whole of Kashgar-Yarkand region, the more useful will she be to us as an obstacle to Russian advance along this line."[75]

By distinctly favouring the Karakoram as India's northern limit and excluding foreign influence from the country south of the Karakoram only as far east as the 79°E long. Lansdowne, in effect, consented to the surrender to China of territory up to 82nd E. longitude, north and east of the Karakoram, or the Yarkand valley and Lingzithang plateaux. The Leh-Yarkand road partly and Lanak la-Keria la-Polur road ran over this territory. Notwithstanding Lansdowne's pronouncement, agreement among the British on this was uncertain, one reason why Elias was called upon to convince Colonel J.C. Ardagh, Secretary to the Viceroy, for one. The territory had a military value. Reasons as to why the British favoured China annexing Indian territories, Elias amplified to Colonel Ardagh ignoring or contradicting those advanced by Colonel Bell and Captain Ramsay :

> "In the first place the 'no-man's land' is uninhabited and except on a section of the Yarkand river below the junction of the stream from Shangshal pass, quite uninhabitable. There would, therefore, be no inducement for Russians to occupy it,,,
>
> "Secondly, as long as Sirikul (Tashkurgan) remains Chinese and Wakhan remains Afghan, this 'no-man's land' would be cut off from Russian territory. By occupying it they would not be extending their own territory but would be occupying an isolated tract beyond their neighbour's frontiers.
>
> "Thirdly, if after a war with China, the Chinese possessions in Turkistan were to fall to Russia, I venture to think the Indus water-parting would form a more rational, a more simply defined and easily guarded frontier than an artificial line farther north. The whole length would be among the most inaccessible heights in Asia, absolutely uninhabitable and only to be crossed at two or three points, except by men on foot

using ropes and axes. It would leave open no such questions as division of tribes, ownership of land, or even rights to pasturage.

"Fourthly, supposing it is decided to take in the 'no-man's land,' we should have to open regular negotiations with China (the most impracticable nation), and have formal delimitation commission to determine an artificial frontier line. If satisfactorily completed, some portions of it would be inhabited, or, at all events, inhabitable country, at easy altitudes, readily accessible from the north, but cut off from our side by height of the Indus water-parting ranges, the passes over which are only practicable for about seven months in the year. At certain points (as on the Yarkand and Karakash rivers) this frontier would have to be guarded by outposts of Kashmiri troops which would be cut off from their base in Ladakh, for some five months of each year; while for the remainder of the year it would be difficult to support and supply them."[76]

The simplest solution of the boundary issue, as long as China occupied Eastern Turkistan, Elias saw, was "to influence the Chinese to claim all the country draining into the Tarim System...i.e., upto the head of the Indus water."[77] A preliminary step towards such a solution, he commended, was to acknowledge the Chinese nationality of the Karakash Kirghiz. So strong were Elias' views that he did not favour any overt or covert act to set at nought British efforts to persuade the Chinese to take over the entire country to the north of the Karakoram. He did not, therefore, approve of Younghusband being accompanied to Shahidulla by an escort of Jammu and Kashmir troops, even though Sir Mortimer had advised him.[78] Elias telegraphed him, calculatedly in the name of Foreign Secretary, against it. In a letter, to Younghusband later, Elias apprehended that "the Chinese might turn the Kashmir sepoys out of Shahidulla," after Younghusband had left. The Chinese, of course, did nothing of the sort, at least immediately, and Younghusband admitted "the presence of the Kashmir troops produced good effect by inspiring confidence into both the Kirghiz and the traders..."[79] Just before his descent into "awal" Hunza, Younghusband and Grombtchevsky met at Khainan-aksai, a camping site between the Taghdumbash Pamir and the Yarkand river, 152 miles from Shahidulla. The Russian had travelled through the Alichur, Great and Little Pamirs and thence to the

Taghdumbash Pamir and the Raskam valley following Younghusband to Shangshal and Aghil passes, both of which he crossed. Grombtchevsky intended to go to Shahidulla en route to Leh and thence by Mangtza lake into Tibet. The route map of his travels Grombtchevsky showed to Younghusband. In it a broad red line enclosed a strip of country running down from the Russian frontier near Tyuksu pass and including the "eastern portion of Wakhan" and the Taghdumbash Pamir and reaching the Yarkand river. This was the "gap" and Younghusband concluded that it was doubtless "the intention of the Russians to drive a wedge between the indefinite eastern boundary of the Afghan territory in Wakhan and the western boundary of China at Aktash."[80] Yet in another despatch on the same day, Younghusband informed the Resident, "...Wakhan has been occupied by Afghan troops and the "gap" I referred to filled up."[81]

For a journey through Ladakh Grombtchevsky sought passport from the Wazir of Gilgit. Grombtchevsky had been appointed by the Russian Imperial Geographical Society to explore Kafiristan but the Afghans had denied his expedition access to the country. He was, therefore, "making for the sources of the Raskam dariya (Yarkand river)" and proposed "to explore the Muztagh as far as Polur." In the event of his expedition "being unable to arrive at Polur along the northern slope of Muztagh," Grombtchevsky earnestly entreated the Resident in Kashmir "to obtain for the expedition a permission to proceed to Polur through Ladakh..."[82] The passport to enter Ladakh was finally denied to Grombtchevsky by the Viceroy himself. But of significance is Grombtchevsky's alternative route to reach Polur *through* Ladakh. He could have travelled, as a Bombay civil servant, A.D. Carey had earlier, by the Lanak la-Mangtza lake-Keria la line, over the eastern Aksai Chin plateaux, or gone all through Aksai Chin via Thaldat and Lake Leighten, a road that Hedin followed later. In either case Grombtchevsky obliquely confirms Ladakh stratched to about 82°E longitude. Another significant reference he makes is to the Muztagh which was one of the names Englishmen used for the Karakoram chain. Polur, as has been noticed, is, however, in the northern part of the Kuen Lun. This was Grombtchevsky's second exploration in and around the Kuen Lun region and an explorer of his repute was hardly likely to trip. In his secret report to Government on his mission of 1889, Younghusband admits that for the range of mountains, which the British claimed formed the watershed of the Indus river system, "though the natives of the country have no name for it, is generally called by us the Hindu Kush in the Western portion, and either the Muztagh or Karakoram mountains in the eastern part."[83] Grombtchevsky's testimony confirms the hypothesis that the Karakoram or Muztagh was no mountain chain by itself but part of the Kuen Lun system.

Grombtchevsky's request to the Wazir of Gilgit disconcerted the British. The Resident in Kashmir counselled Amar Singh" ...it would be well if you directed both the Wazirs at Gilgit and Ladakh not to assist in any way or allow the passage of this or any other Russian Officers through Kashmir territory to Tibet.[84] Grombtchevsky despatched on the 26th of November 1889, a guide to Shahidulla and "taking it for granted that the fort was occupied by Kashmir troops," ordered his messenger to inform the officer commanding the garrison of the arrival of his expedition and to request him to sell him provisions for the use of the expedition. Towards the evening his guide returned and reported :

> "The Chinese who had watched with indifference the construction of the fort, and its occupation by the Kashmiris, late in the autumn, suddenly prohibited the export of flour and other produce from Sanju and Kilian. The Kashmiris, who had anticipated no such prohibition and consequently laid in no supplies, now found themselves in a critical position."
>
> "To obtain provisions through the Karakoram pass from Kashmir, during winter, was out of question. So the Kashmir garrison, 20 in number, hastened to evacuate the fort and departed to Kashmir. Then appeared the Chinese authorities, inspected the fort, arrested the Beg who had been appointed by the Kashmiris, formed a fresh garrison out of the local Kirghiz and having appointed a new Beg went back again to Karghalik."[85]

Supplies were denied by the Chinese both to Younghusband and to the Jammu and Kashmir garrison at Shahidulla. To Younghusband these were resumed after he sent Jan Mohammad on a mission to Yarkand when, it can safely be inferred, the Chinese were formally invited to physically occupy Shahidulla, which they proceeded to do. Hence, the sudden stoppage of supplies to Shahidulla garrison. The most significant part of Grombtchevsky's despatches to the Imperial Geographical Society of Russia is that the Beg of Kirghiz at Shahidulla was appointed by Kashmir officers. Such must have been the practice for years. Turdikol, the Kirghiz Beg, was imprisoned by the Chinese and taken to Kashgar for his role at Shahidulla, second transgression by the Chinese.

For a formal occupation of the fort of Shahidulla, the Chinese despatched, early in December 1889, 15 "sowars" (cavalrymen) under Aziz Beg, "Kakim," or Muslim officer, in charge, of Karghalik. Instead of the cavalry, a guard of 20 Kirghiz was placed in the fort which was converted into a Chinese outpost and supplies were arranged for them.[86] These proceedings were conveyed to the Resident by Raja Amar Singh.[87] On February 8, 1890 the State Council decided to depute the "Naib" (deputy) Wazir of Ladakh to Shahidulla, avowdly to enquire about Russian agents but quite evidently to have a first hand report on the seizure of Shahidulla.[88] The Resident was requested to give his opinion on the issue.[89] Ramsay took notice of the Chinese seizure of Shahidulla. The Chinese he credited with the Inention "to open up communication with... the Kirghiz who inhabit the Karakash valley and the 'no-man's land' laying between the Karakoram range and the Chinese line of outposts at the Kilian, Kukyar and Sanju passes," or the territory to the west of Aksai Chin. He doubted "whether the Kirghiz are Chinese subjects or that we have to some extent intrigued with the subjects of a friendly power,"[90] the latter a veiled reference to China and criticism of Younghusband's proceedings. Some of the Englishmen, like Ramsay, appear to have been appalled by British actions in Jammu and Kashmir. But the Resident was different. He overruled the State Council, his own creature, on the deputation of Raja Ferozdin, "Naib" Wazir, to Shahidulla[91]. At the time they seized Shahidulla the Chinese also began reconstruction of the fort at Bostan, south of Walaghat, or Sanju, boundary pass, to ensure effective occupation of that part of Yarkand valley that lies between Shahidulla and Sanju. Construction of a fort on the Karakoram pass was also contemplated, probably "with the intention," as Ramsay conveyed in his monthly diary," of showing to us that their frontier extended to that point."[92]

China have finally arrived at Shahidulla, several alternative boundary lines occurred to Younghusband as British empire's northern limit. The first he ran "along the spur from the Kuen Lun range, which is crossed by the Sogat and Sokhbulak passes, leading to Raskam, or western part of the Yarkand valley, and would continue along the crest of the Kuen Lun mountains to their western extremity and then, crossing the Yarkand river below the junction of the Ilisu, strike the Kurbu range near the Kurbu pass, and run along it till it met the Muztagh mountains, east of the Khanjerab pass." But, in his secret Report of A Mission to The Northern Frontier of Kashmir, Younghusband dismissed this line, having little to recommend it. The alternative line he ran the whole way along the crest of the Muztagh through the Karakoram, Shangshal and

Khanjerab passes to Kilik where it joined the Hindu Kush. This, of course, was to the British, "the natural and best boundary" which they favoured. Between these two lines there was another which was then laid down as the boundary of Kashmir on official British maps. This line followed the course of the Raskam river. It was given up, there is reason to believe, not because the river is fordable, as Younghusband states, but because, with its considerable economic potential, Yarkand valley was an acceptable quid pro quo for the Chinese to advance their boundary in the arid desert of the Pamirs. Eastward, Younghusband considered it advisable to run the boundary line :

> "from the Karakoram pass north-east through the Karatagh pass, to the bend of the Karakash river, and thus include, as at present laid down on our maps, the Lingzithang plains, up to the eastern Kuen Lun mountains. This tract of country has no practical importance, as the plains are uninhabited and uninhabitable, but it may possibly be gratifying to the Maharaja of Kashmir to feel himself in possession of so many extra square miles of the country."[93]

Such a boundary line split up Aksai Chin into two, the northern and eastern over which roads from Khotan ran over, going to China, and the southern and western remaining in Jammu and Kashmir, limiting it to Lansdowne's 79E longitude towards the east.

To complete the boundary beyond Mintaka over the Taghdumbash and Little Pamir, or cover up the "gap," Younghusband was for the second consecutive year, deputed to the region to thoroughly examine, in communication, as far as possible, with the Chinese officials, all the country up to the Afghan and Russian frontier with a view to ascertaining the exact limits of the Chinese authority. Younghusband was forewarned that Chinese posts "may not in places be situated on the extreme limits of the country over which their dominion claims to extend..."[94] Where this was the case he was to impress upon the Chinese officials the necessity of strengthening and asserting their occupation so that, if possible, there might he no ground for alleging, by Russia evidently, that any unclaimed strip, or "gap," intervened between the Afghan and Chinese territories.

Talks at the highest level also appear to have been conducted in Calcutta's Viceregal Chamber, with all the ceremonial, as Vance Agnew had foreseen four decades earlier. To overcome Tibetan intransigence over Sikkim, the British had seduced to Calcutta the junior Chinese

Imperial Resident at Lhasa, Sheng Tai. So overwhelmed was Sheng with the extravagant reception accorded to him that, on his return to Tibet, Sheng wrote to Lord Lansdowne, "we are of a disposition calculated to bring about a right undertaking between us."[95] Sheng, on his return, was promoted "Chief Resident" in Tibet, which was "an evidence of the approval of his recent doings by the Chinese Government,"[96] The Viceroy went into raptures with the Secretary of State for India over India and China having lately, in the case of Sikkim, "come together in a way that has never occurred before..." No less friendly was the attitude of the British over Eastern Turkistan to become apparent to the Chinese Government, once, as Lansdowne put it in a despatch, the circumstances were communicated to them. These were :

> "...our affording protection last year to Chinese subjects (the Sarekia Kirghiz) after it had been refused them by their own authorities, and by our now refraining to urge the claims of the Maharaja of Kashmir to Shahidulla at a time when the Chinese might, by their refusal to protect the Kirghiz, have been held to have renounced their right to the place."[97]

The Viceroy saw the interest of India and China in Central Asia to be "identical" to keep Russia at bay. Her Majesty's Government was urged, in the secret despatch, to inform the Chinese that the Government of India desire,

> "to see the frontiers of Chinese Turkistan conterminous with those of Afghanistan and Kashmir and its dependencies and Chinese authority definitely asserted up to the Karakoram mountains and to the limits of the Afghan territory on the Pamirs so that no gap may be left through which any third power may push its way. Such an arrangement, we believe, would be advantageous to both countries by preventing the possibility of the encroachment of any third power towards the Hindu Kush on the one hand and towards Sirikul or Tibet on the other."[98]

In the meanwhile British political officers in the dominions of the Maharaja of Jammu and Kashmir were "to regard the limits of the Indus watershed the boundary of His Highness's territories towards the north i.e., the line of natural water parting from a point near the Irshad pass on the west to the recognised Tibet frontier on the east," as the limit of British political jurisdiction. The recognised Tibet frontier was presumably

Lanak La, Carey and other Englishmen having found it so. With some of these issues, the Viceroy also went over with Sir John Walsham. Of considerable importance to the Government of India was the "strip of debatable territory" lying to the north of the Karakoram to which, Lansdowne claimed, Russia intended to extend her influence. The Chinese having lately occupied Shahidulla the British, Walsham was informed, would "acquiesce in their so doing." But, while they had no desire to advance beyond the Karakoram, the British India Government had a very great objection to allowing this strip, a "no-man's land" to the Viceroy, to remain unclaimed and open to Russian incursions. Unabashedly Walsham was advised "that the Chinese should be encouraged as to assert their authority over the tract in question and (westward) up to the limits of Afghan territory."[99] By such means, no gap was left and no temptation offered to Russian exploring parties. Afghan boundary was as then still far to the south and west of the Little Pamir. By proposing that she extend her frontier that far, China was sought to be assigned the intervening territories of the Taghdumbash Pamir and the Yarkand valley, including the area north of the Karakoram pass to Shahidulla, precisely the tracts that Britain gifted away.

China soon after began construction of a "fort" at Sogat to command approaches from the north-west to the Karakash valley and the Lingzithang plains. Chinese intrusion into Sogat was promptly conveyed to the Wazir of Ladakh by Sadiq Joo, the "kardar" of Nubra.[100] Turdikol, the Kashmir appointed Beg, was no more at Shahidulla to prevent the Chinese. The Wazir, Pandit Narayan Kaul, informed the State Council that the Chinese claimed the Karakoram as their boundary.[101] Sadiq Joo's letters were brought to the notice of the deposed Maharaja.[102] The India Office in London commended to the Foreign Office the suggestion of Lansdowne "that the Chinese should be invited to extend their authority upto the limits of Afghan territory on the Pamirs."[103] Notwitstanding Chinese occupation of Shahidulla and Sogat, European travellers continued to treat Shahidulla as the boundary of Jammu and Kashmir.[104] To P'an Ta-Jen, the Amban of Yarkand, direct "overtures" were made by Younghusband on the boundary issue. A map of Kashmir was shown to the Amban on which were marked the Karakoram and Kilian passes. The Viceroy of India, was anxious to come to an understanding with the Chinese Government over Kashmir's boundary with Yarkand, westward of the Karakoram pass, which was then the immediate concern of the British Indian Government. The Viceroy, Younghusband went on to impress upon the Amban, had ever been of opinion :

> "that the best boundary between Kashmir and Yarkand was that formed by the watershed of the Karakoram range, but last year His Excellency had been led to believe that the Chinese considered their frontier extending only as far as the Kilian pass, and that the intervening country was unoccupied by any power, or, in other words, was a tract of 'no-man's land.' This being an unsatisfactory state of affairs, and one that would afford opportunities for lawless proceedings on the part of the Kanjutis, His Excellency was contemplating extending the Indian frontier to the Kilian pass, and annex all the country situated between it and the watershed. He had since, however, learned that the Chinese were undertaking the protection of the trade route, and if he found this to be really the case, he would be unwilling to extend the frontier beyond the Karakoram range."

P'an Ta-jen responded "the Chinese had ever considered the watershed," which he defined as a natural (or literally in Chinese), a heaven-made boundary, "to be the frontier between Kashmir and Yarkand, and that the Chinese were prepared to protect the trade route as far as that range."[105] Distinctly China was coming round to the British view on the boundary, the watershed of the Indus. In the Pamirs, the Amban claimed Sirikul was part of Yarkand district and it was extended by him right upto Mintaka, incorporating thus the whole of Taghdumbash into Eastern Turkistan. Nothing more could have been gratifying to the English. With Younghusband's exposition of British policy to the Amban, Ramsay at Leh agreed only if the Chinese would "effectively occupy the country upto the Karakoram." He, however, saw no such move being made. Instead to avoid further Kanjuti raids, Ramsay credited the Chinese with the intention of moving the Sarekia Kirghiz to the north of the Kilian. This the Kirghiz, would have evaded, being inclined to move west to join their brethren Kirghiz, subjects of Russia, on the Sirikul Pamir.[106] Such a development would have been less than satisfactory to the British.

In Beijing, however, this contrived boundary was far from endorsed by China, not as then. When Sir John Walsham argued that the Chinese and British empires were conterminous in Eastern Turkistan, he was in no uncertain terms told by Prince Ch'ing head of the Tsungli Yamen :

> "...the New Dominion and India could scarcely be

> considered conterminous countries; a large belt of country inhabited by Mohammadan tribes was wedged in between the boundaries of the two Empires"[107]

A little later, on 30th April 1891, the Ministers of the Tsungli Yamen restated this "at first," according to British records. They added that the intervening Mohammadan tribes :

> "owed but slight allegiance to any power. They had formerly constituted an integral part of the New Dominion, but, at present, although nominally subordinate to China, they were not administered by Chinese officials."[108]

The belt of territory inhabited by Mohammadan tribes was the Raskam valley, which, along with Taghdumbash, comprised "doam" Hunza, inhibited by Kanjutis and Karghiz. The two Ministers' statement is significant. It lays to rest another British canard. Whatever its ties earlier with China had been Hunza was not a vassal State of China after she recovered Kashgaria in December 1877.

On 30th September 1890 the Resident in Kashmir was informed by Raja Amar Singh that the Chinese had reached Sogat to build the fort.[109] A communication from the Naib Wazir of Ladakh to the Darbar confirmed construction of the fort had begun at Sogat one march inside Shahidulla, "the frontier of the 'Sarkariwala."[110] By early October 1890, Sogat appeared to have become Chinese customs checkpost.[111] After the roof of the fort was laid, the Chinese departed leaving it in the charge of Khal Beg and 10 Kirghiz.[112] No troops garrisoned the new fort. A Chinese military officer visited the fort and felt there was no need for them.[113] Both these reports were duly sent to the Resident in Kashmir by Raja Amar Singh. Repeated references on the boundary changes obliquely convey Kashmir's refusal to concur with the British. Two years later, in 1892, British traveller, Lord Dunmore, spent a night in the "Chinese fortress" of Sogat. Near its entrance he came across a board on which was inscribed, in large Chinese characters and also in Hindustani, "Any one crossing the Chinese frontier without reporting himself at this fort will be imprisoned."[114] Six miles away at Shahidulla the Chinese quietly pulled down the small guard house or fort. Shahidulla ceased to be the frontier between China and India.

Younghusband's "findings" on the extent of the Chinese domain in the Pamirs being well beyond Aktash and running into Shighnan were dismissed in London by the Foreign and India Offices as "too vague and indefinite to be proposed to China... to which Chinese outposts might advance."[115] A definite line Younghusband was directed by Cunningham to suggest.[116] To propose a definite Anglo-Chinese boundary was not an easy matter. The nomadic Kirghiz, who inhabited the Pamirs, had no definite loyalties. They roamed about the Pamirs and were perfectly ready to march off one year to the Afghans and another to the Russians, according as it suited them best. The Kirghiz of Taghdumbash had in 1889 more than once offered to Younghusband to be taken under British protection. While, the Chinese laid claims over all that portion of the Pamirs which was inhabited by the Kirghiz, on his arrival there, Younghusband found that exactly was not the case. Commencing from the Little Pamir, he found a 'karaul' was stationed at Aktash. From a place being spoken of as a frontier post a legitimate expectation was to find a small fort or a walled enclosure or, at any rate, some soldiers. But Younghusband found nothing of the kind. On the Pamirs a 'karaul', it seemed, merely the headquarters of Beg. No official of Chinese nationality permanently resided at any of these "outer frontier" posts.

> "...the nearest official of Chinese nationality is not to be found further west than the foot of mountains overhanging the Kashgar plain, along which are stationed a series of minor 'karauls.'[117]

The actual Chinese boundary was even in 1890 confined, therefore, to the Kashgar range. On the Little Pamir there was no exact contact point between the Afghan and Chinese territories. On the Great Pamir the boundary was no less indefinite. The frontier and local Beg were at variance as to where the 'karaul' really was.

On the conclusion of his mission a sketch map of the Pamir region showing the boundaries between Afghan and Chinese territories was sent to the Foreign Department by Younghusband, with a list of Chinese equivalents of native names. The list compiled by Chinese knowing Macartney, was incomplete, no such equivalents, being available.[118] While it was understood the boundary would have to be finalised in London or Beijing, the Taotai remarked to Younghusband that a commission would eventually be appointed to settle it. In his view "the matter was by no means a small one, as the frontier extended the whole way *from Shahidulla to the Pamirs* and the boundary of Kanjut with India would have also to be settled."[119] East of Shahidulla, the boundary of Ladakh; it is clear, was not even then at issue.

The very recent expansion of China and Afghanistan into the Pamirs at British instigation and at the expense of Russia is best reflected by the Russian newspaper, "Novoe Vremya." Beginning with the east, and of the times of her former possession of Kashgar, *Novoe Vremya* wrote :

> "...Chinese influence was here very weak, and the Chinese never passed over the west of a chain of posts lying at the foot of the eastern slopes in the valleys of the rivers Kizil-su and Sirikul (Kashgar range)."
>
> "In the beginning of the 1860s the Kashgar Khanate was unexpectedly created...Yakub Beg occupied the country...and taking advantage of the fact that Kokand Khanate was at the time in the state of complete disintegration, this enterprising adventurer moved the line of western posts further into the hills beginning from Chakmak and Ulukchat on the north and ending with Tashkurgan on the south..."
>
> "...In 1878, the Chinese seized Kashgar, and at the same time, as appeared a natural consequence, occupied those points on the west which Yakub Beg had possessed....
>
> "In this way in 1888 Captain Grombtchevsky, in his first expedition, met Chinese Begs already in the valley of Aksu, in the boundaries of Akbaital and Aktash, i.e., on the Little Pamir... the Afghans again invaded the provinces of Badakshan, Shighnan and Roshan which had been given up in 1888...In this way the expedition of M. Grombtchevsky could move southward only by the still unoccupied narrow strip, from 30 to 40 versts broads, (the "gap")...
>
> "Not being satisfied by the recovery of Badakshan and the annexation of Kafiristan, the Afghans strove...to seize the Khanate of Chitral. But when the Khan of Chitral turned for protection of the English, then these latter demanded in exchange the right to keep their own garrison in Mastuj (the chief town of Chitral) (sic) which was instantly accomplished.
>
> "Then in 1889 there took place the deposition of the Maharaja of Kashmir, and the conclusion of a treaty with the Khan of Kanjut by which an Indian garrison was also placed at the chief's place in this Khanate. ...At the present time captain Younghusband, a political traveller,...is already in Kashgar with the object of

> obtaining...from the Chinese....the delimitation of the frontier between Afghanistan and China.
>
> "In this way we find ourselves on the eve of a complete seizure of the Pamir and nobody asks whether Russia agrees to this... Russia as early as 1876, by the annexation of Kokand, acquired rights in the Pamir...
>
> "The chiefs of the tribes inhabiting the Pamir were from ancient times nominees of the Khans of Kokand, and one of them in 1863 was killed in a collision with an armed party from Kanjut in the upper parts of Wakhan; that is close to the lower slopes of the Hindu Kush. On the place where the Kokand General is buried there exists to this day the tomb Bozai Gumbaz. In this way not with China but first of all with Russia must English enter into negotiation."[120]

Some factual errors, such as the imagined treaty between the British and Hunza and the garrisoning of Baltit town by Indian troops, apart, the Novoe Vremya's account of Afghan-Chinese expansion towards the north and west is generally faithful. Its claim that the Pamir chiefs were at one time, nominees of Kokand has substance. Bozai and some others earlier to him were. Bozai's conflict with the Kanjutis was really over the possession of the Little Pamir and his defeat ensured its undisputed ownership for Hunza. China's advance into the Pamirs appears relentless to the Russian newspaper. But the fact is it was a nominal advance.

Political boundaries in the Pamirs, as proposed by Younghusband, were referred to the Secretary of State. The northern line commenced near the junction of the Muztagh and Hindu Kush, which jointly separate the basins of the Indus to the south from those of the Yarkand river and Oxus to the north. Leaving this range at a point west of the Kilik pass, the line was in six different sections. The first two sections of the boundary over the Little and Great Pamir the British considered were "very generally recognised and not likely to be challenged." The "gap" over these Pamirs was covered. The third section along the water parting, separating the basins of the Sirikul (Victoria) and Yeshil Kul lakes too appeared "well defined." The fourth section across the valley of Ghund or Alichur river was considered in all respects as the "most uncertain section...,"[121] it being the region in which the British wished the Afghan-Chinese boundaries to meet but not to delimit or recognise. This boundary line left a projecting tongue formed by the Alichur Pamir. The proposed boundaries were incorporated in a memorandum by the British Foreign

Office and communicated to the Chinese Minister in London with Younghusband's map.[122] The Chinese mission was to inform the Her Majesty's Government "if the frontier thus indicated is recognised by the Chinese Government as correctly describing the limits of Chinese jurisdiction in that direction." In that case the British on their side were ready to recognise it, and to inform the Indian Government of the agreement.."[123] About the time the memorandum was sent to their mission in London, the Chinese in Kashgaria despatched an officer with troops and 500 pony loads of supplies to Alichur. To Younghusband they seemed quite determined upon asserting their authoritiy.[124] In the great game between England and Russia in Central Asia, China was now in the swim up to the ears.

One last attempt was made by the deposed Maharaja, Pratap Singh, to reopen the Shahidulla boundary issue as late as 16th March 1892. The diary of the Wazir of Ladakh for the month of November 1891 contained a reference to the reconstruction of the Shahidulla fort by Turdikol. But this new fort, Pratap Singh noted, had been demolished by the Chinese who had built another fort "on the other side of the State frontier" at Sogat in which some Kirghiz men and 2 or 3 Chinese officials remained as "chowkidars" (watchmen). On 18th December 1891 an order was issued to the Wazir to make full enquiries on the subject and "to show grounds by which it may be proved that Sogat is within the State frontiers." The result of the enquiry Pratap Singh revealed in a detailed memorandum :[125]

"1. Mehta Mangal, late Wazir of Ladakh, had sent a person, named Ahmad, accompanied by 36 men, to Shahidulla Khoja who, on his arrival there, erected some buildings as cantonment. And, after staying for 5 months at Shahidulla Khoja, he came back.

"2. The above named Ahmad is still alive and on his being summoned in the Wazarat, he stated that 28 years ago (in 1863), he was sent with 36 men to Shahidulla Khoja by Mehta Mangal and after staying for 5 months at that place he came back.

"3. Some old men were also questioned on the subject who stated that the State frontier is Shahidulla Khoja.

"4. When Sir Douglas Forsyth went on Yarkand mission, the Kashmir State authorities made arrangements for the supply of provisions etc., upto Shahidulla Khoja."

For these reasons Pratap Singh wrote "Shahidulla Khoja is considered the state frontier." In 1889-90 a Russian officer, evidently

Grombatchevsky, had come to visit Kashmir from Russia via Yarkand and a Dastadar of State Military Department, with a number of irregular troops was sent to Shahidulla with a letter from the Resident to disallow the Russian from coming into the State, the Russian having no passport. "The facts noted in the Wazarat report, the deposed Maharaja reiterated, show that the State frontier is Shahidulla Khoja." But there was a glaring omission on the Wazarat's report. A fort, or a post, evidently in disrepair, had existed at Shahidulla, probably since the rule of the Gyalpos, a mention of which is made, by Adolphe Schlagintweit in 1857.[126]

From the State Council's proceedings it is evident that the Chinese were informed, presumably by State officials, that Shahidulla was Jammu and Kashmir boundary, the fort there having been lately rebuilt by Turdikol.[127] The Khatais (Chinese) "demolished" the fort, took Turdikol prisoner to Yarkand and erected a fort at Sogat. Kashmir's sense of outrage is evident from her officials directly cautioning the Chinese against their encroachment. Being a creature of the Resident, the State Council did not, as it ought to have, urge the British to defend the frontier of Jammu and Kashmir, as was enjoined on them by the Treaty of Amritsar, 1846. The State Council merely directed that the Resident be moved, "it being also essential that the British Joint Commissioner, Ladakh, be requested to state his views after a visit to the spot." This was dilatory. Contemporary English cartographic evidence also upheld Pratap Singh's contention. The latest map of the Pamirs and the surrounding countries, prepared by the Military Intelligence Branch of the Quarter Master General in 1892, had "carried the broken riband upto the Kilian pass" and had thus, in a way "included Shahidulla and Sogat within British dominions." The authority of the Intelligence Branch to issue such a map was questioned, the boundary line on the map being "not in accordance with the *views* of the Government of India...."[128] The map was, of course, promptly superseded.[129]

The Resident overruled not only the deposed Maharaja but ignored the State Council remarking "I do not think I can recommend that the question of the occupation of Shahidulla Khoja by the Kashmir Darbar should be reopened." For him both Shahidulla and Sogat were situated in a district "inhabited by Kirghiz who have for many years paid tribute to China and the water of which flows into Yarkand territory."[130] occupation of Sogat by the Chinese was followed by their notional annexation of Yarkand valley in 1892. A Chinese official visited the Bazar Dara valley in Raskam who, at some place, "marked out the plain of a fort."[131] The Chinese then went to the Karakoram and put a board at

Maldi dawan (sic), Karakoram. Later another Chinese proceeded to the Karakoram pass where he pitched a board. He then set out for "Chinchimmo"-Changchenmo-to inspect the road by which the Russian Prince Galatzin had travelled to Leh. A survey had also been completed from Yarkand to Karakoram and foundation of another fort laid at Ding Tash, near the Kanjut pass (Shangshal ?) and construction work taken up immediately.[132] One of the Chinese "had buried a small wooden mark on the head of the Karakoram pass."[133] The wooden mark was, evidently, to establish ancient rights of China over the Karakoram.

Another report on the construction of a 2 yards by 2 yards pillar on the Karakoram, bearing a Chinese inscription, alerted the Wazir of Ladakh. He petitioned the Darbar recalling his reports on the boundary and Chinese encroachment at Sogat. Since then the Chinese, had moved further southwards and "acting on their own authority" had "established the boundary mark at Karakoram (pass), which is 72 miles from Shahidulla Khoja in spite of the fact that the Sarkar's 'ilaka' (territory) extends upto the latter place..."[134] This petition of the Wazir also reveals that the State Government had a "kardar," an officer, appointed "at the frontier line," obviously Shahidulla. The Wazir conveyed the contents of the inscription found to be in Turki, besides the Chinese. The letters in Turki read :

> "Khan Gha Toba Takta"–The board is under the sway of the Khan, (Khakhan-e-Chin-Chinese Emperor)."[135]

The Darbar was counselled that if no immediate action was taken on the matter "the results of such proceeding will not be favourable to us after the lapse of some period." The Wazir sought orders to depute military guards in the spring of 1893 to Shahidulla and "in accordance with the old practice they will remain there in the State fort..." The posting of the guards at Shahidulla would, the Wazir asserted again, extend the frontier of the Maharaja upto that place. The British Joint Commissioner, Lieutenant W.M. Cubitt, confirmed the Wazir's reports to the Resident, Colonel D.W.K. Barr.[136] The question seemed to the Resident to be one "that may affect the political relations of the Government of India with the Chinese empire." He did not, therefore consider it "expedient to give the Kashmir Darbar any advice on the subject," but merely informed them that the matter was being referred to the Government of India and pending a reply to his communication, "the Darbar should take no action in the matter."[137] From the notings in the Foreign Department, it emerges that in August 1890 the Resident, Colonel Nisbet, was confidentially told that the object of Government was "to induce the Chinese to occupy effectively the country upto the Indus watershed." The Resident was "to let the Darbar known" that he understood "the Indus watershed to be the Kashmir boundary," But Colonel Nisbet, as Cunningham tersely remarked, "probably kept to himself or destroyed the letter written to him...about the northern boundary of Kashmir."[138] That was to avoid embarrassment. Sir Mortimar was different. He observed to Lansdowne :

> "The Kashmir State is now *well in hand*, and I should be inclined to explain to them that any attempt on their part to go beyond the watershed is a mistake. But we should see that the pillar is not over the slope."[139]

The Viceroy was no less unbending. But he made occupation of the territory conditional. He minuted :

> "We are not in a position to commit ourselves as to the position of the boundary between the territories of Kashmir and China in the vicinity of the Karakoram. Her Majesty's Government is, I understand, endeavouring to bring about a settlement of the frontier question between Russia, China and ourselves. In the meanwhile all we can say is that we are not sorry to notice indications of activity on the part of the Chinese. We have always hoped that they would assert effectively their claims to Shahidulla and the tract between the Kuen Lun and Karakoram ranges. We encouraged them to do this in 1890 at the time of Captain Younghusband's mission. But I don't know that we should go the length of saying now that we admit unreservedly their right to claim upto the very summit of the Karakoram.
>
> "It will be best to say that we see no occasion to remonstrate with the Chinese on account of the erection of these boundary marks (provided they are not on this side of the summit) but that it must be clearly understood that no boundary marks will be regarded as having any international value, unless they have been erected *with the concurrence of both powers.*
>
> "We can say this to the Resident and tell him that in principle we favour the idea of getting the 'no-man's land' filled by the Chinese, subject to future delimitation of boundaries.
>
> "Besides this it will be....desirable to let the Chinese

> Government to know that the proceedings of their people are being watched, and that, while we welcome the interest they are showing in these remote places, we cannot allow the ownership of them to be disposed of without reference to us."[140]

The Resident was consequentially told "that the Government of India do not view with disfavour" the indication of activity on the part of the Chinese and "see no occasion to remonstrate with the Chinese Government on account of the erection of these boundary marks provided that they are not on the Ladakh side of the summit."[141] The Darbar was consoled "It does not seem desirable that the responsibilities of the Kashmir State, already heavy, should be increased by the assumption of control over the country beyond the Karakoram..." The purpose behind the deposition of Maharaja Pratap Singh had been two-fold, take over of Gilgit and pull back of the boundary. This was now virtually achieved. In a despatch to the Secretary of State for India, Lansdowne and his Government considered it would be a "matter for congratulation if the Chinese were to assert their claims to Shahidulla and the tract between the Kuen Lun and Karakoram ranges."[142] Nevertheless, it was considered desirable to let the Chinese Government to know that "the proceedings of their officials are being watched" and that, while the Chinese interest in those remote places was welcome, "we cannot allow ownership of them to be disposed of without reference to us and otherwise than by common consent." While, therefore, the immediate British objective of blocking Russia venturing into Ladakh via Raskam and the Karakoram pass was achieved through Chinese advance, ownership of this immense tract was to be subject to a reference to the Government of India and to common consent of India and China. This issue therefore, the India office took up with the British Foreign office.

The Chinese, the Secretary of State of India, Lord Kimberley, proposed, should be intimated that the Indian authorities, acting on behalf of the Kashmir State, would gladly cooperate with the Chinese authorities in Kashgaria "in determining the frontier *on the road from Leh to Kashgar*."[143] Though individual Chinese officials in Kashgaria had rushed as far south as the Karakoram, official Chinese position on the boundary was still a great deal different. It was revealed in a map. Macartney from Kashgar sent to the Resident in Kashmir, published by Hung Ta-jen, late Chinese Minister to the Court of St. Petersburg. It showed the boundary between Chinese and British-Kashmir territories along the Leh-Kashgar road. This boundary line did not run along the crest of the Karakoram pass but was "shown somewhat to the north of the 'watershed' and following the banks of...the Yarkand river which was explored by Captain Younghusband in the summer of 1889."[144] In his map Hung kept Shahidulla out of India but left whole of Lingzithang or Aksai Chin and Vohab plateaux in India. Hung's boundary ran along Aktagh, Kufilong, Sokhbulak pass, Kirghiz Jungle, Kulanuldi, and Yangi dawan. The merit of Hung's map lies in truthfully projecting the ground reality on the boundary as it existed in 1892-1893. Significantly Hung headed a powerful group in Beijing which favoured good relations with Russia.

The great mountain chains running parallel to the Himalaya–Ladakh, Kailash, Gangri, Karakoram, Aghil, Kuen Lun and Hindu Kush–have a remarkable unity on which geographers, including British, notably Burrard, are agreed.[145] These all merge, the Gangri and Kuen Lun with Karakoram at the head of the Karakash valley. The Karakoram also unites with Hindu Kush and Bolor mountains in the Central knot of the Taghdumbash.[146] Of this geographical–and geological–unity the Chinese appear to have been completely and the Indians partly ignorant at the officials talks in 1960. By encouraging the Chinese even nominally to occupy the Taghdumbash, Sirikul and the territories along the Leh-Yarkand line of commerce the British struck at the geographical unity of India. The local tradition in Skardo, narrated to the English explorer, Dr. Longstaff, considered the plateaux, situated amidst these mountain ranges, the Deosai, Depsang, Vohab and Lingzithang, all Changthang, or the northern plain, "whether on this or that side the Karakoram."[147] Of this tradition Colonel Gordon appears to have been aware. Obliquely he refers to the Depsang plain stretching for about 100 miles, from the Saser, south of the Karakoram, to Sogat to the north–near Shahidulla.[148] With this tradition Kenneth Mason, seems to be in agreement. The large plateau he "discovered" north of the Karakoram in the course of his explorations of the watershed, he named as Aghil-Depsang. Though smaller than the southern Depsang, the similarity between the two appeared "most remarkable" to him.[149] Aksai Chin, it has been noted, was originally known as Changthang. To this tradition Burrard lends the weight of his authority. The records of the Survey of India compiled under his direction acknowledge that Changthang extends westwards as far as Skardo, south of the Karakoram.[150]

The mountain chains continued to be called by the name of the

Kuen Lun as late as 1854. The renaming of the southernmost ridge of the Kuen Lun as Karakoram the great Italian explorer, Filippo De Filippi remarks, "is purely due to Europeans."[151] The Russians, notably Valikhanof, in spite of these pronouncements continued to call these mountain ridges by their ancient name of Kuen Lun with the Karakoram a pass over it.[152] Another mountain chain which, like the Kuen Lun, formed part of India's historical boundary that the British split up was the Bolor. Between its two ridges runs up the trough from the Hindu Kush almost to Ferghana. The split facilitated induction of China into the trough.

The British had their own compulsions to invent, or cause to be invented, a separate name for the range known as Karakoiram. This particular ridge of the Angartaksia chains is a stupendous mountain mass, stretching from the east of Lhasa to the Pamirs with a width on the south side of 30 to 60 miles, peaks averaging from 21,000 to 23,000 feet, and round the head of Baltoro glacier dominated by the second highest mountain in the world, Godwin Austin. The head of every valley is the birth place of a glacier. Many of these are of immense size. This great mountain barrier is broken through at only one point, by the Hunza river, a tributary of the Gilgit river. Even this opening is at the north-western extremity of India and at a height of 15,500 feet.[153] For any military force, even a brigade strength, to have marched across it with artillery and every kind of stores was inconceivable.

In contrast, the width of the Kuen Lun westward, at the head of the Keria river, is not much more than 50 miles.[154] Towards the west the ridge recedes and splits in the neighbourhood of Chiraghsaldi pass on the boundary of Jammu and Kashmir.[155] The Schlagintweits called the Kuen Lun as the "secondary range," the principal being Karakoram to denote its superiority. None of the Kuen Lun peaks the Germans saw exceeded the height of 22,000 feet, the mean height of the passes they estimated at only 17,000 feet.[156] The Kuen Lun is cut through north of Aksai Chin by the Keria, Jurungkash, further west by Karakash and beyond by the Yarkand rivers. Colonel Holdich, who was seconded to the Pamir boundary commission, considered the Kuen Lun could be crossed "at frequent points in its length."[157] Mason feels that the Karakoram range has been made to bend out of its normal alignment, almost due east, in order to include the pass.[158] This is more or less, in agreement with Dr. Thomson's view, expressed by him in his "Western Himalayan and Tibet,"[159] and also in his report to Government in 1849, noticed earlier.

Crowned with glaciers, largest outside the Polar regions, these mountain chains are sources of innumerable rivers to the south of the Karakoram ridge—the Hunza, Gilgit, Shyok, Nubra, Chip Chap—and to the north of it—Yurungash, Karakash, and Yarkand. The chains have, therefore, emerged as a watershed which is one of the commonly accepted principles for determining boundaries. In this again the Schlagintweits were in the lead. They considered the Kuen Lun was "erroneously" regarded as the watershed.[160] This, professedly, was one of the major considerations for the British to persuade the Chinese to occupy Sirikul, Taghdumbash, Raskam valley and the territories along the Leh-Yarkand commercial line up to the Karakoram pass. These vast areas were pronounced by the British to be north of the watershed, their water flowing to the Tarim basin. How far does geographical evidence sustain this British and, now, Chinese claim?

Beginning from the eastern end of the boundary, Moorcroft, and his companion in travel, Trebeck, surveyed the Pangong lake. From Moorcroft's description,[161] Dr. Thomson later came, to the conclusion that the lake had originally an outlet at its western extremity, its water having then run through the Tankse valley to the Shyok and the Indus.[162] Godwin Austin surveyed the lake area right upto Rudok. He found that though the lake is 21/2 miles away from the low ridge of Surtok la, the told lake bed extends up within a very short distance of this pass. A rise of 150 feet in the waters will find them again an exit into Tankse.[163] A route, as noticed earlier, leads from the Pangong lake to the Changchenmo valley and beyond to Lingzithang plateaux. The Changchenmo river, the principal tributary of the Shylok, rises in the hills that girdle the Lingzithang and joins the Shyok, a mile or two below the mouth of the Changchenmo valley.[164] Despite this clear watershed the Changchenmo valley was occupied by China in 1962. Another stream, the Chip Chap, also rises in the northeast in Lingzithang and empties into the Skylok near the Rimo glacier. More of this hereafter.

The most important part of the British conceived watershed is the 200 miles long glaciated crest of the Karakoram ridge from the pass to the Hispar in Hunza. This immense sea of ice and snow covers both sides of the Karakoram chain and the glaciers are, in some known instances, interlinked, drawing from each other. The glaciated area is so large and so difficult that not much of it has been surveyed and mapped. Wherever explored, the British belief has been exploded in many instances by Englishmen themselves—Longstaff, Wood and Mason. The Karakoram glaciers are commonly of four types. 1. Longitudinal. 2. Transverse. 3. Cap. 4. Saddle. The saddle types have no definite dividing line and the branch glacier of one type may join the trunk of another. Two major glaciers nearest to the Karakoram pass westward are the Rimo and Siachin, the sources of the Shyok and Nubra respectively. Their waters join those of the Indus. Just across, to the north, rises the Yarkand river. Principally on this score, the Karakoram was given currency as the watershed between, on the south, the Indus and, on the north, the Tarim basin. So it was until Dr. Longstaff's exploration in 1909 and De Filippi's expedition in 1914, blew up this belief. The gigantic glacier, Siachin (Rose), the present day battlefield between India and Pakistan, Dr. Longstaff proved, "has its source north of the Karakoram range." It rises beyond the Gasherbrum peak cuts its way through the Karakoram, flows into the Nubra and thence into the Indus. Burrard reveals that Dr. Longstaff's findings "showed that the northern watershed of the Indus was situated considerably further north than had been believed."[165] Dr. Longstaff was followed to Siachin by the Workman team, Dr. William and Fany Bullock, in 1912. In a report to Government Fany Bullock Workman confirmed Dr. Longstaff's findings.[166] This unexpected development caused a flutter in the Indian Foreign Department. Sir Arthur MacMohan noted :

> "...we understand the watershed of the Indus to be our boundary and have thought that the Karakoram was that wateshed. We are not bound to adhere to the Karakoram if it is proved not to be the watershed, but will claim the real watershed as our boundary."[167]

One of the Italian expedition's members, Colonel Wood, who explored the Shaksgam, north of the Karakoram, "discovered" the Red Range. Wood believed and, a decade later, Major Mason of the Survey of India, confirmed that this Red Range is the watershed. The Yarkand river (Shaksgam channel) cuts through it, and the other branch of the Yarkand river, which starts from the north of the Karakoram pass and along which ran the trade route, pierces this Red Range between Balti Brangsa and Baksambulak in the Yarkand valley.[168] The Red Range, it was found, runs in the west as far as Bazar Dara in Yarkand valley and in the east to the Chip Chap valley. Quite evidently it was this geological finding that influenced Mason to suggest that the northern boundary should not be *finalised* along the Karakoram. This is not all. Rimo is a saddle type glacier. The Yarkand river also issues from Rimo to the north of the Karakoram. Rimo is, therefore, unique, being the only known glacier in the world giving rise to two rivers running in opposite directions.[169] Truly, as Spranger, another member of the De Filippi expedition, described "...this (is a) singular break in the watershed between India and Central

Asia."[170] The Rimo glacier marks the eastern extremity of the great furrow which, De Filippi says, stretches almost unbroken south of and nearly parallel to the Karakoram range, and is filled from, west to east, by the Hispar, Biafo, Siachin (upper half). Tarim Shahr and Rimo glaciers. This furrow, he wrote, appears to continue in the Chip Chap valley and that of the western sources of the Karakash but beyond Rimo there are no more large glaciers and hardly any snowfall.

Burrard implies and Mason approvingly refers to the Nubra and upper Shyok both draining from the *north* of the Karakoram range.[171] The water parting between the Karakash, tributary of the Tarim, and Shyok, tributary of the Indus is not in all places a mountain range. In support of this view Burrard quotes from a letter of Shaw to Sir Roderick Murchison, President of the Royal Geographical Society :

> "What was my astonishment after walking a few yards to find some water trickling westwards towards the mountains. I had, therefore, already passed the imperceptible watershed between the great river systems of the Indus and of Central Asia. Beyond the lake we had just passed, the waters feed the Karakash; while the tickling stream, which I had reached, pierces the great limestone range and much augmented on the way runs through the rocky gorges into the Shyok which is one of the chief sources of the Indus."

Burrard remarks–

> "Thus the great water system of Southern and Central Asia are here separated by no gigantic mountain range but merely by a few yards of level sand at a prodigious height, it is true."[172]

Not only does not a great mountain system separate the watershed here between the Southern and Central Asia but that it is no watershed at all. Reynolds, who followed Johnson into Lingzithang, established this in the course of his surveys and conveyed it to Shaw. Frederic Drew, Wazir of Ladakh, refers to these findings thus :

> "At the extreme south-west corner (of Lingzithang) I have been informed by Mr. Shaw (from his own observations and on the authority of Mr. Reynolds of the Survey) that streams which flow down to the Shyok inter-ramify with those that flow into Lingzithang, that the watershed between is quite unmarked."[173]

Thus, the water of Aksai Chin or Lingzithang flows to India also and not only to Eastern Turkistan as Shaw had claimed. This is what, perhaps, induced Colonel Bell to call the Kuen Lun as the "outer-shed." By implication the Karakoram becomes the "inner-shed and the two together the watershed. Of the Chip Chap tributary of the Shyok, which has its sources in the southwest Lingzithang, the watershed is imperceptible. Writing about this, De Filippi observes :

> "After our second camp by the Chip Chap–whose waters hardly ever come to the surface, but flow under the wide alluviums of the valley bottom–we continued our way eastward following the same trough. But at a certain point we saw water bubbling up among the pebbles, flowing in the direction in which we were going. In other words, we had crossed the watershed; we had passed unwares from one hydrographical basin into another. And this is, indeed, characteristic of the chief valleys of these Tibetan plateaux that they do not have their origin in a mountain crest, a saddle or a rocky pass, but in the alluvial plain. To such an extent that at times, unless we noticed the course of the current, as it bubbles up, we did not know in what direction the slope lay."[174]

Burrard and Mason's agreement on the Nubra and Shyok draining from the north of the Karakoram also appears to be influenced by Captain Trotter's findings during his explorations and surveys in Aksai Chin in 1873 as a member of the Yarkand mission. In his report touching historical and geographical aspects, Captain Trotter noted :

> "...there is a choice of three different roads all leading on to the Lingzithang plains. The most westerly path ascends the Changlung Pangtung pass (18,900 feet), crosses the corner of the plateau and descends into a deep ravine running along the stony and very difficult bed of a stream (which ultimately finds its way into the Shyok river), ascends again and skirts the western border of the gently undulating Lingzithang plain, in traversing which the traveller crosses, almost without knowing it, the watershed between India and Central Asia."[175]

Drew says that there is no outlet for water in the plateaux. It, therefore dries upon the plains.

Yet another aspect of the Karakoram watershed is revealed by De Filippi and Mason. Writing about the water-parting between the Daulatbeg Uldi valley at the southern base of the Karakoram pass and "A" stream flowing north into the Yarkand river, De Filippi observed–

> "The col is so flat that these streams flow indifferently, according as slight obstructions deflect the flow, either to the south to join the Chip Chap and thence the Shyok or to the north to stream "A" and the Yarkand river."[176]

Mason puts it even more vividly :

> "Our own way led over the natural watershed, at the head of the main valley. The divide is hardly perceptible, for small tributary streams trickle among the disintegrating rock, flow in all directions, and finally, as if uncertain whether to take the road to India or Yarkand, separate on the pass and flow both ways. Such is the Indo-Asian watershed."[177]

Finally the Yarkand river branch that springs from the Karakoram glacier, Rimo, is not the principal stream of the river that flows to Yarkand. Tisnaf stream, which takes its rise in the Taghdumbash Pamir, Gordon says, was *traditionally* considered to be the main branch of the river, a view to which Younghusband also refers.[178] Its sources were surveyed by Grombtchevsky in 1888 and 1889.[179]

In Hunza Burrard found what he calls a "curious point" about the nomenclature of the rivers. "On both sides of the Kilik pass, the rivers flowing from the watershed are called Kilik river, that on the Pamir side being generally designated "Jilga." Similarly at the Mintaka, Kharchanai and the Khanjerab passes.[180] All these facts also underline the unity of the region, the mountains, plateaux and drainage. The Karakoram is, therefore, no certain watershed. The British, notably Shaw, Hayward, Elias and Younghusband, projected it so to justify their pulling back India's northern boundary from the Kuen Lun.

References

1. 15th October 1881. Foreign. Pol. A. No. 9 of February 1882.
2. 11th September 1882. Foreign. Secret. E. No. 94 of November 1882.
3. Ney Elias. Explorer and Envoy Extraordinary In High Asia. By Gerald Morgan. p. 117.
4. 13th October 1882. Foreign. Sec. E. No. KW-2-94-96 of November 1882.
5. Undated. Foreign. Sec. E. No. KW-2-94-96 of November 1882.
6. 29th July 1883. Foreign. A. Pol. E. No. KW-309-315 of December 1883.
7. 13th August 1883. Foreign. A. Pol. E. No. KW-309-315 of December

1883.

8. 7th July 1885. Foreign. Secret. F. No. KW-1-775-795 of October 1885.
9. 1st June 1887. Foreign. Frontier. A. No. 127 of June 1887.
10. 22nd April 1888. Foreign. Frontier. A. No. 83 of June 1888.
11. 25th April 1888. Foreign. Frontier. A. No. 85 of July 1888.
12. 29th April 1888. Foreign. Frontier. A. No. 94 of July 1888.
13. Undated. Foreign. Frontier. A. No. KW-76-130 of July 1888.
14. 17th May 1888. Foreign. Frontier. A. No. 93 of July 1888.
15. 21st May 1888. Foreign. Frontier. A. No. 98 of July 1888.
16. 25th May 1888. Foreign. Frontier. A. No. 102 of July 1888.
17. 30th May 1888. Foreign. Secret F. No. 228 of August 1888.
18. 9th June 1888. Foreign. Frontier. A. No. 119 of July 1888.
19. Undated. Foreign. Secret. F. No. 244 of August 1888.
20. 19th July 1888. Foreign. Secret. F. No. 243 of August 1888.
21. Undated. Foreign. Frontier. A. No. 119 of October 1888.
22. 8th August 1888. Foreign. Secret. F. No. KW-2-227-249 of August 1888.
23. 6th September 1888. Foreign. Frontier. A. No. 119 of October 1888.
24. 10th September 1888. Foreign. Frontier. A. No. 124 of October 1888.
25. 7th October 1888. Foreign. Frontier. A. No. 79 of January 1889.
26. Undated. Foreign. Frontier. B. No. 40 of October 1890.
27. Where Three Empires Meet. By E.F. Knight. p. 167.
28. 26th July 1885. Foreign. Secret. F. No. 12 of November 1885.
29. 5th August 1885. Foreign. Secret. F. No. 13 of November 1885.
30. 22nd August 1885. Foreign. Secret. F. No. KW-12-14 of November 1885.
31. *Ibid.* 27th August 1885.
32. *Ibid.*
33. 20th September 1885. General and Political Dept. File No. 1 of 1885. Jammu Achives.
34. 22nd September 1885. General and Political Dept. File No. 1 of 1885. Jammu Achives.
35. 27th September 1886. Foreign. Secret. F. No. 169 of June 1887.
36. *Ibid.*
37. *Ibid.*
38. *Ibid.*
39. 6th January 1887. Foreign. Secret. F. No. 176 of June 1887.
40. 9th April 1887. Foreign. Secret. F. No. 177 of June 1887.
41. 15th November 1887. Foreign. Secret. F. No. KW 238-247 of December 1888.
42. 25th November 1887. Foreign. Secret. F. No. KW 238-247 of December 1888.
43. 6th February 1888. Foreign. Secret. F. No. 283 of April 1888.
44. 23rd February 1888. Foreign. Secret. F. No. 282 of April 1888.
45. 18th April 1888. Foreign. Secret. No. KW 282-283 of April 1888.
46. 19th April 1888. Foreign. Secret. F. No. KW 282-283 of April 1888.
47. 24th April 1888. Foreign. Secret. F. No. 282-283 of April 1888.
48. 11th December 1888. Foreign. Secret. F. No. 116 of March 1889.

49. *Ibid.*
50. *Ibid.*
51. 8th January 1889. Foreign. Secret. F. No. 115 of March 1889.
52. 6th October 1888. Foreign. Frontier-B. No. 13 of November 1888.
53. 31st October 1888. Foreign. Frontier-B. No. 29 of February 1888.
54. 13th May 1889. Foreign. Secret. F. No. 208 of July 1889.
55. 15th August 1889. General & Political. File No. 18 of 1889. (Jammu Archives).
56. 25th May 1889. Foreign. Secret. F. No. KW-3-203-230 of July 1889.
57. *Ibid.*
58. 25th May 1889. Foreign. Secret. F. No. KW-3-203-230 of July 1889.
59. Undated. Foreign. Secret F. No. KW-3-203-230 of July 1889.
60. 25th May 1889. Foreign. Secret. F. No. KW-3-203-230 of July 1889.
61. 25th May 1889. Foreign. Secret. F. No. KW-3-203-230 of July 1889.
62. 30th May 1889. Foreign. Secret. F. No. KW-3-203-230 of July 1889.
63. 3rd June 1889. Foreign. Secret. F. No. 107 of August 1889.
64. 16th June 1889. Foreign. Secret. F. No. KW-3-203-230 of July 1889.
65. 5th July 1889. Foreign. Secret. F. No. 224 of July 1889.
66. 15th August 1889. General and Political. File No. 18 of 1889. (Jammu Archives).
67. 2nd August 1889. Foreign. Secret. F. No. 44 of September 1889.
68. Undated Foreign. Secret. F. No. 47 of September 1889.
69. 26th August 1889. Foreign. Secret. F. No. 184 of October 1889.
70. 26th August 1889. Foreign. Secret. F. No. 186 of October 1889.
71. 28th August 1889. General and Political. File No. 18 of 1889. (Jammu Archives).
72. 2nd September 1889. Foreign. Secret. F. No. 191 of October 1889.
73. 12th September 1889. Foreign. Secret. F. No. 185 of October 1889.
74. 21st September 1889. Foreign. Secret. F. No. KW-1-182-197 of October 1889.
75. 28th September 1889. Foreign. Secret. F. No. KW-1-182-197 of October 1889.
76. 30th September 1889. Foreign. Secret. F. No. KW-2-182-197 of October 1889.
77. *Ibid.*
78. 8th October 1889. Foreign. Secret. F. No. KW-2-59-84 of February 1890.
79. 7th October 1889. Foreign. Secret. F. No. KW-2-59-84 of February 1890.
80. 24th October 1889. Foreign. Secret. F. No. KW-2-59-84 of February 1890.
81. 24th October 1889. Foreign. Secret. F. No. KW-2-59-84 of February 1890.
82. 27th October 1889. Foreign. Secret. F. No. KW-2-59-84 of February 1890.
83. Report of A. Mission To The Northern Frontier of Kashmir in 1889. By Captain F.E. Younghusband. Govt. Printing Press, Calcutta, 1890. p. 92.
84. 15th November 1889. General & Political. File No. 18 of 1889. (Jammu Archives).
85. Undated. Foreign. Frontier. B. No. 129 of September 1890.
86. 23rd December 1889. Foreign. Secret. F. No. 229 of July 1890.

87. 10th January 1890. General & Political. File No. 21 of 1890. (Jammu Archives).
88. 8th February 1890. General & Political. File No. 21 of 1890. (Jammu Archives).
89. 12th February 1890. General & Political. File No. 21 of 1890. (Jammu Archives).
90. 25th February 1890. Foreign. Secret. F. No. 232 of July 1890.
91. 26th February 1890. General & Political. File No. 21 of 1890. (Jammu Archives).
92. 31st March 1890. Foreign. Frontier. B. No. 18 of June 1890.
93. Report of A Mission To The Northern Frontier of Kashmir in 1889. By Captain F.E. Younghusband. Govt. Printing Press, 1890, pp. 90-101.
94. 23rd June 1890. Foreign. Secret. F. No. 222 of July 1890.
95. Undated. Foreign. Secret. E. No. 57 of August 1890.
96. 7th July 1890. Foreign. Secret. E. No. KW-3-57-82 of August 1890.
97. 14th July 1890. Foreign. Secret. F. No. 243 of July 1890.
98. *Ibid.*
99. 17th July 1890. Foreign. Secret. F. No. KW-3-225-245 of July 1890.
100. 22nd July 1890. General & Political. File No. 19 of 1890. (Jammu Archives).
101. 25th July 1890. General & Political. File No. 19 of 1890. (Jammu Archives).
102. 13th August 1890. General & Political. File No. 19 of 1890. (Jammu Archives).
103. 14th August 1890. Foreign. Secret. F. No. 86 of December 1891.
104. 18th August 1890. Foreign. Secret. F. No. KW-1-14-31 of October 1890.
105. 5th August 1890. Foreign. Secret. F. No. KW-3-123-148 of March 1890.
106. 5th September 1890. Foreign. Secret. F. No. 96 of December 1891.
107. Undated. Foreign. Secret. F. No. 204 of February 1893.
108. *Ibid.*
109. 30th September 1890. General & Political. File No. 21 of 1890. (Jammu Archives).
110. 4th October 1890. General & Political. File No. 21 of 1890. (Jammu Archives).
111. 6th October 1890. Foreign. Secret. F. No. 96 of December 1891.
112. 16th October 1890. Foreign. Secret. F. No. KW-3-123-148 of March 1891.
113. 18th October 1890. General & Political. File No. 19 of 1890. (Jammu Archives).
114. The Pamirs. By Lord Dunmore. 1893. Vol. I, pp. 220-25-33.
115. Undated. Foreign. Secret. F. No. 96 of December 1891.
116. 30th October 1890. Foreign. Secret. F. No. KW. 3-123-148 of March 1891.
117. 23rd November 1890. Foreign. Secret. F. No. 133 of March 1891.
118. 23rd December 1890. Foreign. Secret. F. No. 128 of June 1891.
119. 28th December 1890. Foreign. Secret. F. No. KW-3-128-131 of June 1891.
120. 16th January 1891. Foreign. Secret. F. No. 109 of August 1891.
121. 11th March 1891. Foreign. Secret. F. No. 147 of March 1891.
122. 22nd May 1891. Foreign. Secret. F. No. 112 of August 1891.

123. Undated. Foreign. Secret. F. No. 113 of August 1891.
124. 25th May 1891. Foreign. Secret. F. No. KW-2-105-117 of August 1891.
125. 16th March 1892. Foreign. Secret. F. No. 3 of September 1892. Also General & Political. File No. 82 of 1892. (Jammu Archives).
126. Scientific Mission To India And High Asia. By Hermann, Adolphe and Robert De Schlagintweit. 1860. Vol. IV, pp. 231, 258.
127. 4th April 1892. General & Political. File No. 82 of 1892. (Jammu Archives). Also No. 4 of Septempber 1892. Foreign. Secret. F.
128. 21st April 1892. Foreign. Secret. F. No. KW-2-594-600 of August 1892.
129. 29th April 1892. Foreign. Secret. F. No. 596 of August 1892.
130. 21st July 1892. Foreign. Secret. F. No. 5 of September 1892.
131. 16-31st July 1892. Foreign. Frontier. B. No. 104 of November 1892.
132. 1st August 1892. Foreign. Secret. F. No. 870 of September 1892.
133. 6th August 1892. Foreign. Frontier. B. No. 105 of November 1892.
134. Undated. (9th October 1892). Foreign. Secret. F. No. 502 of January 1893.
135. 27th October 1892. Foreign. Secret. F. No. 507 of January 1893.
136. 31st October 1892. Foreign. Secret. F. No. 186 of December 1892.
137. 13th December 1892. Foreign. Secret. F. No. 500 of January 1893.
138. 25th December 1892. Foreign. Secret. F. No. KW-500-510 of January 1893.
139. *Ibid.* 28th December 1892.
140. *Ibid.* 30th December 1892.
141. 16th January 1893. Foreign. Secret. F. No. 508 of January 1893.
142. 18th January 1893. Foreign. Secret. F. No. 509 of January 1893.
143. 15th February 1893. Foreign. Secret. F. No. 58 of June 1893.
144. 23rd July 1893. Foreign. Secret. F. No. 97 of October 1893.
145. A Sketch of Geography and Geology of the Himalaya Mountains and Tibet. By Col. Sir G.S. Burrard and H.H. Hayden. Government Printing Press. 1907-1908, p. 71.
146. Memoir on Indian Surveys. By C.R. Markham. Her Majesty's Stationery Office. London, p. 350.
147. Italian Expedition To The Himalaya, Karakoram and Eastern Turkistan (1913-14). By Filippo De Filippi, p. 406.
148. Roof of The World. By Lt. Colonel T.E. Gordon. (1876) p. 21.
149. Records of The Survey of India. Vol. XXII. Exploration of Shaksgam Valley. 1926. By Major Kenneth Mason. Survey of India. 1928, p. 70.
150. Records of The Survey of India. Volume VIII. Part two. Prepared under the direction of Colonel Sir S.G. Burrard, Surveyor General. 1915, p. 224.
151. Exploration In The Eastern Karakoram And Upper Yarkand Valley. Survey of India Detachment with F. De Filippi's Scientific Expedition of 1914, p. 7.
152. The Russians In Central Asia. By Captain Valikhanof, M. Veniukof and others. English translation (1865), p. 114.
153. Imperial Gazetteer of India. Kashmir And Jammu. (1909), p. 15.
154. Tibet The Mysterious. By Col. Sir T.H. Holdich, p. 273.
155. The Heart of A Continent. By Captain Frank E. Younghusband. (1896),

p. 235.

156. Scientific Mission To India and High Asia. By Hermann, Adolphe and Robert De Schlagintweit. 1860. Vol. II, pp. 494 and 489.
157. Tibet The Mysterious. By Colonel Sir T.H. Holdich. p. 271.
158. Records of The Survey of India Vol. XXII. Exploration of Shaksgam. By Major Kenneth Mason, p. 73.
159. Western Himalaya and Tibet By Dr. Thomas Thomson. (Indian print). p. 434.
160. Scientific Mission To India And High Asia. By Hermann, Adolphe and Robert De Schlagintweit. 1860. Vol. I, pp. 25, 259.
161. Travels in The Himalayan Provinces of Hindustan, Ladakh And Kashmir. By W. Moorcroft. (Indian print). Vol. I, p. 434.
162. 10th October 1849. Foreign. F.C. No. 332 of 29th December 1849.
163. Journal of Asiatic Society. Part II. No. 1. 1868. Notes on Pangong Lake By Captain Godwin Austin. p. 87.
164. Italian Expedition To The Himalaya, Karakoram and Eastern Turkistan (1913-1914). By Filippo De Filippi, p. 288.
165. 3rd April 1912. Foreign. Frontier. B. Enclosure 1 to No. 125 of May 1912.
166. Undated. Foreign. Frontier. B. Notes. 24 of December 1913.
167. 18th April 1912. Foreign, Frontier. B. Notes. No. 125-126 of May 1912.
168. Records of The Survey of India. Vol. XXII. Exploration of Shaksgam Valley. 1926. By Major Kenneth Mason. p. 70.
169. Italian Expedition To The Himalaya, Karakoram & Eastern Turkistan (1913-1914), By Filippo De Filippi. pp. 377, 403.
170. *Ibid.* p. 377.
171. Records of The Survey of India. Vol. XXII. Exploration of Shaksgam Valley 1926. By Major Kenneth Mason. p. 73.[N]
172. A Sketch Of The Geography And Geology Of The Himalaya Mountains and Tibet. By Colonel Sir S.G. Barrard and H.H. Hayden. Government Printing Press. 1907-1908. p. 124.
173. The Jammu and Kashmir Territories. By F. Drew. p. 350.
174. Italian Expedition To The Himalaya, Karakoram and Eastern Turkistan. By Filippo De Filippi. p. 356.
175. Captain H. Trotter's Report on Historical & Geographical Aspects. A Mission To Yarkand. 1875, p. 245.
176. Explorations In The Eastern Karakoram and The Upper Yarkand Valley. The Survey of India Detachment with. De Filippi's Scientific Expedition. 1914, p. 7.
177. Records of The Survey of India. Vol. XXII Exploration of Shaksgam Valley. 1926. By Major Kenneth Mason. p. 21.
178. Roof of The World. By Colonel T.E. Gordon, p. 114. Also The Heart of A Continent By Captain F.E. Younghusband, p. 266.
179. Undated. Foreign. Frontier. B. No. 129 of September 1890.
180. Records of The Survey of India. Vol. VI. 1914. Col. Sir S.G. Burrard. 1913, p. 18.

Chapter 9
England's Second Thoughts over Karakoram Line

Apart from unravelling Hunza China relations, the Baltit papers establish Hunza's sovereign rights over the Taghdumbash Pamir and Sirikul. Sometime in 1886 the Chinese acknowledged Hunza's right to build a fort in Taghdumbash, presumably to control pastures which again belonged to Hunza[1]. The authority of the Hunza Raja was, by and large, recognised by the Begs of Taghdumbash, an undated letter reveals[2]. Three of the four letters, all without dates, but approximately of 1887, 1889 and two of January 1890, marked by the British Agent, Gilgit, as II-a-b-c-d, reveal that "Safdar Ali exercised authority over Sirikul," and "received dues from it."[3] Kuch Mohammad appears to have intrigued with the "Khatais."[4] He was seized, taken to Hunza and finally dismissed and replaced on the orders of Safdar Ali by Khojash[5]. From another letter it is evident that Safdar Ali had proceeded against Kuch Mohammad after the deposition of Khojash, Raja of Kukardan. Kukardan appears to be to the north of the Hindu Kush. Khojash had, on behalf of his people, stated that Kuch Mohammad had seized "their Kanjut."[6] This hardly leaves any doubt that territories north of the Hindu Kush were also known as "Kanjut", besides "doam" Hunza. The Hunza Mirs did not accept the authority of Chinese in their relations with the Kirghiz of Sirikul or Taghdumbash. Even though Safdar Ali was looked upon by the Chinese as "subordinate to the Khakan of China," he appointed his own frontier patrols to keep the Kirghiz under check[7].

China had no real claim whatever to the Little Pamir, north of Chitral and Hunza. With Sirikul and Taghdumbash under Hunza, China was not even contiguous to the Little Pamir. From Hunza, the Irshad pass leads directly into the Little Pamir. Yet China, with British connivance, intended to build forts and appoint "karaul" Begs in Aktash, Bozai Gumbaz and elsewhere in 1892[8]. Territorially Hunza then comprised "awal" and "doam" Hunza, including the Raskam valley. In the context of the impending installation of Nazim Khan as the new Raja, the wording of the "sanad" and, even more importantly, fixing the boundaries of a defeated Hunza were considered "not so pressing" in the Foreign Department[9]. Really, however, it was too early to proceed that far in the context of the Russian advance into the Pamirs. While the British entertained no wish to go beyond the Hindu Kush, yet, it was felt, "it might be as well not to let the Hunza claims to tribute in these regions (Taghdumbash and Sirikul) go by default..."[10] Were China to abandon her claim to the Pamirs Russia, on ethnic and other convenient grounds, would easily, annex Taghdumbash. The Chinese were nowhere in the Taghdumbash Pamir as late as May 1892 when there were reports of their intention to build a fort at Ujadbai[11]. A Hunza fort had certainly existed there earlier, Ujadbai having been on the historic route from Wakhan, via Wakhijrui, to Sirikul and beyond to Central Asia.

Either British intentions to surrender the Taghdumbash to China or the latter's moves to occupy it made even Nazim Khan, the "common" choice of England and China to succeed Safdar Ali, to insist upon his continuing "to receive tribute from the Kirghiz on the Taghdumbash."[12] Confirmed reports were received by the British that a "signed and sealed agreement" was, indeed, reached at Kashgar sometime in 1886 by which "the Sirikulis admitted the claims of the Kanjutis over the whole of Taghdumbash."[13] Yet the British equivocated over Taghdumbash, the Resident in Kashmir felt persuaded to press the Foreign Department that the advantages of a well defined Hindu Kush boundary were too valuable to be relinquished on the ground that the British might, at some future time, be called upon to meet "the improbable contingency of the Russian occupation of the Taghdumbash Pamir." The force of this argument was conceded, yet the Governor General-in-Council did not consider it advisable "that the Hunza claim should, *at present*, be altogether abandoned." An exception was nevertheless, made in the case of China. Were China to hold the Taghdumbash Pamir effectively, "the Government of India will certainly not be disposed, under present conditions, to press that claim against her," Cunningham wrote to Prideaux[14]. At the installation ceremony of Nazim Khan at Baltit, Hunza's claim to Taghdumbash was to be "mentioned" to the Chinese representatives. The right was, admittedly, not without complications for the British. Were the Raja to assert his claim to tribute, or, more appropriately, revenue from Taghdumbash, and were the Kirghiz to refuse to pay, how was the right to be enforced? Its enforcement would necessitate action north of the Hindu Kush range. The Resident went a step further. Were the British, he argued, to contenance the rights of protected States to territories north of the Hindu Kush, like Taghdumbash, would not Russia press the rights of Kokand to the south of the chain?[15] Kokand's rights in the Pamirs were expected by Sir R. Morier to be raised by Russia in negotiations with England.

British calculations were rather rudely upset by Petrovski. The consul general relying on a letter, purportedly written by the Raja Ghazan Khan to him, acknowledging himself, his family and his descendants as vassals of Russian Government[16] implied that Hunza was tributary to Russia. Even more, Russia claimed Sirikul, Chitral and, in fact, the whole of the country in which Kanjutis used then to carry their raids–the entire Yarkand valley. Russia insisted this country was "originally Kanjuti territory" which China had taken away from the Raja. Petrovski's claim coincided with Russian occupation of Aktash, just across Taghdumbash[17]. Whether the consul general really had the letter or not, Russian shadow over these tracts loomed large for England, no less after China eventually took over most of them. For this situation England had to thank herself. Prideaux was directed were Nazim Khan to press for support for the enforcement of his claim over Taghdumbash, his request was to be "refused."[18] The Russian claim, British suspected, was also, perhaps, inspired by the fort, Sanju Kurgan or Bostan, north of Shahidulla, having been built by the Amir of Bokhara, Abu Bakr, and occupied by him several decades earlier[19]. This was only British imagination. Nearer the truth was the consistent Russian claim, voiced by the "Novoe Vremya", to the territories of the Khan of Kokand that were said to have stretched "from the Alai to Kanjut and Yasin..."[20] The "St. Petersburger Herold" wrote in a similar refrain[21].

England being anxious to keep Russia out of the Raskam valley, China was privately furnished with a map carrying a boundary line fancied by Younghusband. Strategic advantages of this boundary were explained to her, so also "the supreme importance to China of preventing Russian encroachments..."[22] Russia openly expressed interest in Sirikul and a design to build a fort on the Taghdumbash Pamir[23]. As a counter Colonel Durand suggested Hunza's claim to the Taghdumbash be raised to British advantage against Russia. Such a claim had been alluded to the Chinese by Dr. Robertson[24]. Russia was, however, forthright. China was seen by Petrovski to have nothing whatsoever to do with Sirikul and the Pamirs considering that her western limits were Sanju, Kilian,

Kukyar, Tung, Yakarak, Ighizyar, Opar and Tashmalik[25]. Russia did not thus recognise British encouraged Chinese encroachments into Vohab plateau, Yarkand valley, Sirikul and Taghdumbash. Macartney pressed that no portion of Sirikul should be ceded to a "foreign power", quite evidently Russia. If commissioners were sent up to delimit Chinese, Russian, Indian (Kashmir) or Afghan frontiers in the Pamirs, "their work", he suggested, "should have nothing whatever to do with Sirikul..."[26] for he saw the Chinese frontier to reach out to Sirikul and the Taghdumbash. Yet when Lord Dunmore traversed the Pamirs in 1893, he had in his possession a Chinese official map of 1892 on which were shown over 20 forts whereas he found none[27]. More, perhaps, as intent rather than ground reality, did the Amban of Tashkurgan claim to the Begs of Sirikul "that from the frontier of Shahidulla...and from Shopakhu all the frontiers and ilaqas of Sirikul up to the frontier of Kepper, which extends to Kashgar, are under the Chinese rule."[28]

While the British were certain that they must cede these and other frontier tracts of Jammu and Kashmir to China or Afghanistan or both, they were less than certain that China could prevent Russian encroachment there or, in the event of an inevitable Russian push, even retain Kashgaria. Ceding these territories to China and her losing them to Russia defeated British policy objective–to build China as a buffer between the Indian empire and Russia. Their dilemma was no less reflected in their map making. Some cartographic principles came to be laid down, for one, indication in a map by symbols of different kinds of boundaries. Thus a definite boundary, as defined by treaty stipulation, was thereafter to be indicated by dot and dash.-.-.-, a boundary that was more or less recognised either by custom or because of physical conditions was to be recognised by the symbol dash, dash - - -. An undefined boundary, which fluctuated or was not known or acknowledged, was to be pointed out by the words "Boundary undefined". But the use of the legend was later dropped. In a new map of India under preparation since 1892, Cunningham suggested in a note addressed to the Surveyor General, dated the 10th June 1892,

> "the present boundary may be indicated with a symbol of the second class along the line as at present shown up to the north-east corner of the Lingzithang plains..."

Ladakh's northern boundary was recognised by custom and because of physical condition–the great mountain chain of the Kuen Lun. Cunningham, therefore, rightly placed this boundary in the second class. But did the boundary line run over the Kuen Lun? The use of the Ladakhi name of Lingzithang and not the Turkish name of Aksai Chin, which British preferred, is suspicious. Another cartographic principle firmed up related to colouring of maps. Colonel Ardagh was of the view that yellow wash on the new map of India should indicate country within the British sphere of influence as well as native states. The yellow wash should, it was proposed, be applied to the northern slopes of the Karakoram–Muztagh, Raskam valley and the Taghdumbash Pamir upto the Chinese posts[29]. Lansdowne agreed but wished it to be made perfectly clear" that all that is meant by the yellow wash is that the country so coloured is within the sphere of our influence, only in this sense that we should not allow any one else to take possession of it."[30]

This was a cartographic elaboration of Lansdowne's earlier argument of England retaining her say in the disposal of territories to the north of the Karakoram given to China. Another and a related doctrine, a military doctrine, came to be propounded by Lansdowne, or, more accurately, by Colonel Ardagh. The passes by which the Hindu Kush-Karakoram are penetrated are not doubt, difficult yet traversable by moderately sized parties. Some control was thought to be necessary, no only to prevent passage of small filibustering expeditions, such as of Colonel Yonoff, but

> "to control and to give us freedom of circulation along what has been spoken of as the northern slope of the glacis, along which it is most undesirable that a Russian force should be allowed to move as freely as it pleases..."[31]

Freedom of circulation here means opportunity to collect military intelligence to the north of the Karakoram. Ardagh fully developed this military doctrine a little later, after he took over as Director of Military Intelligence, British War Office, in the rank of general. Even though, thanks to British blandishments, the Chinese had nominally reached out to the Karakoram pass, Macartney in Kashgar perceived that one day when Russia would have taken over Sirikul and Raskam the British might have to consider the advisability, from a strategic point of view, of either advancing or waiving the claims which the Kanjutis had to the north beyond the British recognised boundary. Were such a contingency to arise England would find Hung Tajen's map to their interest to show that the Chinese frontier never actually extended to the Karakoram[32]. Hung's map showed the Sino-Indian boundary to run along the Yarkand river like many British maps[33]. The Yarkand river was, indeed, the effective boundary wall into the next century, certainly up the end of World War

I. The boundary issue was also being actively considered by China. The district magistrate of Yarkand, into which district were "merged" Shahidulla, Raskam and Sirikul, sought its limits to be clearly defined. The reason for this request was a Russian map on which the Chinese Minister at St. Petersburg, Hsu Tajen, had transcribed Chinese names of places. This map, along with records of explorations by English and Russian explorers, showed Yarkand river as the limit of Chinese jurisdiction. Macartney found some "inaccuracies" in the map—a red line along the Yarkand river between Aktagh and Chong Jungle which a Chinese Official conjectured, might represent the Chinese boundary. The British usually marked their boundaries in red. The Hindu Kush range eastward of Langar was so marked on the map as to place Hunza and Nagar to its north. Finally Aktash was placed to the east of the Sirikul watershed and not to its west, which it is[34].

More likely Chinese apprehensions on Eastern Turkistan frontier with India were the result of their building the boundary pillar on the Karakoram pass without British concurrence which N.R. O'Conor, the British Minister in Beijing, had brought to the notice of the Tsungli Yamen. British objection to Chinese unilateral proceedings was rejected by the Tsungli Yamen. China claimed that the Karakoram was the "south limit of the Yarkand territory." Apparently to project her longstanding ownership of the Jammu and Kashmir territories, Chinese names were, for the first time, given to Shahidulla as Sai Tu La and the Karakoram as the Ka La Hu Lu Mu. The Karakoram was claimed to be "a grazing ground" of Chinese Mohammadan subjects[35]. O'Conor did not find the "tone of the note" of the Tsungli Yamen as "quite satisfactory," but he blamed it for "so much soreness in official quarters over the aggressive policy of Russia in the Pamirs..."[36] O'Conor's explanation is misleading. Russia had inherited rights over the Pamirs. China had conferred lands near Dafdar and the Taghdumbash Pamir in jagir on Sarbuland Shah, a brother of the ex-Mir of Wakhan Ali Mardan Shah. This was contrary to assurances Nazim Khan had received from the Taotai who had "verbally recognised the rights of Hunza to the Taghdumbash Pamir[37]. Calculatedly, it would appear, the Mir of Hunza took up the issue with the British. The reaction of the British Political Agent at Baltit, major B.E.M. Gurdon, was to cast doubt on recognition of Hunza rights by China. This assimilation of Jammu and Kashmir territories by China is also reflected in the Hunza Mir allegedly projecting himself as a vassal of China who, a letter purported to be from Nazim Khan and published in the Peking Gazette of the 1st June 1894, claimed was indebted to Chinese protection and owed his succession to family possessions "to the enjoyment of imperial favour."[38] This and similar subsequent publication of the Mir's polite letters, sent along with gifts of gold dust, were reduced by Chinese to virtual forgeries. On the unilateral construction of the Karakoram boundary mark the Secretary of State for India proposed to "acquiesce" in the Chinese view[39]. In the Little Pamir-Taghdumbash region too this process of assimilation had begun with the construction of huts for sentries to the north of the Kilik and Mintaka passes, which the Russians mistook for British posts[40]. Considering the implications of the construction, of the boundary pillar without approval of the British, the issue remained alive. By 1894 year end, Lord Kimberley, as Secretary of State for Foreign Affairs, considered it inadvisable to raise it at the "present juncture" and proposed to advise O'Conor in Beijing "to defer making any further communication to the Chinese Government on the subject."[41] H. Fowler as the new Secretary of State for India again concurred[42].

British disbelief in China's ability to keep Russia out of Kashgaria inspired Macartney to propose an "intermediary zone between British territory and that which Russia might afterwards acquire in Kashgaria." The proposal had the merit of preventing the Russian boundary becoming conterminous with that of India. Probably, the British feared China might, for a consideration, cede of her own accord to Russia territories informally given to her. Macartney expected once Russian boundary in the Pamirs was fixed, an Anglo-Chinese commission would follow to delimit Afghan-Chinese frontier on the Little Pamir. Such an opportunity could be seized to come to an understanding with the Chinese with reference to the common frontier in the Muztagh-Karakoram region. The Chinese, Macartney proposed, ought to be told of "whatever claims the States of Kashmir and Hunza still have, or recently had, to territory situated on the northern side of these ranges." For the purpose of British requirements,

> "it would be sufficient if the claims of Kashmir and Kanjut, being placed on record in a treaty, were shown to have been waived by us under certain contingencies, for example, so long as the territory claimed and the neighbouring country remained in Chinese occupation. It would not be difficult for China to agree to such a condition, for it would deprive her of the nothing. To us it would be useful as furnishing a basis for negotiations with Russia whenever she should occupy

> Kashgar. Perhaps, when that event comes to pass, it might be possible to arrange for the establishment, under the guarantee of both powers, of a neutral state, which would occupy all the mountain regions between the crest of the Karakoram and the Muztagh ranges on one side and would, on the other, be limited by a line drawn from about Taghdumbash to Kukyar and thence by the skirts of the mountains until *Polur* is reached on the Kuen Lun range. Such places as the Taghdumbash Pamir, the Raskam district and Shahidulla would thus be comprised in a neutral zone..."[43]

Macartney's neutral zone is an admission of British miscalculations on the northern boundary. In the Foreign Department the proposal was dismissed as it did "not appear a very practicable scheme." Nor were the Russians likely to agree to "a neutral state." From it the British appear to have later developed the right to reversion to them of territories informally given to China. The Foreign Department reiterated that as to the question of the relative boundary rights of Kashmir and China on the Karakoram "this would have to be settled by an Anglo-Chinese delimitation commission..."[44] General Brackenbury, Military member in the Viceroy's Council, shared Macartney's views on the delimitation of boundaries. It appeared probable to Brackenbury that Russia would acquire the Taghdumbash Pamir from China at some not very remote date and thus come round to the Hindu Kush. The British should therefore, get the boundaries between Afghanistan and China and between British possessions and China settled and demarcated at an early date[45]. On Taghdumbash, the Secretary of State for India cabled to the Viceroy, Lord Elgin, to take precaution of preventing China from ceding it to Russia[46]. The Chinese attitude was different. The Taotai, Huang Tajen, with the approval of the provincial Governor, acknowledged Hunza rights over the Taghdumbash and "agreed to the collection of taxes..." by the Mir[47]. This was not out of any scruples for fair play, rather it was Hunza was considered a vassal State of China. Hunza's rights to Raskam were claimed to pre-date the return of China to Kashgaria in mid 19th century and acquired during the Mirship of Salim Khan I. After Kashgaria was occupied by China, an agreement was drawn up in the name of Mir Salim Khan II which admitted the rights of Hunza on Raskam and Taghdumbash. During Mir Ghazan Khan's rule, a similar document was signed and sealed by the Sirikulis. This accord was kept in the Baltit fort but was "lost" in 1891 soon after the British invasion of Hunza. The Mir, Nazim Khan, believed it was, along with hundreds of State papers, carried away by the British to Simla. Though there was complete agreement in the Government of India over the limitation of boundaries of China with Afghanistan, Hunza and Jammu and Kashmir, the British Foreign Office in London considered "that the present condition of the Chinese Government is such as to make it impolitic for Her Majesty's Government to bring these questions before them."[48]

Ardagh elaborated his doctrine just as the move to delimit the boundaries of Afghanistan, Hunza and Kashmir with China was initiated. Her defeat in the war against Japan showed to the British how futile it was to rely on China as an ally, or even as a buffer against Russia. Nor was "the precarious nature of China's sovereignty in Kashgaria" lost on the British, maintained as it was by a single line of communication. South of the Uzbel pass Russia had not demarcated her boundary with China "thus leaving herself untrammelled in the natural process of expansion from the Pamirs eastward." Were then Russia to annex Kashgaria, Ardagh was certain "we shall have to conclude a definite agreement regarding the northern frontier of India." The basis of such an agreement was the Karakoram-Hindu Kush as the strategic boundary. But the physical condition of these mountains, their great extent, high altitude, general inaccessibility and sparse population rendered it impossible "to watch the actual watershed..." The measures requisite for security and for information as to the movements of an enemy, Ardagh argued "cannot be adequately carried out unless we circulate freely at the foot of glacis forming the northern slope, along those longitudinal valleys..." For military purposes, therefore, the frontier following the highest watershed was considered by Ardagh to be "defective." The aim was to keep the enemy from "any possibility of establishing himself on the glacis, occupying the longitudinal valleys and there preparing to surprise the passes." Ardagh sought a boundary "which shall leave all these longitudinal valleys in our possession or, at least, under our influence."[49] The value of this sparsely inhabited country was insignificant but its importance as a security to the Indian frontier was seen as considerable. This, in sum, was Ardagh's doctrine. The same principles and arguments, Ardagh foresaw, might have to be applied later to the upper basins of the Indus, the Sutlej and even the Brahmaputra "in the event of prospective absorption of Tibet by Russia."

In effect Ardagh's proposal was and, in the British establishment, came to be seen, as a plea for retention, in one form or another, of the Yarkand valley and the Taghdumbash in the British empire, indeed putting the boundary back over the Kuen Lun. In the Intelligence Branch of the Quarter Master General's Office, Ardagh was understood to suggest that the boundary should start from the westernmost point of Chadirtash (Paik pass) in the Taghdumbash on behalf of Hunza. But the Mir was declared to be tributary of China and the claim hence "a very weak one." Beyond, Hung Tajen's map showed the Chinese boundary to run along the main Hindu Kush range by the Khanjerab and Shangshal passes to a point west of the Muztagh pass thence following the Muztagh river to its junction with the Yarkand river to Aktagh and continued eastward for 140 miles, leaving Aksai Chin within India, before turning south. But the Chinese had set up a boundary pillar on the Karakoram pass and it had "apparently been allowed to remain there for the last four years."[50] As a matter of theory where a mountain formed the line of defence between two conterminous powers, as in the case of India and China, to circulate, it was readily conceded, was an advantage. But in a mass of mountains such as the Karakoram, this advantage was "reduced." No road was seen to exist by which an invasion through this region needed to be feared on a scale that could not with ease be met and crushed. The boundary as it stood along the Karakoram-Hindu Kush remained..." indisputably the strongest in the world."[51] It was, therefore, felt "We should only be courting disaster for ourselves in any attempt to hold the country at the foot of the northern slopes of the Muztagh range, no matter what, or how strong our claims may be to such territory."[52] The Quarter Master General himself dismissed Ardagh's doctrine as "some fanciful military dogma."[53] The view of the commander-in-chief, Sir G.S. White, was no different[54]. Despite these adverse pronouncements by the highest military authorities in India, Ardagh's thesis was, it would appear, rejected more for political considerations. One such consideration would seem to have been the expected Chinese resistance to it. Having been prevailed upon to occupy the glacis, China would have lost face with Russia where she induced to vacate the same territories she was invited to occupy. This appears obliquely to have been referred to by Elias to Ardagh. Yet the doctrine, in course of time, informally reversed British policy on the northern boundary.

What was this glacis which provoked a controversy in the British military establishment? Broadly it comprised the territory sandwiched between the Karakoram and Kuen Lun-Yarkand valley, Taghdumbash, Sirikul and Aksai Chin. Surrounded by several side valleys, or glens, the Yarkand valley is long winding, often a narrow one. Towards the west it reaches out to Tashkurgan in Sirikul[55], where are to be found some of the sources of the Raskam stream. It joins the Yarkand branch, coming down from the Karakoram range, at Chong Jungle to form the Yarkand river which flows down into Yarkand territory to the north. Thornton's Gazetteer estimates the length of the Yarkand Valley from the Karakoram to Yarkand at about 300 miles. Younghusband's estimate is less tentatie. He gives the length of Raskam part of the valley at 180 miles and that of the Yarkand part towards the east at 150 miles, or, in all 330 miles[56]. The width of the valley is not uniform and is not revealed by him or the others. Yet, in spite of the impreciseness of its dimensions, the total area of the Yarkand valley is obviously large.

With an average height between 8,000 and 12,000 feet, Yarkand valley had a large arable area, innumerable pastures, many camping sites and villages which had been inhabited until the end of the 18th century. Water is abundant and potable, vegetation scattered but luxuriant. Yet the distinctive features of the valley are bold, rugged mountains, absolutely barren and, as a rule, so precipitous as to be within a few degrees of the vertical. Ethnically, as noticed, people inhabiting the Yarkand valley were largely of Indian extraction. Descent down the Karakoram north face leads to a broad valley. The plain or the plateau, Vohab to Schlagintweits, or Chilgame as it was called, 16,000 feet, was the habitat of Tibetan antelope, leopard, Kyang, wild Yak and aquatic birds such as geese and ducks. This part of the valley is, therefore, Ladakhi and has nothing in common with Turkistan to the far north. Climatically too, Mason argues, the plateau is Tibetan, (Ladakhi), certainly the Karakoram-Aghil part is[57]. A little to the north of Aktagh the country around Shahidulla was largely different. Over 12000 feet high, Shahidulla was a camping site on the Karakash river, the valley green eastward and northward. Many Kirghiz encampments dotted the valley at Oibuk, Pilatgash, Mirza Abubakr, Ilnagar and Koramalkjilga, all in Sarekia. Besides providing pasturage, land around Oibuk was cultivated until the beginning of the 19th century. At Mirza Abubakr, where the road to Yarkand quits the Karakash valley, were the ruins of a fort, aforementioned. This fort, the British believed, was built by a Badakshan ruler of that name at the beginning of the 19th century to protect the Leh-Yarkand trade line from the depredation of the Kanjutis. This seems to be the Ali Nazar fort of Younghusband, alleged by him to have been built by the Atalik Ghazi of Kashgaria[58] and, according to Bower, by the Amir of Bokhara[59]. Trotter also calls the fort by the name of Ali Nazar but does not claim that it was built by the Atalik, three years earlier in 1870[60]. Grombtchevsky should have claimed it for Bokhara, then Russia's vassal, but did not. He merely called it I-Nazar Kurgan (fort)[61]. That a distant Badakshan and even more distant Bokhara should have built the fort to protect trade, in which neither had a share, is unconvincing. At Ilnagar the Sarekia valley opens out. From there a road took off to the boundary pass of Kokart or Kirghiz Jungle which is on the same ridge as Walaghat, or Sanju, and Kilian passes.

From the Sokhbulak pass in the neighbourhood of Shahidulla, the Yarkand Valley stretches towards Tashkurgan, running almost parallel to the Kuen Lun. The Sokhbulak pass is reached through a considerably green Khal Chushan valley which was inhabited until the Kanjuti raid on the Kirghiz of the Sarekia valley in 1888. On descending the Kokart, or, Kirghiz Jungle pass was the Kashmir Jilga or valley. The next boundary pass was the Chiragsaldi. The Kuen Lun is here split up by the Kulunargu river. The lower part is inhabited, the people who, like the Sarekia Kirghiz, were "denied" protection against the Kanjutis by the Chinese, as the British liked it to be believed, on the ground that they lived outside the Chinese frontier passes[62] and not because they were foreign nationals. A road led from Chiragsaldi to the Tisnaf valley and thence to the Karash-tarim-the cultivated lands of Karash. The remains of a few huts, smelting furnaces and signs of furrows were reminders that around 1810, Karash was a prosperous habitation of a farming community spread over half a mile long grassy stretch with no less than 150 acres of arable land to cultivate[63]. Tributary of the Raskam in this part of the valley is the Surkawat, up which a road led to the Muztagh pass and Skardo beyond to the south. Karul on the Junction of the Surkawat and Raskam was not only populated and cultivated but merchants frequented it on their way to the Muztagh pass and Skardo.

The Shaksgam valley runs longitudinally between the Karakoram and Aghil ranges[64]. This is the territory that Pakistan has gifted to China though the watershed, as noticed earlier, runs over the hills northward. By far the widest portion of the Raskam valley, according to Deasy, is the Chong Jungle, near the confluence of the Shaksgam with the Yarkand river. There the bottom of the valley contains low dense jungle, little grass, and patches of cultivation by the Kanjutis to whom, as Deasy says, it was "ancient home." Younghusband obfuscates that the country to the south belonged to no one in particular[65]. But that was before the watershed was found to be to the north of the Karakoram. It can safely be inferred that up to this point the Yarkand valley was within the limits of Hunza. Beyond, eastwards was Jammu and Kashmir. The assertion of Maharaja Ranbir Singh to the British that his territorial limits extended upto the Kilian range, north-west of Shahidulla, which Johnson upholds, supports this inference[66].

Grombtchevsky entered the Yarkand valley in 1888-89 from the Taghdumbash by the Iliksu pass[67]. Exploring the Shaksgam river valley, along the Shangshal stream, a feeder of Shaksgam, Grombtchevsky stumbled on the Darband fort which controlled the northern entrance to the Shangshal pass over the Hindu Kush in Hunza. It was from here that the Kanjutis used to issue into the Raskam Valley to raid the Kirghiz, Pakhpos and others. Near the fort there were traces of oat cultivation. Everywhere there were traces of irrigation canals, ruined mills, huts and small forts. Continuous raids by Kanjutis had converted the Raskam valley into a wilderness. Azghar was where Grombtchevsky found traces of a considerable village. In the neighbourhood of the Aghil pass the Russian explorer noticed herds of 300 to 400 wild sheep and a score of Kyangs, evidence of Ladakhi fauna. Up the Bazar Dara ravine there were ruins of a small village, a fort and unmistakable signs of mines having been worked there. Again in the neighbourhood of Bazar Dara was Zad in the Kulan Urgi valley which, when Deasy surveyed the Raskam valley in 1898, was the largest permanent encampment of the Kirghiz. Bazar Dara had a fort which, had been taken over by the Chinese alongwith the Sogat "fort" in Ladakh. A "garrison" had been installed by the Chinese in the Bazar Dara fort comprising a few Kirghiz "armed with flags."[68] The eastern end of the Tisnaf valley is approached by Chiragsaldi and Yangi Dawan, passes over the Kuen Lun[69]. The Pakhpos inhabited the numerous valleys and glens on the west bank of the Tisnaf, or the district of Khalastan. The chief town, rather village, was called Chuksu. It had, according to one estimate, 50 houses and, according to another, 200, chiefly of Pakhpos.

Taghdumbash, Little Pamir and Sirikul were the other glacis, all politically one with Hunza. Geographically too these districts have some striking features in common. The valleys and plains comprising the Taghdumbash, Sirikul and Little Pamir are fairly wide as compared with the Yarkand valley, are well watered, the Alpine summer lasting three months. Both Taghdumbash, a crescent shaped Pamir, and Sirikul are situated side by side, north of the Kilik and Mintaka passes, Sirikul farther north. Running almost parallel to the Taghdumbash are the Little Pamir and the Aktash valley. Thus this entire region was a compact one, contiguous to "awal" Hunza. The most easterly of the Pamirs, Taghdumbash commences one branch at the Wakhijrui pass and another at the Khanjerab pass and extends northward to Tashkurgan, where the district of Sirikul begins[70]. Burrard estimated the Taghdumbash to be 60 miles long and one to five miles wide [71]. Kirghiz were the chief inhabitants of this Pamir where a few Sirikulis also lived in the 19th century. South of Tashkurgan no cultivation was possible but the Pamir was covered withlong stretches of fine grass. The two Pamirs, Taghdumbash and Little Pamir, are more elevated, the former 15000 feet, and the latter, including the Aktash valley, around 13000 feet.

Sirikul, ancient Varshdi, is a mountainous district separated from Wakhan and Badakshan by the Sirikul ridge at the western base of which is the plain of Aktash. Colonel Montgomerie estimated Sirikul covers an area of under 10,000 square miles, of which only 2000 square miles are fit for cultivation, divided into several narrow valleys nowhere under 6000 feet in height[72]. Two distinct plains–the Tashkurgan and Tagharma–comprise Sirikul. A low ridge separates the two, Tagharma to the north and Tashkurgan to the south. Practically the two form one large flat. From the dividing ridge the Tashkurgan plain extends southwards to the foot of the Hunza passes over the Hindu Kush[73]. It is 40 to 50 miles long and 5 or 6 miles wide running almost north to south, from Tashkurgan to Ujadbai. Tagharma is a fine open crescent shaped plain about 12 miles long in a north-north-west direction and 7 miles broad. Some 10 miles west is the Bardish pass which divides the Tagharma plain from another and similar plain running parallel to it, the Aktash. The Tagharma plain continues in the same direction right up to the Kizil. Art Uzbel pass which separates it from the Alai. The glacis extends further west from the Taghdumbash to the Little Pamir and Aktash valley. From the Taghdumbash Pamir, Aktash valley was reached by the Paik pass, which was its importance. The "gap" ran over this territory and Sirikul.

The tramp of Yonoff's men over the Aktash valley persuaded the British Indian Government to seriously contemplate delimitation of boundaries in these bleak plateaux to deny a negotiable route to Russian troops to the frontier of the Indian empire[74]. The Chinese "having seized the Pamirs," Russia did not admit her rights there[75]. Russia was convinced that under the 1872-1873 agreement "the whole of the Pamirs to the north of Sirikul and the upper Panja came within the sphere of influence and into the possession of Russia."[76] Actual delimitation work was proposed by England to be preceded by a joint topographical commission to report on the historical and ethnographical aspects of the Pamirs[77]. China, on the other hand, having no real claim whatever to any part of the Pamirs and unable to match the military power of England or Russia to sustain her presence there, saw safety in proposing, from time to time, neutralisation of the Pamirs. After the situation came to a head in the Alichur Pamir in 1891 with the eviction of China from Somatash by the Afghans, the Tsungli Yamen renewed the Chinese proposal to Sir John Walsham in March 1892[78]. But the British had a single point objective in the Pamirs-to extend the Chinese and Afghan frontiers so as to meet on the pulled back northern boundary of India and thus shut out Russia from the Hindu Kush.

That Russia meant business in the face of provocations from China and Afghanistan she made evident by massing her troops in the Alai, Kizil Art, Karakul and the Pamirs close to the frontier of Shighnan and a Russian officer wrote to the ruler of Shighnan to evacuate it being "from a long time a dependency of Kokand..."[79] Mobilisation by Russia followed China's refusal to withdraw all her posts from the Pamirs. Russia, therefore, found China's proposal for neutralisation of the Pamir "as impracticable..."[80] China consequently withdrew her proposal and concluded that partition of the Pamirs was the only feasible plan. In the neighbourhood of Somatash, the Afghans made some 80 or 90 tribal families captives and carried them away to Shighnan. Their release China sought through Britain, England being suzerain of Afghanistan. The Tsungli Yamen pointed out that

> "...(China) took the step of occupying Somatash at the suggestion of the British Government, and, in deference to the British Government, abstained from resenting the insult offered to China by the Amir in driving the Chinese detachment from the post of Somatash..."[81]

Under the menace of an advancing Russian expedition, the Chinese Government at Urumtsi ordered withdrawal of Chinese troops from the contested regions of the Pamirs. By Macartney, the Russians were credited with the intention of annexing Sirikul[82].

Such an intention in regard to the Pamirs Amir Abdul Rehman of Afghanistan too disclosed. Either on his own volition or, more likely, on the persuasion of the British, the Amir acknowledged, as Elias had counselled earlier, Chinese rights up to the Murghabi river in the Alichur Pamir. In the Little Pamir, next to the boundary of Jammu and Kashmir, Wakhijrui pass, the Kotal (pass) itself he assigned to China. To the Aktash branch of the Oxus the Amir held on. Above all Abdul Rehman confined Hunza to the Kilik pass over the Hindu Kush to the south of the Taghdumbash Pamir, and to the Irshad pass[83], to the west. Such a boundary locked the Afghan and Chinese territories over the "gap," to confine Russia far to the north of the Hindu Kush. But as disputes had arisen over the Pamirs, the Amir informed the Government of India of his decision to withdraw from this "rightful frontier," as Sir Mortimer later called it, to a line which Afghanistan could hold[84]. Such a line involved Afghan withdrawal upto 100 miles westward from Baroghil, Darkot, Irshad, Wakhijrui, Avikul, Dasht-i-Murghabi, Taktakoram and Kul-Kudara, to leave the "gap" fully uncovered west of the advanced Chinese boundary. Afghanistan thus gave up her claim to the Little, Great and Alichur Pamirs. Dispute over Pamirs was only a thin veneer to hide the Amirs purpose. Was the threatened withdrawal in response to Russian belligerence? Was it a bargaining gambit for retaining trans-Oxus Shighnan or for a favourable eastern boundary with India? Perhaps, it was for all these. Furnishing a map of these Afghan boundaries to the Government of India, the Amir sought their recognition by Russia, were a conference to be held on the Pamirs[85]. For England such an Afghan boundary was, in more respects than one, "a very awkward proposal."

But proposals for delimitation had come to be stalled for one reason or another. Amidst contending claims of Russia, China and Afghanistan, the India office in London saw the need for a fresh endeavour to restrain Russia in the Pamirs[86]. Sir R. Morier had reason to believe that Russia intended despatching Colonel Yonoff again on another expedition during the ensuing summer of 1893 directed against the Afghan provinces of Shighnan and Roshan, a line of action which, he foresaw, would "undoubtedly place Her Majesty's Government in a very difficult position."[87] There were two aspects of the delimitation. (i) Delimitation of the boundaries of the Afghan provinces and (ii) delimitation of the territory east of Wakhan or part of the so called "gap." As for the first, the British Government could not have repudiated the Agreement of 1872-73 as the basis of delimitation. Sir R. Morier was of the view that it could, however, be rendered less injurious for Afghanistan as England had a lever in the occupation of cis-Oxus Darwaz by Bokhara. But the India Office realised that the Amir Abdul Rehman was least likely to withdraw from trans-Oxus Shighnan and Roshan. As to the second aspect Sir Robert Morier depended on the protocol of 1884 between Russia and China. The protocol "does delimitate the Chinese frontier from Uzbel, then the southern frontier point of Russia with China, to Lake Victoria in a way which, filling up, as it does, the "gap" between the eastern frontier of Wakhan and *admittedly* Chinese territory seems to give us all we desire in the way of avoiding direct contact with Russia." With this view also to India Office differed. That from Uzbel the Chinese boundary would turn due south did not justify the further assumption that it would continue due south not only to lake Sirikul but down to the Hindu Kush.

Yonoff's mission precipitated negotiations, carried on through diplomatic channels. England argued that the agreement solely provided for delimitation of the Afghan frontier to the north. The status quo after the agreement left the Pamirs an unappropriated waste. Of the three, England had the least frontage on the Pamirs, limited to the Hindu Kush. She could and would, as a memorandum by Sir Robert Morier on the Russian expedition to the Pamirs argued, never allow the northern slopes leading up to the passes of the Hindu Kush to be occupied by a power capable of constantly threatening the walls of her "natural" fortress. The Russian view on the Pamirs was different. England was reminded China was not a party to the 1872-73 agreement. On that ground alone, China could not sit in a commission of delimitation[88]. Russia was, therefore, agreeable "to delimit with Her Majesty's Government on the line of the Oxus..." This, quite evidently, meant Afghan withdrawal from trans-Oxus Shighnan and Roshan and of Bokhara from cis-Oxus Darwaz. With China, Russia preferred to deal separately for the Chinese part of the frontier[89]. Consequently Russia backtracked on delimitation, wishing to keep out China. When, therefore, Britain's new Secretary of State for Foreign Affairs, Lord Rosebery, proposed a joint technical commission, as originally suggested by Russia, M. Boutenieff of the Russian mission in London replied that such a commission was no longer favoured by St. Petersburg. That England did not quite relish. Rosebery chose to be bellicose remarking to Boutenieff that he could not remain indifferent to any territorial settlement in the neighbourhood of Britain's north Indian frontier. In fact Britain threatened to send an expedition to the Pamirs similar to that under Yonoff, "if Russians would not join in a technical Commission."[90]

Negotiations did not break down. In January 1893 Russia clarified she was not opposed to a commission. What she objected to was that such a commission should be sent out without previously accurately defined objectives it was to attain. Were a commission to be set up, its composition was equally a contentious issue. From Beijing England was cautioned if China was kept out of such a commission "there is a risk of her separating from us."[91] Discussions were renewed at St. Petersburg on a joint Anglo-Russian commission by Sir Robert Morier to which under some form, to be settled between the two powers, an Afghan commissioner or expert should be adjoined, and which should be instructed, whilst keeping the line of the Oxus generally as the direction the frontier should follow, to ascertain the geographical and historical limits of Badakshan and Wakhan as well as Bokhara so far as the latter claims territory on the left bank of the Oxus[92]. To such a commission, Sir Robert Morier suggested, China might be invited to appoint a commissioner "to take part in the examination of the portion of the frontier which adjoins their territory." It was a limited role for China, yet it involved *de jure* recognition of China's Pamir claims.

One more consideration Sir Robert Morier pressed on Russia. While asserting that England had never contemplated annexation of any portion of the Pamirs, she nevertheless considered to have a perfect right to claim that portion of the Pamirs which is bound on the south by the Hindu Kush and on the north by a line corresponding with the latitude of the Lake Victoria to be drawn from the eastern frontier of Afghan territory to the western frontier of Chinese territory "shall be acknowledged as being within the sphere of British influence, and shall not be disposed of without their will and consent." The territories involved were the Little and Taghdumbash Pamirs and Sirikul, all "doam" Hunza, over which ran the bulk of the "gap" and which formed the northern glacis of the Hindu Kush. What Sir Robert Morier emphasised in regard to them were actually British *de jure* rights, just as Lansdowne had over the area north of the Karakoram pass. For negotiations with Russia, China relied on the 1884 protocol as the basis. Under it the boundary between the two empires was defined from lrkishtan to the Uzbel pass. Beyond this point the boundary ceased to be conterminous, the Chinese line going due south and the Russian line taking a south-westerly direction. While China was agreeable to the delimitation of the land comprised in the angle formed by the two diverging lines, or the "gap," Russia refused to enter into any discussion as to the ownership of this land and endeavoured to make out that the Chinese boundary should not run due south from the Uzbel but turn east and then south[93] to leave the "gap" open.

China agreed to a delimitation commission being set up on condition that Russia withdrew her troops from the Pamir[94]. In the face of the Russian threat, China, through her own officials, ascertained her boundary in the Pamirs. This was found to correspond with the limits of Sirikul ridge of the Bolor range separating the waters of the Oxus from those flowing into Yarkand and Kashgar! The boundary line passes were the Akbirdi, Shindi, Paik and Wakhijrui. Quite evidently Sirikul had to be within China. So Macartney urged[95]. But this boundary left Bozai Gumbaz and Aktash outside China. Of these Bozai Gumbaz commanded roads to Hunza and over Aktash ran part of the "gap." Nor did this boundary line leave England in control of the northern glacis of the Hindu Kush. Russia was agreeable to the boundary east of Wakhan being drawn along the Wakhan river and the Wakhijrui so as to leave the northern slopes of the Hindu Kush, the wall of the Indian fortress, under British control[96]. In Beijing China endeavoured to ensure incorporation into her territories of Aktash, from which Russia had evicted her, a year earlier, in 1892. England also impressed upon China the advantage of her boundary marching with Afghan-Wakhan frontier and thus blocking Russia's access to the Yarkand valley[97]. Another prospect was to include the entire area in Afghanistan. But this the Amir, probably because of the narrowness of the territory involved, which made it militarily untenable, had refused to hold. Other and lesser alternatives were to hand it over to the ex-Mir of Wakhan, Ali Mardan Shah, then living in exile in Gilgit territory, or police it from Hunza[98]. The situation was made curiouser by Russia taking a contradictory stand arguing England had no "right or claim whatsoever to exercise any influence southeast of Lake Victoria..."[99] The line of demarcation of her boundary with China from Uzbel, Russia wanted, should take on easterly direction eventually to abut on the Hindu Kush. Russia, in effect, thus laid claim to Little Pamir, not because she had in the previous year, evicted China from Aktash but because Beijing had surrendered its rights in Hunza[100]. Little Pamir was, therefore, to be Russia's compensation. Implied also is Hunza's ownership of the Little Pamir. In the negotiations at Beijing between Russia and China, Russia made it clear China would have no occasion to consult with the British Government "seeing that the latter power had nothing to do with the northern slopes of the Hindu Kush range."[101] Asking the Amir of Afghanistan to give up trans-Oxus Shighnan and Roshan under the 1872-73 agreement, as a trade off for east of Wakhan territory, proposed by General Brackenbury, was not considered good enough[102]. The trans-Oxus territory was seen by A.E. Miller, Legal member of the Viceroy's Council, as of much consequence to the British, possession of which would give Russia "an easy entrance into Badakshan and a location within striking distance of Chitral over the Baroghil pass."[103]

If Russia could not altogether stop England from closing the gap east of Wakhan, she still made proposals, such as would have secured her Bozai Gumbaz[104], giving her thus access to the Kilik and other Hunza passes. East of the Sirikul lake, diversion of the Russian boundary southwards was seen to confer no advantage on her except to threaten the Hindu Kush passes. To the west of the lake, the British resented "surrender" of the trans-Oxus territory sought by Russia from the Amir under the agreement of 1872-73[105]. But Russia was also apprehensive, and gave vent to her fear, that if the eastward line from the Sirikul lake was conceded to England, "a route would be opened by which Great Britain could invade the Asiatic provinces of Russia."[106] For this reason Russia made it clear that a military agreement between Britain and Russia must precede any settlement of the Pamir boundaries[107]. Such a military agreement was to place England and Russia in a position of mutual and absolute equality with regard to watersheds. Russia was to undertake that her forces would not cross the Murghab limit while Britain was to confine herself to Gilgit, Yasin, Mastuj and Chitral. This implied British withdrawal from Hunza, south of the Hindu Kush to which England would not consent[108]. It was rectified later and Hunza came to be included in the Gilgit territory. Under the final proposals made by Russia, the boundary east of Sirikul lake was to run along natural features and follow the line of latitude until the Chinese frontier. This line was to be actually marked out by a joint commission. The territory to the north of the line was to be administered by Shighnan under Russian influence and to the south by Afghanistan under British superintendence.

The Amir of Afghanistan reluctantly consented to hold east of Wakhan territory but not with troops. He saw this territory as "a long arm extended into a desert"[109] which could be shorn off by Russia whenever she chose. Other options for this territory were considered to be to give it to Chitral, the Mehtar to hold it as a feudatory of the Amir and (2) "exchange" the tract "for the nominal suzerainty" China claimed over Hunza[110]. As to the trans-Oxus territories, Shighnan and Roshan, Russia was assured by Lord Rosebery of the Amir evacuating them on condition that a line to the east of Lake Victoria satisfactory to the British was adopted[111]. Russia, however, insisted east of Wakhan territory must be held by Afghanistan or under its suzerainty to which Rosebery consentd[112]. This was to keep out China. Only odds and ends remained to be tied up. Russia proposed a purely technical mixed commission of delimitation comprising not only Russian and British delegates but also an Afghan representative[113].

With the distinct possibility of the east of Wakhan territory being delimited by the Pamir Commission from the Sirikul lake to the Chinese frontier, the British became concerned about the actual territorial limits of China in the region. By a calculated deflection by Russia of the line that was to run from the Sirikul lake to the Chinese boundary, Paik pass on the Sirikul ridge of Bolor chain in Hunza emerged as the point to which it was seen to reach. The pass, some 20 miles from the Shindi saddle, led to the Yarkand valley from Aksu, over the Kilik and Mintaka. Its possession was vital for Russia to secure access to the Yarkand valley and for England to keep her out of it. Brackenbury unhesitatingly declared Paik to be "in actual Chinese territory."[114] Yet with Sir G.S. White, he urged "that the Paik pass should be excluded from the Russian sphere of influence..."[115] Dunmore had crossed the Paik pass but had found no trace of Chinese there. He put the Russian claim upto the Paik. A Chinese post had existed for a while in Aktash to the north, but it was destroyed by Yonoff in 1892[116]. Paik was, nevertheless, desired by China[117].

By March 1895, an accord on the Pamirs was reached[118] between Russia and England and notes were exchanged between the two governments[119]. Scarcely any modification," as the British claimed, were made in the final draft agreement sent to Russia for approval in 1894. But the few changes that were made were of a vital nature. The east of Wakhan territory was not to be placed under the Amir's suzerainty, as had become evident during the long drawn out negotiations. Nor was it to be annexed by England. It was to "form part of the territory of the Amir."[120] But the Amir was not to build any military posts or fortifications there. Principal commissioners were to be Major General M.G. Gerard, aided by Colonel T.H. Holdich, Major R.A. Wahab for England[121] and Major General Pavalo Schveikovsky assisted by M. Parafidine and Colonel Galkine for Russia[122].

In laying down the boundary line east of the Sirikul lake to the Chinese frontier the first hurdle the Pamir Commission faced was to know the south-western limit of China in the region. Even before his departure for the Pamirs, General Gerard was assailed by doubts as to the actual location of the Chinese boundary. How was he to be assured that the Chinese frontier was "actually reached."[123] The instructions issued to him by the Indian Foreign Department hardly cleared these doubts. Elaborate these instructions were but clear these were not. The Foreign Department itself did not know the Chinese boundary. It was, therefore, preceived in Simla that "delicate questions" might arise in the vicinity of the at present imperfectly known Chinese frontier..."[124] The safe sealing of the "gap," therefore, depended on the determination of the unknown, or non-existent, Chinese boundary in the area.

Once in the Pamirs Gerard grasped that the Chinese boundary was linked to their acquiring sovereign rights over the Hunza territory of Taghdumbash where then they had almost no presence. Was the Chinese boundary to be the Sirikul ridge, separating Little Pamir and the Aktash valley from the Taghdumbash Pamir, passing northward of Kilik pass and from the Wakhijrui pass, north-east towards Tashkurgan[125]? This question was bound to arise. Gerard sought instructions from the Government of India and the Viceroy from the Secretary of State for India. In London the Secretaries of State for Foreign Affairs and India were of one view that Taghdumbash Pamir "is subject to concurrent rights of China and Kanjut." But they hastened to add that no claim was to be proffered on behalf of Hunza "except for the purpose of precaution against China ceding it to Russia."[126] The issue did arise during the proceedings of the Pamir Commission but Gerard was assured by the Russian Commissioner that "the watershed of the Taghdumbash (the Sirikul ridge) is the Chinese frontier." Lord Elgin was not satisfied and urged the HM's Government to further stipulate to Russia "that Taghdumbash should revert to Hunza if China abandons it."[127] Here again reversion of rights over territories ceded by England to China is visualised as a policy.

Actual delimitation of the boundary east of Wakhan was of a strip, estimated by Barackenbury to be 60 miles long and, on an average, 12 miles broad on the left bank of the Oxus and hemmed in by Russia on one side and China on the other. It was at places, as Holdich vouches, just only 8 miles broad and could be ridden across in a morning's ride. For want of natural features suitable for definition, the commissioners were hard put to reconcile the terms of the Anglo-Russian agreement with the geography of the Pamirs. For geographical difficulties too, no boundary pillars or even markstones could be put up at the beginning and towards the end of the boundary line which was officially projected into space. "Amidst this voiceless waste of a vast white wilderness, 20,000 feet above the sea, absolutely inaccessible to man... there the three empires meet," as Holdich, rather metaphorically puts it. For the British empire was way down southeastward, England having gifted away the Taghdumbash, Little Pamir and the Aktash valley, to China and Afghanistan, lest she should be subjected to political upheavals in India on a Russian advance. The "gap" was sealed however fragile the sealing. Holdich concedes, "It is a political intervention—a hedge as it were over which Russia cannot step without violating Afghanistan and the violation of Afghanistan may (or may not) be regarded as a *casus belli*."[128]

One fall out of Safdar Ali's retreat into 'doam' Hunza was that British were forced to espouse Nazim Khan's claim to Taghdumbash and Raskam. In the spring of 1897, Nazim Khan sent a few Kanjutis from Gujal and

Shangshal to reclaim arable parts of Raskam[129]. An initiative like this, directly involving China and indirectly Russia, would not have been taken by the Mir except with, at least, the tacit approval of the British. Justification was found for Kanjuti settlements in Raskam as an inexpensive way of keeping Russia out. Raskam being beyond the Hindu Kush-Karakoram boundary range, were Russia to push into it, no British military intervention, it was for the first time argued, would be called for even though the Tsar's empire would run conterminous with British Indian empire, a prospect the British had never countenanced. Indeed a few among the British establishment contended that in the event of an invasion, areas to the north need not at all be defended. The Mir wrote to the Amban of Yarkanad as the district magistrate, seeking land for cultivation. The Amban saw "something underhand" in the request which was declined with the remark that "there is no land to spare[130]..." The Kirghiz as Chinese subjects were provoked to make similar demands on the Amban of Taskurgan "for permission to cultivate the Raskam valley next year (1898)."[131] The district magistrate of Yarkand proposed to evict the Kanjutis and send them back to their own country. Macartney apprehended, "The proposed action...may raise the whole question of Kanjutis claims on the northern side of the Hindu Kush."[132] Notwithstanding his fears, the Kanjutis were apprehended, carried off to Yarkand and Nazim Khan was directed by the Amban "to prevent his people going to Raskam again."[133] Orders were issued to Begs of the Shakshu and Pakhpo country for "the establishment of a 'karaul' in the Raskam valley."[134] Guided as he, evidently, was by the British Agent at Gilgit, Nazim Khan's response was restrained. To the Taotai it was recalled Raskam lands were farmed by the Kanjutis since the days of Shah Salim I. When the Sirikulis had contested the Kanjut rights in Raskam during Raja Ghazan Khan's rule, Huang Tajen was reminded, "The matter was decided then to our satisfaction."[135] The British had anticipated adverse Chinese response on Raskam but appear to have been surprised by their "determined" opposition[136]. This was one reason, Lord Elgin indicates, why Ardagh's proposal was unanimously rejected[137].

Hunza-China tussle over the Raskam valley snowballed into India-China boundary issue. Even more than China, it was Russia which was positively hostile to Kanjuti colonisation of Raskam. The "gap" having been finally closed by the Pamir Boundary Commission England was inclined to put back, in one way or another, India's northern boundary in Jammu and Kashmir along, at least, the Yarkand river, preferably over the Kuen Lun. Ralph Cobbold, who traversed Hunza, Nagar, the Pamir and

Kashgaria, partly in the company of Deasy in 1897-1898, asserts that both the Taghdumbash Pamir and Sirikul were British territories[138]. What is significant about his assertion was its timing, coincide as it did with the controversy over Raskam. He ignored the nominal possession which the Chinese had then gained of the tract. Deasy, Cobbold relates, was credited by the Chinese with the intention "to erect boundary pillars along the Taghdumbash Pamir whereby the British frontier was to be considerably extended."[139] The pillars were actually put up by Deasy as became known later, two of them 4 miles from the Kilik pass in the Kukturuk valley, and the third some 5 miles south of Ujadbai in the Khanjerab valley, situated to the north of the Hindu Kush, within the country claimed by the Mir of Hunza[140]. Deasy himself refers to Lord Curzon's map published in the Geographical Journal for July 1896. "On this carefully compiled map, showing the Pamirs and adjacent country, a long stretch of Yarkand river is represented by dotted lines whose general direction is about north-north-east."141 Quite evidently the dotted lines represented the boundary. Younghusband acknowledges Hunza collected tribute from the Taghdumbash Pamir and had a fortified post at Darwaza, on the north side of the Hindu Kush. To Younghusband the point at issue was should the frontier line between India and Russia be along the greater watershed dividing the rivers of India from the rivers of Central Asia or should it be allowed to meander along indefinite valleys and ridges on the far side of the boundary formed by nature? No useful object, Younghusband obfuscated, would be attained by England being saddled with "the responsibility of upholding shadowy claims of Hunza over the territory on the northern side of the passes." Yet Younghusband was conscious that lower parts of Raskam were only 8000 feet above the sea level. Crops could be grown there and a suitable spot for permanent military occupation could be found than was to be met anywhere south of Osh.

> "The longer the Russians can be kept from occupying such a position, the more convenient it will be for our dealings with the frontier State which the position immediately touches; and if we are not prepared to occupy the district ourselves, our interest will be best served by seeing that the Chinese occupy it definitely and decisively..."[142]

In the face of Chinese opposition, need for Raskam land for the Kanjutis was, for the first time, and presumably on British promptings, justified on demographic and economic grounds. It was argued that after the British put an end to their raiding propensities Hunza's population had increased and there was not enough ground available south of the Hindu Kush to bring under plough[143]. On compassionate grounds it was conceivable China would be persuaded to accommodate the Kanjutis upon whom she continued to look as her subjects. The Taotai was, indeed, willing to grant "imperial land" to the Mir as "subject" of the emperor[144]. But such a view quite clearly deflected Hunza's sovereign rights over Raskam. When, therefore, Nazim Khan offered to increase his gift, or "tribute," to China by five "miskals" of gold annually he acted in pursuit of his sovereign rights. China insisted, in response, that watershed was the northern limit of Hunza. Russia suspected Kanjuti interest in Raskam was prompted by the British design to make the Yarkand river the boundary of India[145]. Russian interest influenced British officers at Gilgit and Kashgar to work behind the scenes, and leave the dispute, if possible, to be "decided directly between the Chinese and the Kanjutis" without their interference[146]. But Russian influence waxed strongly in Kashgar. The Chinese too worked at cross purposes. After a good deal of prevarication, the Taotai allowed, subject to the concurrence of the Amban of Yarkand, Hunza rights over the Raskam valley. But the district magistrate of Yarkand included Kirghiz too for settlement in Raskam, a condition which was entirely unacceptable to Nazim Khan[147]. Hunza was not willing to whittle down its sovereign rights in Raskam. In a note to the Indian Foreign Department, Deasy detailed these Hunza rights, both in Raskam and Taghdumbash. He had gathered during his explorations in the Raskam Valley that Hunza had extended, westward, from the Aghil pass to the junction of the Bazar Dara and Yarkand rivers, thence along the northern watershed of Raskam valley to Dafdar on the Taghdumbash Pamir and beyond to the Paik peak, close to the Paik pass on the Sirikul range[148]. Petrovski interposed with the Futai, or Lieutenant Governor, of Xinjiang on two grounds. Firstly, Raskam was on the frontier and the presence of the Kanjutis there would have a disturbing influence. Secondly, even if the Chinese allowed the Kanjutis to settle down in the Raskam valley without ceding it to them, they would, in course of time, consider it absolutely theirs. On both counts the Lieutenant Governor agreed with the Russian consul general but argued that the Kanjutis were Chinese subjects who paid "tribute" to the emperor. Surely the Chinese Government would be wanting in their duty if they failed to treat the Kanjutis with kindness. But to make them realise that Raskam belonged to China, the Kanjutis would pay a tax in grain[149]. This condition was, expectedly, unacceptable to the Mir[150]. The issue to him was one of sovereign rather than proprietary rights. But it was on the pretext of poverty of the Kanjutis that the Taotai while granting the land, had declined to accept the five additional "miskals" of gold[151]. Even so the Amban of Yarkand insisted on the payment of 1/10th of the produce as land revenue[152]. The Chinese tactics nettled the British. They viewed their actions as "an interference" in the cultivation of the Raskam valley by the people of Hunza. The rights of Hunza to the Taghdumbash, Khanjerab and Raskam, Captain A.H. MacMahon, the Agent at Gilgit, considered to be "proved beyond doubt." He also, finally, laid to rest the British imagined ghost of Hunza's vassalage to China. Hunza's first dealing with China is disclosed to have begun sometime during the rule of Shah Salim Khan, the eighth ancestor of Nazim Khan who defeated the Kirghiz of the Taghdumbash. This is probably the battle to which Moorcroft alluded to when in Ladakh. To celebrate this victory, Shah Salim Khan erected a stone cairn at Dafdar and sent a trophy of a Kirghiz head to the Chinese with a message that Hunza territory thenceforward extend to Dafdar. The Chinese sent presents which Hunza acknowledged by "a small gift of gold dust and from this originated the custom of annual interchange of presents..."[153] The Chinese presents were substantial and became a source of income to the Mir.

It was immaterial, MacMahon argued with the Foreign Department, whether Hunza occupied Raskam as a tributary of China or not so long as China remained India's neighbour and "it definitely understood that *we claim the reversion of all Chinese rights* to lands claimed by Hunza." Take over by China of trans-Karakoram-Hindu Kush regions was, therefore, conditional. So was demarcation of the northern boundary in Jammu and Kashmir obligatory, as laid down by Lansdowne and taken up with the Secretary of State for India. The Ardagh doctrine, or the strong British desire for sphere of influence in the tracts north of the Karakoram-Hindu Kush, was only, in a sense, manifestation of these. MacMahon went on, however strong the argument might appear at first sight for restricting British frontier to the Hindu Kush on *strategic grounds*,

> "it would be wise, I venture to think, before irrevocably committing ourselves to such a frontier, to carefully consider the wisdom of gratuitously surrendering, in doing so, territory which belongs to the people on whom we will have to depend for active assistance in defending that frontier. Can we reasonably depend upon their assistance if we give them good cause to

> believe that they have lost more than they gained by their past connection with us, and have more to gain in the future from the power who challenges our frontier than from ourselves?"[154]

The Mir was advised to negotiate with the Chinese on Raskam[155]. The Taotai agreed to the occupancy of Raskam lands by the Kanjutis[156], "foregoing an increase of tribute..."Occupancy ought to be accepted on "any terms," MacMahon recommeded to Government at Simla[157], in an apparent reference to their controversial nature. Else, it was evident, were the Mir to reject the Chinese terms and were they to invite in the Sirikulis or Kirghiz that might well provoke a clash. A draft agreement sent to the Mir of Hunza for his signature and seal provided seven sites for Kanjuti occupation. Five of these, Oitughrak, Kuktash, Oprang, Uruklok and Iliksu were all to the south of the Yarkand river, that is, nearer to the Karakoram, and two, Azghar and Ursur, to the north of the river. Together the seven sites virtually comprised the whole of arable Raskam. The Mir was to undertake not to seek more than these seven sites, not to permit foreigners, evidently the British, into them, and not to build himself, or allow foreigners to construct, fortresses and towers on these sites. The Chinese were to be allowed to visit the sites and if Ambans sought to build fortresses and towers, no objection was to be raised by the Kanjutis. After three years of tax-free cultivation, the Kanjutis were to pay 12 "sars" of silver to the "Khan" (emperor). The payment was to be in silver to distinguish it from gold "tribute" and make it a mark of Hunza's true subordination to China. The jurisdiction of Chinese Amban of Sirikul over the southern and of "Wi-Yan" (assistant Amban) of Bazar Dara over the northern sites was to be acknowledged. Every year an official on behalf of the Amban of Yarkand was to visit the sites[158]. Lack of unanimity among Chinese civil and military officials further delayed the Raskam negotiations. The military officials headed by the Titai, commander of troops in Kashgar, opposed grant of four of the seven sites, selected by the Taotai, civil governor, Kashgar, on strategic grounds. The Yarkand Amban had his own views and looked upon Raskam as "a door to Chinese Turkistan."[159]

British failure to secure the Kanjutis their rights in Raskam, partly due to Chinese intransigence but largely because of Russian opposition, precipitated moves on the settlement of the boundary. Her Majesty's Government was no longer of the view that it was "impolitic" to broach it with the Chinese government. Indeed, the Government of India was "urged" by the Foreign office in London "that this should be undertaken."[160] In the Indian Foreign Department one view was to have "some fixed line" as the frontier, which Younghusband was asked to draw[161]. Younghusband's advice expectedly was generally to stick to the crest of the Hindu Kush-Karakoram, the boundary line leaving it only at two places. This view coincided with the one that the Government of India had already expressed. Disadvantages were seen by Younghusband in going down to the Taghdumbash, into the Raskam or from the Karakoram to Shahidulla. But in advance of the Shangshal pass, the Kanjutis had maintained a post at Darwaza. One deviation from the crest that Younghusband favoured was at the peak above Shangshal pass, taking in the Darwaza post and returning to the main ridge, a little north of 36^0. This was thought to make "a perfectly, good and well defined boundary," though not for military considerations. Darwaza was the entry point into the Raskam Valley for people of Shangshal and their large herds and flocks for grazing and collection of salt from the valley. This small deviation, was proposed, to be taken up with the Chinese when the boundary issue was to be discussed. The other departure from the crest was in western Taghdumbash, in the regions of Mintaka and Karachakar–the glacis of the Hindu Kush reaching northward to the Paik pass and beyond to the Russian Pamirs. It was dismissed as being of little value and its addition to Hunza was not seen to be a disadvantage. Though declared to be of "little value," over the area ran the Gilgit-Mintaka-Paik-Kashgar route, control over which enabled England to keep Russia out of reach of the Hindu Kush and Yarkand valley and strike at Kashgar if need arose. But to Cunningham and to other Englishmen, the real bearing of this and the other Hunza claims was to use them "in order to get China to negotiate a boundary and an acknowledgement that Hunza and all on our side of the boundary are British exclusively over which the Chinese have no rights whatsoever."[162] Plainly what Cunningham sought was an end to the informal condominium the British, had in pursuit of their imperial interests, allowed to emerged over Hunza with China. Towards the accomplishment of this objective, the British were to assert Hunza rights over the Taghdumbash and Raskam valley, yielding them in return for Chinese renunciation of sovereignty over Hunza which she had been induced the acquire in the recent past. Towards the east, in Aksai Chin, no boundary line was suggested, the Foreign Department proposed first to consult the Surveyor General. Elgin agreed and the Secretary of State for India was cabled that the Government of India thought it expedient to settle with the Chinese the boundaries of Afghanistan, Hunza and Kashmir.[163] Chinese too had their own understanding of British predilections entirely correct though it was not. In the event of a war with Russia, England was not considered capable of moving a significant number of troops on to the Taghdumbash. But were she able to garrison Azghar and its neighbourhood, England could protect Taghdumbash from Russian seizure and could, at the same time, arrange for her trade with Yarkand being carried on an official footing, as against border trade under the auspices of Kashmir, and so counterbalance Russian influence in Eastern Turkistan. The Amban of Yarkand for one believed, that the British wished to make use of Kanjut "as means for the fulfilment of their ulterior secret intentions with regard to the Taghdumbash Pamir, the latter being the backdoor of Kanjut..."[164] The escalating Anglo-Russian rivalry persuaded the Chinese to order construction of forts in Raskam and even in the districts of Kashgar, Yangi Hissar and Yarkand[165]. After the little war of 1891, Darwaza post had been left unguarded. The Mir was advised to post a garrison[166] to Darwaza to prevent lapse of Hunza claim.

To the Governor General-in-Council "the matter of first importance" was to secure "some line by which China will agree to be bound." The ground situation was that Hunza had extensive rights over Raskam and Taghdumbash, while China claimed to exercise over her a "concurrent jurisdiction of a shadowy sort" that had received definite admission from England. Were the Yarkand district to pass from the possession of China into that of "a more energetic power"–Russia–these acknowledged rights within British borders could scarcely fail to be extremely embarrassing, the Viceroy conveyed to the Secretary of State for India, Lord George Hamilton, in a secret (frontier) despatch. Therefore, for the first time, officially, a boundary line was suggested by the British Indian Government. Beginning at the Little Pamir peak of Pavalo Schveikovsky the proposed boundary took a south-easterly direction, crossed the Karachakar stream at Mintaka Aghazi (north of the Hindu Kush), proceeded in the same direction till it joined, at the Karchanai pass, the crest of the main ridge of the Muztagh range which it then followed passing the Khanjerab pass and continued southward to the peak just north of the Shangshal pass. At this point the boundary left the crest and followed a spur running east approximately parallel to the road from the Shangshal to the Hunza post at Darwaza. The line then turned south through the Darwaza post, crossed the road from the Shangshal pass and then ascended the nearest high spur and regained the main crests, passing the Muztagh, Gusherbrum and the Saltoro passes to the Karakoram. From there for half a degree the boundary passed over the crest. The line then ran over the Laktsung hills and was made to meet a spur running down from the Kuen Lun to separate Ladakh from Tibet[167].

This boundary line made three significant departures from the British conceived Hindu Kush–Karakoram line. The first was at the western end of the line to put Karachakar and the Mintaka valleys, or part of the northern glacis of the Hindu Kush, within the British empire. The deviation ensured British control over the Hunza-Kashgar road via the Paik. The second break from the main crest of the range was around the Shangshal pass so as to leave Darwaza post inside India, as an access to the Raskam Valley. The third deviation from the main Karakoram ridge was east of this pass in Lingzithang. This plateau is midway divided by the Laktsung hills that run parallel, some distance away, to the Kuen Lun. The introduction of the Laktsung hills as the boundary here is sudden for there is not even a mention of it earlier in accessible papers. Such a boundary line left the southwestern half of Lingzithang to the north of the Karakoram in India giving China the northern half or what was loosely called Aksai Chin. This then was the boundary line that the British Minister, Sir Claude Macdonald, was to propose to the Tsungli Yaman at Beijing on the 14th March 1899. Not only did the Macdonald proposal strike a blow at the geographical unity of India but these were most inopportunely made. The "gap" over Sirikul district, Taghdumbash Pamir and Little Pamir, which the British feared, had been already sealed, partly by China advancing her boundary to the Sirikul ridge of the Bolortagh, a proceeding which Russia finally recognised in the course of the working of the Pamir Commission, 1895, and partly by the Commission delimiting the east of Wakhan territory from the Sirikul lake to the Sirikul ridge. China herself collapsed after the transmission of the Macdonald proposal. Other than the Kanjuti wrangle over the Raskam arable land with China, England was in no distress to propose the northern boundary which succeeding British diplomats, Sir Louis Dane and Sir Arther MacMahon, disapproved of insofar as it related to Aksai Chin.

The terms offered by the Chinese for colonisation of Raskam by the Kanjutis put the British in a fix. Notwithstanding contradictory, or "bogus," orders issued by Chinese officials to "appease the Russians," MacMahon, now Assistant Secretary, Foreign Department, noted that Raskam land, including Azghar, was then quickly being given over to the Kanjutis. The acceptance of the terms appeared to him best left to be dealt with after land was taken over. This naturally minimised their importance[168]. But Lord Curzon as Viceroy, saw more in this situation, a fine balance of considerations, "for while, on the one hand, it is desirable to get the Kanjutis into Raskam in order to keep the Russians out, on the other hand, should the latter seize Kashgar, they may claim Hunza as a subject state."[169]

In commending the boundary line to the Tsungli Yamen, Sir Claude Macdonald recalled Hunza's claim to an "extensive tract of land in the Taghdumbash Pamir extending as far north as Tashkurgan..." The Raskam district was no less claimed by the Kanjutis. Hunza rights over part of the Taghdumbash Pamir, it was pointed out, were admitted by the Taotai of Kashgar in a letter to the Mir in February 1896. In 1898 the question of Raskam district was again subject of negotiations between Hunza and the officials of the New Dominion, in which the Chinese admitted that some of the Raskam land should be given to the Kanjutis. The Tsungli Yamen were told that for the sake of avoiding "any dispute or uncertainty in the future," the Government of India proposed that "a clear understanding should be come to with the Chinese Government as to the frontier between the two states." To obtain this clear understanding.

> "it is necessary that China should relinquish her shadowy claim to suzerainty over the State of Kanjut. The Indian Government on the other hand will, on behalf of Kanjut, relinquish her claims to most of the Taghdumbash and Raskam districts."[170]

That British hallucinations over the northern boundary cost India dearly was pointed out to the Tsungli Yamen by Sir Claude Macdonald himself. "...(you) will see by examining this line that a large tract of country to the north of the great dividing range shown in Hung Chun's (sic) map as outside the Chinese boundary will be recognised as Chinese territory."[171] But Hung's map itself arrogated to China no less large territories lying between the Yarkand river and the Kuen Lun-Bolortagh, or the Kashgar, range, thanks to Britannic Majesty.

The Mir was satisfied with the collection of his taxes in Taghdumbash, shadowy though this right was lately growing. But he was more than ever keen to occupy Raskam and sought again the advice of the Political Agent, Gilgit, now Manners-Smith. The Mir was influenced by popular sentiment in Hunza. Given his helplessness Nazim Khan was bluntly told that the Government of India always considered "the country beyond the "natural" boundaries of Kashmir in the direction of Yarkand and Kashgar as being within the sphere of Chinese influence and had no desire to extend its own obligations to these regions..." But China being a friendly power and neighbour, Manners-Smith saw little likelihood of the Government of India objecting to his acquisition of Raskam. The Mir, however, did not fancy signing the agreement and binding himself down to "inconvenient" terms, a view with which the Agent was in full accord. Agreement there was also between the two that whole of Raskam, including Azghar and Ursur on the far, north, side of the Yarkand river should be acquired. Even without Azghar and Ursur, Manners-Smith saw grant of Ruskam down to Yarkand river to answer the purpose desired by Ardagh. But if reversion of rights to England by China was contemplated then, Manners-Smith commanded the Government of India "contend for all that Hunza can fairly claim than to allow a limit to be placed to her claims in regard to Raskam."[172] It can be safely inferred that the Agent had Sirikul in his mind, which was not at all claimed by the British.

Allocation of land to the Kanjutis in the five approved sites had hardly begun in 1898 when in the spring of 1899 it was suspended, Russia threatening "war" on the issue. Nazim Khan was requested to recall his people and not to send them if they had not started for Raskam. Thereafter the Mir was not to make a demand for Raskam. Instead of land Kanjutis were to be given grain[173]. A letter to the this purport was received by Nazim Khan from the Begs of Sirikul also[174]. The threat of war was very real. Russian troops with guns had "actually crossed" the Chinese frontier[175]. Russia had also threatened she would occupy, as "quid pro quo," the village of Tagarma in Sirikul and Yehgin, situated midway between Irkishtan and Ulukchat[176]. Almost simultaneously Raskam was declared "to lay within the boundaries of China." Kanjutis at Kuktash equally vehemently claimed that "the whole of Raskam was subject to Kanjut..."[177] There was nothing new in Russian opposition. In 1898 occupation of Raskam by Hunza was thwarted by Petrovski when a settlement had virtually been reached[178]. The Viceroy saw no reason why Russia should "by threats interfere with a private arrangement" reached by the Chinese authorities on their own initiative. Eviction of Kanjutis could conceivably have been forcible. Nazim Khan was, therefore, advised "to comply with (Chinese) demand...,"[179] rather than risk a conflict with them." Hundreds of men, headed by an Amban, had, indeed, descended on Raskam to evict a few Kunjutis. Once again Nazim Khan was directed to carefully guard the "darbands" (passages) and strong places leading from Raskam to Gujal, like the post of Darwaza[180]. It was consequently garrisoned by the Shangshalis. To the Mir it appeared "curious" that the Chinese should offer him grain instead of "hereditary lands."[181] These adverse developments for the Kanjutis hoist the British with their own petard. They had put Indian territory outside the Indian frontier and beyond the reach of effective support. All that was, therefore, contemplated was to make "representations on behalf of the Kanjutis," and this was conveyed to H.O. Bax Ironside, the British Charge d'Affaires in Beijing[182]. China denied that the Taotai of Kashgar had reached any definite agreement[183]. This position she reiterated later also. The Viceroy confirmed to the Secretary of State that by his letter of 27th April 1898, the Taotai had "distinctly permitted the occupation of Raskam lands" and the draft agreement recited the Taotai's authority[184]. If China failed to enforce her own decision, she was being abundantly cautious, involve as it did alienation of land over which England and Russia had both taken a conflicting stance. Not to give offence to either country was Tsungli Yamen's natural response. To China herself the question was of "no importance."[185]

Direct negotiations between Hunza and China, which the British had assiduously fostered had, quite apparently, failed the Mir[186]. To the Resident in Kashmir MacMahon proposed that the Mir should withhold his annual "tribute" and declare his intention of "breaking off his shadowy relations" with China unless his rights in Raskam were granted[187]. The Russian factor had strongly waxed over Raskam and the Tsungli Yamen plainly admitted that the only difficulty in handing over the land to the Kanjutis "lay in the objections raised by Russia."[188] Russia saw her positions in the Pamirs "in danger of being outflanked and turned." She was, therefore, keen that the relative positions of Russia and England in Central Asia as settled by the Pamir convention should not be unsettled, a view that was expressed in St. Petersburg by the Russian Foreign Minister, Count Mouravieff. England was warned that for encroachments by the Indian Government "Russian Government would be compelled to seek compensation...towards the north,"[189] impliedly Tagharma in Sirikul.

The draft agreement, signed and sealed by Mir Nazim Khan in June 1899, under British advice, was soon after returned. The Taotai considered the Indian government had renounced Hunza's rights to Raskam in return for China relinquishing Hunza "tribute." This erroneous view of his was based on Macdonald's boundary proposal of the 14th March 1899[190]. The Chinese had conveniently failed to distinguish between Hunza's sovereign rights in Raskam, which the British were prepared to renounce, and proprietary rights which they vigorously supported but with which the Mir was not satisfied. In London it appeared that China had "definitely withdrawn the concessions made by them to the Kanjutis..."[191] The Secretary of State for India, Lord George Hamilton, was, therefore, disposed to suggest to the Foreign Office that Russia and China should be distinctly assured "that the British Government make no claim to any territorial rights in Raskam, and have no intention of making any such claim whenever the demarcation of the frontier between the possessions of Great Britain and those of China in that region takes place." But the Russian War Office had positive information which conflicted materially with British, or Hunza, claims for 3000 acres of land in Raskam. The claim of the Mir of Hunza, General Kuropatkin, Russia's Minister of War, detailed to Sir Charles Scott, British Minister at St. Petersburg, comprised lands in Sirikul extending in the northerly direction towards Tashkurgan on the flank of the Taghdumbash Pamir. Kuropatkin produced a large scale Russian map of this part of the Central Asia and drew the attention of Sir Charles Scott "to the red line traced on it to the east of the Pamirs as forming the northern limit of British influence and the demarcation between Kashgar and Kashmir."[192] The line appeared to have included whole of the Taghdumbash Pamir, Raskam-Yarkand valley and Sirikul in British sphere of influence. Russia was pinning down England to her own professed boundary, the Karakoram-Hindu Kush. Scott was asked to obtain from India Office a tracing of a sufficiently large map so as to permit fixing on it exactly the position of lands claimed by Hunza. Only then was Kuropatkin to be satisfied "that the confirmation of the Mir of Hunza's claim to the use of these lands did not signify an extension northward of British influence so as to outflank the Russian position..." Otherwise, it was conveyed to England, "Russia would be obliged to make a corresponding advance and insist on obtaining adequate compensation from China in Kashgar."

One result of these proceedings appears to have been the recall of Kanjutis from Raskam. The Amban of Yarkand warned Nazim Khan, "None of your men should ever come to Raskam."[193] Sir Charles Scott did explain to Count Mouravieff, with the aid of a British map, that lands claimed by Hunza were confined to the area between Sarakamish at one end of the Raskam tributary of the Yarkand river, and Bazar Dara at the other end, and did not, as the Russian military authorities understood they did, extend from the Mariam Pamir (which is not considered a Pamir) northwards to Sirikul. Though Mouravieff assured Sir Charles Scott that Kuropatkin was "quite satisfied,"[194] the "unqualified nature of Russian opposition."[195] remained. In the British Indian Foreign Department, Hunza's rights in Sirikul came to be upheld and Russian objections rejected[196]. H.S. Barnes, Foreign Secretary, acknowledged Hunza's "rather extensive claims" to sovereignty over the Taghdumbash and Raskam" These claims England was prepared to renounce "and to lay down a boundary which leaves Hunza only the western end of the Taghdumbash..." But were China to refuse to recognise proprietary rights of Kanjutis, then Barnes supposed England's offer on the boundary could be withdrawn and Hunza's sovereign claims revived and maintained in both Raskam and Taghdumbash "which probably would not suit the Russians at all."[197] Count Mouravieff was again claimed by the British to have been satisfied by Sir Charles Scott's explanations and reportedly viewed the Raskam issue "as one which exclusively concerned the British and Chinese Governments, and that the Russian Government had no interest in further interfering in the matter."[198] But the Russian War Ministry stayed unconvinced.

British diplomatic support to Hunza therefore, came to be looked down on by Nazim Khan to be no less hopeless than direct negotiations earlier. One last weapon there still was left in British armoury to call off the fiction, British fiction that is, that Hunza was under Chinese suzerainty. This the Mir appears to have urged on the British Agent at Gilgit. The material advantages, which Hunza obtained from the maintenance of a nominal connection with China, Nazim Khan candidly admitted, "are the sole cause" of his caring to continue his relations with Kashgar and Yarkand. These gains were the taxes he levied in Taghdumbash and the Chinese presents, together worth under Rs. 3,000 per annum. He was grateful the Government of India had allowed him to receive Chinese gifts. But he wished to be "still more grateful if he were allowed to break off his connection altogether and were given compensation instead by the Government of India..."[199]

The collapse of Chinese Central authority in 1900 pushed the Raskam negotiations into background[200]. It also revived British anxiety about the trans-Hindu Kush territories were Russia to supplant China in Kashgaria? As late as December 1897, the Government of India had declared itself averse to extending the border beyond the great mountain ranges-Karakoram-Hindu Kush-forming the "natural frontier" of the British empire. But in the changing situation in China, Macartney in Kashgar questioned the relevance of this policy based, as he saw it was, on the pre-supposition that an occupation of the territory beyond the ridges would imply their defence. Raskam and Taghdumbash, Macartney argued, "must become British territory"[201] so as to insulate British boundary from Russian contact on the foot of the Kilik, Mintaka and Shangshal passes, the Hindu Kush glacis remaining thus under British control. Macartney's view was shared by the British Political Agent at Gilgit, who himself was under Nazim Khan's pressure.

To meet the changed situation in China, British policy on Central Asia was reappraised. Macartney favoured England conceding a position of pre-eminence to Russia in Kashgaria. This, he clarified, was not to imply Russian annexation of Eastern Turkistan, "already within her grasp." Nor was it to preclude, in that eventuality, British action somewhere else, say in Tibet. Tibet, indeed, had lately come increasingly to figure, Ardagh onwards, in British thinking. One reason for this was enlarged Russian interest in Tibet another the doctrine of glacis. His earlier proposition of setting up buffer States on the northern boundary in territories ceded or proposed to be ceded, he now declared to be of questionable utility. If some points existed near the crest of the watershed, but situated in the northern glacis, strategically important for the defence of the country behind, these, he fancied, should be occupied on the first favourable opportunity. Everything ought to be done to make the fact patent that these points were considered by the British to be within the Indian frontier. Negotiations with China on the boundary, Macartney urged, should be discarded as useless, both on account of her disorganisation and because of the "paramountcy of Russian influence"[202] in Eastern Turkistan in the face of which China was not a free agent. If it was found advantageous to occupy the points over the glacis, measures could be taken in such good time as to forestall the effect of any treaty which China might be coerced into secretly negotiating with Russia, for the cession of the province, the south western frontier of which was considered by China and Russia to be rigidly the crest of the Muztagh and the Karakoram ranges. Were the Kanjutis to renounce their rights in Raskam and in retaliation stop sending gold "tribute" it was perceived to lead to loss of British prestige, expose as it did British inability to further their suit in the face of Russian opposition.

While dismissive of Macartney on the ground that he was too far away from the centre of Imperial politics to formulate policy, the Viceroy, Lord Curzon, discussed in a minute "our future in these parts and what shape should our present policy assume in order to subserve it." He was not a believer in the policy of an advanced British frontier beyond the Hindu Kush. He thus ruled out retention militarily of territories between the Karakoram-Hindu Kush and Kuen Lun. An advanced frontier beyond the Hindu Kush was seen by him to have no geographical features or value and to possess no military strength. That an advanced frontier would have "no geographical features" Curzon had in mind the Yarkand river boundary from which the British had been virtually beaten out by Russian firmness. But almost in line with the Ardagh doctrine, Curzon saw temporary intervention of small belts of unoccupied, or semi-occupied or neutral territory, that is territories of Jammu and Kashmir informally ceded to China by England, though possessing no permanent value, tended "to keep the Russian and British arms for a while apart, and enables us to negotiate and haggle when the trouble arises." It was also for this lesser reason that the quite legitimate Hunza claims to Raskam were espoused by the British and not "to extend the Indian frontier to Raskam..."[203] Such a policy had, of course, no permanence. Curzon also saw the "as yet undisputed Chinese possession of the Taghdumbash" and "the admitted and as yet unsurrendered Hunza rights in Raskam" all as "pawns in the game, which may be worth something to us and which it is unsurrendered Hunza rights in Raskam" all as "pawns in the game, which may be worth something to us and which it is unnecessary to sacrifice." That Russia would break loose and become conterminous with the British Indian empire, Curzon visualised. No force and no diplomacy could avert it. But on one point Curzon agreed with Macartney that England should find "*a quid pro quo*" in Tibet should Russia seize Eastern Turkistan.

When, therefore, Russia notified the Chinese in Kashgar her intention to build a house in Sirikul, which Macartney and other Englishmen were quick to dub as a fort with Russian troops, already there to be quartered in it[204], Curzon's prophesy appeared to come true. Russian posts were also imagined to come up at Dafdar, once the northern limit of Hunza, Wachcha, some distance eastward of Sirikul, and Kukturuk, the northern glacis of the Hindu Kush in the Taghdumbash[205]. In Raskam too Russia contested the "ancient" rights of Hunza. These were seen to have orginated in the incursions made by the Kanjutis, only about 40 years earlier. Russian view thus far was historically sustainable. But when Russia went on to claim that following the incursions, the Kanjutis obtained from the Chinese authorities the cession of the Raskam lands for their agricultural needs[206], she was far from the truth. Raskam part of the Yarkand valley would appear to have mostly belonged Skardo and Ladakh. Ladakhi outposts have been noticed at Bostan, Kirghiz Jungle and elsewhere. China took advantage of Russian objections, as an excuse for not completing grant of Raskam lands, immediately after the delivery of Macdonald's note proposing the boundary alignment and severance of Hunza's links with her. The latter proposal was quite distasteful to China and one she evaded. The boundary was lost sight of in the prolonged wrangle over Raskam with the result China never replied to Macdonald's proposal. Another outcome of this dispute was that Nazim

Khan had second thoughts about colonisation of Raskam by the Kanjutis. His fears were loss of Kanjuti settlers who would inevitably become "subjects of China or Russia,"[207] Unless, therefore, the tract was "clearly recognised as being within the British sphere,"[208] he preferred to have nothing to do with it. Both the Political Agent in Gilgit and the Resident in Kashmir agreed "that connection between China and Hunza should be severed without delay."[209] In a secret despatch to the Secretary of State for India, Lord Curzon, urged that "a formal notification be made to China that since the Chinese Government have been unable to fulfil their promises to the Mir of Hunza, that State, under the advice of the British Government, withdraws from all relations with China..." The China-Hunza connection was *per se* viewed as harmless as long as China retained Kashgaria. But what if Russia took it over? Would not Russia then cause greater inconvenience to England? Hunza vassalage was a facet of the larger boundary issue and Curzon strongly recommended that China should be informed that as they had not shown any reasons for disagreeing with the proposals of Macdonald, "We shall henceforth assume Chinese concurrence and act accordingly."[210] Nazim Khan's pecuniary loss was to be made good by the Government of India and Kanjuti surplus population settled in Gilgit[211]. The Secretary of State for India, St. John Brodrick concurred with the views of the Government of India. A report was nevertheless sought by him on the effective control exercised by Hunza over western Taghdumbash[212] through which the route led by the Paik pass to Kashgar. It was proposed to be retained in India so that any Chinese action inconsistent with Kanjuti rights was met. Lord Lansdowne, now Secretary of State for Foreign Affairs, was of the same view[213].

But England was hedging, Lord Lansdowne in particular. The extent Hunza exercised jurisdiction beyond the Hindu Kush was well known, both in Calcutta and London. It was known that the Mir collected taxes from Taghdumbash and beyond in Sirikul. This was what an Indian Foreign Department note also admitted[214], and Macartney from Kashgar with the usual British obfuscation, amplified[215]. England had reasons to hedge. There, firstly, was realisation that China would not relinquish territory, even though it was only informally given to her by Britain. For herself China had conceived two watersheds, including one separating the Taghdumbash and Raskam rivers from the tributaries of the Indus to the south as their boundary. The two valleys of the Karachakar and Mintaka, which the British intended to incorporate within their boundary, the Chinese, therefore, claimed as their own. No less importantly, western

Taghdumbash, though it could be defended against China with posts, garrisoned by levies, was considered indefensible as and when Russia seized Chinese Turkistan. British position then on the entire line between Peak Povalo Schveikovsky and Karchnai pass was seen as quite untenable[216]. These reasons prompted Colonel E.G. Colvin, Resident in Kashmir, to suggest a modified boundary line which strictly ran along the watershed, did not require demarcation and excluded western Taghdumbash and Darwaza from British limits. While the modified boundary was seen as quite palatable to the Chinese, Colvin argued it would be better to have this boundary defined with their consent, or deliberate acquiescence "but if the necessity of such definition compels us to impose a frontier on China, then it is equally clear that the frontier selected should be that which is most easily and naturally defensible..."[217] Foreign Secretary, L.W. Dane, did not envisage strict adherence to the watershed. There were advantages, as had been found in the case of Tibet, in having the frontier some distance below the watershed and the Wakhan Russian boundary was not a watershed throughout[218]. There were other factors that, perhaps, influenced Dane's thinking. The Kanjutis of Shanghsal had also extensive grazing rights for 20 miles beyond Darwaza. 5 miles from Darwaza they fetched salt for their consumption. Strict adherence to the watershed excluded this area of Ghorzerab valley[219]. Major B.E.M. Gurdon, Political Agent at Gilgit, obviously under pressure of Nazim Khan, proposed for the reasons mentioned inclusion of Ghorzerab valley within the British boundary. But the Foreign Department was aware were China to be approached for this rectification in Macdonald's boundary line, she would hardly oblige. Curzon sought solution by what he called a "composite agreement." There were three objects British had in view :

1. Recognition of Macartney as consul at Kashgar.
2. Severance of Hunza's connection with China.
3. Secure for Kanjutis a projection of watershed frontier beyond Shangshal.

The British could insist upon the first, argue the second was forced upon them by the inability of the Chinese to hand over Raskam to Hunza, but that in return England agree to the surrender all Hunza rights to the north of the Hindu Kush except for a small perturberance required for subsistence of Shanghsalis[220]. To Curzon it did not matter one bit that the proposed extension lay beyond the Macdonald line. The Viceroy remarked,

> "Equally and still more does the proposed surrender to China lie inside it. China will give less than she will get."[221]

Far from that. Either way there was no giving by China only taking, a little less or more,

The much dreadied Russian take over of Kashgar finally occurred in 1912 in the wake of the overthrow of the Manchu empire and outbreak of disorder in the New Dominion and Tibet. Her Indian possessions Britain did not see threatened by the Czar, even though Russia was now only 150 and 300 miles distant from Srinagar and Simla respectively. But England was quick to recognise political disadvantages from such Russian propinquity and sought, as a measure of compensation, Russian recognition of a new boundary line

> "which will place Taghdumbash, Raskam, Shahidulla and Aksai Chin within our and outside Russian territory."[222]

This was Ardagh's line which the Government of India had rejected in 1897. The revival of this frontier proposal was an abject admission also of a disastrous frontier policy that Britain had ruthlessly pursued for well nigh seven decades under which she gratuitously gave away all of these very territories to China to prevent Russia becoming conterminous with India and in the process deposed the Maharaja of Jammu and Kashmir without any legal or moral right, fought a war with Hunza and Nagar, put to flight Mir Safdar Ali and divided Hunza into two. Hunza did finally reoccupy Raskam in 1914 not so much to forestall embarrassment from Russia. The Kirghiz appeared to have, with or without Chinese encouragement, reclaimed land in Raskam for farming since 1912. With the consent of the British Agent at Gilgit, the Mir sent his subjects to evict the Kirghiz and take over the land and assert his sovereign claims[223]. One manifestation of these sovereign rights was deployment of Hunza levies in Raskam. Another display of the Mir's supremacy was the arrest during World War I of two German military officers, Major Richard Dinkleman and Lt. Bernhard Waurick, in Chinese service, while attempting to escape through the Yarkand valley to Kabul. Their attempt to escape also led to posting of Hunza levies in the northern Hindu Kush glacis of Kukturuk[224]. The Germans were arrested at Takuzbulak in Raskam, near Oprang[225]. When the Germans questioned British right to arrest them in Raskam in China, Nazim Khan claimed that the Chinese recognised his rule in Raskam[226]. The arrests also raised the boundary issue. Major Dinkleman represented that the British regarded "the course of the Raskam river itself" as the boundary between India and China. Their arrests would have been legal, effected as these were on the south bank of the river. But Dinkleman pointed out, the road ran on both sides of the river, some times on the right and some times on the left bank[227]. The German carried a copy of a Younghusband map bearing the legend "north of Raskam extreme limit of Chinese jurisdiction[228]." International law being involved in the arrests, India Office in London queried the Foreign Department[229]. In response the Foreign Secretary, Denys Bray, noted that the northern boundary existed "only on paper." Bray indicated to India Office, Raskam was reoccupied in 1914[230]. Thus the northern boundary rested until in 1950s China cut loose.

References

1. Undated. Foreign. Secret. F.No. 436 of September 1892. Also No. 435.
2. Undated. Foreign. Secret. F.No. 444 of September 1892.
3. Undated. (Numbered 11 a, b, c, d) Foreign. Secret. F.Nos. 423, 424, 425 and 426 of September 1892.
4. Undated. Foreign. Secret. F.No. 427 of September 1892.
5. Undated. Foreign. Secret. F.No. 399 of September 1892.
6. Undated. Foreign. Secret. F.No. 423 of September 1892.
7. Undated. Foreign. Secret. F.No. 457 of September 1892.
8. 27th February 1892. Foreign. Secret. F.No. 273 of July 1892.
9. 7th May 1892. Foreign. Secret. F.No. KW. 1-89-203 of June 1892.
10. 13th May 1892. Foreign. Secret. F.No. 162 of August 1892.
11. 27th May 1892. Foreign. Secret. F.No. 159 of August 1892.
12. 30th May 1892. Foreign. Secret. F.No. 157 of August 1892.
13. 11th June 1892. Foreign. Secret. F.No. 410 of August 1892.
14. 27th June 1892. Foreign. Secret. F.No. 164 of August 1892.
15. 2nd July 1892. Foreign. Secret. F.No. KW. 2-156-198 of August 1892.
16. 2nd July 1892. Foreign. Secret. F.No. 802 of September 1892.
17. 20th July 1892. Foreign. Secret. F.No. 807 of September 1892.
18. 20th July 1892. Foreign. Secret. F.No. KW. 2-156-198 of August 1892.
19. 5th August 1892. Foreign. Secret. F.No. KW. 2-738-872 of September 1892.
20. 30th August 1892. Foreign. Secret. F.No. 346 of December 1892.
21. 13th December 1892. Foreign. Secret. F.No. 7 of March 1893.
22. 2nd January 1893. Foreign. Secret. F.No. 254 of May 1893.
23. 6th January 1893. Foreign. Secret. F.No. 181 of May 1893.
24. 3rd March 1893. Foreign. Secret. F.No. 225 of May 1893.
25. 31st March 1893. Foreign. Secret. F.No. 151 of June 1893.
26. 13th March 1893. Foreign. Secret. F.No. 504 of July 1893.

27. 4th May 1893. Foreign. Secret. F.No. 51 of June 1893.
28. 9th May 1893. Foreign. Secret. F.No. 276 of August 1893.
29. 22nd June 1893. Foreign. Secret. F.No. KWI-344-345 of October 1893.
30. *Ibid.*, 26th June 1893.
31. 10th July 1893. Foreign. Secret. F.No. KW III-493-570 of July 1893.
32. 23rd July 1893. Foreign. Secret. F.No. 97 of October 1893.
33. 9th September 1893. Foreign. Secret. F.No. KW 1-96-102 of October 1893.
34. 8th December 1893. Foreign. Secret. F.No. 166 of March 1894.
35. 31th March 1894. Foreign. Secret. F.No. 32 of August 1894.
36. 3rd April 1894. Foreign. Secret. F.No. 31 of August 1894.
37. 26th May 1894. Foreign. Secret. F.No. 655 of July 1894.
38. 1st June 1894. Foreign. Secret. F.No. 399 of October 1894.
39. 15th June 1894. Foreign. Secret. F.No. 26 of August 1894.
40. 30th July 1894. Foreign. Secret. F.No. 319 of September 1894.
41. 31st December 1894. Foreign. Secret. F.No. 151 of October 1895.
42. 16th January 1895. Foreign. Secret. F.No. 153 of October 1895.
43. 16th April 1895. Foreign. Secret. F.No. 157 of October 1895.
44. 6th July 1895. Foreign. Secret. F.No. KW-150-173 of October 1895.
45. 12th September 1895. Foreign. Secret. F.No. KW. 150-173 of October 1895.
46. *Ibid.*, 14th September 1895.
47. 15th March 1896. Foreign. Secret. F.No. 177 of June 1896.
48. 29th June 1896. Foreign. Secret. F.No. 538 of October 1896.
49. 1st January 1897. Foreign. Secret. F.No. 166 of January 1898.
50. 12th March 1897. Foreign. Secret. F.No. KW 160-169 of January 1898.
51. 14th March 1897. Foreign. Secret. F.No. KW 160-169 of January 1898.
52. 13th April 1897. Foreign. Secret. F.No. KW 1-160-169 of January 1898.
53. 4th October 1897. Foreign. Secret. F.No. KW 1-160-169 of January 1898.
54. 7th October 1897. Foreign. Secret. F.No. KW 1-160-169 of January 1898.
55. Journal of Asiatic Society of Bengal, Vol. XXXVI Part II (1868). A geological paper by Albert M. Verchere, p. 50.
56. The Heart of a Continent. By Captain F.E. Younghusband. (1896), p. 266.
57. Records of The Survey of India. Vol. XXII. Exploration of the Shaksgam Valley. 1926. By Major Kenneth Mason. Dehra Dun-1928, p. 74.
58. 26th August 1889. Foreign. Secret. F.No. 186 of October 1889.
59. 5th August 1892. Foreign. Secret. F.No. KW 2-738-872 of September 1892.
60. Report of A Mission To Yarkand. Historical and Geographical. By Captain-Trotter, Foreign Deptt. Press. (1875), p. 245.

61. Undated. Foreign. Frontier B. No. 129 of September 1890.
62. Report Of A Mission To The Northern Frontier Of Kashmir. By Captain F.E. Younghusband. (1890), p. 25.
63. The Heart Of A Continent. By Captain F.E. Younghusband. (1896), p. 181.
64. Italian Expedition To The Himalaya, Karakoram And Eastern Turkistan. By Filippo De Filippi p. 377[N].
65. 26th August 1889. Foreign. Secret. F. No. 186 of October 1889.
66. Himalayan Frontiers. By Dorothy Woodman. (1969), p. 49.
67. Undated. Foreign. Frontier B. No. 129 of September 1890.
68. In Tibet and Chinese Turkistan. By Captain H.P.P. Deasy (1901), p. 122.
69. Italian Expedition to the Himalaya, Karakoram and Eastern Turkistan. By Filippo De Filippi, p. 438.
70. The Heart of A Continent. By Captain F.E. Younghusband. (1896), p. 274.
71. A Sketch of Geography and Geology of the Himalaya Mountains and Tibet. By Colonel Sir S.G Burrard. Govt. Printing Press. (1907-1908), p. 70.
72. 18th February 1873. Foreign. Secret. No. 30 of April 1873.
73. Report of A Mission To Yarkand. Historical and Geographical. By Captain H. Trotter. Foreign Deptt. Press (1875), p. 268.
74. 19th November 1891. Foreign. Secret. F.No. 125 of January 1892.
75. 20th November 1891. Foreign. Secret. F.No. 182 of January 1892.
76. 3rd January 1892. Foreign. Secret. F.No. 153 of March 1892.
77. 12th March 1892. Foreign. Secret. F.No. 379 of May 1892.
78. 22nd March 1892. Foreign. Secret. F.No. 376 of May 1892.
79. 12th June 1892. Foreign. Secret. F.No. KW-3-115-143 of October 1892.
80. 20th June 1892. Foreign. Secret. F.No. 756 of September 1892.
81. 25th June 1892. Foreign. Secret. F.No. 316 of October 1892.
82. 29th June 1892. Foreign. Secret. F.No. 804 of September 1892.
83. Undated. Foreign. Secret F.No. 320 of October 1892.
84. Undated. Foreign. Secret F.No. 322 of October 1892.
85. Undated Foreign. Secret. F.No. 323 of October 1892. Also 27th July 1892. Secret F. KW 1-314-327 and 322 of October 1892.
86. 1st July 1892. Foreign. Secret. F.No. 63 of August 1892.
87. 1st July 1892. Foreign. Secret. F.No. 64 of August 1892.
88. 3rd September 1892. Foreign. Secret. F.No. 635 of October 1892.
89. 6th September 1892. Foreign. Secret. F.No. 636 of October 1892.
90. 19th September 1892. Foreign. Secret. F.No. 353 of December 1892.
91. 6th February 1893. Foreign. Secret. F.No. 135 of June 1893.
92. 15th February 1893. Foreign. Secret. F.No. 252 of May 1893.

93. 3rd March 1893. Foreign. Secret. F.No. 285 of May 1893.
94. 9th April 1893. Foreign. Secret. F.No. 502 of July 1893.
95. 13th April 1893. Foreign. Secret. F.No. 504 of July 1893.
96. 13th April 1893. Foreign. Secret. F.No. 145 of June 1893.
97. 22nd April 1893. Foreign. Secret. F.No. 155 of June 1893.
98. 29th April 1893. Foreign. Secret. F.No. KW 91-163 of June 1893.
99. 7th May 1893. Foreign. Secret. F.No. 324C of August 1893.
100. 10th May 1893. Foreign. Secret. F.No. 497 of July 1893.
101. 1st July 1893. Foreign. Secret. F.No. 138 of September 1893.
102. 3rd July 1893. Foreign. Secret. F.No. KW 1-493-570 of July 1893.
103. 7th July 1893. Foreign. Secret. F.No. KW III-493-570 of July 1893.
104. 23rd August 1893. Foreign. Secret. F.No. 153 of September 1893.
105. 27th August 1893. Foreign. Secret. F.No. 155 of September 1893.
106. 8th September 1893. Foreign. Secret. F.No. 567 of October 1893.
107. 7th December 1893. Foreign. Secret. F.No. 144 of February 1894.
108. 13th December 1893. Foreign. Secret. F.No. 154 of February 1894.
109. 20th December 1893. Foreign. Secret. F.No. 194 of January 1894.
110. 14th January 1894. Foreign. Secret. F.No. 2 of June 1894.
111. 22nd January 1894. Foreign. Secret. F.No. 195 of February 1894.
112. 2nd February 1894. Foreign. Secret. F.No. 204 of March 1894.
113. 25th April 1894. Foreign. Secret. F.No. 222 of June 1894.
114. 27th April 1894. Foreign. Secret. F.No. KW 1-185-269 of June 1894.
115. *Ibid.*, 27th April 1894.
116. *Ibid.*, 28th April 1894.
117. *Ibid.*, 1st May 1894.
118. 11th March 1895. Foreign. Secret. F.No. 850 of June 1895.
119. 15th March 1895. Foreign. Secret. F.No. 891 of July 1895.
120. 17th March 1895. Foreign. Secret. F.No. KW 1-891-933 of July 1895.
121. 9th May 1895. Foreign. Frontier A.No. KW 8-92-134 of July 1895.
122. 1st June 1895. Foreign. Secret. F.No. 223 of September 1895.
123. 11th June 1895. Foreign. Secret. F.No. KW 1-891-933 of July 1895.
124. 15th June 1895. Foreign. Secret. F.No. 916 of July 1895.
125. 2nd August 1895. Foreign. Secret. F.No. 164 of October 1895.
126. 16th August 1895. Foreign. Secret. F.No. 167 of October 1895.
127. 19th September 1895. Foreign. Secret. F.No. 170 of October 1895.
128. The Indian Borderlands. By Colonel Sir T.H. Holdich. (1901) pp. 284-293.
129. 31st May 1897. Foreign. Secret. F.No. 306 of July 1898.
130. 31st August 1897. Foreign. Secret. F.No. 310 of July 1898.
131. 7th September 1897. Foreign. Secret. F.No. 307 of July 1898.

132. 15th September 1897. Foreign. Secret. F.No. 311 of July 1898.
133. 30th September 1897. Foreign. Secret. F.No. 308 of July 1898.
134. 15th October 1897. Foreign. Secret F.No. 328 of July 1898.
135. - October 1897. Foreign. Secret. F.No. 312 of July 1898.
136. 2nd November 1897. Foreign. Secret. F.No. KW 1-306-347 of July 1898.
137. *Ibid.*, 11th November 1897.
138. Inner Most Asia by Ralph P. Cobbold. (1900) pp. 302, 307.
139. *Ibid.*, pp. 55-56.
140. 15th December 1897. Foreign. Secret. F.No. 172 of May 1898.
141. In Tibet and Chinese Turkistan. By Captain H.H.P. Deasy (1901) p. 101.
142. Undated. Foreign. Secret. F.No. KW-2-160-169 of January 1898.
143. 30th November 1897. Foreign. Secret. F.No. 314 of July 1898.
144. 6th December 1897. Foreign. Secret. F.No. 329 of July 1898.
145. 31st December 1897. Foreign. Secret. F.No. 317 of July 1898.
146. 15th January 1898. Foreign. Secret. F.No. 313 of July 1898.
147. 22nd January 1898. Foreign. Secret. F.No. 316 of July 1898.
148. 15th March 1898. Foreign. Secret. F.No. 175 of August 1898.
149. 15th April 1898. Foreign. Secret. F.No. 334 of July 1898.
150. 27th April 1898. Foreign. Secret. F.No. 339 of July 1898.
151. *Ibid.*
152. 30th April 1898. Foreign. Secret. F.No. 332 of July 1898.
153. 10th April 1898. Foreign. Secret. F.No. 327 of July 1898.
154. *Ibid.*
155. 17th May 1898. Foreign. Secret. F.No. 341 of July 1898.
156. 4th June 1898. Foreign. Secret. F.No. 333 of July 1898.
157. 6th June 1898. Foreign. Secret. F.No. 338 of July 1899.
158. Undated. Foreign. Secret. F.No. 174 of May 1899.
159. 30th April 1898. Foreign. Secret. F.No. 155 of May 1899.
160. 16th July 1898. Foreign. Secret. F.No. KW 1-110-114 of November 1898.
161. *Ibid.*, 18th July 1898.
162. *Ibid.*, 18th July 1898.
163. *Ibid.*, 19th July 1898.
164. - October 1898. Foreign. Secret. F.No. 168 of May 1899.
165. *Ibid.*, Undated.
166. 25th October 1898. Foreign. Secret. F.No. Part II. KW. 154-210 of May 1899.
167. Secret (frontier) despatch from the Govt. of India to the Secretary of State for India. No. 198 of 27th October 1898.
168. 16th February 1899. Foreign. Secret. F.No. Part I. KW-154-210 of May 1899.

169. *Ibid.*, 18th March 1899.
170. 14th March 1899. Foreign. Secret. F.sub encl. 1 (encl. 1) No. 188 of August 1899.
171. *Ibid.*
172. 21st March 1899. Foreign. Secret. F.No. 187 of May 1899.
173. Undated. Foreign. Secret. F. Sub enclosure 5 No. 173 of August 1899.
174. 23rd April 1899. Foreign. Secret. F. Sub enclosure 6. No. 173 of August 1899.
175. 25th April 1899. Foreign. Secret. F.No. 193 of May 1899.
176. 30th April 1899. Foreign. Secret. F.No. 168 of August 1899.
177. 1st May 1899. Foreign. Secret. F. (Enclosure) Sub-enclosure 1. No. 173 of August 1899.
178. 1st May 1899. Foreign. Secret. F.No. 195 of May 1899.
179. 2nd May 1899. Foreign. Secret. F.No. 196 of May 1899.
180. 2nd May 1899. Foreign. Secret. F. Sub enclosure 2 No. 173 of August 1899.
181. 4th May 1899. Foreign. Secret. F. Sub enclosure 4. No. 173 of August 1899.
182. 16th May 1899. Foreign. Secret. F. enclosure 2 No. 180 of August 1899.
183. 24th May 1899. Foreign. Secret. F.No. 171 of August 1899.
184. 28th May 1899. Foreign. Secret. F.No. 174 of August 1899.
185. 29th May 1899. Foreign. Secret. F.No. 210 of September 1899.
186. 6th June 1899. Foreign. Secret. F. Sub-enclosure 3. (enclosure 1) No. 184 of August 1899.
187. 10th June 1899. Foreign. Secret. F.No. 184 of August 1899.
188. 22nd June 1899. Foreign. Secret. F.No. 9 of November 1899.
189. 28th June 1899. Foreign. Secret. F.No. 213 of September 1899.
190. 27th July 1899. Foreign. Secret. F.No. 197 of August 1899.
191. 2nd August 1899. Foreign. Secret. F.No. 222 of September 1899.
192. 9th August 1899. Foreign. Secret. F.No. 11 of November 1899.
193. 10th August 1899. Foreign. Secret. F. Sub enclosure 2 (encl. 1). No. 237 of September 1899.
194. 17th August 1899. Foreign. Secret. F.No. 12 of November 1899.
195. 18th August 1899. Foreign. Secret. F.No. 12-B of November 1899.
196. 18th August 1899. Foreign. Secret F.No. Notes 210-240. September 1899.
197. *Ibid.*, 18th August 1899.
198. 24th August 1899. Foreign. Secret F. No. 14 of November 1899.
199. 6th June 1990 .Foreign. Secret F. Enclosure 1. No. 19 of September 1900.
200. 12th July 1900. Foreign. Secret F. No. 24 of September 1900.
201. 13th August 1900. Foreign. Secret F. Enclosure 2, No. 21 of January 1901.

202. 29th December 1900 .Foreign. Secret F. Enclosure 1. No. 1 of June 1901.
203. 22nd March 1901 .Foreign Secret F. No. Notes 1-2 of June 1901.
204. 16th June 1902. Foreign .Frontier B. Enclusure 1. No. 30 of September 1902.
205. 20th January 1903. Foreign. Secret F. No. 104 of September 1903.
206. 25th February 1903, Foreign Secret F. Appendix to Notes No. 104-110 of September 1903.
207. 14th November 1903. Foreign Secret F. No. 31 of April 1904.
208. 20th February 1904. Foreign Secret F. No. 36 of April 1904.
209. 17th March 1904. Foreign Secret F. No. 37 of April 1904.
210. Secret (frontier) despatch No. 70 from the Govt. of India to the Secretary of State for India of 24th March 1904.
211. 20th June 1904. Foreign. Secret F. No. Notes. 165-202 of February 1905.
212. 16th July 1904. Foreign Secret F. No. 178 of February 1905.
213. 1st August 1904. Foreign. Secret F. No. 182 of February 1905.
214. 12th August 1904. Foreign. Secret F. No. No. 165-202 of February 1905.
215. 2nd October 1904, Foreign. Secret F. Enclosure. No. 191 of February 1905.
216. 12th October 1904. Foreign. Secret F. No. 188 of February 1905.
217. *Ibid.*
218. 7th November 1904. Foreign. Secret F. Notes No. 165-202 of February 1905.
219. 19th December 1904. Foreign Secret F. Notes No. 165-202 of February 1905.
220. 24th December 1904. Foreign Secret F. Notes No. 165-202 of February 1905.
221. *Ibid.*, 2nd January 1905.
222. 12th September 1912. Foreign Secret F. No. 10 of February 1913.
223. 9th June 1914. Foreign. Secret F. No. 6 of October 1915.
224. 31st October 1916. Foreign. Secret F. Notes No. 1-67 of November 1917.
225. 20th November 1916. Foreign Secret F. No. 15 of November 1917.
226. 30th November 1916 .Foreign. Secret F. Encl. 2 No. 66 of November 1917.
227. 1st December 1916 .Foreign. Secret F. Appendix E No. 25 of November 1917.
228. 18th April 1917. Foreign. Secret F. Notes No. 1-67 of November 1917.
229. 26th April 1917. Foreign. Secret F. Notes No. 1-67 of November 1917.
230. 7th September 1917, Foreign. Secret F. Notes. No. 1-67 of November 1917.

Chapter 10
Cavilling Over Aksai Chin

In the moves to negotiate boundaries of Afghanistan, Hunza and Jammu and Kashmir with China, Aksai Chin was very much an area for settlement. Chinese attention was rather ingeniously drawn to Aksai Chin by the British. In December 1895, Macartney had gifted several books to a fomer governor of New Dominion. Among them an atlas of the world and Drew's map of Jammu and Kashmir Territories, as early as 1875, showed the Karakoram as the boundary. A map of Kashmir in the atlas showed Aksai Chin "marked in it as within British territory." A year later Aksai Chin was claimed by the Taotai as belonging "to Chinese Tibet" and Macartney was urged to inform the Indian Government accordingly. Whether Petrovski, as claimed, was or was not at the bottom of the Chinese claim, Macartney's response indicates yet another shift in British policy. Aksai Chin, he informed the Taotai, was, as likely as not, "partly in Chinese and partly in British territory."[1] This, perhaps, was a part of "the nonsense," as he called his talks with the Taotai, of which he committed only an extract "to writing." Most British maps had shown Aksai Chin within India. But Younghusband first divided it in his secret report, "A Mission To The Northern Frontier of Kashmir, 1889," into Lingzithang nearest to the Karakoram and Aksai Chin skirting the Kuen Lun. Keith Johnston's Handy Royal Altas of 1878 had run the boundary "practically the same as on...the Turkistan map...along the Kuen Lun."[2] But in 1894, Sir W.W. Hunter's Atlas of India showed Aksai Chin within Ladakh but divided. The boundary in the east was shown in the atlas to stretch to 80°3' E longitude and a little under 36°N. latitude. This configuration of the boundary split Lingzithang along the Laktsung hills and the spur falling from the Kuen Lun into Lingzithang west and Aksai Chin, the latter comprising north-eastern parts nearest to the Kuen Lun and dividing it further from east Aksai Chin which lies beyond 80°2' E. Macartney's view was not his own. The British Foreign Department justified Aksai Chin being only partly in India. Its own records revealed that "the boundary in the direction of Aksai Chin has never been defined." A new map of India, under preparation in January 1897, depicted only "Aksai Chin (Lingzithang plains) within British limits." The boundary on the 7th edition of the map of Turkistan was "identical with the boundary on the new map of India on this part of the frontier." The British Indian Foreign Department went a step further to, for the first time, claim,

> "There are two distinct localities named Aksai Chin. One is situated in the Lingzithang plains, and the other to the east of our boundaries. The one to the east (Aksai Chin white desert) has never been included within our boundaries. The other Aksai Chin (near the "Soda Plains"), north of the Lingzithang plains, appeared for the first time in the third edition of the map of Turkistan..."[3]

A distinction was sought to be made not only between the plateaux immediately to the north of the Changchenmo valley and the plains to their north and east along the Kuen Lun but an altogether new Aksai Chin, farther east, is projected. The east Aksai Chin had never been included in British maps was not entirely correct, as will be presently seen. But the sudden emergence of east Aksai Chin was certainly an innovation. Earlier to this there had been no mention of it in British records. First references to this, but not under the name of Aksai Chin or even Lingzithang, are by Moorcroft. He conceived the Moghal trade line to Central Asia going over probably the Keria la and Sarekia, the latter far to the west in the Karakash valley. The area was thus a compact one with the jade mine or mines part of it. Even splitting the northeastern Aksai Chin, skirting the Kuen Lun, from the Lingzithang plains was a cartographic "advance." Earlier the British either put Aksai Chin inside their red line boundary or wholly outside it. The reasons for such a devious course were many. The military disadvantage of retaining Aksai Chin had come to be tempered by political factors as had retention of Hunza's trans-Hindu Kush territories. In the case of Aksai Chin and Gilgit it was the steadfast opposition of Maharaja Pratap Singh that led to his deposition in 1889. The break up of Aksai Chin into different parts was, therefore, to meet the Kashmir Darbar half way by holding back Lingzithang in the British empire and thus balance Imperial interests, as far as possible, with those of Jammu and Kashmir State. This consideration is so evident from Younghusband's sneer at Pratap Singh, "...it (the inclusion of Lingzithang in Kashmir) may possibly be gratifying to the Maharaja of Kashmir to feel himself in possession of so many *extra* square miles of country."[4] Ardagh doctrine later came very much into contention and partition of Aksai Chin was canvassed an alternative to shifting the boundary back to the Kuen Lun, as a later day Foreign Department document reveals. The Maharaja's opposition, so open over Chinese occupation of Shahidulla, and China's loss of face, where the boundary again to rest on the Kuen Lun, might well have persuaded A. Stapleton of the Foreign Department to remark that China had "*deliberately* claimed Aksai Chin..."

In the preceding years the British had been guided by the Gazetteer of Kashmir and Ladakh, their own work, which made no distinction between Lingzithang and Aksai Chin. As to whether there was another Aksai Chin to the east, the right authority to know was the Ladakh wazarat (collectorate) at Leh or the Jammu and Kashmir Government. Stapleton, writing on Aksai Chin bypassed both. He had reasons. The British Indian Government had, more or less, conjured the British empire's northern boundary in Jammu and Kashmir. Part, at least, of Aksai Chin, the northeastern and eastern, with routes running into them from Khotan, was to be Chinese. But to avoid northeastern Aksai Chin being confused with the eastern one–and this Stapleton declared to be Chinese–the Surveyor General was to advise Government[5].

Oldest British maps, relying on secondary sources in the absence of explorations and surveys, had shown the northern boundary to rest on one of the ridges of the Kuen Lun. This ridge they later declared to be a separate Chain, the Karakoram, and the boundary. Aksai Chin came thus to be placed outside Ladakh. The first edition of the Turkistan map altered this. Based on a decade of explorations and surveys, the boundary was authoritatively placed on the Kuen Lun chain. But in the second edition of the Turkistan map, it was, as already noticed, pulled back to the Karakoram. The pull back was not, however, considered authoritative. Was it because of the protest of the Kashmir Darbar? Stapleton reveals that the Officer on special duty in Kashmir was informed that "no authoritative delineation of Kashmir frontier will be attempted without previous reference to the Darbar." Clearly Maharaja Ranbir Singh had interposed with the British to be reassured on the boundary, an area of discord between the two. A similar assurance was also held out by the Viceroy. In the third edition of the map of Turkistan, therefore, the boundary was put back on the Kuen Lun.

The 1892 version of Keith Johnson's Royal Atlas put the whole of Aksai Chin in China. There was, however, evidence, the British sweeping the controversy under the carpet, to prove the existence of the more western one (Lingzithang) in Kashmir "but none of any value with regard to that to the east which is within Chinese territory," the Surveyor General, C. Strahan, wrote to the Foreign Department[6]. The only thing of value which, perhaps, Strahan had in mind might well have been the goldmines of Zailik, near the Yurungkash river's sources. There was another goldmine Sorghak, northeast of Aksai Chin, apparently right on the Ladakh boundary which "Pundit" Kishan Singh inspected in 1873. Colonel Gore, also of the Survey of India, was little more forthcoming. The earliest British military intelligence about Aksai Chin and on the routes beyond had come from Mohammad Amin, the dubious guide of the Schlagintweit brothers. A sketch of 1862, based on his information had practically no details south of the Kuen Lun but had Aksai Chin written across it. This appears to be the first use of the Turkish name, Aksai Chin, in an official document. The lithographed map, published in 1868, on the basis of surveys in 1861-62, did not display Aksai Chin but it showed the Chinese boundary running eastwards along the Kuen Lun range up to the margin of the map in longitude 80°5' E with Ladakh marked to the south. That the boundary ran over the Kuen Lun to the north of Aksai Chin and extended 80°5' E clearly included within Ladakh most of the plateaux or plains of Lingzithang which the British later variously called Aksai Chin west or Lingzithang, northeast and east Aksai Chin. As the map ended in the margin at 80°5' E, it still did not show in Ladakh the easternmost part of east Aksai Chin and the mountainous region to the east of east Aksai Chin over which part of the Lanak la-Keria la-Polur route ran. This mountainous region also contains the sources of the Yurungkash and Keria rivers to the north while towards the south its waters flow into the Lake Leighten. The so-called east Aksai Chin of the British started from the spur falling from the Kuen Lun at 80°2' E and extends eastwards to 81°5' E or more. The mountainous region extends further east to 82°E. Stein's map in the "Ruins of Desert Cathay" prepared by the surveyors of the Survey of India, show east Aksai Chin plain to end in the north near the Zokputaran peak. Southward an Aksai Chin valley, or a ledge of territory, stretches further east to 81°4'E. The extreme eastern end of this ledge is covered by the Lake Leighten. That this mountainous region and, consequently, east Aksai Chin, had been in Ladakh was indicated to China at the official level talks in 1961[7]. But by limiting the northeastern boundary of Ladakh to 80°2'E. Indian officials, presumably for want of information, gifted a huge chunk of Aksai Chin, a very valuable chunk, as Strahan implies, to China[8]. The boundary outline in the lithographed map of 1868, was more than confirmed by Major Montgomerie in his trans-frontier map compiled in 1872, partly from Hayward's and partly from Johnson's maps. Montgomerie followed these two maps in omitting Aksai Chin from the position described by Hayward as being near the Ladakh-Khotan route (over the Yangi pass) but entered the road, southward from Keria town via Polur and lake Yeshil Kul, approximately 82°E longitude, for the first time.

> "This is put in dotted and is clearly from *native information*. Astride of this road and above latitude 35° he writes Aksai Chin (White desert)," Gore noted[9].

But Gore was quick to declare "This is evidently speculative as later reconnaissances and surveys of this route show that no open desert lies across the road and that if there is an eastern Aksai Chin it must lie to the west of the road." There was nothing speculative about the maps as Gore suggests. Montgomerie's map was based on evidence that pre-dated developments on the frontier–the overthrow of the Chinese power in Eastern Turkistan and the establishment of the Kashgaria State in 1865 by the Atalik Ghazi. The borders were, therefore, quiescent and the British had no reason to project imaginary boundaries. The lithographed map, on which Montgomerie appears to have heavily relied, was published in 1868, but was based, as noted, on explorations and surveys made in 1861-62. Johnson's surveys were made in 1864 and 1865. But these and Hayward's explorations were only supportive, for neither went eastward beyond the Laktsung hills and the Kuen Lun spur into east Aksai Chin. The other major source material for the map was statedly "native information," evidently collected by Johnson during his survey operations in Lingzithang from his Ladakhi guides, who were not only well acquainted with the boundary but, perhaps, enjoyed official status. Their information was far more reliable and accurate than any British map for the Ladakhis, unlike the British, had no reason to mislead on the extent of Ladakh. Thus not only was the boundary quiescent, the source material for Montgomerie untampered but, no less importantly, the prevailing British policy on boundary too had remained unchanged from the last operative pronouncement of Lord Dalhousie on the disbandment of the aborted second British boundary commission. Some British maps, therefore, incorporated east Aksai Chin in the Indian empire as early as 1860s. These maps and the testimony of Moorcroft that the Gyalpo would throw open to traffic the Polur-Lanak la road, were his submission to the British Government accepted, amply establish the eastern limit of Ladakh east of 82°E. longitude.

Many issues arise out of British obfuscation over Aksai Chin. 1. Are Lingzithang or western, or southern, Aksai Chin, 2. Thaldat, or northern, or northeastern, Aksai Chin, and, 3. East Aksai Chin geographically and politically separate groups of plateaux? Are the Laktsung (eagle's nest in Ladakhi) hills and the spur falling from the Kuen Lun at $80^0 2'$E longitude the true limit of Ladakh to the northeast? So the British claimed. Then how was the Lanak la-Keria la-Polur line, which ran over east Aksai Chin, in Ladakh as testified by Moorcroft and others. Earliest references by Vigne and Dr. Thomson to these plateaux, as noted, are too cursory and, even so, in the case of Vigne, based on what he imagined. Thornton's Gazetteer published, before the formation of Jammu and Kashmir State in 1844, alludes, evidently, to Aksai Chin as the "elevated region," east of Bolor mountains, a frightful desolation,"[10] again a compact region comprising not only Lingzithang but also Yarkand valley. The Schlagintweit brothers placed Aksai Chin "between the Karakoram and the Kuen Lun."[11] They thus geographically treated Aksai Chin as one. Despite their painstaking study of mountains, peaks, plateaux, routes and rivers, they do not make any distinction between Lingzithang, which name they did not use, and Aksai Chin. To them all the plateaux were Aksai Chin, a name which they seem to have coined with the assistance of their guide, Mohammad Amin. Vigne's political view on Aksai Chin–that it was outside Ladakh–was later shared by Colonel H.B. Edwards, Commissioner of Peshawar. Directing enquiries into the murder of Adolphe Schlagintweit, Edwards credited him with "a desire to find a road to Yarkand which need not pass through Ladakh."[12] By incorporating the Karakash valley in Ladakh and putting the boundary over the Kuen Lun in his map, Johnson placed western and northeastern Aksai Chin in the Maharaja's territories. He is silent over east Aksai Chin. This is because it was part of Aksai Chin. Shaw crossed the Lingzithang plains on his way to Kashgar and mentions the plateaux as Lingzithang and Laktsung valleys. He is the first to refer to the Laktsung hills. But he does not call them Ladakh's boundary to the northeast. He wrote "first comes a series of a parallel ridges (Laktsung) with corresponding valleys running N.W. to S.E.... Then a gigantic series of valleys were cut exactly at right angles to all this..."[13] All these valleys and the plains skirting the Kuen Lun the British later referred to as northeastern Aksai Chin. A march away from the Laktsung hills was Thaldat, a staging post and the site of a copious spring of fresh water, the overflow of which formed a little lake. Wild life existed there and Shaw hunted Tibetan antelope and wild yak, common fauna of the Ladakh desert. Thaldat later became one of the many hunting grounds for Englishmen in Ladakh, that were adduced in evidence by Indian officials in support of India's administrative control over Aksai Chin and the Changchenmo valley. Shaw, however, questioned Aksai Chin's political status. Drew traversed Lingzithang, or western and northeastern Aksai Chin, in 1869 as far as the sources of the Karakash river near Yongpa. He fathered the geographical division of the plateaux into (1) Lingzithang or western plains, (2) Kuen Lun or northern plateaux and, (3) Laktsung mountains, running 60 miles northwest and east-south-east, dividing the plains into two. But even he does not mention the Laktsung hills as the political boundary of Ladakh to the east. Though he did not personally travel there, or meet any one who had, Drew says that on its east the northeastern Aksai Chin is bounded by a mountain ridge or, as it came to be called in British records, a spur of the Kuen Lun[14]. Tampering with the historical boundary of India began only with the Forsyth expedition to Yarkand in 1870. Its impact on the Montgomerie map was, therefore, nil. Many surveys in Jammu and Kashmir State were conducted under Montgomerie, then Deputy Superintendent of the Survey of India. With the British boundary policy too Montgomerie later displayed considerable understanding. His map cannot, therefore, be lightly dismissed. It is, however, true, as Gore explained to Government, that explorations and surveys carried out in the closing years of the 19th century and, later, in the early years of the 20th century, establish that there is no plain or desert across the Yashil Kul-Polur part of the Ladakh-Khotan, or Lanak la-Polur route. This is misleading as will be seen.

Heading the expedition to Yarkand in 1870, Forsyth described the "high tableland" to connect the Karakoram and Kuen Lun ranges. He thus brought out their geographical unity. Forsyth passed through most parts of Lingzithang, northeastern and western. From a collective name of the plateaux, he reduced Lingzithang to one of the three plains—Lingzithang, Dipsi Kol and Thaldat[15]. He also mentions the Laktsung hills but not as Ladakh's boundary to the northeast. The route of the Forsyth expedition was the eastern Changchenmo line. Starting from Leh, this road led to Tankse, Pamzal, Nischu, Lingzithang, Laktsung, Thaldat, Khatai pass, Haji Langar and along the Karakash river the Kizil Jilga, Chungtash, Karatagh pass, Chibra Valley, Malikshah to Shahidulla. The route thus covered entire northeastern Aksai Chin. Another road, called the western route, by which the expedition returned from Yarkand, took off from Pamzal in the Changchenmo valley, went to Shamal Lungpa and Samzing Lung to Dehra Gompa and thereafter along the upper valley of the Karakash river. Between them the two lines bound together

Lingzithang and Aksai Chin. Forsyth also questioned the political status of Aksai Chin, as noticed, but does not reveal his grounds. Dr. Cayley called the plateaux Lingzithang[16], which emphasises these were one series of plains, a view Trotter later shared. Trotter referred to them as Lingzithang *or* Aksai Chin. Russian notices of Lingzithang are limited to those of Venukof's[17]. He consistently viewed the huge tableland as one area. To Hedin the area was Lingzithang *and* Aksai Chin as it was officially to the British. The latter he called "the unannexed region...in northwest Tibet,"–unannexed by Kashmir, Tibet or Chinese Turkistan. No boundaries, he remarks, were marked on the map. In vain he, therefore, looked for boundary stones. Yet Hedin himself notes that in Aksai Chin weathering, precipitation, flowing water, storm and wind work together in levelling the land. All heights and ridges are thereby reduced, all hollows are filled up with mud, sand and rubbish. Having looked for boundary stones in such conditions and having not found them, Hedin declared the plateaux as "unannexed,"[18] loyally thus serving his hosts, the British Indian and H.M.'s Governments. The Imperial Gazetteer of India, which was published in 1909, a year before Hedin's Trans-Himalaya, reflects the beginning of change in British thinking on what the Gazetteer calls "the elevated plains of Lingzithang, which lie at the extreme northeastern limit of Kashmir territory."[19] The Gazetteer laid down the Kuen Lun as the northern boundary of the plains leaving their eastern limit undefined. That disposes of Forsyth and the rest.

Earliest account of east Aksai Chin, east of 80°2'E longitude, are in the context of the Lanak la-Polur road by Johnson in 1865. Though he did not go east of the Yangi pass, he, however, confirms that the road, which he named Leh-Ilchi road, passed over "vast plains..." Over the ownership of these plains Johnson is silent. But the fact that he does not say these were Chinese or Tibetan made them Ladakhi for Forsyth had yet to pronounce the no-man's land concept. Presumably for commerce between India and Central Aisa, Johnson considered the highway best. The only difficulty he saw with regard to it was that *a portion* of the road from Spiti passed across Changthan plain of Tibet, occupied by shepherds from Rudok who had closed the route. British interest in it remained unabated because of its commercial potential. In summer the line was free of snow and not "one really difficult pass" was encountered in negotiating it. If still the road could not be commissioned, it was because the British felt thwarted by the Tibetans, the "too independent subordinates"[20] of the Chinese empire. The main line was, however, the Lanka la-Polur road, 40 miles shorter than the Yeshil Kul-

Noh bypass. Stein, who later explored and mapped the region, also called it Polur-Ladakh road and not Polur-Noh route. After crossing Ladakh's present eastern boundary pass of Lanak la, the line entered the Somjeling flat, a very long plain, and passed by the Mangtza lake, south of Aksai Chin. Beyond the lake, the road crossed an easy pass to run over a series of plateaux that comprise east Aksai Chin. Was the Lanak la-Mangtza lake section of the road in Ladakh? Yes if Aksai Chin stretched to the Lanak saddle which then ceases to be boundary pass. From the accessible maps this is, however, not clear, though by all accounts the entire road to Polur passed over Ladakh territory, British obfuscation notwithstanding. Shaw's version of the Lanak la-Polur road over east Aksai Chin is based on native accounts, like Johnson's, but no archival record of his description appears to exist. The first British version of east Aksai Chin is a brief one by Hayward. He described it to stretch far to the east. Beyond he saw a range of mountain peaks. These evidently are the sources of the Keria river, approximately 81^{0}E longitude in Deasy's map, projecting from the Kuen Lun. Hayward's impression was that the Kuen Lun sent down more spurs beyond the one is 80^{0}2'E longitude. Curiously Hayward's map omits the Aksai Chin name altogether, indicating that it was still not well known even among Englishmen. Of Kishen Singh's inaccessible diaries and reports and Shaw's native account, notice is taken by Trotter in his Yarkand mission report. These plains or plateaux, Trotter says, begin soon after the Mongtza lake. Stein also confirms this. The plain nature of the country is evident from the maps of Yarkand mission and Deasy, both prepared by the Survey of India surveyors. In 1873 'Pundit' Kishen Singh traversed this road for the Yarkand mission from Polur to Yeshil Kul and Noh, near Tibet end of the Pangong-tso. Presumably Kishen Singh made no mention of Aksai Chin. This Gore argued, was because no plain crossed this route. This is partly true as from Polur to Yeshil Kul, the road ran along or over hills. But northeast of the Mungtza towards Polur the line passed over plateaux of east Aksai Chin. This is again, albeit obliquely, confirmed by Stein. He departed from the road, two or three marches after Baba Hatim, to visit Lake Leighten. British policy then being equivocal about east Aksai Chin, Trotter put the road outside Maharaja's territories. Trotter gives the bearing of the Polur-Noh bypass as "one and a half to two degrees to the east of the most easterly road...," that is the Yangi dawan route by which Johnson travelled to Khotan. This latter line begins in 79^{0}E longitude[21]. Thus the Polur-Noh bypass ran within 80^{0}5' or 81^{0}E longitude. This puts in Ladakh the entire Aksai Chin, possibly leaving out only the mountainous region farther east than 81^{0}E longitude. Kishen Singh crossed a pass (17000 feet), 35^{0}7' north latitude, which Trotter says is the watershed of the snowy range, noticed from the boundary spur, first by Hayward and then by Hedin. From the north of the pass the Keria river takes its rise. The road to Polur followed this river down as far a Arash (16,000 feet). But again ascended the Ghubolik plain (17,000 feet), south of Polur. The map attached to the Forsyth mission report shows the northern boundary of Ladakh sharply plunge southwards 80^{0}2'E longitude to the neighbourhood of Tashliak Kul, Mangtza and the Lanak la. East Aksai Chin between 80^{0}2' and 81^{0}E longitude is not shown as part of Ladakh. The mountainous region to the east of east Aksai Chin, over which a part of the road to Polur passed, is consequently outside Ladakh. The British boundary red line sunders both from Lingzithang or western Aksai Chin. Yet east Aksai Chin is seemingly shown with its northestern boundary not about Polur but to the south of the Ghubolik plain. The British kept their options open as the map indicates, one reason why east Aksai Chin was shown as unattached or a blank. Trotter appears to have an explanation for Yarkand mission's view on east Aksai Chin. The Polur road, Trotter says, was not used for commerce because of the "fear of Chang-pas, or Tagh-lik, wandering tribe of Tartars, nominally subject to Chinese, and not because the use of the line was proscribed by the Gyalpo. The inhabitants of Keria town and Polur are credited by Trotter to have gone as far south as Ghubolik to procure sulphur. They, he says, also went west of this towards the head of the Yurungkash river where they searched for gold and jade. All these territories being south of Polur, were in Ladakh but by 1870s would appear to have been used by the Khotanese for mining. Stein in the early years of the 20th century confirmed mining of gold there by the Khotanese slave labour. Trotter credited the Khotanese to claim territory far to the south, up to Yeshil Kul! But out of fear of Chang-pas they never ventured that far south. Chang-pas too, Trotter obfuscates, feared the Turks and did not wander farther north than Rikong Chumik ridge. This ridge runs southeast to northwest and divides east Aksai Chin into two, northern and southern parts. Trotter declared the northern portion, from the ridge to the Ghubolik plain, as "neutral" territory, never occupied by one or the other party, and the southern part he assigned to Tibet. But this fanciful disposal of Aksai Chin appears to have evoked no response from the British Indian Government.

The issue of ownership of east Aksai Chin is somewhat cleared by the map of a German cartographer, Joseph Chavanne. This map, compiled in 1880, appears to show the whole of Aksai Chin, east Aksai Chin including, and the mountainous region farther east, in Ladakh 82°E longitude. Northward the boundary seems to run over the northern, and not the southern, ridge of the Kuen Lun, putting Shahidulla inside Ladakh and the boundary a little farther north. Polur and Sorghak are, agreeably with other evidence, shown on the north foot of the Kuen Lun's northern ridge. North of them and across is inscribed "Khotan."[22] This, indeed, was the boundary on the ground with Tibet and Chinese Turkistan during Maharaja Ranbir Singh's rule (1857-1885), Yarkand mission report map notwithstanding. Arrowheads are marked on the map by the Indian Ministry of External Affairs to show what is calls the "traditional Indian alignment," along 80°2'E longitude. This is the British fixed boundary of the Indian empire. It is not the historical boundary of India. From the arrowheads, placed in 1960 when the official level talks were first held, it does not seem the Ministry was, at least then, well informed about the true frontier of India in Ladakh. These, for example, divide Aksai Chin into western and eastern and leave eastern Aksai Chin out of Ladakh. Pal, far to the south, is placed well within Tibet when, as noticed earlier, it was the frontier point near Rudok, recognised by the Tibetans themselves.

The height of east Aksai Chin and the hill region to its east is 16,000 to 17,500 feet. It is somewhat green as compared with Lingzithang to the west of the Kuen Lun spur 80°2'E longitude. Water too there is little more comparatively. The only adverse factor, therefore, was its height. For these reasons Carey, who was the first European to traverse it from Lanak la to Polur in 1885, considered the route negotiable, including by a battery of artillery.[23] The Chinese, being completely ignorant of the road, panicked when he descended the Kuen Lun into Keria town. Unlike the Chinese, the Russians were aware of the road and a month before Carey's arrival at Keria Prjevalsky, the celebrated Russian explorer, had attempted to negotiate it. Another Russian, Roborovsky, Deasy latter reveals, had nearly perished in exploring the region. Though Kishen Singh was the first to explore the Polur-Noh bypass in 1873, it was Deasy who surveyed and mapped it in 1898. Deasy claimed he was not permitted by the Chow Kuan, the Chinese district magistrate of Keria, to travel to east Aksai Chin[24] by the Polur-Lanak la route. The people of Polur had petitioned him against the travel on grounds of "difficulties and dangers of the road." In Nula village Deasy was counselled that the route of Aksai Chin was impracticable and had been closed by orders." He was not allowed to repair it. Evidently Deasy's brief was to throw open the Polur-Lanak la line to traffic. British policy reversal, first noticed in Taghdumbash, had begun. For his refusal to assist in repairs to the road, the Taotai was rough shod over by Macartney in Kashgar. Russia is presented by Macartney to have pressured China to prevent Deasy's journey. China was warned Russia would interfere.[25] Russia perceived that the English had some secret intentions on Aksai Chin country and that Deasy was commissioned to open the Polur-Aksai Chin road. Yet Russia did not entirely succeed. Deasy journeyed by another route, the Keria-Sorghak-Kara Sai line to the east of the Polur-Lanak la highway. The Keria-Sorghak-Kara Sai road is placed in Deasy's map in Khotan. The ban on travel appears to have been effectively enforced by Ladakh until British intervention began in 1870, one reason why the envoy of the Khotan Badshah, Habibullah, first sent to Leh by this road, was seized and sent back in 1865. The road was seldom used and whenever used it were the Ladakhis who alone journeyed by it, evidently with the consent or on behalf of the Ladakh Government. This is established by the Chow Kuan's refusal to provide protection to Deasy beyond the limit of Keria district and his[26] readiness to permit transport of supplies by the Polur road "to meet the expected Ladakhis," journeying by east Aksai Chin. China was not apparently willing to trespass into Ladakh despite Macartney's intervention at Kashgar. While in Polur, Deasy made enquiries on the use of the road. He was informed that within living memory it were only Ladakhis who, on the rare occasions that the road was used, had crossed the mountains to Polur.[27] The rare use of the highway had thus remained within the discretion of the Ladakh authorities. The two events tend to suggest that the Chow Kuan's resistance to Deasy's travel was not entirely because of Russian pressure but also on account of the ban on the use of the road. That the prohibition on the use of the road was real is established by another event, significant in more than one way. Travelling by the Keria-Sorghak-Kara Sai route, Deasy's Khotanese carriers mutinied,[28] refusing to go beyond Kara Sai to Kumboyan, Yepal Ungur, Baba Hatim and Yeshil Kul, travel over which would have attracted penal action, the Polur-Lanak la road passing over them. Violation of the restraint was punishable with death. Chinese assertion at the official level talks in 1860 that Deasy upheld China's right over Aksai Chin thus falls flat. Their claim that sentinels had been posted to guard the road[29] is not substantiated by the accounts of Deasy, and later, of Hedin (1908) and Stein (1909).

Deasy's proceeding's help locate some boundary points in the mountainous region of east Aksai Chin. That Keria-Sorghak-Kara Sai or their neighbourhood was Ladakh's northern boundary in these parts agrees with Polur being on Ladakh boundary. Sorghak was, perhaps, visited by Kishen Singh as a boundary point rather than the site of a goldfield for there were many other goldfields in the region, notably Zailik to the southwest which he did not investigate. That the Khotanese carriers refused to go beyond Kara Sai is strong enough evidence of its being a boundary point to the east of Sorghak. Far to the south of Sorghak, Deasy noticed ruins of, probably, a fort or a military post over the Baba Hatim pass but stopped short of calling it Chinese. A firm boundary point far to the south of Baba Hatim was in the neighbourhood of Yeshil Kul lake where Deasy was arrested by Tibetan guards and, under escort, deported to Ladakh.[30] Thus between Yeshil Kul to the south and Keria-Sorhak-Kara Sai to the north, the mountainous area and east Aksai Chin were Kashmir territory or, as the British pretended, a "no man's land." That it was Kashmir territory becomes again evident from the impending policy initiatives of Sir Louis Dane and Sir Arthur MacMahon. Chinese officials in 1960 made much of the proceedings and report to the Chinese Government of Chow Kuan of Keria. While all Chinese claims are tall, the Chow Kuan himself and the Khotanese carriers by their mutiny unmistakably identified Keria-Sorghak-Kara Sai as the sourthern limit of Chinese Turkistan in this region. Again, the Chow Kuan wished Deasy to survey Khotan-Tibet boundary accurately but "on no account to place it too far south."[31] Tibet and Khotan did not then have a common boundary in the region and Aksai Chin was, indeed, too far away from Khotan.

Hedin, who twice explored Aksai Chin in 1906 and 1908, gives a figurative account of the dimensions of the eastern plateaux. Like Crosby earlier in 1903, Hedin did not travel by the Lanak la line but by the road that directly leads east from the Lingzithang plains. North of the spur 80°2'E longitude, he says "a large flat plain extends..." A march later Hedin found "the country was open eastwards to the horizon. Only in the far distance one snowy mountain appeared in this direction but the longitudinal valley extended along the north or south side..." Again he notes, "Far in the east the country is quite open. Here giants riding on Indian elephants would have room enough to play a game of polo in grand style, and the swift footed 'jambas' dromedaries might run till they were tired, for even the restless west wind finds no obstacle in its path."[32] In this valley, he suspected lake Leighten, Yeshil Kul and Pul-tso to lay. Here Hedin came across the typical Ladakhi fauna, the kayangs and antelopes but of human beings he saw not a sign. Like the other parts of

Aksai Chin, the eastern plains contain several lakes, mostly of brackish water. Of these an important lake is the Leighten at the eastern end of the valley. A little beyond eastwards, nestling in the hills, is the Yeshil Kul. The Leighten lake to the south and the Keria river to the north between them divide the "imperceptible" drainage. Westward of the Leighten lake, British maps of the 19th century showed the high plain as "Aksai Chin desert" but a later day trans-frontier map of the Survey of India, Stein says, "rightly"[33] showed it as an unsurveyed blank. The sources of the Yurungkash river are to the west of the Keria. Indian officials were aware in 1960 that the river's catchment area was very much in Ladakh until 1820. The boundary then rested on the north ridge of the Kuen Lun. The area thereafter appears to have been selectively encroached upon by the Turks of Khotan. Towards the end of the 19th century mining of gold at Zailik, near the upper stream of the Yurungkash, was certainly carried on by Turks rather than the Ladakhis. The ascendancy of the British in Ladakh after 1870s might well have induced the boundary in the northeast to be gradually encroached upon from Polur southwards as in the Karakoram pass region. Hedin, however, clearly places the "frontier of Yarkand" north of the Kuen Lun[34] in this region. The Jammu and Kashmir Government's land settlement report for Ladakh for the Year 1908 puts the entire Lingzithang, western and northeastern, within India as a look at the settlement map unmistakably reveals, but excludes the Aksai Chin further east, beyond 80⁰2'E longitude.[35] Was the boundary shown with the free consent of the State whose Maharaja remained deposed and whose previous representations on Chinese encroachments into Shahidulla and Sogat first and the Karakoram later were cast into the dustbin of history? Even the inclusion of northeastern Aksai Chin in Ladakh probably followed Dane's initiatives. It is not unlikely the State was not permitted to undertake settlement operations in east Aksai Chin. On the road, traversing the east Aksai Chin plains, Hedin says Keria la was known to the Chinese in 1791. De Rhins claimed that this road really went from the Pangong-tso and Noh to Tengri Nor from Polur. But this line between the Keria la and Noh was far too circuitous and two or three days journey longer than the main Lanak la-Keria la route and on this score alone unacceptable as a line of contact or commerce. Hedin also refers to Professor George Wagener to suggest that emperor Chin Lung opened the road as a line of commerce from Lhasa[36]. Deasy saw no trace even of such a line. Even if opened, the road was never in use, a fact attested to by Moorcroft in 1820. He only states that the route was used by Moghals.

Stein, who followed Hedin into these bleak areas and surveyed and mapped them, significantly calls the territories, southwestward of the watershed of the Keria river, as Aksai Chin. From Stein's account east Aksai Chin appears to be six marches[37] or 90 to 120 mile long. He returned to western Ladakh crossing the spur 80°2'E longitude into the neighbourhood of Amtogor lake where now the Chinese road from the Yangi dawan forks and then leads to the Lanak la to the south. Stein's finding and of Hedin earlier admit that Aksai Chin did not end with the spur falling southeast from the Kuen Lun but extends well beyond 81°E longitude to the sources of the Keria to the north and Baba Hatim to the east. The division of Aksai Chin was, therefore, artificial and arbitrary and the northeastern limit of Ladakh reached well beyond 80°2' to 82°E longitude. The British boundary policy then was not to commit themselves to any definite limits to the north and northeast in Jammu and Kashmir. This is also evident in the map of Eastern Turkistan in the Aitchison's Treaties, 1909 print. The map shows east Aksai Chin a blank or no-man's land. Montgomerie's map, therefore, indefinitely ended in the margin, the Polur-Yeshil Kul section of the road shown dotted or uncertain. For this very reason Gore ignored the descriptive of Trotter and the Yarkand Mission Report map to claim that "there is no Aksai Chin to the east of the spur above mentioned." Tibet had no commercial or any other contact with Khotan, an Islamic country. Whatever trade was carried on by the Lanak la-Polur line was that between Ladakh and Khotan, which itself must have been insignificant, as and when it flourished. But the route was historically seen and used as a military road. Gore, therefore only confuses. He concluded his note to Government causing greater confusion : "...there is a plain south of the Kuen Lun somewhere east of Thaldat and west of the dividing spur which runs south from the Kuen Lun in about 80°25' which is called Aksai Chin." This, of course, is at least, part of what the British called northern or northeastern Aksai Chin. Based on the views of Strahan and Gore, the British Indian Foreign Department concluded : "Aksai Chin implies 'the Great *Chinese* white desert.' There is no certainty as to its dimensions." Montgomerie had merely called it Aksai Chin (white desert). The Foreign Department made it "Chinese." Aksai Chin's dimensions also were uncertain to the Foreign Department. Yet the boundary was soon to be fixed having definite coordinates. Rather generously the British, for their political compulsions, conceded that "a portion (of Aksai Chin) undoubtedly lies within the boundary *claimed* by Kashmir." What was this boundary that Kashmir claimed if not whole of Aksai Chin, western, northern and eastern? At best this was the British policy in 1898 and 1899. In the next few years for the very Russian factor, which they had dreaded that far, British boundary policy was to swing to the other extreme-seeking to incorporate every nook and corner of Jammu and Kashmir into the British empire.

The issue of the ownership of Aksai Chin would have rested where Strahan and Gore had claimed it to be but for the emergence of a new factor that altogether changed British perceptions and, ultimately, British policy on the boundary. Perceptive Englishmen, Ardagh and Curzon, had anticipated Russian interest in Tibet. Dorjiev (Dorji), a Buriat Mongol from Russian Central Asia, who had arrived in Tibet in 1880 to study Buddhism at the Drepung monastery, came to wield enormous influence over the Dalai Lama in the closing years of the 19th century that alarmed the British Indian Government and, indeed, the Whitehall itself no less[38]. Deasy's surveys and mapping of the mountainous region, east of the road to Polur, and east Aksai Chin were conducted in this background. British interest in the Polur-Lanak la line, its bypass and in and near Aksai Chin areas was more than commercial though well suited the road was to the interests of commerce. Yet for 180 years its use had remained proscribed. Even so Hedin specifically mentions that the Keria pass was "well known to the Ladakhis and natives of Eastern Turkistan."[39] It was the possible military use of the road that worried the British for it was by this line that Sultan Said of Kashgaria had wished to join Mirza Haidar in Ladakh. It indicates, as Holdich points out, "that this road was a recognised route then..."[40] It is now certain that the belief of Dzungars, under Tsringdondob, advanced through Lingzithang or Western Aksai Chin to the Lanak la to invade Tibet in 1716-17 is incorrect[41]. Petech agrees with Hedin that the route for this invasion of Tibet was the Polur-Lanak la line[42]. Despite serious difficulties, chiefly on account of elevation, 6000 Dzungars, armed with swivel guns and mounted on camels[43], had successfully negotiated the road. The difficulties encountered were less than those confronted in the Lingzithang plateaux. The Dzungars took road and succeeded, Mirza Haidar advised Sultan Said to avoid using the Ladakh routes, including the Polur-Lanak la highway. The only hard part of this line, Hedin considered, was that between Selling-tso and Yeshil Kul, south of the Keria la. The route running diagonally, linked Lhasa with Khotan, passing over the Naktsang province.

Such a road in Russian hands would have put paid to British influence in Tibet, whatever it was, and the security of the British empire would have been seriously threatened. The question arises if the Dzungars invaded Tibet by the Polur-Lanak la road why were the neighbouring

Changchenmo lines, eastern and western, running across the Lingzithang plateaux proscribed? The answer may well be that Polur-Lanak la road lay over Aksai Chin across which also ran the Changchenmo roads. These routes were, therefore, a single line. From the accounts of travellers, explorers and surveyors it is evident that by whatever name they called them, the plateaux were one. To prevent roads from Central Asia converging directly on Indian territory, the British contrived a Turkish name for Lingzithang to obliquely suggest it was not a part of Ladakh but of Eastern Turkistan. They then assiduously built up their records to suggest Ladakh's eastern limit terminates at 80^{0}2'E longitude for which there is no independent evidence on record. It is for the first reason China claims that Aksai Chin is in Eastern Turkistan, not in Tibet though geographers are unanimous that these plateaux are a continuation of the great Changthang plain of Tibet, politically separated since the treaty of Tingmosgong of 1683.

For better or for worse–for worse it has now turned out–China, for this reason, emerged as a factor for settling an unsettled boundary. The actual boundary line proposed by Ardagh started from the peak Povalo Scheikovsky (Little Pamir) included in the basins of the Dangabash and its affluents above Dafdar in the Taghdumbash Pamir. It then took in Raskam district and the whole of the Karakash valley, including Shahidulla, to put the frontier back on the Kuen Lun[44]. Only Sirikul was left out. Were China to resist such a line, Ardagh's alternative boundary was to leave out Raskam and the Karakash valley, including Shahidulla. This latter line with Lord Elgin's concurrence was proposed to the Secretary of State for India. The Kuen Lun line would have been "strongly resented"[45] by China. It might, it was feared, "precipitate Russian advance" than put (England) in good position[46]. The boundary proposals from the Viceroy to the Secretary of State for India required to be explained on a large scale map. The Foreign Department had a map, based on the views of Younghusband from Hunza eastwards to 76^{0}E, that is a little to the east of Shangshal. Surprisingly beyond this point no large scale map was available to trace the boundary of Aksai Chin eastward. Besides how far east was the boundary to be drawn on a new map? Cunningham saw the frontier involved was that between Kashmir and Khotan alone[47]. Quite evidently Tibet was far to the south, 35^{0}N latitude, to have had common boundary with India south of the Kuen Lun. So was Khotan far to the north, 37^{0}N latitude. If still Khotan was acceptable, it was because China was amenable to British influence. It would have been, as the British themselves observed, "imprudent to start any boundary question with regions of Tibet." This perception of Tibet, however, soon changed. But how far north did Tibet reach to its northwest? This, probably, was one of the issues to be settled by Deasy's and, later, by Hedin's explorations. Strahan helped to construct the boundary line on a small map beyond Shangshal along the watershed up to 79°E longitude[48]. With the aid of another old small map by Trotter the frontier line was carried forward from 79°E, a little above 35°N latitude, along the Laktsung hills to meet the spur running south-east from the Kuen Lun range, which on British maps, it was pronounced, "forms the boundary between China and Kashmir[49]." There was no compelling reason for the British as then to commit themselves on the whole northern boundary in Jammu and Kashmir. Their immediate problem had been to effectively cover up to so-called gap. That the Pamir Commission had ensured. Yet Cunningham, contrary to considered British policy to leave out, from immediate consideration, Aksai Chin, a "no man's land tending to be Kashmir's," rushed the issue. He thus foreclosed British options to meet any future contingency that might threaten the British empire in India as soon occurred in Tibet. This was particularly relevant to Ladakh's northeastern limit. Needlessly, Cunningham placed the boundary over the Laktsung hills and the spur falling from the Kuen Lun. This fictitious boundary line is the genesis of the Chinese claim against India.

In less than a decade highly place Englishmen from the Viceroy, Lord Hardinge, to Sir Arthur McMahon, looked askance at this tactical limit when they perceived Russia threatening India from both Kashgaria and Tibet. Otherwise too it was unconvincing. In Hedin's tracing, two spurs, at a considerable distance from each other, are thrown from the Kuen Lun into Aksai Chin. Why was the first, or the western, and not the second, the eastern, near Lake Leighten 81°5'E, the boundary? The jugglery over the maps and over the spur was too obviously to keep out both the northeastern and the further east Aksai Chin from Jammu and Kashmir. Through northeastern Aksai Chin ran two routes, from the Hindutash and Yangi passes while through east Aksai Chin passed the more important and militarily strategic Lanak la-Polur line. The boundary thus finalised was short of what even Hung Ta-Chen had in 1893 acknowledged was the northeastern limit of Jammu and Kashmir. That itself was not the historical boundary line.

From an assortment of maps the Survey Department prepared a single map showing the proposed boundary from the Peak Povalo Schveikovsky to the point $80^{0}2'E$ and $35^{0}N$ where the Laktsung range joins the spur running southeast from the Kuen Lun "which spur is now regarded as the eastern boundary of Kashmir."[50] From the Peak Povalo Schveikovsky the finalised boundary has already been noticed up to the Karakoram pass. From this pass the boundary followed the crest of the Karakoram ridge for half a degree, and then turned south a little below the 36th parallel. Rounding then what in the British maps was shown as the source of the Karakash river, the boundary ran northeast to a point east of Kizil Jilga in central Lingzithang plains and from thence went in a south-easterly direction to the Lakstung hills until that meets the spur running southeast from the Kuen Lun, a little farther than 80^{0} E longitude[51]. But political developments overturned this boundary proposal. The turn of the century saw the collapse of Chinese central authority (1900). Kashgaria exclusively came within the Russian sphere of influence.[52] In Tibet England's response was the Younghusband military expedition to Lhasa in 1904. Within Kashgaria, Russia sought to move towards Khotan, just north of Aksai Chin. As a counter, Sir Louis Dane, Secretary, Foreign Department, proposed "a move into western Tibet" what with Britain admittedly at war with Lhasa. A preliminary step to this he saw in the completion of the Hindustan-Tibet road, which had been left incomplete to spare Tibetan susceptibilities. Once the road was complete upto the Shipki la on the boundary, "we might then be able to establish the Kuen Lun range as our future frontier,"[53] confidently Dane asserted, reviving, in effect, the Ardagh proposal and going beyond. One change he, nevertheless, contemplated in the Ardagh line. West of Aksai Chin, unlike Ardagh, Dane implied the Karakoram-Muztagh would remain the boundary. To the Viceroy, Dane explained that the arguments against the adoption of the Kuen Lun as the "ultimate frontier of India," north of Kashmir, "do not apply with the same force farther eastward..." The British, notably, Salisbury, had recognised that it would be impossible to allow Russian influence to be firmly established in Tibet on the northern glacis of the Himalaya. What Dane favoured was thus not only restoration of the Kuen Lun boundary over Aksai Chin but extending this boundary to

> "...the desert waste between this and the inhabited portion of Tibet which is, at present, practically a no man's land..."[54]

Dane imagined Russia at any moment occupying Kashgaria and, as the inheritor of Chinese claims, to fill up the "blank," or the "no man's land" of east Aksai Chin desert, "if we have not anticipated her by establishing our influence in Western Tibet..." Opposed as it still was to the dominant British thinking, Dane's proposition appeared inconceivable to the stop-gap Viceroy, Lord Amphill. "I cannot for a moment regard," Lord Ampthill minuted, "the extension of our frontier towards the Kuen Lun mountains and annexation of Western Tibet as within the sphere of practical policy." His reason Ampthill revealed. "His Majesty's Government would have a fit if we proposed anything of the kind and the unanimous voice of the British nation would be against it."[55] Nevertheless the British Indian army establishment admitted that in a military sense "it would be highly disadvantageous to us for Russia to penetrate into western Tibet or even as far as Khotan and that the Kuen Lun range is theoretically an admirable barrier to such pretensions." But it saw the proposition would involve extending "existing liabilities and means."[56] Nor did Dane's view find favour with Lord Kitchener, Commander-in-Chief[57]. The Royal Geographical Journal for June 1904 coincidently published a paper by the American traveller, Crosby, who had explored east Aksai Chin. It was Crosby's view "that the Tibetan northern plateau with its escarpment, the Kuen Lun range, may well be taken as bulwark and barrier between two great empires" British and Russian. With this view of Crosby, the President of the Royal Geographical Society concurred[58]. Younghusband, who had emerged as Britain's "authority" on India's northern boundary, saw the Kuen Lun as "our dipomatic frontier"[59] farther east in Tibet, hinting occupation of east Aksai Chin by Tibet. A related consideration for Dane to draw attention to Aksai Chin was British keenness to define the northern limits of Tibet now that Russia was advancing towards it.

Western Tibet that Dane had proposed England should annex was not Tibetan territory. It was east Aksai Chin, including the hilly region over which ran the road from Khotan via Polur, and, perhaps, some adjoining Tibet territory. Occupation of this Kashmir territory or, as Dane later clarified, extension of British influence to it, would have interposed England between Russian held Khotan and Tibet blocking the Polur-Lanak la-Noh route. If the semi-nomadic Dzungar tribesmen with their primitive organisation could achieve the almost impossible feat of successfully invading Tibet in 1717 from the northwest could not Russia with the means of a modern State at her disposal succeed in a similar exercise? It was asked. Given its strategic significance in the context of Khotan and Tibet, Aksai Chin emerged as a pawn the and Anglo-Russian imperial game. Contemporary proceedings on map making, including over a map of the northwest frontier of India for England's Parliament members, abundantly reveals perceptible change in British thinking. Dane wanted the map for Parliament members to be so colour washed as to leave Shahidulla as the first Kashgar post. Thence the boundary was to run along the Kuen Lun leaving Lingzithing in Kashmir and (east) Aksai Chin doubtful[60]. The western half of Lingzithang was to be colour-washed. This boundary line was contrary to 1898 proposals made to the Secretary of State and proposed by Macdonald to China in 1899. In these proposals only western Lingzithang had been proposed to be retained. For the rest of Aksai Chin India was not to have even a "doubtful" claim. The Foreign Department agreed that there was considerable evidence, though of "ancient date," of Kashmir claims to western Aksai Chin. Justification was seen, therefore, to colour wash this area "to the Kuen Lun range on the north and as far to the east as is shown on the old map of Turkistan, i.e., up to the range dipping first southeast and then southwest, then southeast again from the Kuen Lun."[61]

To such a boundary line "north of the Karakoram," Clarke in the Foreign Department was opposed, pointing out the Chinese had erected "a boundry pillar on the pass in 1890[62]." But this argument was rejected by Dane. In a map where Chinese and Russian pretension were concerned, Dane wished, "we should be careful not to cut down our claims." For defensive purposes too he considered it desirable that "we should hold as large a stretch of the Karakoram waste as possible to prevent others improving the road and so reducing the difficulties of access." These very arguments had poor Ramsay pressed on Sir Mortimer Durand only to be rebuffed time and again. Regrettably the British had surrendered sovereign rights in Raskam and Dane saw no reason "why we should give up any more especially as we have Times Atlas to support us."[63] Probably to bring about greater agreement among Englishmen who had influenced decision making on the northern boundary, Younghusband, Resident in Kashmir, was asked "what the *true* boundary of Kashmir is." The boundary marked by Dane on his map was from Gasherbrum, west of the Muztagh, Kashmir Jilga, southwest of Shahidulla, Sogat, southeast of Shahidulla, and thence along the Kuen Lun ridge via Khushk Maidan, taking in the whole of western Aksai Chin, the line going east thereafter. Younghusband's boundary was not entirely truthful. He stuck to the line from the Karakoram, rounding the Karakash source, but thereafter ran it east slightly different than the Laktsung limit[64]. Clarke favoured Younghusband's line on the ground that it agreed with the boundary proposed to the Secretary of State[65]. But Dane, while agreeable to eastern boundary of Ladakh being as shown, sought to know Younghusband's reasons for his northern boundary of Kashmir[66]. Surely Younghusband was bound to consult old Gazetteers and ascertain the present practice as to jurisdiction, factors which British officers had continued to ignore. Clearly Dane wished Younghusband to fall in line with his views. If necessary a considered response from Younghusband, Dane suggested, could wait till a Russian officer, then in India, was conducted through Ladakh to Kashgaria which would provide an opportunity for ascertaining limits of Chinese jurisdiction. Younghusband's considered response was, however, no more encouraging than his initial one. He had marked the boundary on the basis of what "appeared" to be the watershed. Besides, he pointed out, there was not a single Kashmir subject in Lingzithang for the Kashmir Government to have jurisdiction over[67]. Whether there were any Chinese subjects in Lingzithang, Younghusband was silent about. Silent also Younghusband was on as to whether China had acquired any jurisdiction south of Shahidulla, since it occupation by her in 1889, or attained any claim to territories bordering the Karakoram more substantial than a mere notice board or a boundary pillar on the pass[68]. After the passage of the Russian officer, Younghusband admitted there was no Chinese subject living until Sogat was reached and even there Chinese presence was limited to fair weather season, as had been Kashmir's at Shahidulla. When some years later the De Filippi expedition descended down the north face of the Karakoram to explore the upper Yarkand valley and beyond the western and northeastern Aksai Chin no passports were sought. De Filippi just did not see the Chinese anywhere[69]. The argument among Englishmen was however, cut short by the Secretary of State for India. The boundary line was once again to be pulled back to the Karakoram. Its return to the Kuen Lun crest could have been prompted by only one consideration, to revive, in course of time, Kashmir's "doubtful" claim to east Aksai Chin with the intention to interpose British territory between Khotan and Tibet. If this premise is correct—and there is reason to believe correct it is—then the British imposed limit of Kashmir's territory at 80°2E is proved to be arbitrary and Kashmir territory did reach out to Lake Leighten, beyond 81°E, and to Yeshil Kul itself farther than 82°E Longitude. Lake Leighten is very much in eastern Aksai Chin while Yeshil Kul nestles in the hills to the east of the Leighten. Such a northeastern boundary puts the entire Polur-Lanak la road in Jammu and Kashmir territory. Stein gives the northwesternmost limit of Tibet to have been the southern chain in the Kuen Lun astride which is the Baba Hatim pass. But this is clearly an exaggeration. One point is significant. While both Wellby and Stein freely travelled upto Lake

Leighten, Deasy was seized by Tibetan guards in the neighbourhood of Yeshil Kul. The watershed between the Keria river to the north and the Lake Leighten is around an elevation south of the Keria's sources. On the high plain east Aksai Chin itself drains into the Leighten, as Stein found[70].

Dane failed because he could not move British policy makers to abandon a policy that had earned England nothing but enmity of native Indian States, notably Kashmir. A change in policy did not, however, take long to come about. Developments hastened it. Longstaff's discovery knocked out the Karakoram as the watershed. A state of anarchy prevailed in Chinese Turkistan after the revolution and entry of Russian troops. British feared Russian occupation would be permanent.[71]. England was unwilling militarily to get involved and, therefore, virtually became reconciled to Russian occupation of Sinkiang. All she sought, as a memo by R.T. Nugent of the British Foreign Office, reveals, was "adequate compensation elsewhere,"[72] in Tibet specifically as Secretary of State for India, Lord Crewe, suggested. A solution was seen by the Foreign Office in reaching a new Anglo-Russian convention on this basis with a clause regulating and defining the Mir of Hunza's rights in Raskam and the Taghdumbash Pamir and the still more shadowy claims of the Chinese Government in Hunza (to which the Russian Government would presumably succeed)." Such a convention involved change in the status of Tibet. Justification for this was seen in (1) China's own forward policy, that is making her hold over Tibet effective from nominal, her weakness and friendliness of the Dalai Lama to the British and (2) Russia's forward policy, or advance, in to Mongolia and the New Dominion. China was, therefore, categorically told England would "refuse to tolerate any attempt on their part to consolidate their administration in Tibet and limit the extent of their relations with the Tibetan authorities..." The second and, perhaps, more potent reasons "for utilising this moment for a forward movement in Tibet, is the forward movement of Russia in Mongolia and the New Dominion," a second Foreign Office paper discloses.[73] To counter Russia in Eastern Turkistan, Sir Arthur MacMahon, Secretary. Foreign Department, considered it necessary in the first place "to obtain a frontier more satisfactory to us and our interests than the existing India-China boundary." Britain, he wrote, must claim the Taghdumbash Pamir and Raskam in the interests of Hunza and Shahidulla in those of Kashmir. Hunza had acknowledged rights in the two former places

> "and Shahidulla properly belongs to Kashmir who occupied it until 1890 when the Chinese took advantage

> of Kashmir's carelessness (!) to build a post there. We somewhat carelessly refrained from protest (!)"[74]

The boundary line proposed by Ardagh on military considerations in 1897 was seen by MacMahon to "exactly suit our political requirements and is the boundary which we should claim from Russia as a preliminary to any other negotiations respecting New Dominion." Return of Aksai Chin was to be without the usual limit in the east to the Laktsung hills and the spur. This implied inclusion of east Aksai Chin right up to and including Yeshil Kul. Lord Hardinage agreed, calling the proposals respecting the frontier as "appropriate."[75] To avoid past disagreements McMahon made it clear that no boundary posts were visualised to be set up in the intervening territories sought to be restored to Jammu and Kashmir. This ensured concurrence of the Military as their resources were not to be stretched. Politically, McMahon considered the proposed boundary rectification as "most important," as safeguarding the interests of Jammu and Kashmir and Hunza "while interposing a further barrier of barren, inhospitable country between ourselves and Russian territory."[76] The barren, inhospitable country was the entire Aksai Chin or nearly so. The Army Department and the Commander-in-Chief, Mcreagh, agreed.[77] In the event of the Russian annexation of Eastern Turkistan, the first step (as a preliminary to negotiations) was seen by Hardinge and conveyed by him to the Secretary of State for India, as "recognition of a boundary line which will place. Taghdumbash, Raskam, Shahidulla and Aksai Chin within our and outside Russian territory." To obtain this object, the Viceroy revived the Ardagh line of 1897. The Secretary of State was conveyed :

> "A good line would be one commencing from Paik peak, running eastward to Chang pass, leaving Taghdumbash and Dehda (Dafdar) on British side, thence along crest of range through Sargon pass and crossing Yarkand river to crest Kuen Lun range north of Raskam and along crest of the range through...Kukahang, Dozak, Yangi, Kilik passes to Sanju or Grim (Walaghat) from there along Kuen Lun watershed to Tibet frontier crossing Karakash river, including Aksai Chin plain in British territory[78]."

This, indeed, was very largely but not completely the historical boundary as it had existed and was recognised before British intervention began in the 19th century. Only Sirikul it left outside India and did not specifically mention the eastern limit of Aksai Chin. But without east

Aksai Chin, it would not have been possible to interpose British territory between India and lately arrived Russia in Khotan. There is, besides, ample archival evidence to suggest that, like Dane earlier, McMahon was keen to restore entire Aksai Chin to Jammu and Kashmir so as to thrust it between Khotan and Tibet. Besides, Hardinge vent his fear that Russia would reopen "the old Khotan trade route–Polur road–to stifle India's Tibet trade. This boundary line appears to have been again pressed upon the Secretary of State for India by the Viceroy in a telegram dated the 14th October 1915. What then was the status of northern boundary line of India in Jammu and Kashmir? This is well argued by Denys Bray, Foreign Secretary to the British Indian Government, in a letter to J.E. Shuchkburgh, Secretary, Political Department, India Office, London, dated 7th September 1917 in connection with the arrest of two German military officers south of the Yarkand river, in Raskam valley. Bray remarked "These (boundary) limits, however, exist only on paper and have been indicated by us not as the result of any treaty or engagement with China, nor as finally and definitely marking the bounds of our sphere of influence, nor altogether as forming a scientific or strategic border but partly because they follow a lofty and well defined watershed and partly in order to assign some limit to China's indefinite political relations in that neighbourhood."[79] Recalling the Macdonald proposals, their virtual rejection by China and the new basis for negotiation twice proposed by Hardinge, Bray contended the Government of India could not be regarded as absolutely bound by a border line

> "Which we have ourselves laid down without the concurrence of the other partly concerned, which we have already more than once altered, without reference to this other party, and the substantial pushing forward of which we have already advocated..."

It was, as Bray aptly summed up the argument, "our self-imposed boundary."

The ground situation was that the boundary line ran eastward from the Paik peak of the Sirikul (Bolor west) range to the Mintaka, Kilik, Khanjerab and Shangshal, descended northward to incorporate Raskam in Hunza, returned to the Hindu Kush-Karakoram range west of Muztagh, thence ran eastwards to the Karakoram pass, over this ridge north-eastward to the Kuen Lun, eastward to 80°2'E before turning south. On the upper Yarkand valley, Lord Lansdowne's stipulation that it could only be disposed of with the consent of India remained operative. The state of the boundary is best expressed by Wood in a communication in

1923 to the Surveyor General of India "...the boundary between Chinese Turkistan, and Kashmir is indefinite."[80] Clearly China's possession of areas north of the Karakoram is not recognised. Dr. Emil Trinkler, a German geologist, probably the last foreigner to investigate the Lingzithang plains, east and west, or Aksai Chin, did not find any Chinese there in 1927[81]. So the northern boundary in Jammu and Kashmir rested until Chinese encroachments began in 1950s leading to subsequent large scale annexations.

The boundary dispute is, but ought not to be, limited to territories China either surreptitiously or forcibly seized between 1954 and 1962. A large one the territorial conflict is, related as it is to the vast areas that England persuaded China to occupy until 1890s after which British policy on the northern limits of India dramatically changed in favour of reverting to the Kuen Lun as the boundary in the north. It is evident that these areas, notably Aksai Chin, vast in extent, are not real estate, an aspect that is best reflected in the British coined phrase "not a blade of grass grows" in them, which Nehru, at the height of the Sino-Indian boundary crisis of early 1960s, borrowed. The British, wishing to unburden themselves of other people's territories, had reason to indulge in such semantics. Nehru had only his failure to hide. Principal problem in Lingzithang is its height, 16,000 to 17,000 feet, and lack of fresh water and, therefore, of vegetation. In the Taghdumbash Pamir and Little Pamir, cold is exacerbated by high velocity winds. Vohab is largely rocky and no less wind swept. Comparatively, therefore, the most hospitable lands are the Karakash valley, the Raskam and above all, Sirikul. Permanent human habitations could be, and must have been, extended in these valleys and highlands since these came to be occupied by China. Present day technologies can regain considerable tracts of these lands for productive purposes. Yet with all the severity of the elements, nature has not altogether made them the lands of dolorous that Hedin represented Lingzithang, at least, to be.

Nature has gifted them with immense wealth which, despite exploitation, must remain substantial. For ages the Kuen Lun range of mountains has been noted for mineral wealth. So also the Hindu Kush and the Pamirs. As early as 1859 Captain Reverty, a surveyor, specifically mentioned Gilgit, Chitral, Yasin, Hunza and Nagar as sources of gold. Prospects of discovery of gold in Hunza and Nagar are far greater[82]. Gold was collected in these little principalities from river-beds. It was this gold that the Rajas of Hunza and Nagar sent as tribute to the Maharaja of Jammu and Kashmir. Johnson was the first in the 19th century to speak of the wealth of the Kuen Lun in gold, silver, iron, lead, copper, antimony, salt, soda, sulphur, saltpetre and even coal[83]. Rock salt is found in the Yarkand valley. Gold was so abundant that while it sold in Khotan for Rs. 9 to Rs. 10 per "tola" (about 12 grams), it fetched in Kashmir Rs. 17 to Rs. 18 per "tola." On his way to Khotan, Johnson saw the Yongpa river-bed goldfield in the Kuen Lun[84]. Presence of gold and copper in the Kuen Lun range was also noticed by Albert Verchere, a geologist, of which he makes a reference in the Journal of the Asiatic Society in 1868[85]. The Thokjalong goldfield was a celebrated one. It was with this gold that coin was stuck in the name of Aurangzeb on the conclusion of the peace treaty of Tingmosogong in 1683. This mine is now in Tibet. Another and equally well worked goldfield was the Zailik mine near the headwaters of the Yurungkash river. Exploring the sources of the Yurungkash in the Kuen Lun mountains in 1906-08 Stein went up the upper most gorge and found the Zailik valley with extensive gold pits bored into precipitous cliffs of conglomerates, evidently worked since long ages[86].

As noted earlier soda was mined in Lingzithang and its neighbourhood. Bellew proceeding to Yarkand with the Forsyth mission in 1873 was informed that some 2,40,000 lbs of soda had that year been collected in the adjoining areas of Nubra for despatch to Kashmir[87]. In the Yarkand valley there were several sites where ferrous and non-ferrous ores had been mined and smelted in local furnaces. One such site Younghusband mentions was Karash Tarim[88]. There copper and iron were mined. In Bazar Dara there were traces of gold. The jude mine near Shahidulla was noticed by every European traveller. Grombtchevsky, who also visited the mine, thought it was "very insignificant" as compared with the "massive rocks of jade sticking out of water at Pil (Tash-Khan), on the left bank of the Raskam[89]. Deposits of rock salt were known to occur in the Yarkand valley. It was, probably, this salt that Kanjutis mined in the Ghorzerab valley for their use. Curzon's map of the Yarkand valley indicated occurrence of petroleum. Even more significant than all these mineral resources of Lingzithang, the Yarkand valley, Hunza and Nagar, are the reportedly extensive deposits of radio-active minerals, notably uranium, in the Vohab plateau. China was reported to be mining this uranium north of the Karakoram. Of this mining the Soviets were aware as early as 1950s.

A highway led in the last century from Hunza over the Sirikul plain to the Alai, far to the north. A branch route from Shahidulla joined it in Sirikul. This is the line that India can easily build as a commercial road to Central Asia, were the territories now under *de facto* control of China wrested from her. Through Lingzithang, Yarkand valley and Sirikul, India could reach Kirzil Art and beyond to Osh and the Alai in present day Tajikistan. This Central Asian highway could run over the Karakoram pass, which is practically free of snow, to Shahidulla, Kirghiz Jungle, down the Yarkand river to the Alai. A variation could be a railway line from Leh to the Pangong lake, Lanak la and across the Lingzithang plains to Shahidulla. The Karakoram highway recently built by China from Kashgar to Gilgit is part of the road to the Alai over which Colonel Yonoff had staged his *promenade militaire*. Its alignment from Kashgar appears to be over the Gez defile and then by Sirikul and the Khanjerab river to Ujadbai. Thereafter it, ascends the Hindu Kush, crossing it by the Khanjerab pass, 15,800 feet, into Hunza and along the Hunza river to Gilgit. By far the easiest route will be the Lanak la-Polur line which could extend direct to Rampur in Himachal Pradesh. Any or all these highways will give India direct access to Central Asia, relieving her of dependence on Iran through which trade is, at present, carried on. The commercial and political impact of such an Indian road will be a factor in international relations.

19th century witnessed intense rivalry, commercial, political and military, between England and Russia in Central Asia to which China was a mute witness and, sometimes, courtesy Britain, a rival of Russia. After 1950s Anglo-Russian contest has come to be replaced by Sino-Indian rivalry with Pakistan playing supporting role to China. Though Moorcroft was the first in recent times to grasp the strategic importance of Ladakh in the context of China, yet it had long before been underscored by the Tibetans; Moorcroft's analysis of Ladakh's significance in any conflict against China remains valid today, 177 years after he wrote his memorable despatches to the East India Company's officials. Indeed Ladakh has emerged even more important now, in the later half of the 20th century, than it was Moorcroft's time. This is so because Ladakh is central to India's defences. It was not for its unproductive deserts that China seized Lingzithang in late 1950s and followed this seizure with the annexation of the Changchenmo valley and its neighbouring areas. A look at the map reveals that China has thus strengthened her position in Xinjiang, eliminating any potential intervention or subversion from the south, that is from Ladakh or Gilgit. Even more China has achieved. Any threat, real or imaginary, of Indian intervention in Tibet to restore to this helpless country it natural and traditional status of a true buffer State or of containing any Chinese threat to northern India, from the Lanak la to the Nathu la, has been eliminated. It is India—not China notwithstanding an unsure hold over Xinjiang and Tibet—which is militarily at a disadvantage all along the long, tenuous boundary line between the two countries. In any future hostilities China can attack India at will by the Junglang high road, Demchok, Shipki la—the Hindustan—Tibet road—and the Niti route—the Mughal road. The airfields China has built in Lingzithang, or in Tibet itself, bring northern India well within their striking distances, assuming hostilities will be limited to conventional warfare. Restore Lingzithang to India and the Chinese stand outflanked. A mere brigade of well equipped troops over the Lanak la and another in Gilgit can achieve this. Kao had this military strength during his campaign. Sitting pretty in Tibet, China dominates not only India but also south and south-east-Asia. From a military point of view, therefore, passession of Lingzithang is of supreme importance to India. In fact India cannot feel safe as long as China remains in Tibet. This is the cru of the boundary dispute. It has nothing to do, as some analysts in India presume, with China lacking a direct road link between Tibet and Xinjiang. Such a road exists via Keria, Sorghak, Kara Sai. The road probably ends in mountainous northern Tibet. Be that as it may, no self-respecting sovereign country can allow seizure of territories for such or any other purpose.

By herself, mutual confidence building measures notwithstanding, China will never leave Lingzithang, Vohab, the Yarkand valley, Taghdumbash and Sirikul so as to restore India's northern boundary to its historically appointed place–the crests of the Kuen Lun and Bolor ranges. China will need to be coerced to secure the return of Lingzithang, or her hold on Tibet and Xinjiang has to break down. Much, therefore, depends on the future of China herelf. India by herself has, as yet, hardly any credible option. And when she has, India could denounce the Tingmosgong treaty of 1683, which China any way has violated, and lay claim to western Tibet which even Dane had contemplated India-China negotiations must, in the meanwhile, take note of British stipulations under which the surreptitious give-away of the trans-Karakoram-Hindu Kush Indian territories took place. One stipulation, first pronounced by Lord Lansdowne and repeated in one form or another by the British Indian Foreign Department, was that the rights of China to these territories were not absolute but conditional. Reversion of these territories to India was very much envisaged. The other condition was that the relative boundary rights of India and China in the Karakoram region were to be determined by a boundary delimitation commission. Here the British gave themselves enough elbow-room to have as much of the Ardagh boundary as possible. Ardagh doctrine, therefore, remains relevant to any boundary settlement in Jammu and Kashmir.

References

1. 15th October 1896. Foreign. Secret. F. No. KW. 2-160-169 of January 1898.
2. 14th December 1896. Foreign. Secret. F. No. KW. 2-160-169 of January 1898.
3. 7th January 1897. Foreign. Secret. F. No. KW. 2-160-169 of January 1898.
4. Report of A Mission To The Northern Frontier of Kashmir. By Captain F.E. Younghusband. 1889, p. 101.
5. 7th January 1897. Foreign. Secret. F. No. KW. 2-160-169 of January 1898.
6. 8th February 1897. Foreign. Secret. F. No. KW. 2-160-169 of January 1898.
7. Report of the Officials of India and China. Ministry of External Affairs publication. 1961, p. 46.
8. *Ibid.*, p. 1.
9. 8th February 1897. Foreign. Secret. F. No. KW. 160-169 of January 1898.
10. A Gazetteer Of The Countries Adjacent to India. By Edward Thornton. 1844. Vol. 1, p. 239.
11. Scientific Mission To India And High Asia. By Herman, Adolphe and Robert De Schlagintwiet. 1860. Vol. 11, p. 487.
12. *Ibid.*, Vol. 1, p. 58.
13. Visits To High Tartary, Yarkand And Kashgar. By Robert Shaw. 1871, p. 90.
14. The Jammu and Kashmir Territories. By Frederick Drew. 1875. (Indian print). pp. 336, 342, 344 and 350.
15. 2nd December 1870. Foreign. Pol. A. No. 382 of January 1871.
16. 19th August 1870. Foreign. Pol. A. No. 469 of December 1870.
17. English Dominions in Asia. By M. Venukof. Tr. By F.C. Daukes. 1876, p. xxx and xxxii.
18. Trans-Himalaya. By Sven Hedin. 1910, Vol. 1, p. 93.
19. Imperial Gazetteer. Provincial Series. Jammu and Kashmir. Government Press. 1909, p. 15.
20. Report Of A Mission To Yarkand in 1873. Foreign Department Press. 1875, p. 248.
21. The Chinese Threat. Publication Division. Government of India Press. 1963. Map No. 2.
22. *Ibid.*, Map No. 12.
23. 29th September 1885. Foreign. Secret. F. No. 298 of May 1886.
24. In Tibet And Chinese Turkistan. By Captain H.H.P. Deasy. 1901, p. 164.
25. 15th June 1899, Foreign. Secret. F. No. 123. Enclosure I of September 1899. 31st July 1899. Foreign. Secret. F. No. 84 August 1899.
26. 31st May 1899. Foreign. Secret. F. No. 144 of July 1899.
27. In Tibet And Chinese Turkistan. By Captain H.H.P. Deasy. 1901, p. 172.
28. *Ibid.*, p. 167.

29. Report Of The Officials of India And China. Ministry of External Affairs Publication. 1961, p. 77 (CR).
30. In Tibet And Chinese Turkistan. By Captain H.H.P. Deasy. 1901, p. 63.
31. *Ibid.*, p. 165.
32. Trans-Himalaya. By Sven Hedin. 1910. Vol 1, pp. 94-97.
33. Explorations in Central Asia. 1906-8. (Read at the Royal Geographical Society. 8th March 1909), p. 56.
34. Southern Tibet. By Sven Hedin. Vol. III, p. 40.
35. The Chinese Threat. Publication Division. Government of India Press. 1963, Map No. 10.
36. Southern Tibet. By Sven Hedin. Vol. III, p. 58.
37. Memoir On Maps of Chinese Turkistan. By Sir Aurel Stein. Trigonometrical Survey Office. 1923, p. 22.
38. A Short History of Tibet. By H.E. Richardson. 1962, p. 83.
39. Southern Tibet. By Sven Hedin. Vol. III, p. 60.
40. Tibet The Mysterious. By Sir Thomas Holdich, p. 62.
41. Himalayan Frontiers. By Dorothy Woodman. 1969, p. 66.
42. China And Tibet. By L. Petech. 1950. P. 28. Southern Tibet. By Sven Hedin. Vol. III, pp. 38-40-58.
43. Pioneer, 29th July 1904. Foreign. Secret. E. No. Notes. 1398-1445 of February 1904.
44. 22nd April 1897. Foreign. Secret. F. No. KW. 1-160-169 of January 1898.
45. 30th April 1897. Foreign. Secret. F. No. KW. 1-160-169 of January 1898.
46. 24th May 1897. Foreign. Secret. F. No. KW. 1-160-169 of January 1898.
47. 10th August 1898. Foreign. Secret. F. No. KW. 1-110-114 of November 1898.
48. 16th August 1898. Foreign. Secret. F. No. KW. 1-110-114 of November 1898.
49. 25th August 1898. Foreign. Secret. F. No. KW. 1-110-114 of November 1898.
50. 4th September 1898. Foreign. Secret. F. No. KW. 2-110-114 of November 1898.
51. Foreign. Secret (Frontier) despatch from the Government of India to the Secretary of State for India. No. 198 of 27th October 1898.
52. 29th December 1900. Foreign. Secret. F. Encl. 1 to No. 1 of June 1901.
53. 21st May 1904. Foreign. Secret. E. Notes. No. 1398-1445 of February 1905.
54. *Ibid.*, 9th June 1904.
55. 11th June 1904. Foreign. Secret. E. Notes. 1398-1445 of February 1905.
56. 25th June 1904. Foreign. Secret. E. Notes. 1398-1445 of February 1905.
57. 28th June 1904. Foreign. Secret. E. Notes. 1398-1445 of February 1905.
58. 11th July 1904. Foreign. Secret. E. Notes. 1398-1445 of February 1905.
59. 29th August 1904. Foreign. Secret. E. Notes. 1398-1445 of February 1905.
60. 25th March 1907. Foreign. Secret. F. Appendix to notes. No. 40-51 of February 1908.
61. 30th March 1907. Foreign. Secret. F. Appendix to notes. No. 40-51 of February 1908.

62. 1st April 1907. Foreign. Secret. F. Appendix to notes. No. 40-51 of February 1908.
63. 1st April 1907. Foreign. Secret. F. Appendix to notes. No. 40-51 of February 1908.
64. 11th May 1907. Foreign. Secret. F. Appendix to notes. No. 40-51 of February 1908.
65. 16th May 1907. Foreign. Secret. F. Appendix to notes. No. 40-51 of February 1908.
66. 16th May 1907. Foreign. Secret. F. Appendix to notes. No. 40-51 of February 1908.
67. 31st May 1907. Foreign. Secret. F. Appendix to notes. No. 40-51 of February 1908.
68. 8th June and 30th August 1907. Foreign. Secret. F. Appendix to notes. No. 40-51 of February 1908.
69. 8th February 1923. Foreign. Frontier B. No. 33. File No. 483 F. 1923. Also Explorations in the Eastern Karakoram and the Upper yarkand Valley. Survey of India detachment with the De Filippi Scientific Expedition. Report by Colonel H. Wood. 1922, p. 15.
70. Ruins of Desert Cathay. By Sir M.A. Stein. 1912, p. 458-459.
71. 15th July 1912. Foreign. Secret. F. No. 63-166 of September 1912.
72. 26th August 1912. Foreign. Secret. F. No. 23 of February 1913.
73. *Ibid.*,1st September 1912.
74. *Ibid.*, 9th September 1912.
75. 10th September 1912. Foreign. Secret. F. Notes. 1-67 of February 1913.
76. 11th September 1912. Foreign. Secret. F. Notes. 1-67 of February 1913.
77. 12th September 1912. Foreign. Secret. F. Notes. 1-67 of February 1913.
78. 12th September 1912. Foreign. Secret. F. No. 10 of February 1913.
79. 7th September 1917. Foreign. Secret. F. Notes. 1-67 of November 1917.
80. 9th April 1923. Foreign. Frontier. B. No. 1-29. File No. 483. F. 1923.
81. Himalayan Frontiers. By Dorothy Woodman. 1969, p. 83.
82. Journal of the Asiatic Society of Bengal. Vol. XXVIII. Nos. III to V. 1859, p. 329.
83. 22nd April 1866. Foreign. Pol. A. No. 136 of June 1868.
84. Undated. Foreign. Pol. A. No. 137 of June 1868.
85. Journal of the Asiatic Society of Bengal. Vol. XXXVI. Part II Nos. I to III. 1867.
86. Explorations in Central Asia. By Sir Aurel Stein. (Read at the Royal Geographical Society, London. 8th March 1909). Also, Memoir on maps of Chinese Turkistan. By Sir Aurel Stein. Great Trigonometrical Survey of India, p. 21.
87. Kashmir and Kashgar. By H.W. Bellew. 1875, p. 151.
88. The Heart of A Continent. By Frank E. Younghusband. 1896, p. 181.
89. Grombtchevsky. Proceedings of the Russian Imperial Geographical Society. Undated. Foreign. Frontier B. No. 129 of September 1890.

Appendix I

Text of the Treaty of Tingomsgong of 1683.

The treaty is a two-sided accord between Ladakh and Tibet and Ladakh and Moghal Kashmir. The treaty with Tibet covered Bashahr's interest while the accord with Kashmir provided for Kulu. The text of the treaty is largely based on the "Antiquities of Indian Tibet," Archaeological Survey of India, Imperial Series, Volume L. Part (volume) 11. By Dr. A.H. Francke. p. 115, partly on "A study of the Chronicles of Ladakh," and research paper published in the Indian Historical Quarterly. Vol. XXIII of September 1973 no. 3 both by Dr. Luciano Petech. Articles, As at the beginning King Skyid-lde-ni-ma-mgon gave a separate kingdom to each of his sons, the same delimitation still to hold good.

2. Tibetans have come to consider that since Tibet is a Buddhist and Kha-chul (Kashmir) is a non-Buddhist country and since Buddhist and non-Buddhist religions have nothing in common and are hostile to each other, if at the frontier the king of La-dvags does not prosper Bod (Tibet) also cannot enjoy prosperity. (This being so), the occurrences of the recent war should be considered things of the past. The king, (on the other hand) shall in future keep watch at the frontier of Buddhist and non-Buddhist peoples and out of regard for the doctrine of Buddha must not allow an army from India to proceed to an attack (upon Tibet).

3. As to the privileges of Kha-chul (Kashmir) (the following agreement was come to) :– The fine wool of goats of Manh-ris-skor-gsum shall not be sold to any other country; the price of fine and coarse wool mixed shall be fixed at eight 'nag'* to two repees (or) the price of fine and coarse wool mixed shall be fixed at forty 'nag'* to one rupee (to be paid in both money and kind); the Byan-(than) people shall not be allowed to use the 'nag'* or Ron (Indus gorge?); it shall not be said of the wool of Byan-(than) that it contains soil, stones or moisture.

4. To Ruthog proper none but the court merchants (of Ladakh) are to be admitted. (Regarding) the goat wool (trade) :– four Kashmiri merchants shall reside at Dpe-thub, and do the trading with Kashmiris of Kashmir. Besides these

---

* 12 'nag = 1 'batti' or 4 lbs.

men, who are called Kha-chul-hygro-rgya, no Kashmiri of Kashmir shall be allowed to go to Byan-than. Those Ladakhi-Kashmiris who go to Byan-than shall not be allowed themselves to go down to Kashmir with loads of wool of goats.

5. Regarding Mnah-ris-skor-gsum...it shall be set apart to meet the expenses of sacred lamps and prayers (offered) at Lha-sa; but at Menser the king shall be his own master, so that the kings of Ladakh may have wherewithal to pay for lamps and other sacrifices at the Gans-mtsho (lake); it shall be his private domain. With this exception the boundary shall be fixed at the Lha-ri stream at Bde-mchog.
6. From Tibet the Government trader shall come with two hundred loads of tea; and nowhere but by La-dvags shall rectangular tea-bricks be sent across the frontier. Should the government trade fail to come every year, then the above stipulations shall no longer be binding.
7. The king of La-dvags, on the other hand, shall, on the occasion of the Lo-phyag (biennial embassy) offer presents to the clergy. This embassy has to be sent with presents to ordinary lamas, the quantity is not fixed, but to the Bla-bran steward shall be given ten *thur-zo*-of gold, ten *sran* of scent (saffron), six pieces of calico from Hor (the Moghal empire? Or Turkistan?); and one piece of cotton cloth. Throughout their sojourn (the members of the Lo-phyag) shall receive (daily) rations. For the road (shall be supplied) (beasts of burden, to carry) 200 loads, 25 riding horses; 10 men (to act as) groom, cook and servant. There (in Tibet) the horses shall have fodder without restriction.
8. A corollary of the peace treaty was that Bashahr reaped the fruit of its loyal and effective support to Ganden in the form of the cession by Ladakh of upper Kinnaur.

The second accord–

9. Likewise, the king of La-dvags had to send his filial share to Kashmir every year, and alongwith that 18 piebald horses, 18 pods of musk, and 18 white yak, tails, whilst it was also settled that 500 bags of rice, being the revenue accruing to the king of La-dvags from his 'jagir' (Naushahr) should every year be sent up from Kha-chul.

The king of Ladakh. De-legs-rnam-rgyal, had to accept (at least outwardly) Islam...He was also compelled to have a coin of Moghal type struck in Kashmir for Ladakh... Other terms imposed by the Moghals were that the king should give one of his sons as a hostage, build (or repair) a mosque at Leh and grant Kashmiri merchants the monopoly of the wool trade.

The Moghal's ally, Kulu, received upper Lahaul.

Appendix II

The Persian text of the treaty of 2 Asuj 1899 Sambat, corresponding with the 15 August 1842, text reproduced from Golabnama* :

"On this auspicious occasion, the second day of the month of Asuj in the year 1899 we the officers of Lhasa. viz., firstly Kalon, Surkhang, and, secondly, Bakshi Sapju, commander of the forces of Kha-quan-i-Chin, on the one hand, and on behalf of Sri Maharaja Sahib Raja-e-Rajgan, Raja Sahib Bahadur Raja Golab Singhji, two officers, firstly, Sahib-i-Mukhtar-al-Daulah, Diwan Harichand, and secondly Wazarat-panah, Wazir. Ratnu on the other, held in mutual concord, assembly of reconciliation, agreement and treaty and after swearing on the friendship and amity and sincerity of the parties and swearing repeatedly upon Qonhaq sahib, it was agreed upon that :

1. The bounds of peace and treaty and unity between Sri Maharaja Sahib Bahadur Raja Golab Singhji, and Khaqan-i-Chin and Lama Guru Sahib Lhasawala on dint of cleanness of heart, will, remain firm and coherent from this day till eternity. Upon Qonhaq-sahib by all manner of means, no deviation, disregard and error will occur.
2. As regard the boundary of the country of Ladakh, including suburbs, fixed of ancient days, we will at all have no concern and nothing to do.
3. We will export shawl 'pashm' and tea according to the old tradition by way of Ladakh yearly.
4. If any one of Sri Raja Sahib Bahadur's enemies come to our quarters and territories, we will not entertain the word of the said enemies and will give no shelter in our country to the aforesaid men.
5. Whatever traders of Ladakh will come to our territories shall meet no hindrance and whatever we stipulate in writing on the face of the contract about solidarity and friendship, unity and fixation of the frontiers of Ladakh territory and keeping open of the road for the traffic in shawl, 'pashm' and tea, will not in the least be infringed by us.
6. "To this agreement and vow, Qonhaq Sahib, Gaitri and Pissi and Zohmian and Khashal Shah stand witness.
7. "The treaty written on the second day of Asuj of the year 1899."

The Tibetan version* of the treaty is :

Kalon Surkhang and investigating officer Depon Pishi on behalf of his Holiness the Dalai Lama and his officials and Shri Khalsaji Absarani Shri Maharaja.

---

* Translation by Sukhdev Charak.
* Text from The Founding of The Kashmir State. By K.M. Panikkar. pp. 85, 86, 87.

Lala Golana, the representative of Khashur Shag Golam Mohammad through an interpreter Amir Shah (on behalf of Golab Singh) have arrived at Ladakh and discussed the terms of peace treaty.

1. In the first place the two contracting parties have decided to sink all past differences and ill-feeling and to consider the friendship and unity between the two kings reestablished for ever.
2. This peace treaty between Shri Maharaja Golab Singh and Shri Guru Lama of Lhasa has been restored and there will be no cause for enmity in future in the two nations regarding their respective frontier.
3. "Shri Maharaja Sahib has declared, invoking God as his witness, that he will not deviate from the terms of this agreement.
4. "It is agreed that the two brothers kings of Ladakh and the Queen shall remain peacefully, in Ladakh and shall not indulge in any intrigue, besides trying to promote the friendly relations between the two nations.
5. The Ladakhis shall send the annual tribute to His Holiness the Dalai Lama and his Ministers unfailingly as heretofore and the Shri Maharaja Sahib will not interfere with this arrangement.
6 "No restriction shall be laid on the mutual export and import of commodities, e.g. tea, piece-goods, etc. and trading shall be allowed according to the old established custom.
7 "The Ladakhis shall supply the Tibetan Government traders with the usual transport animals and arrange for their accommodation as heretofore, and the Tibetans will also do the same to the Ladakhis who come to Tibet with the annual tribute.
8. "It is agreed that no trouble will be occasioned to the Tibetan Government by the Ladakhis.
9. "We invoke God to bear witness to this agreement whereby the friendly relations between Shri Maharaja Sahib and the Lhasa officials shall continue as between members of the same family. This is sent on the second day of the month of Asuj year 1899 (Sambat).

Text of the second and substantive treaty between Lahore and China. Translation of the Tibetan text. The treaty was signed by the officials of the Maharaja of Lahore, Sher Singh, and Raja Golab Singh, on behalf of the former by the officials of the Governor of Kashmir, Shiekh Mohinddin, and the latter by the commander-in-chief of the western area (Dewan Harichand), and for the Dalai Lama of Lhasa by Kalon Surkhang and Depon Shabeho Bakshi in Ladakh.

1. There will never be on any account in future, while the world lasts, any deviation even by the hair's breadth or any breach in the alliance, friendship, and unity between the king of the world (Sher Singh) Sri Khalsaji Sahib (and Golab Singh) Shri Maharaja Sahib Raja-e-Rajgan Raja Sahib Bahadur, and the Khagan (Emperor) of China and the Lama Guru Sahib of Lhasa (the Dalai Lama).
2. We shall remain in possession of the limits of the boundaries of Ladakh and the neighbourhood subordinate to it, in accordance with the old customs,

and there shall be no transgression and no interference in the country beyond the old established frontiers.

3. We shall hold our own respective frontiers, relations of friendship and the bond of common interests shall grow closer from day to day.
4. There are several kinds of witnesses to this agreement. The Rajazadas shall, if they remain faithful, loyal and obedient receive greater consideration.
5. In case the Rajas of Ladakh should desire to send their usual presents to the Lama Guru Sahib of Lhasa, this will not concern us and we shall not interfere.
6. From the other side (arrangements) shall continue in accordance with the old custom and the traders who proceed to Changthang country shall receive considerate treatment and a supply of "begar" in accordance with the old custom and shall not be interfered with. The traders from Ladakh shall in no case interfere with the subjects of Changthang.

Written on the second of the month of Assuj, year 1899.

British version and the English text* of the treaty of 1842. The text is a translation, probably from Persian, by J.C. Erskine sub-commissioner, N.W.F.*

The following chiefs having assembled in the city of Leh on 28 Assuj, 1899, Sambat corresponding with 17th October 1842. Kalon Surkhang and Dewan Pishi on the part of the Chinese and Shah Gholam on the part of the Ruler of Lahore, and Rutnoo Wazir and Harichand on the part of Raja Golab Singh, besides others of inferior note belonging to both parties. It was mutually agreed that a treaty of amity and peace should be concluded between the Chinese and Sikhs, the conditions of which, as under mentioned, were recorded in writing in the presence of the chief aforesaid and likewise Sibchu Tudpun (Tukpun) Peesy and Lamha Wazir, both confidential advisers of the Viceroy of Lhasa.

1. That the boundaries of Ladakh and Lhasa should be constituted as formerly the contracting parties engaging to confine themselves within their respective boundaries, the one to refrain from any act of aggression on the other.
2. That in conformity with ancient usage, tea and pashm shawl wool shall be transmitted by the Ladakh road.
3. Such person as may in future proceed from China to Ladakh or from Ladakh to China not to be obstructed on the road.
4. That no renewal of the war between the chiefs of the Raja and of those of the Viceroy of Lhasa shall take place.
5. That the above mentioned conditions shall remain in force without interruption and whatever customs formerly existed...(shall) continued to prevail.
6. It is understood that in signing the above treaty the contracting parties are bound to a true and faithful observance of all provisions thereof by the solemn obligations attached to the Holy Place called Gangri (Mt. Kailash) to the Lake Mantalai (Mansarovar) and the Temple of Kojoor chu in China (Tibet).

---

* Text from : The Founding Of The Kashmir State, pp. 87, 88, 89.

* Foreign. SC. No. 62 of 24th May 1843.

Appendix III

Treaty of Amritsar of 16th March 1846. Text :

Treaty between the British Government and the Maharaja Golab Singh concluded at Amritsar.

Article 1. The British Government transfers and makes over, for ever, in independent possession to Maharaja Golab Singh, and the heirs male of his body, all the hilly or mountainous country, with its dependencies, situated to the eastward of the river Indus, and westward of the river Ravi, including Chamba and excluding Lahaul, being part of the territory ceded to the British Government by the Lahore State, according to the provisions of Article 4 of the treaty of Lahore, dated 9th March 1846.

Article 2. The eastern boundary of the tract transferred by the foregoing article to Maharaja Golab Singh shall be laid down by commissioners appointed by the British Government and Maharaja Golab Singh respectively, for that purpose, and shall be defined in a separate engagement, after survey.

Article 3. In consideration of the transfer made to him and his heirs by the provisions of the foregoing articles, Maharaja Golab Singh will pay to the British Government the sum of seventy five lakhs of rupees (Nanakshahi), fifty lakhs to be paid on ratification of this treaty, and twenty five lakhs on or before the 1st of October of the current year, A.D. 1946.

Article 4. The limits of the territories of Maharaja Golab Singh shall not be at any time changed without the concurrence of the British Government.

Article 5. Maharaja Golab Singh will refer to the arbitration of the British Government any disputes or questions that may arise between himself and the Government of Lahore, or any other neighbouring State, and will abide by the decision of the British Government.

Article 6. Maharaja Golab Singh engages for himself and heirs, to join with the whole of his military force, the British troops, when employed within the hills or in the territories adjoining his possessions.

Article 7. Maharaja Golab Singh engages never to take or retain, in his service any British subject, nor the subject of any European or American state, without the consent of the British Government.

Article 8. Maharaja Golab Singh engages to respect, in regard to the territory transferred to him, the provisions of Article 5, 6 and 7, of the separate engagement between the British Government and the Lahore Darbar, dated 11th March 1846.

Article 9. The British Government will give its aid to Maharaja Golab Singh in protecting his territories from external enemies.

Article 10. Maharaja Golab Singh acknowledges the supremacy of the British Government and will in token of such supremacy, present annually to the British Government one horse, twelve perfect shawl goats of approved breed (six male and six female), and three pairs of Kashmir shawls.

This treaty consisting of ten articles, has been this day settled by Frederick Currie Esq. and Brevet-Major Henry Montagomery Lawrence, acting under the directions of the Right Honourable Sir Henry Hardinge, G.C.B. Governor General, on the part of the British Government and by Maharaja Golab Singh in person, and the said treaty has been this day ratified by the seal of the Rt. Hon'ble Sir Henry Hardinge, G.C.B. Governor General.

Done at Amritsar, this 16th day of March in the year of our Lord 1846...

Index

K